Hegel and the Hermetic Tradition

HEGEL

and the Hermetic Tradition

GLENN
ALEXANDER
MAGEE

Cornell University Press

Ithaca and London

First published 2001 by
Cornell University Press

Printed in the United States
of America

Library of Congress
Cataloging-in-Publication Data

Magee, Glenn Alexander, 1966-

  Hegel and the hermetic tradition /
Glenn Alexander Magee.
    p. cm.
  Includes bibliographical references
and index.
  ISBN 0-8014-3872-1
  1. Hegel, Georg Wilhelm Friedrich,
1770-1831. 2. Hermetism—History—
19th century. I. Title.
  B2949.H37 M34 2001
  193—dc21
                                00-012973

Cornell University Press strives to use
environmentally responsible suppliers
and materials to the fullest extent
possible in the publishing of its
books. Such materials include veg-
etable-based, low-VOC inks and acid-
free papers that are recycled, totally
chlorine-free, or partly composed of
nonwood fibers. Books that bear the
logo of the FSC (Forest Stewardship
Council) use paper taken from forests
that have been inspected and certified
as meeting the highest standards for
environmental and social responsibil-
ity. For further information, visit our
website at
www.cornellpress.cornell.edu.

Cloth printing
10 9 8 7 6 5 4 3 2 1

FSC FSC Trademark © 1996 Forest Stewardship Council A.C.
      SW-COC-098

Contents

List of Illustrations p.ix
Acknowledgments p.xi
Abbreviations and Conventions p.xii

Introduction
1. Hegel as Hermetic Thinker p.1
2. Scholarship on Hegel and the Hermetic Tradition p.4
3. What is Hermeticism? p.8
4. Hegel: A Metaphysical View p.14
5. The Plan of This Book p.17

Part One
The Sorcerer's Apprenticeship

Chapter One: *A Brief Overview of the Hermetic Tradition*
1. The Earliest Hermeticists p.21
2. Meister Eckhart p.23
3. Nicholas of Cusa p.26
4. Renaissance and Reformation p.28
5. Agrippa p.30
6. Bruno p.33
7. Franck and Weigel p.34
8. Böhme p.36

Chapter Two: *The Hermetic Milieu of Hegel's Early Years*
1. Rosicrucianism and Freemasonry p.51
2. Goethe the Alchemist p.57
3. Swabian Pietism and F. C. Oetinger p.61
4. Hegel's *Lehrjahre* p.70
5. Pantheism, Hölderlin, and Schelling p.76

Chapter Three: *The Mythology of Reason*
1. The Absolute Religion p.84
2. Speculation and Recollection p.88
3. Speculation as "Mythic" p.91
4. Further Parallels Between Speculation and Myth p.96
5. Imagination and the Symbolic Forms p.98
6. The "Divine Triangle" and the Triangle Diagram p.104
7. Summary of the Argument Thus Far p.119

Part Two
Magnum Opus

Chapter Four: Hegel's Initiation Rite: *The Phenomenology of Spirit*
1. Initiation p.127
2. Hermetic Influences
   a) Jena p.132
   b) The Hermetic Subtext to Hegel's Preface p.134
   c) Böhmean Elements in the *Phenomenology* p.138
   d) Alchemical Elements p.145
   e) The Foaming Chalice p.146

Chapter Five: The Kabbalistic Tree: *The Science of Logic*
1. The Project of Hegel's *Logic* p.150
2. Böhmean Influences on the *Logic* p.157
3. The Kabbalah p.165
   a) The Kabbalistic Writings p.165
   b) Hegel's Knowledge of Kabbalism p.166
   c) *Bereshith* . . . p.168
   d) Language and Method in the Kabbalah p.175
4. Ramon Lull and the Tradition of *Pansophia* p.177

Chapter Six: The Alchemist's Laboratory: *The Philosophy of Nature* and *Philosophy of Subjective Spirit*
1. Introduction p.187
2. The Four Elements p.191
3. Aether p.196
4. The Alchemical Opus p.200
5. Hegel and Alchemy p.209
6. Hegel on Mesmerism and ESP p.213

Chapter Seven: "The Rose in the Cross of the Present": Hegel's Philosophy of Objective and Absolute Spirit
1. Introduction p.223
2. Hegel's Philosophy of Religion: The Influence of Mysticism p.223
3. Hegel's Philosophy of History: The Influence of Isaac Luria and Jewish Eschatology p.227
4. Joachimite Mysticism and the End of History p.236
5. Hegel and Prussian Rosicrucianism p.247

Bibliography p.259
Index p.279

Illustrations

1. Hegel's triangle diagram p.111
2. Key to triangle diagram p.112
3. From an eighteenth-century manuscript known to Goethe p.114
4. *Mercurius redivivus* p.115
5. "Speculation" graphically depicted p.121
6. The "Tree of Life" as rendered by Brucker p.171
7. The dove of Spirit returning to God (the Father) p.208
8. The Lurianic Sephiroth p.231
9. The Three Ages of Joachim de Fiore p.239

Acknowledgments

I thank the individuals who have taught me Hegel: Martin J. De Nys, Wayne J. Froman, Thelma Z. Lavine, Donald Phillip Verene, and Richard Dien Winfield. Thanks are also owed to four men who have never been my teachers but whose work has been the principal influence on my interpretation of Hegel's system: Eric Voegelin, J. N. Findlay, Errol E. Harris, and G. R. G. Mure. Their way of reading Hegel is currently unfashionable, but I believe that it is substantially correct.

I am grateful to the Earhart Foundation for a generous grant that enabled me to continue work on this book during the academic year 1998–99. I would also like to thank the Emory University Department of Philosophy for funding my research in Germany during the summer of 1996. I thank the staff of the Staatsbibliothek Preussischer Kulturbesitz in Berlin for allowing me to consult Hegel's manuscripts and other materials. Otto Pöggeler at the Hegel-Archiv in Bochum was also kind enough to point me in the direction of some useful literature. I also thank Marsha Keith Schuchard, who lent me her expertise on the Hermetic tradition.

In particular I must express my gratitude to Donald Phillip Verene. His generosity, support, good advice, and, above all, good taste have meant a great deal to me. I also thank David Carr, Ann Hartle, Donald Livingston, Donald Rutherford, and Cynthia Willett, all of Emory University, for their support, kindness, and constructive criticism. I am also grateful to Tom Darby and Cyril O'Regan for their thoughtful remarks on an earlier draft of this work, and to Chris Matthew Sciabarra for his efforts on my behalf.

Special thanks must also go to Catherine Rice, my editor at Cornell. Her support and enthusiasm have meant much to me.

Greg Johnson has been a great help at all stages of my writing. Indeed, he suggested the project in the first place; therefore, I dedicate it to him.

Atlanta, Georgia   G. A. M.

Abbreviations and Conventions

Butler=*Hegel: The Letters*, trans. Clark Butler and Christianne Seiler (Bloomington: Indiana University Press, 1984).
EL=*Encyclopedia Logic*. Reference is by Hegel's paragraph number; e.g., "EL § 9."
Geraets=*The Encyclopedia Logic*, trans. T. F. Geraets et al. (Albany: State University of New York Press, 1991).
Hoffmeister=Johannes Hoffmeister, *Briefe von und an Hegel*, 4 vols. (Hamburg: Felix Meiner Verlag, 1952–81). Reference is by Hoffmeister's letter number, e.g., "Hoffmeister #15".
Knox=*Philosophy of Right*, trans. T. M. Knox (Oxford: Clarendon Press, 1952).
LHP=*Lectures on the History of Philosophy*, 3 vols., trans. E. S. Haldane (London: Kegan Paul, Trench, Trübner, 1892).
LPR=*Lectures on the Philosophy of Religion*, 3 vols., ed. and trans. Peter C. Hodgson et al. (Berkeley: University of California Press, 1984).
Miller=*The Phenomenology of Spirit*, trans. A. V. Miller (Oxford: Oxford University Press, 1977). Reference is by Miller's page number, not paragraph number. The paragraph numbers in Miller do not exist in Hegel's original and simply provide a reference for J. N. Findlay's commentary, which forms an appendix to the translation; or *The Science of Logic*, trans. A. V. Miller (London: George Allen and Unwin, 1969). Which text is being referred to is clear from the context.
Nisbet=*Lectures on the Philosophy of World History*, trans. H. B. Nisbet (Cambridge: Cambridge University Press, 1975).
Petry=*Hegel's Philosophy of Nature*, 3 vols., trans. M. J. Petry (London: George Allen and Unwin, 1970); or *Hegel's Philosophy of Subjective Spirit*, 3 vols., trans. M. J. Petry (Dordrecht: D. Reidel, 1978). Which text is being referred to is clear from the context.
PG=*Phänomenologie des Geistes*, hrsg. v. Hans-Friedrich Wessels und Heinrich Clairmont (Hamburg: Felix Meiner, 1988).
PN=*Philosophy of Nature*. Reference is by Hegel's paragraph number.
PR=*Philosophy of Right*. Reference is by Hegel's paragraph number.
PS=*Philosophy of Spirit*. Reference is by Hegel's paragraph number.
VIG=*Die Vernunft in der Geschichte*, hrsg. v. Johannes Hoffmeister (Berlin: Akademie Verlag, 1966).

VPR=*Vorlesungen über die Philosophie der Religion*, 3 Bde., hrsg. v. Walter
Jaeschke (Hamburg: Felix Meiner, 1983–87).
Wallace=*Hegel's Philosophy of Mind*, trans. William Wallace (Oxford:
Clarendon Press, 1971).
Werke=G. W. F. *Hegel: Werke*, 20 Bde., hrsg. v. Eva Moldenhauer und Karl
Markus Michel (Frankfurt am Main: Suhrkamp, 1986).
WL=*Wissenschaft der Logik*, 3 Bde., hrsg. v. Hans-Jürgen Gawoll (Hamburg:
Felix Meiner, 1986–92). This includes the 1812 edition of *Das Sein*, but
unless otherwise noted, reference to "WL 1" is always to the 1832 edition
of *Das Sein*, hrsg. v. Hans-Jürgen Gawoll (Hamburg: Felix Meiner, 1990).
z=*Zusatz*

Unless otherwise noted, reference is by page number.

When referring to specific texts by Hegel, such as the *Philosophy of
Nature*, I have italicized their titles. I have not italicized the names
of the individual Hegelian sciences, but I have adopted the
familiar convention of capitalizing words that have a
special technical meaning in Hegel's philosophy,
e.g. "the Absolute," "Being," "Logic,"
"the Concrete," Substance."

Hegel and the Hermetic Tradition

Introduction

> God is God only so far as he knows himself: his self-knowledge is,
> further, a self-consciousness in man and man's knowledge of God,
> which proceeds to man's self-knowledge in God.
> —Hegel, *Encyclopedia of the Philosophical Sciences*

1. Hegel as Hermetic Thinker

Hegel is not a philosopher. He is no lover or seeker of wisdom—he believes he has found it. Hegel writes in the preface to the *Phenomenology of Spirit*, "To help bring philosophy closer to the form of Science, to the goal where it can lay aside the title of '*love* of knowing' and be actual knowledge—that is what I have set before me" (Miller, 3; PG, 3). By the end of the *Phenomenology*, Hegel claims to have arrived at Absolute Knowledge, which he identifies with wisdom.

Hegel's claim to have attained wisdom is completely contrary to the original Greek conception of philosophy as the love of wisdom, that is, the ongoing pursuit rather than the final possession of wisdom. His claim is, however, fully consistent with the ambitions of the Hermetic tradition, a current of thought that derives its name from the so-called *Hermetica* (or *Corpus Hermeticum*), a collection of Greek and Latin treatises and dialogues written in the first or second centuries A.D. and probably containing ideas that are far older. The legendary author of these works is Hermes Trismegistus ("Thrice-Greatest Hermes"). "Hermeticism" denotes a broad tradition of thought that grew out of the "writings of Hermes" and was expanded and developed through the infusion of various other traditions. Thus, alchemy, Kabbalism, Lullism, and the mysticism of Eckhart and Cusa—to name just a few examples—became intertwined with the Hermetic doctrines. (Indeed, Hermeticism is used by some authors simply to mean alchemy.)[1] Hermeticism is also sometimes called theosophy, or esotericism; less precisely, it is often characterized as mysticism, or occultism.

It is the thesis of this book that Hegel is a Hermetic thinker. I shall show that there are striking correspondences between Hegelian philosophy and Hermetic theosophy, and that these correspondences are not accidental. Hegel was actively interested in Hermeticism, he was influ-

---

1. Antoine Faivre, *Access to Western Esotericism*, vol. 1 (Albany: State University of New York Press, 1994), 35.

enced by its exponents from boyhood on, and he allied himself with Hermetic movements and thinkers throughout his life. I do not argue merely that we *can* understand Hegel as a Hermetic thinker, just as we can understand him as a German or a Swabian or an idealist thinker. Instead, I argue that we *must* understand Hegel as a Hermetic thinker, if we are to truly understand him at all.

Hegel's life and works offer ample evidence for this thesis.

There are references throughout Hegel's published and unpublished writings to many of the leading figures and movements of the Hermetic tradition. These references are in large measure approving. This is particularly the case with Hegel's treatment of Eckhart, Bruno, Paracelsus, and Böhme. Böhme is the most striking case. Hegel accords him considerable space in his *Lectures on the History of Philosophy*—more space, in fact, than he devotes to many significant mainstream thinkers in the philosophic tradition.

There are, furthermore, numerous Hermetic elements in Hegel's writings. These include, in broad strokes, a Masonic subtext of "initiation mysticism" in the *Phenomenology of Spirit*; a Böhmean subtext to the *Phenomenology's* famous preface; a Kabbalistic-Böhmean-Lullian influence on the *Logic*; alchemical-Paracelsian elements in the *Philosophy of Nature*; an influence of Kabbalistic and Joachimite millennialism on Hegel's doctrine of Objective Spirit and theory of world history; alchemical and Rosicrucian images in the *Philosophy of Right*; an influence of the Hermetic tradition of *pansophia* on the system as a whole; an endorsement of the Hermetic belief in *philosophia perennis*; and the use of perennial Hermetic symbolic forms (such as the triangle, the circle, and the square) as structural, architectonic devices.

Hegel's library included Hermetic writings by Agrippa, Böhme, Bruno, and Paracelsus. He read widely on Mesmerism, psychic phenomena, dowsing, precognition, and sorcery. He publicly associated himself with known occultists, like Franz von Baader. He structured his philosophy in a manner identical to the Hermetic use of "correspondences." He relied on histories of thought that discussed Hermes Trismegistus, Pico della Mirandola, Robert Fludd, and Knorr von Rosenroth alongside Plato, Galileo, Descartes, and Newton. He stated in his lectures more than once that the term "speculative" means the same thing as "mystical." He believed in an "Earth Spirit" and corresponded with colleagues about the nature of magic. He aligned himself, informally, with "Hermetic" societies such as the Freemasons and the Rosicrucians. Even Hegel's doodles were Hermetic, as we shall see in chapter 3 when I discuss the mysterious "triangle diagram."

There are four major periods in Hegel's life during which he seems to have been strongly under the influence of Hermeticism, or to have actively pursued an interest in it. First, there is his boyhood in Stuttgart, from 1770 to 1788. As I shall discuss in detail in chapter 2, during this period Württemberg was a major center of Hermetic interest, with much of the Pietist movement influenced by Böhmeanism and Rosicrucianism (Württemberg was the spiritual center of the Rosicrucian movement). The leading exponents of Pietism, J. A. Bengel and, in particular, F. C. Oetinger were strongly influenced by German mysticism, Böhmean theosophy, and Kabbalism.

Most Hegel scholars have not thought it necessary to consider the intellectual milieu of his boyhood. Hegel is almost universally understood simply within the context of the German philosophical tradition—as responding to Kant, Fichte, and Schelling. Needless to say, the influence of Kant, Fichte, and Schelling was important, but it was not the only influence on Hegel. Part of the reason other sources of influence are missed or ignored is that few scholars are familiar with the complexities of religious life in eighteenth-century Germany. Those who are familiar are almost always from disciplines other than philosophy, and almost always German. (The study of German Pietism is almost exclusively the province of German-speaking scholars.) The religious and intellectual life of Württemberg is, however, the obvious place to begin to understand Hegel's own intellectual origins, characteristic ideas, and aims.

Hegel has to be understood in terms of the theosophical Pietist tradition of Württemberg—he cannot be seen simply as a critic of Kant. Indeed Hegel, as I will argue, was *always* a critic of Kant and never a wholehearted admirer precisely because he was "imprinted" early on by the tradition of *pansophia*, which was very much alive in Württemberg, and by Oetinger's ideal of the truth as the Whole (see chapter 2). He could not accept Kant's scepticism, nor could Schelling, and for identical reasons. Yet they both recognized the power of Kant's thought and labored hard to move from his premises to their own conclusions, to circumvent his scepticism at all costs, in the name of the speculative ideal of their youth.

From 1793 to 1801 Hegel worked as a private tutor, first at Berne, then at Frankfurt. As I shall discuss in chapter 3, Hegel's biographer Karl Rosenkranz referred to this period as a "theosophical phase" in Hegel's development. During this time, Hegel appears to have become conversant with the works of Böhme, as well as Eckhart and Johannes Tauler. Also during this period Hegel became involved in Masonic circles.

In Jena (1801–7), Hegel's interest in theosophy continued. He lectured at length, and approvingly, on Böhme and Bruno. He composed several pieces, which have only come down to us in fragmentary form, employing Hermetic language and symbolism (see chapters 3 and 4). His lectures on the Philosophy of Nature during this time reflect an ongoing interest in alchemy. It is likely that Schelling, who had come to Jena sometime earlier, introduced Hegel to his circle of friends, which included a number of Romantics who were heavily interested in Hermeticism. Schelling himself was an avid reader of Böhme and Oetinger, and likely encouraged Hegel's interest.

The final "Hermetic" period of Hegel's life is his time in Berlin, from 1818 until his death on November 14, 1831. This is contrary to what one might expect. It might be assumed that Hegel's "Hermeticism" was merely an aberration of youth, which the "arch rationalist" moved away from as he matured. Surprisingly, precisely the reverse seems to be the case. In Berlin, Hegel developed a friendship with Franz von Baader, the premiere occultist and mystic of the day. Together they studied Meister Eckhart. The preface to Hegel's 1827 edition of the *Encyclopedia of the Philosophical Sciences in Outline* makes prominent mention of Böhme and Baader. His revised 1832 edition of the *Science of Logic* corrects a passage so as to include a reference to Böhme. His preface to the 1821 *Philosophy of Right* includes alchemical and Rosicrucian imagery. His 1831 *Lectures on the Philosophy of Religion* show the influence of the mystic Joachim of Fiore, as well as certain structural correspondences to the thought of Böhme. In sum, all the evidence indicates that in the last period of his life, Hegel's interest in the mystical and Hermetic traditions *intensified*, and that he became more bold about publicly aligning himself with Hermetic thinkers and movements.

The divisions of Hegel's philosophy follow a pattern that is typical of many forms of mystical and Hermetic philosophy. The *Phenomenology* represents an initial stage of "purification," of raising the mind above the level of the sensory and the mundane, a preparation for the reception of wisdom. The *Logic* is equivalent to the Hermetic "ascent" to the level of pure form, of the eternal, of "Universal Mind" (Absolute Idea). The *Philosophy of Nature* describes an "emanation" or "othering" of Universal Mind in the form of the spatio-temporal world. Its categories accomplish a transfiguration of the natural: we come to see the world as a reflection of Universal Mind. The *Philosophy of Spirit* accomplishes a "return" of created nature to the Divine by means of *man*, who can rise above the merely natural and "actualize" God in the world through concrete forms of life (e.g., the state and religion) and through speculative philosophy.

2. Scholarship on Hegel and the Hermetic Tradition

It is important to note that these claims would not have been particularly controversial in the decades after Hegel's death. In the 1840s, Schelling publicly accused Hegel of having simply borrowed much of his philosophy from Jakob Böhme. One of Hegel's disciples, Friedrich Theodor Vischer once asked, "Have you forgotten that the new philosophy came forth from the school of the old mystics, especially from Jacob Böhme?"[2] Another Hegelian, Hans Martensen, author of one of the first scholarly studies of Meister Eckhart, remarked that "German mysticism is the first form in which German philosophy revealed itself in the history of thought" ("philosophy" for Hegelians generally means Hegel's philosophy).[3] Wilhelm Dilthey noted the same continuity between German mysticism and speculative philosophy.[4]

Perhaps the most famous nineteenth-century study of Hermetic

2. See Ernst Benz, *The Mystical Sources of German Romantic Philosophy*, trans. Blair R. Reynolds and Eunice M. Paul (Allison Park, Pa.: Pickwick Publications, 1983), 2.
3. Ibid., 2.
4. Ibid., 2.

aspects in Hegel was Ferdinand Christian Bauer's *Die christliche Gnosis* (1835).[5] Bauer's was one of the first works to attempt to define Gnosticism and to distinguish between its different forms. The term *Gnostic* is used very loosely even in our own time, and very often what would more properly be termed "Hermetic" is labeled "Gnostic" instead. (I will discuss the differences between the two in the next section.) After a lengthy discussion of Gnosticism in antiquity, Bauer argues that Jakob Böhme was a modern Gnostic, and that Schelling and Hegel can be seen as Böhme's intellectual heirs, and thus as Gnostics themselves. *Die christliche Gnosis* is about the closest thing to a book on Hegel and the Hermetic tradition that has yet been published, though, as I have said, Bauer's focus is on gnosticism, not Hermeticism.[6] In 1853, Ludwig Noack published a two-volume work, *Die Christliche Mystik nach ihrem geschichtlichen Entwicklungsgange im Mittelalter und in der neueren Zeit dargestellt*, in which he dealt with the Idealists as modern representatives of mysticism.

Later discussions of Hegel's connection to Hermeticism are often coupled with similar discussions of Schelling. This is the case with Ernst Benz's *Mystical Sources of German Romantic Philosophy*, a brief but indispensable text by the leading scholar in this highly specialized field. In 1938, a German scholar named Robert Schneider published *Schellings und Hegels schwäbische Geistesahnen* in Würzburg. Most of the copies of Schneider's book were destroyed during the allied firebombing of Würzburg on March 16, 1945. Schneider was destroyed along with them. His book is a valuable study of the theosophical Pietism prevalent in Württemberg during Hegel and Schelling's youth.

Other works by German scholars dealing with the relationship of mysticism or Hermeticism to German Idealism and Hegel include Josef Bach's *Meister Eckhart der Vater der Deutschen Spekulation. Ein Beitrag zu einer Geschichte der deutschen Theologie und Philosophie der mittleren Zeit* (1864); Gottfried Fischer's *Geschichte der Entdeckung der deutschen Mystiker, Eckhart, Tauler u. Seuse im 19. Jahrhundert* (1931); Emanuel Hirsch's *Die idealistische Philosophie und das Christentum* (1926); Fritz Leese's *Philosophie und Theologie im Spätidealismus, Forschungen zur Auseinandersetzung von Christentum und idealistischer Philosophie im 19. Jahrhundert* (1919), and *Von Jakob Böhme zu Schelling. Zur Metaphysik des Gottesproblems* (1927); Wilhelm Lütgert's *Die Religion des Deutschen Idealismus und ihr Ende* (1923); and Heinrich Maier's *Die Anfange der Philosophie des deutschen Idealismus* (1930). There has also been a fair amount of Dutch literature on the topic, including G. J. P. J. Bolland's *Schelling, Hegel, Fechner en de nieuwere theosophie* (1910); J. d'Aulnis de Bourrouill's *Het mystieke*

---

5. The bibliography contains full information on all the works mentioned in this introduction. Generally I have mentioned only books here. Both books and articles are listed in the bibliography.

6. M.-M. Cottier refers to Hegel's philosophy as "Une Gnose christologique" in his *L'Atheisme Du Jeune Marx: Ses Origines Hegeliennes* (Paris: Vrin, 1969), 20–30. Eric Voegelin has also argued, critically, for Hegel as a "gnostic thinker," for instance in *Science, Politics, and Gnosticism* (Washington, D.C.: Regnery Gateway, 1968), 40–44, 67–80.

karakter van Hegel's logica; and H. W. Mook's *Hegeliaansch-theosofische opstellen* (1913).

In French, Jacques d'Hondt's *Hegel Secret* (1968) is an extremely important study of Hegel's relationship to Hermetic secret societies such as the Masons, Illuminati, and Rosicrucians.

There is also an important body of English-language literature on Hegel and mysticism, beginning with George Plimpton Adams's *The Mystical Element in Hegel's Early Theological Writings* (1910). Frederick Copleston authored a useful article, "Hegel and the Rationalization of Mysticism" in 1971. Perhaps the most widely read English-speaking interpreter of Hegel, J. N. Findlay was himself a theosophist, and his interpretation of Hegel is attuned to its mystic-Hermetic aspects. In Findlay's *Hegel: A Re-Examination* (1958), he suggests tantalizingly that Hegel was a "nineteenth-century representative of some *philosophia Germanica perennis.*"[7] H. S. Harris's two-volume intellectual biography of Hegel, *Hegel's Development* (1972/1983), contains asides regarding Hegel's relationship to Eckhart, Böhme, Baader, and alchemy. Recently, Cyril O'Regan has published a massive and groundbreaking study of the mystical roots of Hegel's philosophy of religion, *The Heterodox Hegel* (1994).

Thus far, however, the most influential English-language account of Hegel's Hermeticism is Eric Voegelin's. In his essay, "Response to Professor Altizer's 'A New History and a New but Ancient God,'" Voegelin admits that "For a long time I studiously avoided any serious criticism of Hegel in my published work, because I simply could not understand him." The turning point came with Voegelin's study of gnosticism, and the discovery that, "by his contemporaries Hegel was considered a gnostic thinker." Voegelin goes on to claim that Hegel's thought "belongs to the continuous history of modern Hermeticism since the fifteenth century."[8] Voegelin's principal statement on Hegel's Hermeticism is a savagely polemical essay, "On Hegel: A Study in Sorcery," referring to the *Phenomenology of Spirit* as a "grimoire" which "must be recognized as a work of magic—indeed, it is one of the great magic performances."[9]

Voegelin's claims are unique in that he does not simply claim that Hegel was *influenced* by the Hermetic tradition. He claims that Hegel was *part of* the Hermetic tradition and cannot be adequately understood apart from it. Unfortunately, however, Voegelin never adequately developed his thesis. He never spelled out, in detail, how Hegel is a Hermetic thinker. Voegelin has, however, encouraged other scholars to develop his thesis more systematically (and more soberly). David Walsh, for instance,

7. J. N. Findlay, *Hegel: A Re-Examination* (New York: Oxford University Press, 1958), 49.
8. Eric Voegelin, "Response to Professor Altizer's 'A New History and a New but Ancient God'" in *The Collected Works of Eric Voegelin*, vol. 12, *Published Essays, 1966–1985,* ed. Ellis Sandoz (Baton Rouge: Louisiana State University Press, 1990), 297.
9. Eric Voegelin, "On Hegel: A Study in Sorcery," *Published Essays, 1966–1985,* 222; cf. Voegelin's *Science, Politics, and Gnosticism,* 68–69, and his *Order and History,* vol. 5, *In Search of Order* (Baton Rouge: Louisiana State University Press, 1987), 54–70.

has written an important doctoral dissertation entitled *The Esoteric Origins of Modern Ideological Thought: Boehme and Hegel* (1978), in which he makes strong claims about Hegel's indebtedness to Böhme.[10] Gerald Hanratty has also published an extensive two-part essay, entitled "Hegel and the Gnostic Tradition" (1984–87).

Yet for all this scholarly activity, there has never been a systematic, book-length study of Hegel as Hermetic thinker that takes into account not only his intellectual development but also the entirety of his mature system until the present book.[11]

I consider this work not only a continuation of the tradition of scholarship I have sketched out above but also as a contribution to an ongoing project in the history of ideas pioneered by such writers as Voegelin, Frances Yates, Antoine Faivre, Richard Popkin, Allan Debus, Betty Jo Teeter Dobbs, Paul Oskar Kristeller, D. P. Walker, Stephen McKnight, and Alison Coudert (see bibliography). These scholars argue that Hermeticism has influenced such mainstream rationalist thinkers as Bacon, Descartes, Spinoza, Leibniz, and Newton and has played a hitherto unappreciated role in the formation of the central ideas and ambitions of modern philosophy and science, particularly the modern project of the progressive scientific investigation and technological mastery of nature.[12]

It is surely one of the great ironies of history that the Hermetic ideal of man as magus, achieving total knowledge and wielding Godlike powers to bring the world to perfection, was the prototype of the modern scientist. Yet, as Gerald Hanratty writes, "the widespread recourse to

10. See David Walsh, *The Esoteric Origins of Modern Ideological Thought: Boehme and Hegel* (Ph.D. Dissertation, University of Virginia, 1978). See also *The Mysticism of Innerworldly Fulfillment: A Study of Jacob Böhme* (Gainesville: University Presses of Florida, 1983), "The Historical Dialectic of Spirit: Jacob Böhme's Influence on Hegel," in *History and System: Hegel's Philosophy of History*, ed. Robert L. Perkins (Albany: State University of New York Press, 1984), 28, and "A Mythology of Reason: The Persistence of Pseudo-Science in the Modern World," in *Science, Pseudo-Science, and Utopianism in Early Modern Thought*, ed. Stephen A. McKnight (Columbia: University of Missouri Press, 1992).

11. In addition to Hegel's published writings, the primary sources I have relied on include letters, manuscripts, lecture notes, student notes, and reports by contemporaries of remarks made by Hegel. Remarks culled from student notes have been published as the *Zusätze* to the *Encyclopedia of the Philosophical Sciences*, and the published editions of Hegel's lectures on the history of philosophy, art, religion, and world history are also largely made up of student notes.

12. In addition to Bacon's use of Rosicrucian images, Descartes's search for the Rosicrucians, Spinoza's debts to Kabbalism, Leibniz's fascination with Rosicrucianism, Kabbalah, and alchemy, and Newton's fascination with millennialism and alchemy, there is also evidence that Kant was interested in the visions of Emanuel Swedenborg; Schelling was interested in Böhme, Swedenborg, and Mesmer; Schopenhauer was interested in Böhme, Swedenborg, and Lavater; William James was interested in Swedenborg, Fechner, spiritualism and ESP; C. S. Peirce was interested in Swedenborg and Böhme; C. D. Broad was interested in ESP; and, today, Michael Dummett is interested in tarot cards (Michael Dummett, *The Visconti-Sforza Tarot Cards* [New York: G. Braziller, 1986]).

magical and alchemical techniques inspired a new confidence in man's operational powers. In contrast with the passive and contemplative attitudes which generally prevail during earlier centuries, Renaissance alchemists and Magi asserted their dominion over all levels of being."[13] Hermeticism replaces the love of wisdom with the lust for power. As we shall see, Hegel's system is the ultimate expression of this pursuit of mastery.

3. What is Hermeticism?

Whether or not Hegel can be understood as "Hermetic" depends on how Hermeticism is defined. In truth, Hermeticism is difficult to define rigorously. Its adherents all tend to share certain interests—often classed as "occult" or "esoteric"—which are held together merely by family resemblances. In part, my argument for Hegel's Hermeticism depends on demonstrating that Hegel's interests coincide with the curious mixture of interests typical of Hermeticists. These include alchemy, Kabbalism, Mesmerism, extrasensory perception, spiritualism, dowsing, eschatology, *prisca theologia*, *philosophia perennis*, Lullism, Paracelcism, Joachimism, Rosicrucianism, Masonry, Eckhartean mysticism, "correspondences," secret systems of symbolism, vitalism, and "cosmic sympathies."[14]

There is, however, one essential feature that I shall take as definitive of Hermeticism. Ernest Lee Tuveson, in his *The Avatars of Thrice Greatest Hermes: An Approach to Romanticism* suggests that Hermeticism constitutes a middle position between pantheism and the Judaeo-Christian conception of God. According to traditional Judaeo-Christian thought, God utterly transcends and is infinitely distant from creation. Furthermore, God is entirely self-sufficient and therefore did not have to create the world, and would have lost nothing if He had not created it. Thus the act of creation is essentially gratuitous and unmotivated. God creates out of sheer abundance, not out of need. This doctrine has proved dissatisfying and even disturbing to many, for it makes creation seem

13. Gerald Hanratty, "Hegel and the Gnostic Tradition: II," *Philosophical Studies* (Ireland) 31 (1986–87): 301–25, 308. Walsh writes that "The empirical investigation of nature received its impetus from the conviction of Neoplatonic Hermeticism that reality is a hierarchy of occult or hidden sympathies uniting the whole and ultimately emanating from the divine One" (Walsh, "A Mythology of Reason," 146).

14. Antoine Faivre writes that "Hermeticism" has come to be used "to designate the general attitude of mind underlying a variety of traditions and/or currents beside alchemy, such as Hermetism [the religion of the *Corpus Hermeticum*], Astrology, Kabbalah, Christian Theosophy, and *philosophia occulta* or *magia* (in the sense these two words acquired in the Renaissance, that is, of a magical vision of nature understood as a living being replete with signs and correspondences, which could be deciphered and interpreted)." See Faivre, "Renaissance Hermeticism and Western Esotericism" in *Gnosis and Hermeticism*, ed. Roelof van den Broek and Wouter J. Hanegraaf (Albany: State University of New York Press, 1998), 110. Faivre distinguishes between "Hermeticism" and "Hermetism," the latter term designating the *Corpus Hermeticum* and its intellectual milieu.

arbitrary and absurd. Pantheism, by contrast, so thoroughly involves the divine in the world that *everything* becomes God, even mud, hair, and dirt—which drains the divine of its exaltedness and sublimity. Thus, pantheism is equally dissatisfying.

Hermeticism is a middle position because it affirms *both* God's transcendence of the world and his involvement in it. God is metaphysically distinct from the world, yet God needs the world to complete Himself. Thus the act of creation is not arbitrary or gratuitous, but necessary and rational. Consider these lines from the "Discourse of Hermes to Tat: The mixing bowl or the monad" (*Corpus Hermeticum* 4): "If you force me to say something still more daring, it is [God's] essence to be pregnant with all things and to make them. As it is impossible for anything to be produced without a maker, so also is it impossible for this maker [not] to exist always unless he is always making everything. . . . He is himself the things that are and those that are not."[15] Consider also *Corpus Hermeticum* 10: "God's activity is will, and his essence is to will all things to be."[16] Finally, consider *Corpus Hermeticum* 14: "For the two are all there is, what comes to be and what makes it, and it is impossible to separate the one from the other. No maker can exist without something that comes to be."[17] Thus, according to Hermeticism, *God requires creation in order to be God.*[18] This Hermetic account of creation is central to Hegel's thought as well.

But there is more. Hermeticists not only hold that God requires creation, they make a specific creature, man, play a crucial role in God's self-actualization. Hermeticism holds that man can know God, and that man's knowledge of God is necessary for God's own completion. Consider the words of *Corpus Hermeticum* 10: "For God does not ignore mankind; on the contrary, he recognizes him fully and wishes to be recognized. For mankind this is the only deliverance, the knowledge of God. It is ascent to Olympus."[19] *Corpus Hermeticum* 11 asks, "Who is more visible than God? This is why he made all things: so that through them all you might look on him."[20] As Garth Fowden notes, what God *gains* from creation is recognition: "Man's contemplation of God is in some sense a two-way process. Not only does Man wish to know God, but God too desires to be known by the most glorious of His creations, Man."[21] In short, it is man's end to achieve knowledge of God (or "the wisdom of

15. *Hermetica*, trans. Brian Copenhaver (Cambridge: Cambridge University Press, 1992), 20.
16. Ibid., 30.
17. Ibid, 56.
18. Tuveson, however, goes too far in *identifying* this position with Hermeticism, rejecting other aspects—such as interest in alchemy and correspondences—as "accidental" and "not truly" Hermetic. Ernest Lee Tuveson, *The Avatars of Thrice Great Hermes: An Approach to Romanticism* (Lewisburg, Pa.: Bucknell University Press, 1982), 15–16; 34.
19. Copenhaver, 33.
20. Ibid., 42.
21. Garth Fowden, *The Egyptian Hermes: A Historical Approach to the Late Pagan Mind* (Princeton, N.J.: Princeton University Press, 1986), 104.

God," theosophy). In so doing, man realizes God's own need to be recognized. Man's knowledge of God becomes God's knowledge of himself. Thus the need for which the cosmos is created is the need for self-knowledge, attained through recognition. Variations on this doctrine are to be found throughout the Hermetic tradition.

It is important to understand the significance of this doctrine in the history of ideas. On the standard Judaeo-Christian account of creation, the creation of the world and God's command that mankind seek to know and love him seem arbitrary, because there is no reason why a perfect being should want or need anything. The great advantage of the Hermetic conception is that it tells us *why* the cosmos and the human desire to know God exist in the first place.

This Hermetic doctrine of the "circular" relationship between God and creation and the necessity of man for the completion of God is utterly original. It is not to be found in earlier philosophy. But it recurs again and again in the thought of Hermeticists, and it is the chief doctrinal identity between Hermeticism and Hegelian thought.

Hegel is often described as a mystic. Indeed, even he describes himself as one (see chapter 4). But mysticism is a broad concept that subsumes many radically different ideas. All forms of mysticism aim at some kind of knowledge of, experience of, or unity with the divine. If we ask what kind of mystic Hegel is, the answer is that he is a Hermeticist. Hermeticism is often confused with another form of mysticism, Gnosticism (particularly in recent Hegel scholarship).[22] Gnosticism and Hermeticism both believe that a divine "spark" is implanted in man, and that man can come to know God. However, Gnosticism involves an absolutely negative account of creation. It does not regard creation as a part of God's being, or as "completing" God. Nor does Gnosticism hold that God somehow needs man to know Him. Hermeticism is also very often confused with Neoplatonism. Like the Hermeticists, Plotinus holds that the cosmos is a circular process of emanation from and return to the One. Unlike the Hermeticists, Plotinus does not hold that the One is completed by man's contemplation of it. (Centuries later, however, the Neoplatonism of Proclus and of the Renaissance was influenced by Hermeticism.)

Another parallel between Hermeticism and Hegel concerns the initiation process through which the intuitive portion of the intellect is trained to see the Reason inherent in the world. As Fowden notes, Hermetic initiation seems to fall into two parts, one dealing with self-

---

22. See for example Gerald Hanratty, "Hegel and the Gnostic Tradition: I," *Philosophical Studies* (Ireland) 30 (1984): 23–48; "Hegel and the Gnostic Tradition II," *Philosophical Studies* (Ireland) 31 (1986–87): 301–25; Jeff Mitscherling, "The Identity of the Human and the Divine in the Logic of Speculative Philosophy" in *Hegel and the Tradition: Essays in Honor of H. S. Harris*, ed. Michael Baur and John Russon (Toronto: University of Toronto Press, 1997), 143–61. Mitscherling's understanding of Gnosticism derives from the Messina Colloquium on the Origins of Gnosticism. As Roelof van den Broek points out, however, the Messina Colloquium defines Gnosticism so broadly "it loses all concrete substance." See Broek, "Gnosticism and Hermetism in Antiquity" in *Gnosis and Hermeticism*, 4.

knowledge, the other with knowledge of God.[23] It can easily be shown, simply on a theoretical level, that these two are intimately wedded. To really know one's self is to be able to give a complete speech about the conditions of one's being, and this involves speaking about God and His entire cosmos. As Pico della Mirandola puts it, "he who knows himself knows all things in himself."[24] Also, in the Near East it was typical to portray God as hovering strangely between transcendence and immanence. The attainment of enlightenment involved somehow seeing the divine in oneself, indeed becoming divine.

We do not really know anything about the Hermes cult that may have employed the Hermetic texts as its sacred writings. We know little or nothing of their rites of initiation or how they lived. We can, however, say that Hermetic initiation differed from initiation into, for example, the Eleusinian mysteries in classical Greece. We also happen to know quite little about what happened at Eleusis, but it does seem to be the case that illumination there consisted in the participation in some kind of arresting experience which was intended to change the initiate permanently.[25] We do not know what that experience was, but we do know that it could be had by young and old, rich and poor, educated and uneducated. This is not the case with Hermetic initiation. Salvation for the Hermeticists was, as we have seen, through gnosis, through understanding. This could be attained only through hard work, and then it could be attained only by some. Hermes is quoted in *Corpus Hermeticum* 16 as stating that his teaching "keeps the meaning of its words concealed," hidden from the discernment of the unworthy.

However, it would be a mistake to treat the Hermetic initiation as purely intellectual. Enlightenment does not occur simply by learning a set of doctrines. One must not only know doctrine, but have the real-life experience of the truth of the doctrine. One must be led up to illumination carefully; one must actually explore the blind alleys that promise illumination but do not deliver. Only in this way will the true doctrine mean anything; only in this way will the initiate's life actually change. Fowden writes that Hermetic initiation is envisaged as "a real experience, stretching all the capacities of those who embark upon it," and he quotes *Corpus Hermeticum* 4, stating that "it is an extremely tortuous way, to abandon what one is used to and possesses now, and to retrace one's steps towards the old primordial things."[26] We will see in chapter 4 that Hegel preserves both the intellectual and emotional moments of this Hermetic conception of initiation.

Enlightenment, for the authors of the *Hermetica* and for Hegel, is not just an intellectual event; it is expected to change the life of the enlight-

23. Fowden, *The Egyptian Hermes*, 106.
24. Giovanni Pico della Mirandola, *Oration on the Dignity of Man*, trans. A. Robert Caponigri (Chicago: Regnery Gateway, 1956), 28.
25. Joseph Campbell, *Transformations of Myth Through Time* (New York: Harper and Row, 1990), 189ff.
26. Fowden, *The Egyptian Hermes*, 106.

ened one. Philosophy, for Hegel, is about living.[27] In brief, the man who achieves *Selbstbewusstsein* is the man who becomes *selbstbewusst*: confident, self-actualized, no longer an ordinary human being. Klaus Vondung writes that "The Hermeticist does not need to escape from the world in order to save himself; he wants to gain knowledge of the world in order to expand his own self, and utilize this knowledge to penetrate into the self of God. Hermeticism is a positive Gnosis, as it were, devoted to the world."[28] To know everything is to in some sense have control over everything. This is what I term the ideal of man as magus, and it is unique to the *Hermetica*. See, for example, *Corpus Hermeticum* 4: "All those who heeded the proclamation and immersed themselves in mind [*nous*] participated in knowledge and became perfect [or "complete," *teleioi*] people because they received mind. But those who missed the point of the proclamation are people of reason [or "speech," *log<ik>on*] because they did not receive [the gift of] mind as well *and do not know the purpose or the agents of their coming to be.*"[29] In other words, the men of complete self-understanding who know even the "purpose or the agents of their coming to be" are perfect human beings. If Hegel did not believe that man could literally become God, he certainly believed that the wise man is *daimonic*: a more-than-merely-human participant in the divine life.

In the *Corpus Hermeticum* we find a kind of "bridge position" between Egyptian occultism and the modern Hermeticism of Hegel and others. Instead of conceiving words as carrying literal occult power, words come to be seen as carrying a kind of *existential empowerment*. The ideal of Hermetic theosophy becomes the formulation of a "complete speech" (*teleeis logos*, "perfect discourse" or perhaps "Encyclopedic discourse," which means, of course, "circular" discourse). When acquired, the complete speech, which concerns the whole of reality, will radically transform and empower the life of the enlightened one. So Hegel writes in a fragment preserved by Rosenkranz,

> Every individual is a blind link in the chain of absolute necessity, along which the world develops. Every individual can raise himself to domination over a great length of this chain only if he realizes the goal of this great necessity and, by virtue of this knowledge, learns to speak the *magic words* which evoke its shape. The knowledge of how to simultaneously absorb and elevate oneself beyond the total energy of suffering and antithesis that has dominated the world and all forms of its development for thousands of years—this knowledge can be gathered from philosophy alone.[30]

27. H. S. Harris, *Hegel's Development*, vol. 2, *Night Thoughts* (Oxford: Oxford University Press, 1983), 191ff.
28. Vondung, "Millenarianism, Hermeticism, and the Search for a Universal Science." In *Science, Pseudo-Science, and Utopianism in Early Modern Thought*, ed. Stephen McKnight, (Columbia: University of Missouri Press, 1992), 132.
29. Copenhaver, 16–17; emphasis added.
30. Karl Rosenkranz, *Georg Wilhelm Friedrich Hegels Leben* (Darmstadt: Wissenschaftliche Buchgesellschaft, 1969), 141. The fragment is referred to by Harris and Knox as "The Supposed Conclusion of the System of Ethical Life." See H. S. Harris and T. M. Knox, *System of Ethical Life and First Philosophy of Spirit* (Albany: State University of New York Press, 1979), 178.

Another parallel between Hermeticism and Hegel is the analysis of the divine into a set of "modes" or "moments." Hermeticists do not rest content with the idea of an unknowable God. Instead, they seek to penetrate the divine mystery. They hold that it is possible to know God in a piecemeal fashion, by coming to understand the different aspects of the divine. The best example is Kabbalism, both in its Jewish and Christian forms. Lull, Bruno, Paracelsus, Böhme, Oetinger, and many others in the Hermetic tradition hold this belief.

Another parallel between Hermeticism and Hegel is the doctrine of internal relations. For the Hermeticists, the cosmos is not a loosely connected, or to use Hegelian language, externally related set of particulars. Rather, everything in the cosmos is internally related, bound up with everything else. Even though the cosmos may be hierarchically arranged, there are forces that cut across and unify all the levels. Divine powers understood variously as "energy" or "light" pervade the whole.[31] This principle is most clearly expressed in the so-called *Emerald Tablet* of Hermes Trismegistus, which begins with the famous lines "As above, so below." This maxim became the central tenet of Western occultism, for it laid the basis for a doctrine of the unity of the cosmos through sympathies and correspondences between its various levels. The most important implication of this doctrine is the idea that man is the microcosm, in which the whole of the macrocosm is reflected. Self-knowledge, therefore, leads necessarily to knowledge of the whole.

To summarize, the doctrines of the *Hermetica* that became enduring features of the Hermetic tradition can be enumerated as follows:

1. God requires creation in order to be God.
2. God is in some sense "completed" or has a need fulfilled through man's contemplation of Him.
3. Illumination involves capturing the whole of reality in a complete, encyclopedic speech.
4. Man can perfect himself through gnosis: he becomes empowered through the possession of the complete speech.
5. Man can know the aspects or "moments" of God.
6. An initial stage of purification in which the initiate is purged of false intellectual standpoints is required before the reception of the true doctrine.
7. The universe is an internally related whole pervaded by cosmic energies.

To make clear the parallels between these doctrines and Hegel's, here is a preview of what I will be arguing in the rest of this book:

1. Hegel holds that God's being involves "creation," the subject matter of his *Philosophy of Nature*. Nature is a moment of God's being.
2. Hegel holds that God is in some sense "completed" or actualized through the intellectual activity of mankind: "Philosophy" is the final stage in the actualization of Absolute Spirit. Hegel holds the

31. Fowden, *The Egyptian Hermes*, 77.

"circular" conception of God and of the cosmos I referred to earlier, involving God "returning to Himself" and truly becoming God through man.

3. Hegel's philosophy is *encyclopedic*: he aims to end philosophy, for all intents and purposes, by capturing the whole of reality in a complete, circular speech.

4. Hegel believes that we rise above nature and become masters of our own destiny through the profound gnosis provided by his system.

5. Hegel's *Logic* is an attempt to know the aspects or "moments" of God as a system of ideas. In a famous passage of the *Science of Logic*, Hegel states that the Logic "is to be understood as the system of pure reason, as the realm of pure thought. This realm is truth as it is without veil and in its own absolute nature. It can therefore be said that this content is the exposition of God as He is in his eternal essence before the creation of nature and a finite Spirit" (Miller, 50; WL I, 33–34).

6. Hegel's *Phenomenology of Spirit* represents, in the Hegelian system, an initial stage of purification in which the would-be philosopher is purged of false intellectual standpoints so that he might receive the true doctrine of Absolute Knowing (Logic-Nature-Spirit).

7. Hegel's account of nature rejects the philosophy of mechanism. He upholds what the followers of Bradley would later call a doctrine of "internal relations," as against the typical, modern mechanistic understanding of things in terms of "external relations."

4. Hegel: A Metaphysical View

Given the evidence for Hegel's place in the Hermetic tradition, it seems surprising that so few Hegel scholars acknowledge it. The topic is often dismissed as unimportant or uninteresting (it is neither). Usually, it is treated as relevant only to Hegel's youth (which is false). Surely one reason for this attitude is disciplinary specialization. Few scholars of the history of philosophy ever study Hermetic thinkers. Another reason is the recent tendency among influential Hegel scholars to argue that it is wrongheaded to treat Hegel as having *any* serious interest in metaphysics or theology at all, let alone the sort of exotic metaphysics and theology that we find in Hermeticism. This is the so-called "non-metaphysical reading" of Hegel. As Cyril O'Regan has pointed out, it goes hand in hand with an "anti-theological" reading.[32] For instance, David Kolb writes, "I want most of all to preclude the idea that Hegel provides a cosmology including the discovery of a wondrous new superentity, a cosmic self or a world soul or a supermind."[33] But this is exactly what Hegel does.

The phrase "non-metaphysical reading" seems to have originated with Klaus Hartmann who, in his influential 1972 article "Hegel: A Non-Metaphysical View," identified Hegel's system as a "hermeneutic of cate-

---

32. See Cyril O'Regan, *The Heterodox Hegel* (Albany: State University of New York Press, 1994), 86.
33. David Kolb, *Critique of Pure Modernity: Hegel, Heidegger, and After* (Chicago: University of Chicago Press, 1986), 42–43.

gories."[34] Other well-known proponents of Hartmann's approach include Kenley Royce Dove, William Maker, Terry Pinkard, and Richard Dien Winfield.

The non-metaphysical/anti-theological reading relies on ignoring or explaining away the many frankly metaphysical, cosmological, theological, and theosophical passages in Hegel's writings and lectures.[35] Thus the non-metaphysical reading is less an interpretation of Hegel than a revision. Its advocates sometimes admit this—Hartmann, for instance— but more often than not they offer their "reading" in opposition to other interpretations of what Hegel meant. It is, furthermore, no accident that the same authors finish out their "interpretation" by tacking a left-wing politics onto Hegel, for they are, in fact, the intellectual heirs of the nineteenth-century "Young Hegelians" who also gave non-metaphysical, anti-theological "interpretations" of Hegel. The non-metaphysical reading is simply Hegel shorn of everything offensive to the modern, secular, liberal mind. This does not, however, imply that I am offering an alternative "right Hegelian" reading of Hegel. I am simply reading Hegel. In so doing, I hope to contribute to the "nonpartisan, historical and textual analysis" of Hegel's thought called for by Louis Dupré.[36]

Such a reading, I am convinced, places Hegel's philosophy squarely in the tradition of classical metaphysics. In this view, I am in accord with the broadly "ontotheological" interpretation of Hegel offered by Martin Heidegger, who coined the term, and by such scholars as Walter Jaeschke, Emil Fackenheim, Cyril O'Regan, Malcolm Clark, Albert Chapelle, Claude Bruaire, and Iwan Iljin.[37] "Ontotheology" refers to

34. "Klaus Hartmann, "Hegel: A Non-Metaphysical View," in Hegel: A Collection of Critical Essays, ed. Alasdair MacIntyre (Notre Dame: University of Notre Dame Press, 1972), 124.

35. Non-metaphysical/anti-theological readers of Hegel must somehow explain passages such as the following: "God is the one and only object of philosophy. [Its concern is] to occupy itself with God, to apprehend everything in Him, to lead everything back to Him, as well as to derive everything particular from God and to justify everything only insofar as it stems from God, is sustained through its relationship with Him, lives by His radiance and has [within itself] the mind of God. Thus philosophy is theology, and [one's] occupation with philosophy—or rather in philosophy—is of itself the service of God" (LPR 1:84; VPR I:3–4).

36. Louis Dupré, foreword to O'Regan, The Heterodox Hegel, ix.

37. Martin Heidegger, "The Onto-Theo-Logical Constitution of Metaphysics," in Identity and Difference, bilingual ed., trans. Joan Stambaugh (New York: Harper and Row, 1969); Walter Jaeschke, Reason in Religion: The Formation of Hegel's Philosophy of Religion, trans. J. Michael Steward and Peter Hodgson (Berkeley: University of California, 1990), Die Religionsphilosophie Hegels (Darmstadt: Wissenschaftliche Buchgesellschaft, 1983), "Speculative and Anthropological Criticism of Religion: A Theological Orientation to Hegel and Feuerbach," Journal of the American Academy of Religion 48 (1980): 345–64; Emil Fackenheim, The Religious Dimension of Hegel's Thought (Bloomington: Indiana University Press, 1967); Malcolm Clark, Logic and System: A Study of the Transition from "Vorstellung" to Thought in the Philosophy of Hegel (The Hague: Martinus Nijhoff, 1971); Albert Chapelle, Hegel et la religion, 3 vols. (Paris: Éditions Universitaires, 1964–71); Claude Bruaire, Logique et religion chrétienne dans la philosophie de Hegel (Paris: Éditions du Seuil, 1964); Iwan Iljin, Die Philosophie Hegels also kontemplative Gotteslehre (Berne: Francke, 1946).

the equation of Being, God, and logos. Hegel's account of the Absolute is structurally identical to Aristotle's account of Being as Substance (*ousia*): it is the most real, independent, and self-sufficient thing that is. Hegel identifies the Absolute with God, and does so both in his public statements (his books and lectures) and in his private notes—and with a straight face, without winking at us.[38] Hegel does not offer the categories of his Logic as mere "hermeneutic devices" but as eternal forms, moments or aspects of the Divine Mind (Absolute Idea). He treats nature as "expressing" the divine ideas in imperfect form. He speaks of a "World Soul" and uses it to explain how dowsing and animal magnetism work. He structures his entire philosophy around the Christian Trinity, and claims that with Christianity the "principle" of speculative philosophy was *revealed* to mankind.[39] He tells us—again with a straight face—that the state is God on earth.

I see no reason not to take Hegel at his word on any of this. I am interested only in what Hegel thought, not in what he *ought* to have thought. To be sure, Hegel's appropriation of classical metaphysics and Christianity *is* transformative; Hegel is no ordinary believer. But his metaphysical and religious commitments are not exoteric. He believes that his Absolute and World Soul, and so forth, are *real beings*; they are just not real in the sense in which traditional, pious "picture-thinking" conceives of them.[40] If Hegel departs from the metaphysical tradition in

38. In a July 3, 1826, letter to Friedrich August Gottreu Tholuck (1799–1877), Hegel writes, "I am a Lutheran, and through philosophy have been at once completely confirmed in Lutheranism." See *Hegel: The Letters*, trans. Clark Butler and Christianne Seiler (Bloomington: Indiana University Press, 1984), 520; cf. Johannes Hoffmeister, *Briefe von und an Hegel*, 4 vols. (Hamburg: Felix Meiner, 1952–61). Hoffmeister numbers the letters. This is number 514a. Henceforth, references to Hegel's letters will be written as follows: "Butler, 520; Hoffmeister #514a." In 1826 a small controversy erupted in Berlin when a priest attending Hegel's lectures complained to the government about allegedly anti-Catholic statements made by Hegel. Hegel responded: "Should suit be filed because of remarks I have made from the podium before Catholic students causing them annoyance, they would have to blame only themselves for attending philosophical lectures at a Protestant university under a professor who prides himself on having been baptized and raised a Lutheran, which he still is and shall remain" (See Butler, 532). In an 1829 review of K. F. Göschel, *Aphorismen über Nichtwissen und absolutes Wissen im Verhältnisse zur christlichen Glaubenserkenntnis*, Hegel makes it clear that he is pleased to have his work regarded as a "Christian philosophy." *Berliner Schriften, 1818–1831*, ed. Eva Moldehauer and Karl Markus Michel (Frankfurt am Main: Suhrkamp, 1986).

39. In the *Lectures on the History of Philosophy*, Hegel notes that "the Arians, since they did not recognize God in Christ, did away with the idea of the Trinity, and consequently with the principle of all speculative philosophy" (LHP 3:20). J. N. Findlay writes that "[Hegel's] whole system may in fact be regarded as an attempt to see the Christian mysteries in everything whatever, every natural process, every form of human activity, and every logical transition" (*Hegel: A Re-Examination*, 131).

40. In the *Encyclopedia Logic*, Hegel writes of picture-thinking: "Finding itself displaced into the pure realm of the Concept, it does not know *where* in the world it is" (EL § 3; Geraets, 27).

anything, it is in dispensing with its false modesty. Hegel does not claim to be merely searching for truth. He claims that he has found it.

5. The Plan of This Book

In this book I will be concerned to do two things:

1) To demonstrate the *influence* of the Hermetic tradition on Hegel—by way of remarks made in his texts and lectures, works he is known to have had access to, and individuals he is known to have corresponded with or met.

2) To situate Hegel's thought *within* the Hermetic tradition; to show that Hegel self-consciously appropriated and aligned himself with Hermeticism; to show that Hegel's thought can best be understood as Hermetic. This is the most radical element of my thesis.

What will emerge from my discussion is, I hope, a radically new picture of Hegel's thought. It will no longer be possible to treat him as an "arch rationalist," as many still do, let alone to read him in a non-metaphysical or anti-theological manner.

Chapter 1 is devoted to an overview of the Hermetic tradition up until the seventeenth century, dealing mainly with Germany. Chapter 2 starts with the early seventeenth century and covers up to and including Hegel's youth. I will be concerned in chapter 2 mainly with the intellectual milieu Hegel was born into. Chapter 3 is central to my account. It presents an overall interpretation of Hegel's thought in light of his Hermetic connections. Chapters 4 through 7 cover Hegel's major writings.

In these chapters, I will not be concerned to present an "intellectual biography" of Hegel. Such a work has already been written by H. S. Harris, and I do not intend to try to surpass it. The study is text-centered, although I have sketched-in important details about Hegel's life throughout. In terms of my treatment of Hegel's intellectual development, I have not made fine distinctions between "stages" in his thinking. Developmental readings which speak of "early" and "late" periods in a thinker's life very often stem from an inability to see the underlying identity or common tie between texts which are superficially different (e.g., in their use of different philosophical vocabularies). In the case of *great* thinkers—like Plato, Aristotle, and Hegel—I think that there is very little development. Great minds do not, for the most part, change (though in chapter 7 I will discuss one important way in which I believe Hegel did change his mind, and his allegiances). The different works produced by great philosophers over a lifetime are usually variations on a theme, or themes. To borrow Hegel's language, one must learn to see the identity in difference.

Part 1. The Sorcerer's Apprenticeship

A Brief Overview of the Hermetic Tradition

1. The Earliest Hermeticists

This chapter presents a brief account of the major figures and movements in the Hermetic tradition up to the end of the seventeenth century, with special attention given to thinkers Hegel read and discussed and thinkers who were part of, or influenced, the Hermetic tradition in Germany. Chapter 2 will be primarily devoted to the Hermetic context of Hegel's early development.

The first major philosopher who shows signs of Hermetic influence is Proclus (412–85). Speaking of Proclus in his *Lectures on the History of Philosophy*, Hegel refers to the *Corpus Hermeticum*: "Proclus studied everything pertaining to the mysteries, the Orphic hymns, the writings of Hermes [*die Schriften des Hermes*], and religious institutions of every kind, so that, wherever he went, he understood the ceremonies of the pagan worship better than the priests who were placed there for the purpose of performing them" (LHP 2:433; *Werke* 19:467).

Hegel admires Proclus as a "profoundly speculative man" and states that with him the Neoplatonic philosophy "has at last reached a more systematic order" (LHP 2:434, 435; *Werke* 19:468, 469). What Hegel seems to admire chiefly in Proclus is his use of the dialectic and the triadic form. Proclus attempts to demonstrate, according to Hegel, "the many as one and the one as many," and how, "all determinations, and particularly that of multiplicity, are resolved into themselves and return into unity" (LHP 2:436; *Werke* 19:470). What Proclus adds to the Plotinian system is teleology. Plotinus, like the Hermeticists, offers a circular account of the cosmos as emanating from the One and then returning back to it through the speculative activity of the philosopher. Unlike the Hermeticists, however, he also holds that the One is entirely self-sufficient and emanates the world not out of need, but out of superabundance. Thus the One is in no way completed by the return. Proclus, however, follows the *Hermetica* in teaching that the One must emanate creation in order to be complete. According to Hegel, Proclus's philosophy displays the "self-development" of the One (LHP 2:435; *Werke* 19:470). Hegel describes in detail the three spheres, each "complete in itself," which constitute the moments of the One (LHP 2:440; *Werke* 19:474). In short, Hegel sees much of himself in Proclus.

As Antoine Faivre notes, from the end of the Roman world until the Renaissance, the Latin *Asclepius* was the only portion of the *Corpus Hermeticum* available in the West.[1] During this period of nearly a thousand years, the primary transmission of Hermetic ideas to Europe was through alchemy. During the Middle Ages Hermes Trismegistus was given as the author of scores of occult works, and even medical texts. Prominent among this "pseudo-Hermetic" literature were the various Arabic texts attributed to Hermes. The most famous of these works was the *Emerald Tablet*. A very short work (about a page long) it was nevertheless extremely influential, particularly on alchemy. According to the text, Apollonius of Tyana discovered the tomb of Hermes Trismegistus and, inside, an engraved emerald tablet still clutched in his gnarled hands. The text of the tablet then follows. It consists of twelve propositions. The initial one is the most famous: "In truth certainly and without doubt, whatever is below is like that which is above, and whatever is above is like that which is below, to accomplish the miracles of one thing." Others are clearly alchemical in nature: "Separate the earth from the fire and the subtle from the gross, softly and with great patience."[2] The oldest known version of the *Emerald Tablet* dates from the eighth century A.D. Arab Spain functioned as a conduit for this and other Islamic-Hermetic texts to Christian Europe.

In the late twelfth century, a book appeared in Western Europe entitled *Book of Propositions or Rules of Theology, said to be by the Philosopher Termegistus* (also known as the *Book of Twenty-four Philosophers*). It contained twenty-four propositions, the second of which subsequently enjoyed a long career, borrowed by a succession of other authors: "God is an infinite sphere whose center is everywhere, and whose circumference is nowhere."[3] As Brian Copenhaver notes, this work became a favorite of Albertus Magnus and his student Thomas Aquinas.[4] Aquinas was supposed to have authored a work in which it was claimed that Abel, the son of Adam, carved esoteric teachings on stones, which then passed into the hands of Hermes Trismegistus, and then to Thomas.[5]

Among the Hermetic thinkers of the High Middle Ages whom I shall discuss later in the text are Joachim de Fiore (1135–1202), a Calabrian monk who developed a mystical theory of history that came to exercise an influence on German Pietism and Hegel; Ramon Lull (1235–1316), who was perhaps the first individual to develop a systematic science for the achievement of *pansophia*—universal wisdom; and Meister Eckhart (ca.1260–ca.1327), one of the fathers of the German mystical tradition.

---

1. Faivre, *The Eternal Hermes*, 18.
2. David Fideler, *Jesus Christ, Son of God: Ancient Cosmology and Early Christian Symbolism* (Wheaton, Ill.: Quest, 1993), 233.
3. This passage is highly descriptive of many kinds of mystical philosophy. Ronald Gray takes it as Spinozistic! See Gray, *Goethe the Alchemist* (Cambridge, U.K.: Cambridge University Press, 1952), 72.
4. Copenhaver, xlvii.
5. Faivre, *Eternal Hermes*, 94.

The first significant German figure who can be called "Hermetic" is Albertus Magnus (1193/1206–1280), the teacher of Thomas Aquinas. Albert was a renowned alchemist who mentions Hermes Trismegistus by name in twenty-three of his writings. Another of his students, Dietrich of Freiburg (also known as Theodoric of Freiburg; ca.1250–1311) melded Albertian alchemical theory with the Neoplatonism of Proclus. Dietrich held a version of emanation theory in which a transcendent God gives rise to the One. Contra Plotinus, he identified the One with the *Logos* that informs all the levels of creation, including man, the "image of the One."[6]

The fourteenth century in Germany, known as the "century of heresy,"[7] witnessed a tremendous flowering of mysticism. Virtually no centers of higher learning existed in Germany until the fourteenth century, and as a consequence it was necessary for German thinkers to go to Italy and France to be educated. Thus, among other things, Hermetic philosophy—which had seeped into France and Italy through Arabic Spain—gradually found its way into Germany. The Rhineland was already a haven for freethinkers and mystics. The region produced its own homegrown mysticism in the form of the so-called *Frauenmystik*, which included figures such as Hildegard of Bingen (1098–1179). Her *Book of Divine Works* (1163–73) includes the memorable image of creation as an act of God making countless mirrors in which to behold Himself.

2. Meister Eckhart

Johannes Eckhart, better known as Meister Eckhart, was born in Hocheim near Gotha about 1260 and died about 1327. No one has demonstrated direct Hermetic influences on Eckhart, but his thought exhibits certain "Hermetic" features and was co-opted by German Hermeticists in later times. Eckhart's significance for German philosophy and intellectual culture in general cannot be overstressed. Ernst Benz writes that

> the German language of the High Middle Ages was essentially poetic. German literature of the Middle Ages was the literature of the *Minnesang*, of the troubadours, of the *Heldenlied*, of epic songs such as the *Nibelungenlied*, which means that it was a language of images, allegories, parables, not a language of abstract concepts and philosophical and logical terms. There was no philosophical terminology in the German language, and there were no German translations of Latin philosophical or theological treatises. . . . The German language of the Middle Ages did not take part in the scholastic development of philosophy, theology, and the sciences. It is only with . . . Meister Eckhart that all this changed.[8]

6. Lewis White Beck, *Early German Philosophy* (Cambridge, Mass: Harvard University Press, 1969), 39.
7. Ibid., 41.
8. Ernst Benz, *Mystical Sources*, 8.

Eckhart was a Dominican monk and university professor, initially at Paris and then at Cologne. Part of his duties in Cologne consisted in preaching to convents of Dominican nuns. The sisters did not know Latin, and so Eckhart was forced to translate Latin philosophical and theological terms into German. (For instance, Eckhart was the first to translate the Latin *actualitas* as "werkelichkeit.") Given the rather unusual nature of his thought, he was also forced to employ common words in an uncommon way, and to employ metaphors and images of all kinds (thus, words like *abyss* [*Abgrund*] took on philosophical or mystical meaning). For the first time, through Eckhart, philosophy began to speak German. Benz writes that "Meister Eckhart is indeed the creator of a new German philosophical and theological terminology; and since his own theology was a mystical one, founded on mystical experiences and intuitions, it is truly with mystical speculation that philosophical speculation in German began."[9]

Eckhart preached that *intelligere*, knowing, is the basic attribute of the divine. Like Aristotle's Unmoved Mover, Eckhart's God thinks His own thought, but unlike Aristotle's God, Eckhart's is thoroughly involved with the world. In fact, it is hard to see where the difference between God and the world is to be drawn at all for Eckhart, for he taught that apart from God there is nothing.[10] Like so many mystics, Eckhart conceived God as the "coincidence of opposites." By collapsing the distinction between God and World, Eckhart obviously opened himself up to the charge of pantheism—but actually his philosophy is much more radical than simple pantheism.

In his tenth sermon, Eckhart preached that just as a son requires a father to give him existence, so the father is not father without the son. Similarly, God would not be God without creation: God must create to actualize His nature.[11] (This is one of the innovations of the *Hermetica*.) Just as in Hegel more than five hundred years later, God the Father is conceived as "abstract" and "incomplete" apart from na-

9. Ibid., 10. Benz gives as examples of philosophical terms originating in early German mysticism *Abbild, Anschauung, Bild, Bildhaftigkeit, entbilden, entichen, Entichung, ergründen, Erkennen, Erkenntnis, Form, Gestalt, Grund, Ichheit, das Nichts, Nicht-Ich, nichtigen, Nichtigkeit, Sein, das Seiende, Ungrund, Urgrund, Vernunft, Vernünftigkeit, Verstand, Verständigkeit, Verständnis, Wesen, Wesenheit.*

10. Eckhart, Sermon 21, in J. M. Clark, *Meister Eckhart, An Introduction to the Study of His Works with an Anthology of His Sermons* (London: Thomas Nelson and Sons, 1957), 230.

11. In the *Philosophy of Spirit*, in one of the *Zusätze*, Hegel remarks that "According to Christianity, God has revealed Himself through Christ, His only begotten Son. Picture-thinking takes this proposition to mean that Christ is merely the organ of this revelation, as if that which is revealed is something other than the source of the revelation. However, the true meaning of the proposition is rather that *God has revealed that His nature consists in having a Son*, i.e., to differentiate, to limit Himself, yet to remain with Himself in His difference; to contemplate and reveal Himself in the Son, and through this unity with the Son, through this being-for-self in the other, to be absolute spirit. Consequently, the Son is not the mere organ, but the very content of the revelation" (PS § 384, Z; Petry 1:57; emphasis added).

ture. Nature or creation is the Son. The "return" of the Son to the Father is the Holy Spirit and, again as in Hegel, this specifically denotes mankind. In Sermon 12 Eckhart declares, "When all creatures pronounce His name, God comes into being."[12] God requires mankind to complete the "circle" of His being. We can fulfill this function because, as a part of nature, we too are the "Son" and possess a divine "spark" within us (Sermon 20). To find this spark, affirm its existence, and strive to develop and increase the divine within us, is to hold up a mirror to creation: the *Logos* informing the world can reflect on itself through human self-knowledge.[13] Eckhart writes: "If I had not been, there would have been no God" (Sermon 4).[14] Human self-reflection is the actualization of God.

Eckhart comes quite close in many places to affirming that man is God. He writes in one place: "The soul cannot bear to have anything above it. I believe that it cannot bear to have even God above it. If he is not in the soul, and the soul is not as good as he, it can never be at ease."[15] Not surprisingly, in July 1326 Eckhart was brought up on charges of heresy, but he was subsequently cleared. The charges were reopened the following year, however, but Eckhart died before anything came of it. In 1329 a papal bull, *In Agro Domenico*, condemned a number of Eckhart's theses. As a consequence, Eckhart's pupils were frightened into retreating from some of their master's more speculative ideas, at least publicly.[16]

Franz von Baader reports that he heard Hegel exclaim, upon reading a certain passage in Eckhart, "*da haben wir es ja, was wir wollen!*" ("There, indeed, we have what we want!").[17] Hegel quotes Eckhart not once in his published writings, and only once in his 1824 *Lectures on the Philosophy of Religion*: "The eye with which God sees me is the same eye by which I see Him, my eye and His eye are one and the same. In righteousness I am weighed in God and He in me. If God did not exist nor would I; if I did not exist nor would He" (LPR 1:347–48).[18]

Quite a number of authors have attempted to argue for the decisive

12. Clark, *Meister Eckhart*, 184; quoted in Beck, *Early German Philosophy*, 52.
13. In Karl Rosenkranz's discussion of Hegel's early Jena Philosophy of Spirit, he writes: "Hegel still loved, even now, as we already saw above, in his first exposition of metaphysics [the Triangle fragment—see chapter 3], to present the creation of the universe as the *utterance* of the absolute *Word*, and the return of the universe into itself as the *understanding* of the Word, so that nature and history become the *medium* between the uttering and the understanding of the Word—a medium which itself, as other-being, vanishes" (Rosenkranz, *Hegels Leben*, 193).
14. *Meister Eckhart: A Modern Translation*, trans. Raymond Bernard Blakney (New York: Harper and Bros., 1941), 231.
15. Ibid., 163.
16. Beck, *Early German Philosophy*, 46.
17. Günther Nicolin, ed., *Hegel in Berichten seiner Zeitgenossen* (Hamburg: Felix Meiner, 1970), 261.
18. This is actually a "quilt quotation" made up of lines from several of Eckhart's sermons (certainly the reference to "the concept" looks suspiciously like an Hegelian interpolation).

influence of Eckhart on Hegel.[19] Such arguments have been based partly on the fact that we know Hegel to have read Eckhart in the years 1795–99 and 1823–24,[20] but they are mainly based on the striking parallels between Hegel's language and Eckhart's. At one point in the *Encyclopedia*, Hegel writes, "God is God only in so far as He knows himself; this self-knowledge is, further, a self-consciousness in man and man's knowledge of God, which becomes man's self-knowledge in God" (ps § 564; Wallace, 298). I shall return to the issue of Hegel's debt to Eckhart in chapter 7.

3. Nicholas of Cusa

Nicholas of Cusa (1401–64) is another mystic whose influence on the Hermetic tradition was important. He stands also as a transitional figure between the Middle Ages and the Renaissance. Forgotten by mainstream philosophy until the nineteenth century, Cusa influenced such figures in the Hermetic countertradition as Bruno.[21] As a young man, Cusa was educated by the Brothers of the Common Life at Deventer. There, as Ernst Cassirer writes, "for the first time, Cusa was touched by the spirit of German mysticism in all its speculative depth and in its moral and religious force."[22] Gerard Groote, the founder of the brotherhood, was associated with Ruysbröck, who was profoundly influenced by Eckhart.

Like Eckhart, Cusa would teach that God is the coincidence of opposites. (He was also the first author to refer to God as *Absolutum*.) Indeed, Cassirer writes that in many places, Cusa seems to do nothing more than "repeat thoughts that belong to the solid patrimony of medieval mysticism. Cusa constantly refers to the sources of this mysticism, especially to the writings of Meister Eckhart and the Pseudo-Dionysius."[23] Cusa also held the perennial Hermetic-mystical doctrine of "internal relations" (important for German Idealism, with which the term is associated): the view that everything is involved with or connected to everything else.

Cusa is most famous for his doctrine of "learned ignorance," which he

---

19. Benz, *Mystical Sources*; Ernst Lichtenstein, "Von Meister Eckhart bis Hegel: Zur philosophischen Entwicklung des deutschen Bildungsbegriff," in *Kritik und Metaphysik*, ed. Friedrich Kaulbech and Joachim Ritter (Berlin: de Gruyter, 1966), 260–98; Cyril O'Regan, "Hegelian Philosophy of Religion and Eckhartian Mysticism," in *New Perspectives on Hegel's Philosophy of Religion*, ed. David Kolb (Albany: State University of New York Press, 1992) and *The Heterodox Hegel*; G. Ralfs, "Lebensformen des Geistes: Meister Eckhart und Hegel," in *Kant Studien*, suppl. no. 86 (1966); W. Schultz, "Der Einfluss der deutschen Mystik auf Hegels Philosophie," in *Theologie und Wirklichkeit* (Kiel: Lutherische Verlagsgesellschaft, 1969), 147–77.
20. See O'Regan, "Hegelian Philosophy of Religion and Eckhartian Mysticism," 110; also see H. S. Harris, *Hegel's Development*, vol. 1, *Toward the Sunlight* (Oxford: Oxford University Press, 1972), 230.
21. Beck, *Early German Philosophy*, 58.
22. Ernst Cassirer, *The Individual and the Cosmos in Renaissance Philosophy*, trans. Mario Domandi (New York: Harper and Row, 1963), 33.
23. Ibid., 8.

set forth in a work of the same name (1440). "Learned ignorance" involves knowing that we do not know God, meaning, technically, that we can predicate nothing univocally of God. We can "know" God through a series of *contradictory predicates* (hence God as "coincidence of opposites"), but this sort of knowledge, of course, seems thoroughly paradoxical to our limited human capacities. For instance, Nicholas asserts in *Of Learned Ignorance* that God is both Maximum *and* Minimum: since to be the Maximum is to be everything that can be, in the fullest sense, God as Maximum must also be *as small as He can be*, and hence Minimum.[24] Cusa understood the relation of God to world in terms of the first two persons of the Trinity: creator is to creature as Father is to Son. Holy Spirit constitutes the unity of these two. As the identity of Unity and Plurality, God must contain the whole wealth of existence "contracted" into Himself.

To say that all things are "contracted" into God means that every individual thing has its meaning or significance through its relation to the whole, and thus, as noted earlier, everything is bound up with and related to everything else. To Cusa, this was equivalent to saying that every individual thing is itself the universe, contracted into one set of relations knitted together at one unique point in the cosmos.[25] The parallel to Leibniz's doctrine of monads is obvious. Thus, we find in Cusa a situation quite similar to Eckhart, where the distinction between God and World has been collapsed in the very process of upholding the transcendence or otherness of God. Cusa also taught that the mind of man is structurally isomorphic with the mind of God. The major difference between human *mens* and divine is that while God creates things with His mind, we create only images or ideas of things. God creates an actual world, whereas man creates a mental world, a world of ideas. We can, however, through physical labor, bring our ideas to fruition in reality with exactitude, through our use of mathematics. There is, then, an analogy between man and God, and Cusa is not shy about exploiting it and treating man as a "little God."

In *De visione Dei* (1453) Cusa takes advantage of the ambiguity of the phrase "the vision of God" to make a truly mystical point, very much in line with Eckhart and also with the Hermetic tradition. For Cusa, God's vision and our vision of God are one and the same. This is an idea we find in Eckhart: "The same knowing in which God knows Himself is none other than the knowing of each detached spirit."[26] God reveals Himself in a multiplicity of "points of view." *What God is* can only be approached somehow through an insight into the many individual "thoughts" *of* or *on* God, into which God has "specified" Himself. Thus our "vision" of God is God's vision of Himself. To open ourselves to the divine is to open ourselves to the particularity through which the divine

24. Nicolas of Cusa, *Of Learned Ignorance*, trans. Germain Heron (New Haven, Conn.: Yale University Press, 1954), 12.

25. Cusa, *Of Learned Ignorance*, 82.

26. Eckhart, *In diebus suis placuit*, in *Deutsche und lateinischen Werke*, vol. 1, ed. Josef Quint (Stuttgart: Kohlhammer, 1963), 162.

unfolds. (In the *Phenomenology of Spirit*, Hegel writes that the Absolute must be conceived in "the whole wealth of the developed form. Only then is it conceived and expressed as an actuality" [Miller, 11; PG, 15].) Again, this is the same Hermetic doctrine of God requiring creation, and specifically man, for His actualization. It is the doctrine that flowers fully in the Böhmean-Hegelian theosophy. Lewis White Beck notes in his *Early German Philosophy* that Cusa's "theory of the polarity but unity of man, God, and nature is elaborated by Schelling (who, we know, was actually influenced by reading Nicholas)."[27] Beck also makes the claim that the *Naturphilosophie* of the late eighteenth and early nineteenth centuries, as well as theosophy and Protestant mysticism, have their roots in Cusa. However, Hegel never mentions Cusa anywhere in his published writings or in his lectures.[28]

4. Renaissance and Reformation

In 1460, fourteen out of the fifteen "philosophical" *Hermetica* were brought to Florence from Macedonia by a monk employed by Cosimo de'Medici to locate manuscripts for him. Remarkably, Cosimo ordered Marsilio Ficino (1433–99) to interrupt the translation he was preparing of Plato's dialogues to begin work immediately on a Latin translation of the *Corpus Hermeticum*. Ficino's translation, entitled *Pimander* (after the first of the treatises) and printed for the first time in 1471, had an incredibly wide circulation. It went through sixteen editions up until the end of the sixteenth century.

In the preface to *Pimander*, Ficino presented his own genealogy of wisdom, which he culled from a variety of sources, including the church fathers Augustine, Lactantius, and Clement. It began with Hermes Trismegistus and Zoroaster, and traced a direct line to Plato. Subsequent to his translation of the *Hermetica*, Ficino developed his own magical philosophy of occult correspondences, described in detail by Yates in *Giordano Bruno and the Hermetic Tradition*.

The next major event in the history of Hermeticism was the rediscovery by Europeans of the Jewish Kabbalah after the expulsion of the Jews from Spain in 1492. Jewish trade and social networks served as a conduit for Kabbalistic teachings. I shall discuss the Kabbalah at length in chapters 5 and 7. First to make significant use of the Kabbalah was Pico della Mirandola (1463–94). Pico, a younger contemporary of Ficino, joined Kabbalah and Hermeticism in the words of Antoine Faivre, "through the basic theme of Creation through the Word."[29] Yates writes that "for the Renaissance mind, which loved symmetrical arrangements, there was a certain parallelism between the writings of Hermes Trismegistus, the

27. Beck, *Early German Philosophy*, 71.
28. David Walsh notes that although there is no evidence that Hegel ever read Cusa, he was indirectly influenced by him through J. G. Hamann and Giordano Bruno. See Walsh, *Boehme and Hegel*, 326. See also Josef Stallmach, "Das Absolute und die Dialektik bei Cusanus im Vergleich zu Hegel," *Scholastik* 39 (1964): 495–509.
29. Faivre, *The Eternal Hermes*, 98.

Egyptian Moses, and Cabala which was a Jewish mystical tradition supposed to have been handed down orally from Moses himself."[30] With Pico, who acquired numerous followers, the tradition of "Christian Kabbalism" begins.

In 1486, Pico, at the tender age of twenty-three, went to Rome with "nine hundred theses": precepts derived, he claimed, from the perennial philosophy of the ages. He hoped to debate the theses in public. Instead, he created such a scandal that he was forced to publish an *Apology* in 1487. Along with the *Apology*, he published the famous *Oration on the Dignity of Man*, in which the "man as magus" thesis is argued for most eloquently. The *Oration* opens with the famous lines from *Asclepius* 1.6: "a great wonder, Asclepius, is man."

Johannes Reuchlin (1455–1522), also called Capnion, was one of the great figures of the Renaissance in Germany. Reuchlin was a Swabian— a fact that Hegel himself was careful to note. He studied for a time in Italy and made the acquaintance of Pico della Mirandola. Reuchlin subsequently became a Christian Kabbalist himself and did even more than Pico to promote study of the Kabbalah in the Christian world. Reuchlin's first Kabbalist work, *De verbo mirifico*, appeared in 1494. His *De arte Cabalistica* (1517) was the first in-depth study of the Kabbalah by a gentile author. During the twenty-three years that separated Reuchlin's two major works, many more Kabbalist treatises had come to light, which Reuchlin was able to utilize in writing *De arte Cabalistica*. In this later work, Reuchlin refers to the Kabbalah as "an alchemy transforming external perceptions into internal, then into images, opinion, reason, intuition, spirit, and, finally, light."[31] As Joseph Blau has written, "from Reuchlin's time no writer who touched on cabalism with any thoroughness did so without using him as a source."[32]

Reuchlin's work did much to increase study of the Kabbalah. As Ernst Benz notes, his ideas were preserved in the circles of "Swabian theosophical scholars."[33] In his *Lectures on the History of Philosophy*, Hegel praises Reuchlin for single-handedly rescuing Hebrew philosophy from the flames: "There was in hand a project to destroy all Hebrew books in Germany by an imperial decree; Reuchlin deserves great credit for having prevented this" (LHP 3:113; *Werke* 20:15). Reuchlin's vision of a congruity between the Greek, Jewish, and Muslim traditions would become a cornerstone of Hermetic thought in the next two centuries, especially as espoused by the Rosicrucian movement.

The same year that *De arte Cabalistica* was published, Luther nailed his "Ninety-five theses" to the door of the castle church at Wittenberg on October 31 or November 1. The Catholic church had not been particularly tolerant of Hermeticism (as the cases of Pico and Bruno illustrate),

30. Yates, *Giordano Bruno*, 84.
31. G. Mallery Masters, "Renaissance Kabbalah" in *Modern Esoteric Spirituality*, ed. Antoine Faivre and Jacob Needleman (New York: Crossroad, 1995), 142.
32. Joseph Leon Blau, *The Christian Interpretation of the Cabala in the Renaissance* (New York: Columbia University Press, 1944), 60.
33. Benz, *Mystical Sources*, 47.

and the Lutherans were little better. During the sixteenth century, Lutheranism was a considerable impediment to the dissemination of Hermetic philosophy in Germany, but it spread widely nonetheless. Luther himself, although he rejected mystical "excesses," incorporated vivid quasi-mystical imagery in his sermons. (Commenting on Luther's condemnation of Aristotle for rejecting Plato's theory of Ideas, Lewis White Beck writes, "Only if Plato is thought of in terms of Neoplatonism, and Neoplatonism is seen through the eyes of Christian mystics, is such a strange judgement intelligible at all in a man like Luther."[34]) Oddly enough, though, Luther had nothing but praise for alchemy:

> The science of alchemy I like very well, indeed, it is truly the natural philosophy of the ancients. I like it not only for the many uses it has in decorating metals and in distilling and subliming herbs and liquors, but also for the sake of the allegory and secret signification, which is exceedingly fine, touching the resurrection of the dead at the Last Day. For, as in a furnace the fire retracts and separates from a substance the other portions, and carries upward the spirit, the life, the sap, the strength, while the unclean matter, the dregs, remain at the bottom, like a dead and worthless carcass . . . even so God, at the day of judgement, will separate all things through fire, and righteous from the ungodly.[35]

Still, Luther's followers were not entirely pleased with the next major figure of German Hermeticism, Theophrastus Bombastus von Hohenheim, called Paracelsus (1493–1541). Alchemy, whether in its practical or mystical form, flourished in Germany, and Paracelsus is definitely the most significant figure in the history of German alchemy. In his own time Paracelsus's name became inseparably linked with alchemy, and his doctrines, as well as others often erroneously attributed to him, exercised a great influence over esoteric philosophy in Germany. Hegel drew on Paracelsus in composing his *Philosophy of Nature*, though in the *Lectures on the History of Philosophy* he compares him unfavorably with Böhme, stating that Paracelsus was "much more confused, and without Böhme's profundity of mind" (LHP 3:191; *Werke* 20:94). I shall discuss Paracelsus more fully in chapter 6.

5. Agrippa

Of almost equal importance with Paracelsus was Henricus Cornelius Agrippa von Nettesheim (1486–1535). Agrippa is most famous for his massive work *The Occult Philosophy* (*De occulta philosophia*), written sometime after 1510 and published in 1533. *The Occult Philosophy* was an attempt at a complete synthesis of Hermetic philosophy, alchemy, and Kabbalah (Agrippa had read Reuchlin). Agrippa offered his work as a

---

34. Beck, *Early German Philosophy*, 93; see Luther, *Heidelberg Disputation*, Thesis 36, *Early Theological Writings*, trans. James Atkinson (Philadelphia: Westminster Press, 1962), 281.
35. Quoted in J. W. Montgomery, "Cross, Constellation, and Crucible: Lutheran Astrology and Alchemy in the Age of Reformation," *Ambix* 11 (1963): 65–86.

remedy for the "chaotic" state of learning in his day—in short, his *Occult Philosophy* was to be a realization of the *pansophic* idea of a "superscience."

In 1530, Agrippa published *The Vanity of the Sciences* (*De vanitate scientiarum*). In this work, Agrippa presents himself as a skeptic, launching arguments against the possibility of any knowledge and the efficacy of any of the sciences, including the occult sciences. *The Vanity of the Sciences* was widely read by humanists and exercised an influence on Montaigne, among others. Three years later, however, Agrippa would publish *The Occult Philosophy*, arguing for Kabbalah as a *prisca theologia* and for the power of magic based on Kabbalah. Could Agrippa have simply changed his mind? This is certainly a possible explanation but not a very satisfying one. As Yates suggests in *Giordano Bruno and the Hermetic Tradition*, Agrippa probably suppressed *The Occult Philosophy* for twenty-three years because he realized, quite rightly, that its doctrine would be considered dangerous by many. Agrippa's reputation as a "black magician," which reached ridiculous extremes after his death, is testament to the legitimacy of this concern. In the interim, he published *The Vanity of the Sciences* as, perhaps, a kind of "safety device": if anyone challenged him on the contents of *The Occult Philosophy* he could always point to the arguments of *The Vanity of the Sciences* and insist that he was a mere chronicler of occult lore and did not mean to be taken seriously.[36] In other words, *The Vanity of the Sciences* was Agrippa's "exoteric doctrine."[37]

Agrippa received his Hermetic education in Italy, under the tutelage of scholars trained in the tradition of Pico and Ficino. In Italy, Agrippa made the acquaintance of Cardinal Egidius of Viterbo and of Agostino Ricci, both of whom were interested in using Christian Kabbalah to advance the Catholic reform movement. Through them and others Agrippa had access to much of the Kabbalist literature (including Reuchlin's *De Verbo Mirifico*). As Yates notes, Agrippa's *The Occult Philosophy* "belongs to the tradition of Christian Kabbalah, because it leads up, in the third book on the supercelestial world, to the presentation of the Name of Jesus as now all-powerful, containing all the powers of the Tetragrammaton [the four-letter Hebrew name of God], 'as is confirmed by Hebrews and Cabalists skilled in the Divine Names.' "[38]

Agrippa divides *The Occult Philosophy* into three major sections: Natural Magic (based on a quasi-Aristotelian physics), Celestial Magic (based on a Pythagoreanized mathematics), and Ceremonial Magic (based in

36. Yates, *Giordano Bruno*, 131; as Andrew Weeks points out, Agrippa published a revised version of *The Occult Philosophy* just two years prior to his death. See Weeks, *German Mysticism from Hildegard of Bingen to Ludwig Wittgenstein* (Albany: State University of New York Press, 1993), 123.

37. John Trithemius, abbot of Saint James of Heroipolis, wrote to Agrippa in 1510 that "this one rule I advise you to observe, that you communicate vulgar secrets to vulgar friends, but higher and secret to higher, and secret friends only. Give hay to an ox, sugar to a parrot only; understand my meaning, lest you be trod under oxen's feet, as oftentimes happens." See Agrippa, *The Three Books of Occult Philosophy*, ed. Donald Tyson and trans. James Freake (St. Paul, Minn.: Llewellyn Publications, 1995), lvii. I have altered the translation.

38. Yates, *Giordano Bruno*, 37.

what Agrippa calls "theology"). Like alchemy, Agrippa's magic is both an art and a philosophy.

The theory of "Natural Magic" is founded on the doctrine of the four elements. Agrippa draws on Ficino's *De vita coelitus comparanda* (1489) for his account of the occult virtues, which are inculcated in things through the rays of the stars, communicating the influences of Ideas from the "World Soul." Agrippa then explains how we can use our knowledge of this world-system to manipulate occult sympathies.

Agrippa divides "Celestial Magic" into arithmetic, music, geometry, optics, astronomy, and mechanics. He accepts the Pythagorean claim about the higher reality of number, and thus ranks Celestial Magic higher than Natural Magic, which concerns mundane, earthly objects. Basically, Agrippa's Celestial Magic is a kind of numerology, in which the adept exploits certain numerical correspondences between things. Agrippa gives an account of the symbolic and magical significance of the numbers from one to twelve. He also includes a discussion of gematria, the science of attaining wisdom and occult prowess through the substitution of numbers for the letters in words of power.[39] For this practice, Hebrew is the most powerful language. There is nothing here that is original with Agrippa: Kabbalists had for centuries practiced gematria, the most famous of them being Abraham Abulafia (1240–ca.1291). There follows an account of the use of celestial images or symbols in magic, primarily in the preparation of talismans. The images—of the planets, zodiacal signs, and even demons—were to be engraved on certain specially prepared objects and then "activated" through magic, which can be practiced only by a highly developed adept, who becomes thereby a "co-operator" with God and can "do all things."[40] Here we are again confronted with the Hermetic doctrine of man's "divinization," which we have seen in Pico, Eckhart, and shall see again in Bruno, and others.

The highest level of magic, however, Agrippa reserves for the third book of *The Occult Philosophy*. Ceremonial Magic is a practical Kabbalah designed to give the adept divine powers to invoke and manipulate demons and spiritual guides. Agrippa derives much of his account of this "spirit world" from the Kabbalah. He gives the names of the *Sephiroth* and their significance, and relates each to the angelic powers. Agrippa accepts the standard Hermetic microcosm-macrocosm analogy, and so his account of the intelligible structure of the cosmos is also an account of the structure of man. Thus, to master the occult philosophy and become an adept is to attain self-knowledge.

Agrippa had a far-flung influence but led a singularly unhappy life and in death was excoriated as an evil necromancer. The legendary character of Doctor Faustus, as well as the tale of the "sorcerer's apprentice," were based on him. In 1567, many years after Agrippa's death, a fourth book of

39. J. L. Blau discusses Reuchlin's use of gematria. See Blau, *The Christian Interpretation of the Cabala*, 8.
40. Quoted in Yates, *Giordano Bruno*, 136.

De occulta philosophia, "Of Magical Ceremonies," was published, claiming to be a key to the previous three books. It was denounced by Agrippa's pupil Johann Wierus as spurious, and most scholars have accepted that judgment. Curiously, we know from the auction catalog of Hegel's library, compiled in 1832, that Hegel possessed a copy of that work.[41]

6. Bruno

One of the major thinkers influenced by Agrippa was Giordano Bruno (1548–1600). Bruno's influence in Germany was significant enough for Hegel to devote a section of his *Lectures on the History of Philosophy* to him. (Hegel also discusses Ficino and Pico in his *Lectures*, although quite briefly and in no depth; LHP 3:112; *Werke* 20:14–15). The auction catalog of Hegel's library reveals that Hegel owned Bruno's works.[42] Hegel's remarks on Bruno in the *Lectures* fill roughly eighteen pages in the Suhrkamp edition of his works.

Bruno took Ficino's lily-white, Christianized magic of correspondences and developed it into the basis for a new Hermetic religion. His aim, in fact, was to return Renaissance occultism to its pagan Egyptian roots. Bruno conceived himself as the messiah of this new religion. Its central teaching was a familiar idea, that the "All" is One.[43] This must certainly have appealed to Hegel, for in his schooldays, he and friends such as Hölderlin adopted a pantheist outlook, their motto being *hen kai pan* (One and All; I shall discuss this more fully in chapter 2).[44]

In his *Lectures*, Hegel refers to Bruno as a "noble soul" who has "a sense of indwelling, and knows the unity of its own Being and all Being to be the whole life of thought" (LHP 3:121–22; *Werke* 20:24). Hegel compares Bruno with Proclus: "With Proclus in the same way the understanding, as substantial, is that which includes all things in its unity" (LHP 3:124; *Werke* 20:26). Calling Bruno a "very original mind," Hegel states that his philosophy is "on the whole certainly Spinozism, Pantheism" (LHP 3:123; *Werke* 20:25). And: "This system of Bruno's is . . . objective Spinozism, and nothing else; one can see how deeply he penetrated." Summarizing this Spinozism-Pantheism, Hegel writes

> The main endeavor of Bruno was . . . to represent the All and One [*das All und Eine*], after the method of Lullus, as a system of classes of regular determinations. Hence, in the manner of Proclus he specifies three spheres: First, the original form (*huperousia*) as the originator of all forms; secondly, the physical world, which impresses the traces of the Ideas on the surface of matter, and multiplies the original picture in countless mirrors set face to face; thirdly, the form of the rational world, which individualizes numerically for the senses the shadows of the Ideas, brings them into one,

41. *Berzeichniss der von dem Professor Herrn Dr. Hegel und dem Dr. herrn Seebeck hinterlassen Bücher-Sammlungen* (Berlin, 1832). In the collection of the Staatsbibliothek Preussischer Kulturbesitz, Berlin.
42. Ibid.
43. Yates, *Giordano Bruno*, 248.
44. Harris, *Toward the Sunlight*, 96ff.

and raises them to general conceptions for the understanding. The moments of the original form itself are termed Being, goodness (nature or life), and unity. (LHP 3:134–35; *Werke* 20:36)

Another summary passage employs language strikingly like the later preface to the *Phenomenology of Spirit* (1807): "The unity of life he thus determines as the universal, active understanding (*nous*), which manifests itself as the universal form of all the world, and comprehends all forms in itself. . . . It is the artist within, who shapes and forms the material without. From within the root or the seed-grain it makes the shoot come forth; from this again it brings the branches, and from them the twigs, and from out of the twigs it calls forth the buds, and leaves, and flowers" (LHP 3:124; *Werke* 20:26; cf. *Phenomenology of Spirit*, Miller, 2; PG, 4.)

In the end, Hegel, as he does with all of his predecessors, points out the fatal flaws that prevent Bruno from arriving fully at wisdom. In this case, Hegel's analysis is fascinating for it is nearly identical to his critique of Kant: "But while the system of Bruno is otherwise a grand one, in it the determinations of thought nevertheless at once become superficial, or mere dead types, as in later times was the case with the classification of natural philosophy . . . [Bruno's] twelve forms laid down as basis neither have their derivation traced nor are they united in one entire system, nor is the further multiplication deduced" (LHP 3:137; *Werke* 20:39).

Bruno sojourned for a time in Germany, holding a university professorship in Wittenberg from 1586 to 1588. Bruno claimed to have founded a sect among the Lutherans there that he called the "Giordanisti." While in Wittenberg, Bruno wrote *Lampas triginta statuarum* (ca.1586–88), an attempt to extend the magical memory system that was his life's work. Bruno's stay in Wittenberg resulted in a lasting influence of his memory system on German Hermeticism. I will suggest in chapter 3 that Hegel was influenced by this tradition of "memory magic." The mnemotechnic art of memory was of ancient origin and originally had little or no occult connotation. However, in the Renaissance it became integrated into the new Hermetic philosophy, as discussed in detail by Yates in *The Art of Memory*. It was thought that the techniques of *ars memoria* could be used to reawaken the adept's latent knowledge of the structure of the cosmos and the nature of the occult influences. The structure of Bruno's memory system was set out in his first work, *De Umbris Idearum* (1548), and remained basically constant throughout his career. The goal of this system was self-transformation, self-actualization: the adept who "recollected" the cosmic forces described by Bruno would acquire a new and powerful personality.

7. Franck and Weigel

Sebastian Franck and Valentin Weigel are two lesser-known, but still influential figures in German Hermeticism. Luther referred to Franck (1499–1542/3) as "the devil's most cherished slanderous mouth."[45]

45. Quoted in Beck, *Early German Philosophy*, 149.

Franck was essentially a pantheist who held God to be immanent in nature. Like many mystics, he taught that man is imbued with an ember of the divine personality. However, Franck held the unusual position that God *just is* what He reveals Himself to be, under different aspects in the spiritual lives of individual men. "God is for us," Franck contends, "just as we represent him."[46] Beck remarks that "Franck's ontology of mind and spirit is not sufficiently developed for him to know, or for us to be sure, that he is here adumbrating a thesis of later transcendental philosophy. . . . He does not and could not work this out; but his philosophical heir is Schelling."[47] The presence of God within us is a "natural light," which Franck calls Spirit. He makes a distinction between what he calls the church "visible" and "invisible." The "invisible church" is constituted by the Holy Spirit, through the loving hearts of all men. This conception of the invisible church, stated here by Franck for perhaps the first time, will later be important for the Rosicrucians and Freemasons, and for their intellectual heirs, Schelling, Hölderlin and Hegel.

Valentin Weigel (1533–88) makes frequent reference in his works to Paracelsus and Eckhart. He refers nineteen times to "Mercurius" or Hermes Trismegistus. As Andrew Weeks notes, Hermes Trismegistus represents for Weigel "the compatibility of natural and supernatural, of pagan and Christian knowledge."[48] Weigel was also deeply influenced by Cusa, and by an anonymous mystical tract called the *Theologia Germanica*, which he made the subject of a commentary in 1571. The *Theologia Germanica* was written around 1350 by a cleric in Frankfurt am Main who belonged to the Teutonic Order. The work achieved a wide circulation when it was discovered and printed in 1516 by Luther. The *Theologia Germanica* teaches that God requires man to redeem the world, but to achieve this man must first come to know God. God is a perfect whole, and knowing the whole requires emptying the mind of images. God is One, but the text also says that He is All, "and must be All."[49] Evil occurs when human beings break away from the whole and turn their minds and hearts to the limited, the partial. "All knowledge limited to separate parts will come to nought when the Whole is perceived," states the anonymous author.[50] The *Theologia Germanica* holds that strict obedience to God's law does not oppress, rather it is the realization of true freedom.[51]

Drawing on Paracelsus, Weigel states that "All corporeal things are an excrement or coagulated smoke . . . from the invisible stars; the same smoke has three substances: sulphur, mercury, and salt."[52] Following

---

46. *Paradoxa* (1534); quoted in Beck, *Early German Philosophy*, 151.
47. Beck, *Early German Philosophy*, 151.
48. Andrew Weeks, *Valentin Weigel* (Albany: State University of New York Press, 2000), 55.
49. *The Theologia Germanica of Martin Luther*, trans. Bengt Hoffman (New York: Paulist Press, 1980), 126.
50. Ibid., 82.
51. Ibid., 71, 136. See also Weeks, *Valentin Weigel*, 50.
52. Quoted in Weeks, *Valentin Weigel*, 111.

Cusa and the *Theologia Germanica*, he holds that all creatures are contained within God. Man, however, is unique. He contains within himself the characteristics of all creation. Weigel uses the term *Begriff* to designate the "enfolding" within man of the nature of all things. *Begriff* comes from *begreifen*, which in modern German means "to understand," but literally means "to grasp." *Der Begriff* (in modern German, "concept") is "the grasped." Man is the "quintessence," the fifth element, rising above the four elements.

For Weigel, the mental restraint necessary to achieve knowledge of God involves pure consciousness or self-knowing, not a knowledge of particular things. In being absolutely passive, however, it is absolutely active, for this type of knowledge is precisely God's knowledge (Weigel conceives God as the "Nothing and All"). So, the mystic does not come to know God but to *become God's knowing*. This, as we have seen, is a perennial Hermetic theme. Also present in Weigel is the ideal of wisdom as a knowledge of all things, as well as the conception of the "invisible church" first put forward by Franck. Weigel's ideas exercised a great influence on German mysticism and philosophy, and were spread by writers such as Johann Arndt, Gottfried Arnold, and Leibniz.

8. Böhme

Jakob Böhme (1575–1624) began to write just before the publication of the first Rosicrucian manifestos. He was a native of Görlitz, in Lusatia on the borders of Bohemia. Böhme was a simple shoemaker who, in 1600 had a mystical vision: looking at a gleam of light reflected on a pewter vessel, he felt himself able to peer into the inner essence of all things. In a letter, he described the experience:

> The gate was opened unto me, so that in one quarter of an hour I saw and knew more than if I had been many years together at a University; at which I did exceedingly admire, and I knew not how it happened to me; and thereupon I turned my heart to praise God for it. For I saw and knew the Being of all beings; . . . also the birth or eternal generation of the Holy Trinity; the descent and origin of this world.[53]

For twelve years he remained silent, and when he did write for the first time in 1612, it was only a personal exercise; he never intended his work to be copied and read by others. During the intervening years, there is evidence that Böhme read the alchemists, especially Paracelsus. In Böhme's first work, *Aurora* (*Morgenröthe im Aufgang*), he both denies and claims expertise in alchemical theory in the same passage: "Do not take me for an alchemist, for I write only in the *knowledge* of the spirit, and not from experience. Though indeed I could here show *something else*, *viz.* in *how many* days, and in *what hours*, these things must be prepared; for gold cannot be made in one day, but a whole month is requi-

---

53. Jakob Böhme, letter to Caspar Lindner, in *Jakob Böhme: Essential Readings*, ed. Robin Waterfield (Wellingborough, England: Crucible/Thorsens, 1989), 64.

site for it."[54] Andrew Weeks speculates that Böhme did actually experiment with alchemy, perhaps with one of his wealthy friends.[55] Böhme was also acquainted with the writings of the mystics (e.g., Weigel), and possibly some Kabbalistic works.[56]

Böhme's Görlitz was, as Pierre Deghaye puts it, "rich in spiritual heterodoxy and Hermeticism."[57] The medical doctors of Görlitz were mainly Paracelsians. There was even a minor scandal over their Paracelcism, which erupted in 1570.[58] This scandal only increased the appetite of the citizens, particularly of the nobility, for Hermetic and alchemical philosophy, in which they were widely known to dabble. Supernatural events were frequently reported in or near Görlitz: giant meteors crashed to earth at propitious times, grain was said to rain from the sky, etc.[59]

One important influence on the underground Hermetic culture of Görlitz was Dr. Balthasar Walter, a Christian Kabbalist and alchemist who befriended Böhme after 1612. Walter had traveled to the Orient in search of wisdom, but declared that he had found it only with Böhme. It is through Walter that Böhme probably first became deeply immersed in the Kabbalah. Another influential acquaintance of Böhme was Dr. Tobias Kober, a Paracelsian physician, who may have been the source of Böhme's Paracelcism. Another friend was the alchemist Johann Rothe, who was well-versed in medieval mysticism, including Tauler.

Böhme is a turning point in the history of Hermetic philosophy. Hermeticism and Christianity had always been strange bedfellows, and as we have seen, much of Hermetic thought—such as its conception of the divine or semi-divine status of man—is heretical by Christian standards. Bruno even went so far as to advocate the abandonment of Christianity and the return to a Hermetic, "Egyptian" religion. Böhme, in effect, acted to prevent the self-destruction of Hermetic philosophy in the face of its clear conflict with the dominant, orthodox faith. David

54. *Aurora*, in *Sämtliche Schriften*, ed. Will-Erich Peuckert and August Faust (Stuttgart: Fromann, 1955), vol. 1, chap. 22, § 105. (All references to Böhme's works will be given by chapter and paragraph number.) English translation: *Aurora*, trans. John Sparrow, ed. C. J. Barker and D. S. Hehner (London: John M. Watkins, 1914), 610. Sparrow's translation was originally published in 1656. It is the only English translation of the entire work. I have included page numbers from Sparrow, because his paragraph numbers do not correspond to those in the German.
55. Weeks, *Boehme: An Intellectual Biography of the Seventeenth-Century Philosopher and Mystic* (Albany: State University of New York Press, 1991), 57; H. H. Brinton has remarked that "Böhme did more than borrow a large part of his vocabulary from alchemy, he took over the whole alchemistic world-view, which he developed into a philosophic system." See Howard Haines Brinton, *The Mystic Will* (New York: Macmillan, 1930), 81.
56. The influence of Kabbalah on Böhme's works seems to increase with time. Ernst Benz believes that Böhme's sources for Kabbalism were probably oral (Benz, *Mystical Sources*, 48).
57. Pierre Deghaye, "Jacob Böhme and His Followers," *Modern Esoteric Spirituality*, 210.
58. Weeks, *Boehme*, 29.
59. Ibid., 31.

Walsh writes that "For the new occult philosophy to work, the old Christian philosophy must be redirected. The individual with the theoretical genius to effect their reconciliation and, thereby, become the transmitter of the new symbolism to the modern world was Jakob Böhme."[60]

Walsh summarizes the radical "redirection" of Christian philosophy, and the key to Böhme's thought, as follows: "The crucial shift is from the idea of all reality as moving toward God to the idea of God himself as part of the movement of reality as well."[61] This is the core of Böhme's Hermeticism: the conception of God not as transcendent and static, existing "outside" the world, impassive and complete, but as an active *process* unfolding within the world, within history. What initiates this process in the first place? Böhme held that God is moved by the desire to reveal Himself to Himself, but that this self-revelation is psychologically impossible unless an *other* stands opposed to Him.[62]

In a later work, Böhme wrote, "No thing can be revealed to itself without opposition [*Wiederwärtigkeit*]: For if there is nothing that opposes it, then it always goes out of itself and never returns to itself again. If it does not return into itself, as into that from which it originated, then it knows nothing of its origin."[63] In short, the "other" is necessary for God's self-consciousness. Without self-consciousness God would not be God, for His knowledge would be incomplete. This other "limits" God; by "othering," God limits Himself, giving Himself discernible "boundaries." Although it is not clear that Böhme thinks God exists at all apart from creation, the mind can *think* Him apart, can think Him as transcendent—but as transcendent God is merely a "dark inchoate will for self-revelation"[64] which Böhme calls the *Ungrund* (a conception not far removed from Eckhart's *Abgrund*, or Abyss).[65]

God does not know Himself through the world qua *absolute other*, however. An absolute other would be so foreign as to be unknowable. Instead, God in creation "others Himself," corporealizes Himself, a process that reaches its consummation with Christ. It is through Christ

60. David Walsh, "A Mythology of Reason," 151.

61. Ibid., 152; Jürgen Habermas has remarked that Böhme was the first to "historicize" God or the Absolute; i.e., to claim that it develops through time. See Habermas's "Das Absolute und die Geschichte: Von der Zweispältigkeit in Schellings Denken" (Bonn: Ph.D. dissertation, Rheinische Friedrich Wilhelms Universität, 1954), 2.

62. To borrow terms from Gershom Scholem's treatment of Isaac Luria, Böhme's theosophy conceives God as "macro-anthropos" and man as "microcosmos." See Scholem, *Major Trends in Jewish Mysticism* (New York: Schocken Books, 1946), 269.

63. See Jakob Böhme, *Vom Göttlicher Beschaulichkeit*, in *Sämtliche Schriften*, ed. Will-Erich Peuckert (Stuttgart: Frommann, 1955–61), vol. 4, chap. 1, § 8. Hegel quotes this passage in his *Lectures on the History of Philosophy* 3:203; *Werke* 20:106.

64. Walsh, "A Mythology of Reason," 154.

65. The term *Ungrund* seems to appear first in Böhme's treatise, "On the Incarnation of Christ."

that the nature of God and the world is revealed to man. Through Christ, we can reflect on our nature as divine products, and this reflection constitutes a "return" to the source; God's will to self-revelation is fulfilled with His creation's knowledge of Him. As Walsh puts it succinctly, "Böhme is the herald of the self-actualizing evolutionary God."[66] And F. Ernest Stoeffler writes, "To Böhme God was that ultimate Mystery which moves deliberately and constantly toward self-understanding through progressive self-actualization. Philosophy, then, as Böhme understood it, becomes basically the history of the ultimate Mystery striving to know itself."[67]

Böhme's first work, which came to be known simply as *Aurora*, was titled *Morgenröthe im Aufgang*, which Weeks translates as "Morning Glow, Ascending." The preface to *Aurora* employs the metaphor of the "tree of revealed truth," which is a kind of intellectual history leading up to Luther and the Reformation. Böhme includes himself in his metaphor, claiming that before the tree is at last consumed by fire, it will sprout one final branch, a final and consummate revelation of the truth of the tree, from its root. As Böhme writes later in *Aurora*, "this book is the first sprouting or vegetation of this twig, which springs or grows green in its mother, like a child that is learning to walk, and is not able to run apace at the first."[68]

Aurora is a fragmented, inconsistent text. At times its outlook appears pantheistic, even proto-Spinozistic. Böhme writes in the second chapter: "In the Holy Ghost alone, who is in God, and also in the whole nature, out of which all things were made, in Him alone can you search into the whole body or corporeity of God, *which is nature*; as also into the Holy Trinity itself."[69] And:

> But here you must elevate your mind in the *spirit*, and consider how the *whole nature*, with all the powers which are in nature, also the width, depth and height, also heaven and earth, and all whatsoever is therein, and all that is above the heavens, is together the *body* or corporeity of God; and the powers of the stars are the fountain veins in the natural body of God *in this world*.[70]

This is not pantheism, however. It is Hermeticism in its classical form, just as I described it in opposition to pantheism in the introduction: what is claimed is *not* that all the things in the world are divine or are "full of gods," but that the world as a whole is a part of God's being. Nature is the "body of God," but God is more than just His body. Along with Eckhart, Cusa, and Hegel, Böhme reads the second person of the Trinity, the "Son," as equivalent to nature. This is unusual enough in Hegel, but in an untutored seventeenth-century shoemaker it is quite radical indeed.

66. Walsh *The Mysticism of Innerwordly Fulfillment*, 1.
67. F. Ernest Stoeffler, *German Pietism During the Eighteenth Century* (Leiden: E. J. Brill, 1973), 110.
68. *Aurora*, chap. 21, § 63; Sparrow, *The Aurora*, 563.
69. *Aurora*, chap. 2, § 12; Sparrow, *The Aurora*, 53.
70. *Aurora*, chap. 2, § 16; Sparrow, *The Aurora*, 55–56.

Böhme writes: "But the Father *everywhere* generates the Son out of all his powers."[71] In chapter 16, Böhme speaks of the deity being "continually generated" (*immer geboren*).[72]

I wish now to examine the details of Böhme's theory of divine self-manifestation, as it develops throughout his writings, in *Aurora* and beyond. For Böhme, God is One, but within Him is generated a trinity of worlds: the dark world, the light world, and the elemental world. The third world functions to "reconcile" the first two. Darkness yearns for Light; the unmanifest strives to become manifest. In its yearning, there is kindled within the Darkness a fire. Light is the pure principle of openness, of manifestation without any hiddenness. Fire is the actualization of the pure principle of Light in reality. With the kindling of fire (the alchemical agent of change), a reconciliation is reached between Darkness and Light. The fire burns, but within Darkness: the self-revelation will be of an entity that maintains its integrity, its identity—and thus always an element of inwardness—in and through its manifestation; presence will carry with it a concomitant absence. Böhme writes in *Mysterium Magnum* that "the eternal free will has introduced itself into darkness, pain, and source; and so also through the darkness into the fire and light, even into a kingdom of joy; in order that the Nothing might be known in the Something."[73] Böhme further details the divine self-manifestation in terms of what he calls the seven "source spirits."

Böhme's account of the spirits—their order, their relationships, even their names—varies from work to work. The following is a kind of amalgamation of the various accounts, following *Aurora* most closely. Böhme's seven source spirits are Sour, Sweet, Bitter, Heat, Love, Tone, and Body. In addition to referring to them as "source spirits" (*Quellgeister*), Böhme also calls them "properties" (*Eigenschaften*), "qualities" (*Qualitäten*), and "forms" (*Gestalten*). All of these spirits are "contained" within God as *Ungrund*, in potentia. God as *Ungrund* is both *Alles* and *Nichts*. The first three spirits—Sour, Sweet, and Bitter—form a primordial Trinity of conflict within the Godhead, preceding its manifestation. They are a triad of the unmanifest God or God-in-Himself. Sour (*Herb*) is a negative force, a "cold fire,"[74] the will of God to remain unmanifest, unrevealed. This is the first stage of desire, as described above: a primitive, egoistic will to self-assertion without self-reflection. But opposed to Sour there is Sweet (*Süss*): a positive force that contrasts with sourness as expansion, or opening outward, contrasts with contraction, or inwardness. Sour is a "pull" to remain in-itself, unmanifest; Sweet is a "push" to exteriorize, go out and become for-itself. Sour is the "Eternal No"; Sweet is the "Eternal Yes." Sour is a pucker; sweet is a kiss. The third source-spirit, Bitter (*Bitter*) is a kind of compromise: a going-out

---

71. *Aurora*, chap. 7, § 43; Sparrow, *The Aurora*, 138.
72. *Aurora*, chap. 16, § 12; Sparrow, *The Aurora*, 412.
73. *Mysterium Magnum*, (1623), in *Sämtliche Schriften*, vol. 7, chap. 26, § 37.
74. "Cold fire," as Julius Evola points out, is an alchemical term. See Julius Evola, *The Hermetic Tradition*, trans. E. E. Rehmus (Rochester, Vt.: Inner Traditions, 1995), 37.

that preserves and seeks identity. Bitter reconciles Sour and Sweet because it is the being of a being that freely gives itself or opens out, but simultaneously collects and preserves its manifestations as the revealed aspects of one identical being.

This triad is referred to by Böhme as a "wheel of anguish."[75] Böhme at times identifies it with the Holy Trinity, with the Paracelsian triad of Salt, Mercury, and Sulphur, and he conceives it as Hell. Basarab Nicolescu refers to it as the "death of God to Himself inasmuch as He is the God of pure transcendence."[76] The "wheel of anguish" is, in fact, the birth of God. In *Mysterium Magnum*, Böhme refers to God before this process, God as *Ungrund*, as "the dark nature" and states that "in the dark nature he is not called God."[77]

The triad Sour-Sweet-Bitter describes the birth of the living God, the birth of life itself, and the fundamental nature of all living beings. Sour-Sweet-Bitter gives way to Heat (*Hitze*). Heat is vitality, the inchoate living force that has arisen through the conflict of Sour-Sweet-Bitter. It is the first and most basic outward (that is, worldly) manifestation of the conflict of God in-Himself. It is as if Böhme conceives of Sour-Sweet-Bitter as rubbing up against one another, giving rise to Heat. This Heat then gives way to what Böhme calls the Flash (*Schrack*). The Flash is not one of the source spirits. Instead, it is literally the *force* of the preceding four spirits taken together: it is the *ignition* produced by their activity, and it is *life* and real being, burgeoning, growing, now separated, externalized, leading on to other things—"positive" and "external" things.[78]

The Flash is a will to the creation of self-revealing essence—a determinate nature that is open, not closed, to itself—for which Böhme uses the alchemical designation *Tinctur*. The first four spirits taken together constitute a kind of vector of manifestation. Picture a lightning flash, consisting of the four in dynamic interaction.[79] The Flash also represents mystical vision of the kind Böhme had in 1600: the invisible world is illuminated to the mystic in this Flash.

What the flash produces is a "hot fire," which Böhme calls Love (*Liebe*). Heat, the warmth of exteriorized life, is not inert, nor even stable (yet). It is still a *seeking*, it is Love. What began as a drive towards manifestation continues. Love is the Tinctur in which all the preceding spirits are united in joyful ecstasy. This is an externalization seeking fulfillment—it is an individuation through self-manifestation. Love's desire is for complete illumination, display, and representation to itself. This

75. *Mysterium Magnum*, chap. 3, § 11.
76. Basarb Nicolescu, *Science, Meaning, and Evolution: The Cosmology of Jacob Böhme*, trans. Rob Baker (New York: Parabola Books, 1991), 29.
77. *Mysterium Magnum*, chap. 7, § 14.
78. Hegel refers to it in his *Lectures on the History of Philosophy* as the "Absolute Generator" (*das absolut Gebärende*) (LHP 3:208; *Werke* 20:111).
79. In Kabbalah, a lightning flash is often spoken of as "zigzagging" its way through the ten *Sephiroth* of the "Tree of Life," representing the process of emanation.

seeking (Love) issues in a phenomenon that is a kind of "eject" of the seeking—a kind of significant epiphenomenon. This is Sound or Tone (*Schall* or *Ton*). As separate from Love, but as a product of Love, Tone has the potential of making Love manifest to itself. Love manifest to itself is the completion of the cycle.

It can easily be seen already that the spirits are not absolutely separate from one another, but, to use Hegelian language, are "moments" of a whole. Tone is the "song of Love"; Love is the desire for fulfillment energized by the Flash, ignited by Heat; Heat is the energy produced by the unity in opposition of Sour and Sweet within Bitter. With Tone, the life of God (and the life of life) is ready for fulfillment: having given rise to a "speech" or "expression" of itself (Tone), the process becomes a thing definite to itself. Body (*Corpus*), the seventh spirit, encompasses the other six. It represents the "concretization" of the process through its self-expression. This concretization is the completion of the cycle, but as involving the cycle's self-awareness it includes the cycle as well. Böhme writes in *Aurora*, "The Seventh Spirit of God in the divine power is the corpus or body, which is generated out of the other six spirits, wherein all heavenly figures subsist, and wherein all things image and form themselves, and wherein all beauty and joy rise up."[80] For Böhme, no spirit can really be without a "body," without giving rise at some point to its own concretization. All things strive to become fully specified and concrete, including God. Böhme also calls *Corpus Leiblichkeit*, and also sometimes *Begreiflichkeit*, "the graspedness" (in modern German, "intelligibleness"; recall Weigel's *Begriff*).

Böhme refers to spirit's activity of creating a body or a determinate being for itself as *Magia*.[81] In *Six Mystical Points*, he writes that

> Magic is the mother of eternity, of the being of all beings; for it creates itself, and is understood in desire. . . . Its desire makes an imagination, and imagination or figuration is only the will of desire. . . . True Magic is not a being, but the desiring spirit of the being. . . . Magic is the greatest secrecy, for it is above Nature, and makes Nature after the form of its will. It is the mystery of the Trinity, viz. it is in desire the will striving towards the heart of God.[82]

Body is also a return to the original spirit, Sour. Sour was the expression of the desire of God to contract into a hard, self-contained, and self-absorbed center, without external expression. In fact, however, God as *Ungrund* could not achieve this desire for concretization and integrity without self-expression. Through the cycle, consummated in Body, the original will, now heavily qualified, has actually been fulfilled: God is now a concrete, self-subsistent entity, but through His othering and self-expression. As Nicolescu puts it, "The loop is thus closed: the seventh

---

80. *Aurora*, chap. 11, § 1.
81. *Six Mystical Points* (*Kurtze Erklärung von sechs mystischen Puncten;* 1620), in *Sämtliche Schriften*, vol. 4, Point 5, §5.
82. *Six Mystical Points*, Point 5, §§ 1–6.

quality rejoins the first. . . . The line changes into a circle: paradoxically, in the philosophy of Jakob Böhme, the Son gives birth to the Father."[83]

Böhme himself employs circle metaphors to characterize his system (much as Hegel will do with his own system). Of the seven source spirits, Böhme writes at one point, "These seven generatings in all are none of them the first, the second, or the third, or last, but they are all seven, every one of them, both the first, second, third, fourth, and last. Yet I must set them down one after another, according to a *creaturely way* and manner, otherwise you could not understand it: For the Deity is as a wheel with seven wheels made one in another, wherein a man sees neither beginning nor end."[84]

Standing as an intermediary between God and creation is Wisdom (*Sophia*). It is referred to by Böhme as the "mirror" of God (recall Eckhart's mirror, and Hildegard's many mirrors). The mirror reflects God back to Himself, but in sensual, imagistic form, as the created world. This is necessary for Böhme, because, as *Aurora* maintains, what God projects in his creative will to self-revelation is in fact his *corporealization*. In short, the products of God, including God's Wisdom, *must* take sensuous form.

As with gnostic conceptions of the *Logos*, Böhme's Wisdom is conceived as active.[85] It is the source of the further specifications of God's corporeality. Further, Böhme's Wisdom is conceived metaphorically as female.[86] For Böhme, God's desire for self-manifestation echoes throughout creation as a desire inherent in all things. Like God as *Ungrund* (which, in proto-Hegelian language, Böhme describes as God "in Himself"), each thing is first merely an egoistic, infantile desire to exist for itself, but then this gives way to a desire for self-awareness. Böhme analyzes God's Wisdom—which is simultaneously the thought of God, the process of creation and the essence of created nature—into a sevenfold cycle of desire.[87] In God, these seven are as one, but our limited human capacities require us to know God and creation in a piecemeal (*stückweise*) fashion.

Returning to Böhme's conception of Tone, the "epiphenomenon" or song of love through which Body is actualized and the process of self-manifestation is completed, Böhme conceives the highest form of Tone in nature to be the speech of man. It is through human speech, human thought, that God achieves his highest and most consummate self-knowledge, for we are the beings who in thought and speech can reflect

83 . Nicolescu, *Science, Meaning, and Evolution*, 32.

84. *Aurora*, chap. 23, § 18; Sparrow, *The Aurora*, 615–16; see also chap. 13, § 71–74.

85. Deghaye, "Böhme and his Followers," 224.

86. Böhme may have been influenced here by the Kabbalistic conception of *Shekinah*, which is the tenth *Sephirah*. *Shekinah* is conceived as female and containing all the other *Sephiroth* in herself as in a body.

87. Walsh writes that the seven spirits in Böhme correspond "to the last seven *Sefiroth* [of the Kabbalah] which exemplify the order of the cosmos" (Walsh, *Boehme and Hegel*, 84–85).

on the whole of the cycle of creation. As Arthur Versluis states, "Ultimately, God comprehends himself through man. The mystery of divine nature is, finally, the mystery of human nature as well."[88] Böhme's account of the order of creation is quite complex, and I can only indicate some of the most important points here.

In words that call to mind the *Emerald Tablet*, Böhme writes at one point of the unity of all things: "When I take up a stone or clod of earth and look upon it, I see that which is above and that which is below, indeed [I see] the whole world therein."[89] He writes in *Clavis* (1624): "The whole visible world is a joyful spermatic [*eitel spermatischen*] active ground; each essence longs for the other, the above for the below and the below for the above, since they are separated from one another, and in such hunger they embrace one another in the desire."[90] Böhme describes the "world's existence" as "Nothing else than coagulated smoke from the eternal aether, which thus has a fulfillment like the eternal."[91]

Before men, God created angels. The angels aid God in the formation of all things according to the seven spirits, for, as Böhme writes in *Aurora*, "All the creatures are made and descended from these qualities."[92] Among the angels, Lucifer was the most magnificent. However, Lucifer, representing the "Sour" quality of in-drawing, broke away from God, thinking himself able to create through the ember of divine fire within him. Lucifer represents the will to isolation, cutting-off, a selfishness that all things exhibit. As Walsh puts it, Lucifer "can 'imaginate' his angry fire into all things and by hardening their wills can extinguish the divine light within them."[93]

Man, for Böhme, is a microcosm containing all the seven spirits within himself. Böhme speaks of man receiving God's Wisdom (*Sophia*, again, conceived as female) as wife. In man's soul there "hovers the revelation of the divine holiness, as the living outflowing Word of God with the eternally known Idea, which was known in divine Wisdom from eternity as a *Subjectum* or form of the divine imagination."[94] The first man was androgynous and possessed supernatural powers. He/She could procreate at will by the power of imagination, could exist without eating or sleeping, and could alter the essences of objects through magic words (a power which suggests alchemical transmutation).[95] In naming the animals, Adam drew on the essence of each, for in the *Natursprache* (nature language) of Adam, the being of a thing is captured in its name.[96] In Böhme's telling of the myth of the Garden of Eden, man *must* fall be-

88. Arthur Versluis, *Wisdom's Children* (Albany: State University of New York Press, 1999), 133.
89. *Mysterium Magnum*, chap. 2, § 6.
90. Quoted in Walsh, *Boehme and Hegel*, 241.
91. *Six Theosophical Points* (*Von sechs theosophischen Puncten*; 1620), in *Sämtliche Schriften*, vol. 4, Point 1, chap. 2, § 19.
92. *Aurora*, chap. 2, § 1; Sparrow, *The Aurora*, 50.
93. Walsh, *Boehme and Hegel*, 227.
94. Quoted in ibid., 237–38.
95. *Mysterium Magnum*, chap. 17, § 43.
96. Ibid., chap. 35, § 56.

cause the unity man enjoys with God in paradise is an *unthinking, unreflective*, and thus inferior unity. Man must become alienated from God and *return* to a higher state of unity, in *full consciousness* of his nature and the nature of God.

How did the fall come about? Adam wanted knowledge of each of the spirits of nature. In the garden, the Tree of Good and Evil represents disharmony, a separation of the spirits of nature into units under the sway of the "Eternal No," withdrawn into themselves, spurning unity. Adam's eating of the fruit of this tree is symbolic of a transformation of imagination. In what Böhme calls *Lust*, imagination and desire are in harmony. But Adam broke this happy equilibrium when his imagination was perverted into a base and sensualistic form. At this point *Lust* becomes *Begierde*, an infinite, negative, insatiable striving.[97] Adam's action constituted a turning away from divine unity. Immediately, Adam's nature was radically altered and he desperately sought reunification with the divine. This desire manifested itself first in shame, in awareness of the exposure of his bodily imperfection. The revulsion that Adam and all human beings feel about their condition of lack, degradation, and frailty *just is* the urge to reunite with God.

Wisdom was revealed yet again to men, however, through a man, Jesus Christ, who was perfectly married to *Sophia*. Christ is the second Adam. Through Christ's passion, death, and resurrection (which Böhme makes equivalent to the work of alchemical transmutation)[98] a secret teaching has been revealed to man, which can show him the way to at-one-ment with the divine. The interpretation of the Scriptures opens up the possibility of man the microcosm's self-knowledge—what Böhme has striven to accomplish in his work. Böhme writes in *Aurora* that "you need not ask, Where is God? Hearken, you blind man; you live in God, and God is in you; and if you live holily, then therein you yourself are God."[99] Through our self-reflection nature reaches a kind of closure: its pure, eternal forms are identified for what they are. Given that we are natural beings, our contemplation of the forms of nature amounts to nature's holding up a mirror to itself, and given that the nature of nature is the thought of God, it is a mirror held up to God. Thus, through our human understanding, God is fully actualized: He achieves self-awareness and closure.

Böhme does not present philosophical arguments. How then does he explain his access to this wisdom? He holds the view that before his fall, Adam was privy to the Wisdom of God, "But yet when he fell, and was set into the outward birth or geniture, he knew it no more, but kept it in remembrance only as a dark and veiled story [*sondern als eine dunkele und verdeckte Geschichte im Gedächtnis behalten*]; and this he left to his posterity." Buried in our subconscious (a word which, of course, Böhme did

---

97. For a discussion of this, see Antoine Faivre, *Theosophy, Imagination, Tradition*, trans. Christine Rhone (Albany: State University of New York Press, 2000), 106.

98. *De Signatura Rerum* (1622), in *Sämtliche Schriften*, vol. 6, chap. 11, § 6.

99. *Aurora*, chap. 22, § 46; Sparrow, *The Aurora*, 594.

not know) are significant images—"dark and veiled stories"—which are keys to the meaning of the cosmos, and these images are common to all men—to Adam's "posterity." Böhme claims, as Walsh puts it, "that it should not be considered impossible for someone to talk about the creation of the world as if he were there, because the Spirit which is in us is the same which breathed into Adam form eternal and which sees it all in the light of God."[100] Using a kind of "active imagination" to recollect these latent symbols, Böhme worked out his theosophy.

In *Access to Western Esotericism*, Faivre ranks "imagination" as "the essential component of esotericism."[101] The idea of occult correspondences that figures so largely in Hermeticism depends on "a form of imagination inclined to reveal and use mediations of all kinds, such as rituals, symbolic images, mandalas, intermediary spirits."[102] But this imagination does not create from nothing, rather it "recalls" images and associations from the collective unconscious of the race. Imagination depends on memory. Faivre writes that "it is especially under the inspiration of the *Corpus Hermeticum* rediscovered in the fifteenth century that memory and imagination are associated to the extent of blending together. After all, a part of the teaching of Hermes Trismegistus consisted of 'interiorizing' the world in our mens, from whence the 'arts of memory' cultivated in the light of magic, during and after the Renaissance."[103] As we have seen, the occult philosophy of Bruno depended on the relationship of imagination to memory. Böhme continues this tradition by developing his theosophy entirely in terms of images that carry both a literal (often alchemical) and figurative sense.

Böhme was attacked during his lifetime, and even briefly imprisoned, but he managed to exert a great influence over a small group of friends, mainly from the local nobility, who copied and distributed his manuscripts and acted to protect him as much as they could. In his *Kabbalah*, Gershom Scholem writes that "In certain circles, particularly in Germany, Holland, and England, Christian Kabbalah henceforward assumed a Böhmean guise."[104]

At first, Böhme's theosophy had little following in Germany, but became quite popular in England, first through the translation and publication of his works by John Sparrow (1615–65). It was John Pordage (1608–81) who was the center of the first Böhmean movement in England (called "behemism" there). From this group was formed the Philadelphian Society, led by Jane Lead (1623–1704), a visionary with whom Pordage had a liaison after the death of his wife in 1668. With Lead's death, the Böhme movement in England more or less died out.

100. Walsh, *Boehme and Hegel*, 139; cf. *Description of the Three Principles of God's Being* (*Beschreibung der drey Principien Göttliches Wesens*; 1619), in *Sämtliche Schriften*, vol. 2, chap. 7, § 7.
101. Faivre, *Access to Western Esotericism*, 21.
102. Ibid., 12.
103. Ibid., 13.
104. Gershom Scholem, *Kabbalah* (New York: New American Library, 1974), 200.

Böhme's thought was kept alive, however, by solitary figures such as the theologian William Law (1686–1761) and the poet and painter William Blake (1757–1827).

It was through French Hermeticists such as Louis Claude de Saint-Martin (1743–1803), who translated Böhme into French, that Böhme eventually came to make an impact on German thought, but as Heinrich Schneider notes, "in the German secret societies [Böhme's ideas] had never been forgotten."[105] I will have more to say about these societies in the following chapter. Böhme's theosophy became quite influential in Pietist circles, until by the end of the seventeenth century Böhmeanism, as F. Ernest Stoeffler states, "constituted a considerable challenge to established Lutheranism."[106] Böhme's first German follower of note was Johann Georg Gichtel (1638–1710), who had been a student of Philipp Jacob Spener, the "father" of German Pietism. Gichtel published an edition of Böhme's works in 1682, as well as works of his own in which he developed Böhme's theosophy. Quirinus Kuhlmann (1651–89), a chiliast with messianic aspirations, was introduced to Böhme by Friedrich Breckling (1629–1710), the same man who had taught Gichtel. Kuhlmann eventually turned up in Moscow to preach his evangel and was promptly burned at the stake. Böhme also influenced Pierre Poiret (1646–1719), who, though a French Protestant, was a pastor in Germany. Poiret edited the writings of Antoinette Bourignon (1616–80), a mystic who announced herself as "the Virgin" Böhme had prophesied as appearing at the end of time.

The radical Pietist Gottfried Arnold (1666–1714) published his landmark work *Impartial History of Churches and Heretics* in 1699. Arnold shocked many by arguing that it was the heretics—among whom he gave prominent place to Böhme—who represented the true religion. Standing in antithetical relationship to Arnold was Ehregott Daniel Colberg (1659–98). Without actually using the term, Colberg attacked the influence of the Hermetic tradition in Germany. Colberg attacks Böhme, Paracelsus, astrology, alchemy, and mysticism as such, seeing in all of them a common element: the desire of man to make himself God. Significantly, Colberg also attacks Pietism, seeing in it the same tendencies.

Ernst Benz has written that "In a certain sense one can refer to the philosophy of German Idealism as a Böhme-Renaissance, when Böhme was discovered at the same time by Schelling, Hegel, Franz von Baader, Tieck, Novalis and many others."[107] Baader (1765–1841), called "Böhmius redivivus," is often still regarded as Böhme's principal interpreter. He would become perhaps the most significant and influential Hermeticist of the nineteenth century. Baader, who studied mineralogy under

105. Heinrich Schneider, *Quest for Mysteries: The Masonic Background for Literature in Eighteenth-Century Germany* (Ithaca, N.Y.: Cornell University Press, 1947), 81.
106. Stoeffler, *German Pietism*, 168.
107. Ernst Benz, *Adam der Mythus vom Urmenschen* (Munich: Barth, 1955), 23.

Alexander von Humboldt, discovered Böhme in 1787 and made it his project to revive the mystical tradition. Indeed, it is Baader who should receive much of the credit for the awakening of interest in mysticism in the nineteenth century. He was not, however, as faithful a disciple of Böhme as was, for instance, Oetinger. A devout Catholic, he believed in a transcendent God and strongly opposed pantheism, or any other attempt to immanentize God. The world, Baader held, is a product of God's thought and utterly dependent on him. Like Oetinger, he interpreted nature as an "emblem book" and advocated an organic model of reality, rejecting mechanistic materialism. In politics, Baader was anti-egalitarian, anti-capitalist, and advocated the subjection of the state to the church. His collected works run to sixteen volumes.

Hegel was an avid reader of Baader.[108] Clark Butler refers to "Hegel's abortive courtship of von Baader" and writes that "despite apparent differences, Hegel sought to persuade both the public and von Baader himself that their positions were reconcilable."[109] Baader did not share this view, but he did do Hegel the honor of dedicating his lectures on Böhme's *Mysterium Magnum* to him. In 1824, Baader stated in a letter that Hegel's system was a "philosophy of dust."[110] Nevertheless, he shared Hegel's opposition to scientific rationalism and to the philosophy of Kant. Hegel even stated in print that he and Baader shared the goal of translating Böhme's eccentric, sensualistic theosophy into "scientific" terms (see chapter 5).

In *Hegel's Development*, H. S. Harris writes that "I am inclined to believe in Böhme's influence upon Hegel from 1801 onwards."[111] It is possible, however, that Hegel could have encountered Böhme's work as early as the mid to late 1790's, in the midst of what Rosenkranz has termed his "theosophical phase" (see chapter 3). David Walsh has argued that Hegel's use in the *Phenomenology of Spirit* of such terms as *element, aether, expansion*, and *contraction* has its roots in his acquaintance with Böhme and Paracelsian alchemy.[112] I will deal with the *Phenomenology's* further debts to Böhme in chapter 4. Hegel refers to Böhme explicitly in his *Science of Logic* (1832 edition), *Philosophy of Nature, Lectures on the Philosophy of Religion*, and elsewhere.

Hegel's most famous treatment of Böhme is in his *Lectures on the History of Philosophy* of 1805. There, Hegel couples Böhme with Francis Bacon as the twin representatives of "Modern Philosophy in its First Statement." He makes the transition from Bacon to Böhme by remarking, "We now pass on from this English Lord Chancellor, the leader of

---

108. Butler, 572; Hoffmeister #699.
109. Butler, editorial comment, 570.
110. *Berichten*, 401. Quoted in Butler, 571.
111. Harris, *Night Thoughts*, 85.
112. Walsh, "The Historical Dialectic of Spirit," 28. Walsh believes that only the influence of Böhme can explain why Hegel believes that history has a structure, and that it is to be understood in terms of the development of Spirit.

the external, sensuous method in Philosophy, to the *philosophicus teutonicus*, as he is called—to the German cobbler of Lusatia, of whom we have no reason to be ashamed. It was, in fact, through him that Philosophy first appeared in Germany with a character peculiar to itself: Böhme stands in exact antithesis to Bacon" (LHP 3:188; *Werke* 20:91).[113]

Hegel's discussion of Böhme in the *Lectures* occupies twenty-eight full pages in the Suhrkamp edition of his works—significantly more space than he devotes to important mainstream figures such as Locke, Hobbes, Hume, Rousseau, and Jacobi. Hegel's account of Böhme's theosophy is quite faithful and positive and shows that Hegel was familiar with several of Böhme's works. Hegel draws comparisons between Böhme and Proclus, Bruno, and Paracelsus. It is clear that he sees much of his own thought in Böhme's peculiar, imagistic theosophy. Hegel writes that although it "appears strange to read of the bitterness of God, of the flash, and of lightning," once we have "the Idea" in hand, "then we certainly discern its presence here" (LHP 3:193; *Werke* 20:95).[114] Hegel writes, further, that,

> Böhme's chief, and one may even say, his only thought—the thought that permeates all his works—is that of perceiving the Holy Trinity in everything, and recognizing everything as its revelation and manifestation . . . in such a way, moreover, that all things have this divine Trinity in themselves, not as a Trinity pertaining to the ordinary conception, but as the real Trinity of the Absolute Idea. (LHP 3:196; *Werke* 20:98)[115]

Hegel notes that Böhme regards the Trinity as "the absolute Substance" (*die absolute Substanz*; LHP 3:212; *Werke* 20:115).

Hegel's major objection to Böhme is well known: "Böhme's great mind is confined in the hard knotty oak of the senses—in the gnarled concretion of ordinary conception—and is not able to arrive at a free presentation of the Idea" (LHP 3:195; *Werke* 20:98). From this, some commentators have concluded that Hegel decisively rejects Böhme's theosophy. However, H. S. Harris finds that Hegel's criticism is "quite consistent with his evident desire [discussed earlier in section two above] to show that the older alchemical tradition of Paracelsus (and probably Böhme himself) contained symbolic expressions of important speculative truths."[116] In other words, Hegel rejects the "sensuous" manner in which Böhme's theosophy is presented, but accepts the inner core of its

113. Hegel mentions in the same passage that *philosophia teutonica* was once used as a term for mysticism.

114. Later, Hegel writes that "the principle of the Concept [*Begriff*] is living within him, only he cannot express it in the form of thought" (LHP 3:197; *Werke* 20:100).

115. Compare this comment to J. N. Findlay's observation about Hegel's system: "[Hegel's] whole system may in fact be regarded as an attempt to see the Christian mysteries in everything whatever, every natural process, every form of human activity, and every logical transition" (Findlay, *Hegel: A Re-Examination*, 131).

116. Harris, *Night Thoughts*, 399.

teaching. As Walsh puts it, "such qualifications aside, when Hegel comes to the content of Böhme's speculation he is clearly a believer."[117]

I will have something to say about Hegel's relation to Böhme in every chapter that follows, so deep is Hegel's debt to him.[118]

117. Walsh, "The Historical Dialectic of Spirit," 18.
118. I concur with Cyril O'Regan when he suggests "massive structural correspondences" between Hegel and Böhme. See Cyril O'Regan, *The Heterodox Hegel*, 18–19.

The Hermetic Milieu of Hegel's Early Years

One has only to say the words "College of Tübingen" to grasp *what*
German philosophy is at bottom—a *cunning* theology. . . . The
Swabians are the best liars in Germany, they lie innocently.
—Friedrich Nietzsche, *The Anti-Christ*

1. Rosicrucianism and Freemasonry

In the introduction and chapter 1, I have dealt with the fundamental
concepts of Hermeticism and the first 1,600 years of the Hermetic tradition. In this chapter I shall deal in part with events in the seventeenth
century, but in the main with the late eighteenth, the so-called
Goethezeit, the period of Hegel's youth. Histories of this period often
portray Hermeticism as on the decline. This is far from true. If anything, the eighteenth century saw a renaissance of Hermeticism.

By far the most important event in the history of seventeenth-century
Hermeticism was the appearance of the Rosicrucian manifestos. The
first appeared in the town of Kassel in Brunswick in 1614. Titled *Fama
Fraternitatis* and totaling only thirty-eight pages, the work was addressed
to "all the learned in Europe," and named as its source "the praiseworthy
order of the Rose Cross." The *Fama Fraternitatis* had been circulating in
manuscript throughout Europe since at least 1610,[1] and some of the
Rosicrucian texts were being circulated in manuscript form among certain like-minded individuals in Tübingen as early as the 1590s.[2] The
Fama was later republished with two other works—*Reform of the Universe* and *Short Reply to the Esteemed Fraternity of the Rose-Cross*—in a volume totaling 147 pages, by Adam Haselmayer, a follower of Paracelsus
and notary public to Archduke Maximilian.

The three works modestly proposed the "General Reformation of
the Entire World." The Rosicrucian manifestos centered around the
legendary figure of Christian Rosenkreuz, who was supposed to have
been born in 1378, taught the Hermetic art by Arabs, and died in

1. Roland Edighoffer, "Rosicrucianism: From the Seventeenth to the Twentieth Century," in *Modern Esoteric Spirituality*, 186. See also Donald R. Dickson,
The Tessera of Antilia (Leiden: Brill, 1998), 18.
2. See J. Montgomery, *The Cross and the Crucible*, 2 vols. (The Hague: Nijhoff,
1973), 204ff; also Will-Erich Peuckert, *Die Rosenkreutzer: Zur Geschichte einer
Reformation* (Jena: E. Diederichs, 1928), 96–99.

1484. These writings contain, in the words of Antoine Faivre, "traces of the Christian Kabbalah, Pythagoreanism, and a strong dose of Paracelsism."[3]

The second Rosicrucian manifesto, *Confessio Fraternitatis*, appeared in 1615. The third and most famous Rosicrucian work, *The Chemical Wedding of Christian Rosenkreuz*, an allegorical prose poem laden with alchemical imagery, appeared in 1616. The principal author of these works, and perhaps the "inventor" of Rosicrucianism, seems to have been Johann Valentin Andreae (1586–1654), a native of Württemberg. Andreae's father was a clergyman and practicing alchemist. Johann Valentin's mother was later court apothecary to the duke. His grandfather, Jakob Andreae, had a hand in drafting the *Formula of Concord* of 1580, which aimed at unifying Lutherans and Calvinists. It was Jakob who created the Andreae family coat of arms: a St. Andrew's cross with four roses. Johann Valentin was trained as a pastor at the Tübingen *Stift*, but was expelled following a political scandal.

According to Heinrich Schneider, the Rosicrucians, "declared that unification with God was demonstrable and possible already on earth. For that demonstration they were leaning upon a modification of enlightened natural philosophy which upheld that nature in its teleological structure was a gradual revelation of God."[4] Given that Böhme's first work was not even written until 1612, it is not plausible that he influenced the Rosicrucians. Rather, it is more likely that the Rosicrucian movement influenced Böhme. Schneider has suggested that "Böhme took up the Rosicrucian pansophy and the reformatory plans connected with it."[5] Andrew Weeks notes that Böhme incorporated two Rosicrucian slogans into his writings: the "age of the rose" and the "new reformation."[6]

The Rosicrucian movement involved members of many different religious denominations. The Rosicrucians held a doctrine of *prisca theologia*, the position that there is one true, trans-denominational, trans-cultural theology, an account of divine being revealed by God to man in the remote past. They believed that if this ancient wisdom could be recovered it would unify the world's religions.[7] Two images are associated with Rosicrucianism, owing to the ambiguity of the German *Rosenkreuz*: a red cross, and a cross with roses, usually blooming from the center. The meaning of these images has provoked much speculation. The Rosicrucians were supposed to adopt the dress and manners of the different lands into which they traveled, a fact which Julius Evola takes as symbolic of the belief in *prisca theologia* or

3. Antoine Faivre, *Access to Western Esotericism*, 64. For a discussion of the influence of the *Corpus Hermeticum* on Rosicrucianism, see Roland Edighoffer, "Hermeticism in Early Rosicrucianism," in Broek, 197–215.
4. Heinrich Schneider, *Quest for Mysteries: The Masonic Background for Literature in Eighteenth-Century Germany* (Ithaca, N.Y.: Cornell University Press, 1947), 45.
5. Heinrich Schneider, *Quest for Mysteries*, 43.
6. Weeks, *Boehme*, 95.
7. Allison Coudert, *Leibniz and the Kabbalah*, 8.

philosophia perennis.[8] Antoine Faivre offers the following list of impor-
tant authors who helped disseminate Rosicrucian ideas: Robert Fludd
(1574–1637), Julius Sperber (?–1619), Elias Ashmole (1617–92),
Michael Maier (ca.1566–1622), Samuel Hartlib (1595–1662), Jan Amos
Comenius (1592–1670), John Heydon (*The Holy Guide*, 1662), and
Theophilus Schweighardt (*Speculum sophicum-Rhodo-Stauricum*, 1618).[9]

The Rosicrucian manifestos captured the imagination of scores of
intellectuals throughout Europe, many of whom desperately tried to
make contact with the "order" and to join their ranks. Descartes and
Bacon were two such seekers.[10] Some, like Robert Fludd, even wrote
their own "Rosicrucian" works in hopes of earning the favor of the order.
Eventually, Andreae became disgusted with the furor he had created and
sought to distance himself from those who were now calling themselves
"Rosicrucians." In 1619, Andreae published *Christianapolis*, which called
for a "new reformation." There was no longer any talk of Rosicrucians,
but as Frances Yates puts it, "A rose by any other name . . ."[11]

Christianapolis preached a mysterious doctrine of "theosophy," which
involved a theory of "mystical architecture." In *Christianapolis*, as in the
Rosicrucian writings, Andreae places a strong emphasis on medicine
and healing, perhaps reflecting the influence of Paracelsian medicine.
Andreae now issued a call for the formation of "Christian Societies" or
"Christian Unions." Such groups, which were similar to Swabian Pietist
societies, were actually formed, but the "Societas Christiana" came to an
end with the outbreak of the Thirty Years War.[12] In 1628 Andreae
attempted to restart the organization in Nuremberg. Leibniz is supposed to have joined a Rosicrucian society in Nuremberg in 1666, and it
may have been the very one founded by Andreae.[13] The precepts of Leibniz's proposed "Order of Charity" are, according to Yates, "practically a
quotation from the *Fama*."[14] I shall discuss a later incarnation of the
Rosicrucian movement, and Hegel's connections to it, in chapter 7.

It is uncertain when Freemasonry was founded, or what its original
purpose was. It nevertheless became a repository for Hermetic philosophy, even employing the symbolic figure of Hermes Trismegistus in
some of its rituals.[15] The Freemasons numbered among their members
some of the most prominent minds in Europe, and flourished in Germany. Masonic historians distinguish between "Speculative" and "Opera-
tive" Masonry, the latter actual stonemasonry, indicating that the society

8. Evola, *Hermetic Tradition*, 161. One is also reminded of part 3 of Descartes's
Discourse on Method, in which he recommends, as a matter of prudence, obedience to the laws and customs of the country in which one finds oneself. See
below for Descartes's relation to Rosicrucianism.
9. Faivre, *Access to Western Esotercicism*, 65.
10. See Yates, *Rosicrucian Enlightenment*, 118–29.
11. Dickson, *Tessera*, 147.
12. Dickson considers Andreae "the forerunner of Philipp Jakob Spener and
German Pietism" (ibid., 19).
13. Yates, *Rosicrucian Enlightenment*, 154.
14. Ibid., 154.
15. Faivre, *The Eternal Hermes*, 177.

probably developed from craft guilds. With the inception of Speculative Masonry, the rites and trappings of the stonemasons took on a symbolic, and metaphysical significance. The Rosicrucians came to exercise an influence over Freemasonry, helping to make it even more mystical.

The first lodges in Germany were established in the 1730s and were of the Franco-Scottish "speculative" variety. The Stuarts, while in France, were intimately involved in the spread of Masonry throughout Europe. It is from them that the "Scottish Rite" of Masonry originates. The Scottish Rite involves further, higher degrees over and above those offered by other lodges. Scottish Rite Masonry exhibits connections with such aspects of Hermetic thought as alchemy and Kabbalism. An offshoot of the Scottish Rite, the so-called "Strict Observance" Masonry, maintained that Masonry originated in Scotland as a survival of the Knights Templar. It is claimed that before his execution the last Grand Master of the Templars, Jacques de Molay, assigned Hugo von Salm, a canon of Mainz, the mission of smuggling important Templar documents into Scotland. De Molay's hope was that the Templars could be reactivated there under another name. That name, according to the tradition, is Freemasonry. Strict Observance Masonry incorporated references to the Templars into its rites and degrees.

Like the Rosicrucians, the Masons believed in the fundamental identity of all religions. Beneath the superficial differences of religions was supposed to lie a *prisca theologia*. According to Schneider, "The aim of the lodges was the creation of a new man through membership in a communion mirroring a rational universe of freedom and love, just as primitive Christianity had once sought to call into being children of God for the Kingdom of God."[16] Indeed the conception of an invisible church—an idea advanced, as we saw in the last chapter, by the mystic Sebastian Franck—was one of the precepts of Masonry.[17] Edmond Mazet writes that Masonry would lead its members, "each through proper understanding of his own faith, to this transcendental truth."[18] Indeed, Masonry would come to "incorporate" Rosicrucianism, investing its higher degrees with Rosicrucian imagery.[19]

In 1738 Pope Clement XII, alarmed by the ecumenical nature of Freemasonry, issued a papal bull excommunicating Freemasons. Among other things, the Masons were accused of denying Christ's divinity (an accusation also leveled against the Knights Templar in 1307). The pope also claimed that the forces behind Masonry were identical with those that incited the Reformation. (Some have suggested that the Rosicrucians were intended as a Protestant counterpart to the Jesuits.[20])

The Masonic lodges differed in the messages they imparted to their members. Many were Hermetic or mystical in character, and politically conservative. Others were vehicles of Enlightenment secularism and

16. Heinrich Schneider, *Quest for Mysteries*, 57.
17. Ibid., 100.
18. Edmond Mazet, "Freemasonry and Esotericism," *Modern Esoteric Spirituality*, 249.
19. Yates, *The Rosicrucian Enlightenment*, 218.
20. Weeks, *Boehme*, 95.

rationalism, and by the end of the eighteenth century these had grown in number. Christopher MacIntosh points out that recent scholarship has tended to focus on the "enlightened" strain of Masonry, and to ignore the mystical, which was also quite strong. Indeed, as MacIntosh points out, these two were not mutually exclusive. Many "enlightened" German Masons actively engaged in alchemy, and saw no contradiction in it.[21]

In the final four decades of the eighteenth century legions of famous men in Germany aligned themselves with Masonry, including Bürger, Claudius, Fichte, Goethe, Herder, Klinger, Knebel, Lessing, Novalis, Rheinhold, Schelling, and Schiller. Many of these men published works dealing explicitly with Masonry. Fichte, for example, became a Mason in Zürich in 1793. There had been no lodge in Jena since 1764, so he joined the Günther Lodge of the Standing Lion at Rudolstadt in Thuringia (which was about eighteen miles from Jena). In 1799 Fichte worked with Ignaz Aurelius Fessler (1756–1839) on the development of various higher degrees for the lodge in Berlin.[22] As part of his work, Fichte wrote two lectures on the "philosophy of Masonry," which he presented to Johann Karl Christian Fischer. In 1802–3, Fischer published the lectures as "Letters to Constant" in two volumes of a journal entitled *Eleusinians of the Nineteenth Century, or Results of United Thinkers on the Philosophy and History of Freemasonry*. The format of "letters" to Constant (a fictitious non-Mason) was imposed on the text by the publisher, along with other arbitrary and ill-conceived changes. The lectures have since been published in a form that approximates Fichte's original, though his manuscripts have been lost.[23]

In 1778, Lessing published his *Ernst and Falk: Dialogues for Freemasons* (*Freimaürgespräche*). Lessing's *Nathan the Wise* (1779), a play with some broadly construed Masonic themes was a great influence on Hegel.[24] Among other things, the play presses the Masonic theme of a unity of the world's religions, and thus of an "invisible church." In act IV, scene 7, the Christian Friar praises Nathan, a Jew:

> *Friar*: O Nathan, Nathan! You're a Christian soul! By God a better Christian never lived!
> *Nathan*: And well for us! For what makes me for you a Christian, makes yourself for me a Jew!

The first letter we possess of Goethe's, written in 1764 when he was sixteen, has him applying earnestly for admission to a Masonic lodge.[25] He was not permitted Masonic membership, however, until 1780, when,

21. Christopher MacIntosh, *The Rose Cross and the Age of Reason* (Leiden: E. J. Brill, 1992), 2, 45.
22. See William R. Denslow, *10,000 Famous Freemasons*, vol. 2 (Trenton, Mo.: The Educational Bureau of the *Royal Arch Mason Magazine*, 1958), 46.
23. Roscoe Pound, *Masonic Addresses and Writings of Roscoe Pound* (New York: Macoy Publishing and Masonic Supply Company, 1953), 111–13; Pound also prints a translation of Fichte's text, pages 130–98.
24. Harris, *Toward the Sunlight*, 38.
25. Richard Friedenthal, *Goethe: His Life and Times* (London: Weidenfeld, 1963), 31.

on June 23 he was initiated into a lodge in Weimar. In 1782 he was the recipient of "Higher Templar Degrees of the Rite of Strict Observance."

According to Heinrich Schneider, the German Masonic lodges were
"teeming with magical, theosophical, mystical notions."[26] Schneider
notes that much of their lore was Kabbalistic in origin.[27] The German
Masonic movement was strongly influenced by the writings of the
French Mason and Böhmean, Louis Claude de Saint Martin. About
1770, the year of Hegel's birth, a "Hermetic Rite" was established, based
on the doctrines of the *Hermetica*.[28] Hermes Trismegistus himself
appears in such German Masonic rites of the eighteenth century as that
of the "Magi of Memphis."[29] In general, the higher degrees of Masonry
were (and are) strongly mystical. Schneider has claimed that the
Enlightenment is partly responsible for this. The Enlightenment quest
for universal knowledge and power over nature led to a revival of mysticism and occultism, for these had always promised to deliver just those
boons. In a reaction against the implicitly (and sometimes explicitly)
anti-spiritual, anti-religious rationalism of modern science, certain individuals sought a truer enlightenment in Hermeticism, and hoped to
make these secret societies into secret weapons. Schneider writes: "Long
before Kant's important answers to the great problems of human life,
the mystics in the secret societies had transformed these societies into
anti-Enlightenment organizations and, in thus keeping alive the mystical traditions, had made possible the later merging of German idealism
and mysticism. . . . This mystical movement was the conservative revolution of the eighteenth century, and if in its beginnings its character
was not exactly Christian, it was undoubtedly religious."[30]

The individuals known as the Illuminati were the reaction to this
reaction. The Illuminati were founded in 1776 as a means to advance the
ideals of the Enlightenment: opposition to traditional religion, superstition, and feudalism, and advocacy of scientific rationalism and the rights
of man. Initially they were led by their founder, Adam Weishaupt
(1784–1830), a law professor at the Bavarian University of Ingolstadt.
Weishaupt, however, proved inept at organization and he soon dele-
gated a great deal of authority to Freiherr Adolph von Knigge (1752–96),
who mounted a highly successful membership drive in 1781. Weishaupt's
jealousy of Knigge's abilities led to their break three years later.
Weishaupt appears to have endowed the order with Hermetic trappings
merely as window dressing, to entice members and, perhaps, to discour-
age the authorities from investigating.[31] Members were encouraged to

26. Heinrich Schneider, *Quest for Mysteries*, 22.
27. Ibid., 102.
28. Faivre, *Access to Western Esotericism*, 80.
29. Faivre, *The Eternal Hermes*, 189. Faivre notes that the rite may originally
have been French in origin.
30. Heinrich Schneider, *Quest for Mysteries*, 76–77.
31. Klaus Epstein's account of the history of the Illuminati and its suppression
makes for fascinating reading. See Epstein, *The Genesis of German Conservatism*
(Princeton, N.J.: Princeton University Press, 1966), 88–95; 100–104.

believe that their superiors possessed some special secret that they would be made privy to in time.

At its height, the Illuminati included literati like Goethe and Herder, as well as numerous other public figures and members of the aristocracy: Karl-August, duke of Weimar, the Prussian reformer Karl von Hardenberg, Duke Ferdinand of Braunschweig, Duke Ernst of Gotha, the publisher C. F. Cotta, Count Johann Cobenzl, and many others. The order thus managed to insinuate itself into the governments of Austria and Germany. Not surprisingly, Weishaupt and company made the infiltration of the educational system a top priority. The staff of the Karlsschule in Stuttgart included several Illuminati.

The influence of the order was short-lived, however. In 1784 Elector Karl Theodor of Bavaria, seeing the Illuminati as a threat to religion, issued a proclamation commanding them to disband. In 1785 Weishaupt was forced out of his professorship at Ingolstadt and went to live with a friend, Jakob Lanz, in Regensburg. While out walking together one day they were caught in a sudden downpour and Lanz was struck by lightning and killed. The Illuminati membership list was found on his body, constituting proof positive that the order had defied the elector's proclamation. The elector then issued a second proclamation commanding all Illuminati to register with the government and promising a full pardon if they did so. This put the order in a terrific bind. The members could not possibly know how complete a list the government had obtained, so if they registered they risked imprisonment or worse (if Karl Theodor's promise was disingenuous). On the other hand, if they did not register and their names were on the list, they risked imprisonment (or worse). In this impossible situation the order self-destructed, as most members chose to obey the elector's edict. Although rumors of the influence of the Illuminati continue to this day, it was never—so far as we know—officially reactivated, and if it was reactivated there is no evidence that it regained anything like the influence it had from 1776 to 1785.

Most of the Illuminati were also Masons. Jacques D'Hondt in his *Hegel Secret* provides a fascinating discussion of the influence of the Enlightenment ideals and terminology of the Illuminati on the young Hegel.[32] I shall discuss some his conclusions in section 4 here, as well as in chapter 7.

2. Goethe the Alchemist

The life of Johann Wolfgang von Goethe (1749–1832) provides a fascinating case study of an eighteenth century Hermeticist. His example makes it vividly clear that an eminent scientist and man of letters could still be deeply immersed in Hermeticism as late as the second half of the eighteenth century.

Most scholars treat the Enlightenment as a single, unitary phenomenon: the effort to emancipate mankind from tradition, superstition, and

---

32. See Jacques D'Hondt, *Hegel Secret* (Paris: Presses Universitaires de France, 1968), 62–114.

despotism. But in fact the Enlightenment took radically different shapes in different countries. This is especially true of Germany. Christopher MacIntosh writes that when the Enlightenment "fell on German soil it often took root in strange and contradictory ways."[33] An example of this is the German phenomenon of the "Enlightened despot," exemplified by Frederick the Great. In particular, the scientific spirit of the Enlightenment took longer to gain ground in Germany. Well into the time of Hegel and Goethe, Hermeticism was still seen in many quarters as a progressive influence. Alchemy survived much later in Germany than it did in the rest of Europe.

Ronald Gray, who has produced an entire study of the influence of alchemy on Goethe, writes that "At the time of Goethe's birth, in ... Mannheim, alchemy was all the rage. Many of the most respectable citizens had established alchemical laboratories, and so widespread was the enthusiasm that the city authorities felt themselves obliged to suppress it by law, on the grounds that the numerous ill-guarded fires and the waste of labour and materials were dangerous, and harmful to the economy of the state."[34] As a young man, Goethe read Paracelsus, Basil Valentine, van Helmont, Swedenborg, and the Kabbalah.[35] In particular, as Gray notes, Goethe was influenced by an anonymous alchemical work entitled *Aurea Catena Homeri* (ca.1723).[36] Goethe's letter to E. Th. Langer of May 11, 1770, discusses the Emerald Tablet of Hermes Trismegistus.[37] Goethe's notebook from Frankfurt and Strasbourg contains many references to Paracelsus and Agrippa.[38] According to Richard Friedenthal, for Goethe "alchemy was a thing of the present, not of the past, a still living survival from the middle ages."[39] Indeed, Gray claims that "The degree to which alchemy had established control over Goethe's interests in early manhood can scarcely be over-emphasized."[40]

In September of 1768, Goethe, exhausted, took leave from Leipzig University and spent the winter at home. He was much of the time in the company of Susanna von Klettenberg, who belonged to the sect of Herrnhuter, a Pietist movement founded by the notorious Hermeticist Count von Zinzendorf (1700–60). An alchemical adept, Klettenberg introduced Goethe to the *Opus Mago-Cabbalisticum et Theosophicum* of Georg von Welling.[41] Together, they engaged in alchemical experiments in Goethe's father's attic. Friedenthal describes their work in dramatic detail:

33. MacIntosh, *The Rose Cross*, 15.
34. Gray, *Goethe the Alchemist*, 4.
35. Friedenthal, *Goethe*, 66–68; see also Gray, *Goethe the Alchemist*, 5.
36. Gray, *Goethe the Alchemist*, 5.
37. Ibid., 182.
38. Ibid., 6.
39. Friedenthal, *Goethe*, 67. See also Gray's entire *Goethe the Alchemist*. Gray claims that Goethe probably encountered much of alchemy in a Böhmean formulation, though he probably never encountered Böhme's thought directly.
40. Gray, *Goethe the Alchemist*, 7.
41. This work was based on Paracelsus and Böhme. Goethe is also known to have read Kabbalistic works. See Friedenthal, *Goethe*, 66.

The pious Fräulein von Klettenberg stood with the young Goethe in front of a wind furnace, with sand-bath and chemical flasks. They stirred up the 'ingredients of Macrocosm and Microcosm.' They tried to produce silicic acid by melting quartz pebbles from the river Main. They discussed mysterious salts, to be conjured up by unheard-of means, a 'virgin soil' with extraordinary powers. . . . Even in his [later] natural science he remained far truer to the world of *prima materia* and the *Chemical Marriage*, as the text-book of the Rosicrucians was called, than subsequent opinion has been willing to admit.[42]

In later years, Goethe was far more critical of alchemy: "It is a misuse of genuine and true ideas, a leap from the ideal, the possible, to the reality, a false application of genuine feelings, a lying promise, which flatters our dearest hopes and aspirations."[43] However, Goethe's disapproval appears to have extended only to the actual practice of laboratory alchemy. He continued to be influenced by alchemical theory and symbolism. In 1795 he composed an alchemical fairy tale laden with Hermetic imagery of all sorts—such as, for instance, the image of the *ouroboros* (the snake biting its tail).

The conception of a unity of the world's religions is joined in Goethe's thought, as it is in Rosicrucianism and Freemasonry, to a quasi-pantheistic nature mysticism. In words that call to mind Schiller's poem *Die Freundschaft* (1782), which is quoted—or rather deliberately misquoted—by Hegel in the final passage of the *Phenomenology of Spirit*, Goethe writes in the *Sorrows of the Young Werther* (1774):

From the inaccessible mountains across the desert that no foot has trodden, and on to the end of the unknown ocean, breathes the spirit of the eternally creating One, rejoicing in every speck of dust that hears Him and is alive. —Ah, in those days, how often did my longing take the wings of a crane that flew overhead and carried me to the shore of the uncharted sea, to drink from the foaming cup of the infinite that swelling rapture of life, and to taste but for an instant, despite the limited force of my soul, one drop of the bliss of that being which produces all things in and by means of itself.[44]

David Walsh notes that "Goethe made frequent use of the idea of unifying opposites in the sense derived from the alchemical symbolism, both in his literary and scientific writings."[45] His aim, as Gray puts it, was "an incorruptible permanence which embraces in itself all opposites."[46] Goethe writes: "I was pleased to imagine to myself a divinity [*Gottheit*] which reproduces itself from all eternity, but since production cannot be thought of without multiplicity [*Mannigfältigkeit*], this divin-

42. Friedenthal, *Goethe*, 67; in Hegel's lectures on the *Philosophy of Nature* of 1803, he discusses a "Virgin Earth," mentioning in this context "the elders," whom H. S. Harris argues refers to Paracelsus, Böhme, and the alchemists (*Night Thoughts*, 274).
43. Quoted in Gray, *Goethe the Alchemist*, 66–67.
44. Goethe, *The Sorrows of the Young Werther*, trans. Bayard Quincy Morgan (New York: Frederick Ungar Publishing, 1957), 69.
45. Walsh, *Boehme and Hegel*, 326.
46. Gray, *Goethe the Alchemist*, 11–12.

ity necessarily appeared to itself at once as a Second Person [*ein Zweites*], whom we recognize by the name of the Son."[47] The similarity to Böhme's doctrine is obvious here.[48] Goethe continues, speaking of the Father and Son: "These two had now to continue the act of creation, and appeared to themselves again as a Third Person [*im Dritten*], who was now just as living and eternal as the whole. But with this the circle of divinity was closed, and even they would have found it impossible to create again a being fully equal to themselves."[49]

Gray has described Goethe's color-theory as, "entirely alchemical in conception."[50] The color-theory, which had a great influence on Hegel's later *Naturphilosophie*, was influenced by the alchemical teaching that all colors arise from the opposition of darkness and light.[51] Goethe himself acknowledges the influence of alchemy on the *Farbenlehre*: "He who ponders this matter more deeply," Goethe states, "will be so much the better able to relate these remarks with the secret philosophy and experience of the chemists."[52] Furthermore, Goethe acknowledged the importance of the form of "triplicity" in his color-theory, a triplicity which, of course, figures prominently in Hegel and, as we have seen, in Böhme and his followers: "If one has rightly understood the separation of blue and yellow," Goethe states,

> and has sufficiently considered in particular the development towards red, whereby the opposed sides incline towards one another and combine in a third being, then a certain secret significance will become apparent, to wit that a spiritual meaning can be read into these two separated and opposed beings, and one will scarcely refrain, when one sees them producing green below, and red above, from thinking in the former case of the earthly, and in the latter case of the heavenly creatures of the Elohim.[53]

Goethe's botanical theory, the doctrine of the so-called *Urpflanze*, is also heavily influenced by Böhme and alchemy. Goethe's search for the *Urpflanze* led him to postulate a sequence of seven stages of plant development, moved by the twin forces of "diastole" and "systole." Rolf Christian Zimmerman has argued that Goethe's conceptions of diastole and systole derive from Oetinger's conceptions of expansion and contraction.[54] Robert Schneider speaks of these concepts as part of the "old

47. Quoted in Gray, *Goethe the Alchemist*, 50.
48. The more immediate source may have been the thought of Oetinger. See Robert Schneider, *Schellings und Hegels schwäbische Geistesahnen* (Würzburg-Aumühle: Konrad Triltsch Verlag, 1938), 136.
49. Quoted in Gray, *Goethe the Alchemist*, 50.
50. Ibid., 128.
51. Walsh, *Boehme and Hegel*, 94.
52. Quoted in Gray, *Goethe the Alchemist*, 127.
53. Quoted in ibid., 122
54. Rolf Christian Zimmerman, *Das Weltbild des jungen Goethe: Studien zur hermetischen Tradition des deutschen 18. Jahrhunderts*, 2 vols. (Munich: Fink, 1969, 1979), 1:187. Oetinger actually employed the terms *systole* and *diastole*. The "contraction/expansion" theory originates, not surprisingly, with Böhme. See Walsh, *The Mysticism of Innerwordly Fulfillment*, 60–61.

vitalistic tradition" and points out that they crop up later in Schelling's *Weltalter*.[55] David Walsh has also compared Goethe's seven stages to Böhme's seven source-spirits.[56]

The *Urpflanze* is conceived by Goethe as a *microcosm* of the universe. The seven stages of plant development mirror the seven stages of the unfolding and division of creation as a whole. But all the parts and stages are simply the modes of one fundamental form. Goethe believed that each stage of the plant's development was understandable as a transformation of the primordial leaf. Gray writes that Goethe held this observation (which has been disputed by most botanists) to be "confirmation of his belief that the whole was present in all of its parts."[57] Again, we are reminded of a similar position in Hegel. Goethe also believed in the reality of an *Urtier*, of which all animals are modifications, though he did not develop this theory as extensively as he did that of the *Urpflanze*.

Goethe was an active and enthusiastic Mason. He even composed songs and orations in honor of deceased Masonic brethren, in which he elaborated his own views of the true mission of Masonry.[58] Some of these views may be inferred from his 1784 fragment *Die Geheimnisse*, a fable about a spiritual order of knights (modeled, it seems, on the Templars). The knights are led by a *Humanus*, who unites in his person the underlying "truth" of the various religious faiths—again, we find the conception of the invisible church. More than once in *Die Geheimnisse*, Goethe uses the imagery of the cross and roses. Goethe's name and reputation served to lend a measure of respectability to Hermeticism throughout his lifetime. Many were undoubtedly introduced to aspects of Hermeticism through Goethe, and his work was a major conduit for the indirect influence of alchemy, Böhme, Kabbalah, and various other Hermetic offshoots.

3. Swabian Pietism and F. C. Oetinger

Laurence Dickey has argued recently that the approach of going "back to the text" with Hegel's work is misguided, for so much of the intellectual context of what Hegel wrote is unfamiliar to us.[59] The Germany of Hegel's youth consisted of almost two thousand sovereign states, cities, dukedoms, and bishoprics. There was no centralized government, and no center of intellectual and spiritual life. Thus any German thinker must be understood in terms of his local context. Dickey argues that Hegel must be understood in the context of what he calls the "Protestant civil piety" of Old Württemberg. This tradition involves, among

---

55. Robert Schneider, *Geistesahnen*, 103. For the *Weltalter* passages see F. W. J. Schelling, *Sämtliche Werke*, vol. 8, ed. K.F.A. Schelling (Stuttgart: J. G. Cotta'scher, 1856–58), 231, 320, 327.
56. Walsh, *Boehme and Hegel*, 94.
57. Gray, *Goethe the Alchemist*, 74.
58. Heinrich Schneider, *Quest for Mysteries*, 123.
59. Laurence Dickey, *Hegel: Religion, Economics, and the Politics of Spirit 1770–1807* (Cambridge: Cambridge University Press, 1987), vii–viii.

other things, the goal of establishing the kingdom of God on earth through a transformation of society. Robert Schneider, in fact, refers to the "kingdom of God" (*Das Königreich Gottes*) as the "consummate idea" of Swabian Pietism.[60]

Schneider's *Schellings und Hegels Schwäbische Geistesahnen* was the first major study of the influence of Swabian theosophy on German idealism. He refers to the widespread scholarly ignorance of Hegel's Swabian roots as an "embarrassing situation" (*Zwangslage*) and argues that Schelling and Hegel were influenced by such aspects of Swabian cultural life as the *Geschichtstheologie* of Johann Coccejus (1603–69), mystical pantheism, Paracelcism, and theosophical *Naturphilosophie* (especially that of the Böhmean F. C. Oetinger).[61]

In Hegel's own time his Swabianism was the subject of some discussion, as well as ridicule. Karl Rosenkranz writes that "In Berlin it was the case that much that was attributed to Hegel as a person was typical of all Swabians, and was not regarded as being in any way peculiar to him so long as he lived in southern Germany. This is true of his warm, unpretentious manner, his intuitive openness, the directness of his speech, and the straightforwardness, matter-of-factness and sincerity of his mental attitude."[62] In the year following Hegel's death, O. H. Gruppe (writing under the pseudonym "Absolutulus von Hegelingen") played Aristophanes to Hegel's Socrates with his play, *The Wind, or an Entirely Absolute Construction of World History Through Oberon's Horn*, in which Hegel's Swabian origins were lampooned. Understanding Hegel's Swabian roots is indispensable for making sense out of his philosophical presuppositions and attachments.

The Duchy of Württemberg was an extremely insular state, which, after turning Protestant in 1534, became fertile ground for many forms of religious enthusiasm, including mysticism and Hermeticism. Indeed, the Swabians are *the* mystical people of Germany, notorious for their interest in esoteric, theosophical, and occult strains of thought. Reuchlin, Andreae, Oetinger, Hahn, Mesmer, Schiller, Schelling, Hegel, and Hölderlin were all Swabians. Wiedmann writes of the Swabians, "Reserved and uncommunicative, they conceal deep within themselves a quiet faculty for brooding and meditating."[63] Pierre Deghaye states that "Swabia is accustomed to reconciling opposites."[64] Württemberg, Laurence Dickey claims, was a land of "both-and" rather than "either-or."[65] "The Swabians," writes Heinrich Schneider, "always search for the totality of being behind the reality

60. Robert Schneider, *Geistesahnen*, 146. See chapter 7 for a discussion of the "Kingdom of God" in relation to Hegel, Schelling, and Hölderlin.
61. Ibid., 5.
62. Rosenkranz, *Hegels Leben*, 22.
63. Franz Wiedmann, *Hegel: An Illustrated Biography*, trans. Joachim Neugroschel (New York: Pegasus, 1968), 14.
64. Deghaye, "Jacob Böhme and His Followers," 236.
65. Dickey, *Hegel*, 11.

with its confusing multiformity, and beyond the rationale with its sharp antithesis of truth and Essence."[66] Robert Schneider writes of the Swabian "mental attitude" (*Geisteshaltung*), which continually points toward *die Ganzheit des Seins.*[67]

Even well into the nineteenth century, little of the scientific spirit of the Enlightenment had seeped in. Walsh writes: "The influence of the Enlightenment, to the extent it had made itself felt in Württemberg, was integrated with a theosophic philosophy of nature and a speculative Pietism which was concerned with the progressive revelation of the divine structure of history."[68] Indeed, for this reason, Robert Schneider holds that the influence of the *Aufklärung* on the young Hegel has been very much exaggerated.[69] We may think of biblical scholarship and "speculative philosophy" as widely different activities, but to the Pietists of Württemberg they were intimately connected.

Just what exactly is "speculative Pietism"? Defining Pietism itself is rather difficult, for it existed in Germany (and elsewhere) in a variety of forms. Lewis White Beck characterizes Pietism as "the public re-emergence of a more or less continuous effort in Germany to achieve a simpler, less dogmatic, and more moralistic Christianity than that to be found in any of the established churches."[70] The Pietists were inspired by a variety of sources. One highly significant source of inspiration was Böhme. By the end of the seventeenth century, Böhme's followers had become a thorn in the side of the established church. In Württemberg in 1681 Pastor Johann Jakob Zimmerman of Bietigheim was dismissed from his post for "Böhmeanism." A similar fate befell Ludwig Brunnquell of Grossbotwar in 1679. Despite this, Böhmeans in Württemberg were generally treated with more tolerance than anywhere else in Germany.

The strain of "Böhmean Pietism" became particularly strong in the eighteenth century, when many Pietist thinkers became active opponents of the mathematical and mechanical model of science and advocated instead a Böhmean "vitalistic philosophy of nature."[71] These religious mystics, some of whom, like Böhme, had no formal education, came to exercise a wide influence, and by the middle of the eighteenth century, as Beck puts it, "a Pietistic patina spread over almost all of German culture."[72] In addition to the open, Pietist religious societies, which were tolerated by the Duchy of Württemburg, secret societies flour-

66. Heinrich Schneider, *Quest for Mysteries*, 62–63. Here Schneider is actually explicating the views, with which he is in sympathy, of H. O. Burger in his *Schwabentum in der Geistesgeschicte* (Stuttgart and Berlin, 1933).
67. Robert Schneider, *Geistesahnen*, 23.
68. Walsh, *Boehme and Hegel*, 296.
69. Robert Schneider, *Geistesahnen*, 7.
70. Beck, *Early German Philosophy*, 157. This is indeed the case, for these "Pietist" concerns are to be found in such German mystics as Eckhart, Hildegard, Seuse, Tauler, Joachim, and others.
71. Ibid, 159.
72. Ibid., 10.

ished there as well.[73] Some of these societies were alchemical in nature. Alchemy was quite popular at the Württemberg court in the seventeenth century. The *Schwäbischen Magazin*, one of the most important publications in Swabian literary life, published works on theosophy and alchemical *Naturphilosophie* including Ph. M. Hahn's anonymous work, "Von Gottes Dreyeinigkeit und von der Versöhnung."[74]

I will have more to say about the influence of Swabian Pietism and Hermeticism on Schelling and Hegel in section 4 of this chapter. In the rest of this section, I will discuss the life and thought of Oetinger, who exercised considerable influence on both Schelling and Hegel.

Friedrich Christoph Oetinger (1702–82), virtually unknown to English-speaking scholars, ranks as the second most important figure in Württemberg Pietism after Johann Albrecht Bengel (1687–1752).[75] Stoeffler writes that "By most estimates [Oetinger] was, in fact, the most original theologian of the eighteenth century in Württemberg, and perhaps in all of Germany."[76] Robert Schneider has characterized Bengel as "the philosopher of history who anticipated the work of Schelling and Hegel."[77] Bengel believed that he was the herald of a "final age" of man in which God would achieve perfect self-actualization in the world, history would end, and all reality would be absorbed into God. Specifically, Bengel held that this would occur in 1836. Bengel and his followers, who called themselves "The Free" (*Die Freien*), proclaimed the perennial ideal of the invisible church, which would prepare man for the end of time. (I will have more to say about Bengel in chapter 7.)

Oetinger, after undergoing a conversion experience in 1721, entered the theological seminary in Tübingen, where Hegel would study sixty-seven years later. Oetinger was decidedly unimpressed by the Wolffian philosophy of rationalism and mechanism that was popular at the time, and yearned for something more. Discussing his intellectual frustrations with Johann Kaspar Oberberger, the proprietor of the powder mill in Tübingen, the latter gave Oetinger the works of Böhme. It was not long before Oetinger openly declared himself a disciple of Böhme. Indeed, Oetinger's first book was a commentary on Böhme: *Aufmunternde Gründe zur Lesung der Schriften Jacob Böhmens* (1731).

---

73. Heinrich Schneider has drawn interesting parallels between German Freemasonry and Pietist sects in his *Quest for Mysteries*, 48–49.

74. Ronald Gray notes that as a consequence of Böhme's influence on Pietism, it is possible to say that "wherever in Germany Pietism was strong . . . there was likely to be also some belief in the validity of alchemy" (Gray, *Goethe the Alchemist*, 4).

75. One place English-speaking scholars *have* encountered Oetinger is in Hans-Georg Gadamer's *Truth and Method*, in which Oetinger's doctrine of *sensus communis* is discussed briefly. To be sure, Gadamer appropriates Oetinger for his own purposes and says nothing of the role played by *sensus communis* in Oetinger's Böhmean theosophy. See *Truth and Method*, 2nd rev. ed., trans. Joel Weinsheimer and Donald G. Marshall (New York: Crossroad, 1989), 27–30, 485.

76. Stoeffler, *German Pietism*, 107.

77. Robert Schneider, *Geistesahnen*, 38.

Oetinger is also known to have visited a circle of Jewish Kabbalists at Frankfurt am Main, who introduced him to Knorr von Rosenroth's *Cabala Denudata*, as well as to the messianic Kabbalism of Isaac Luria. Through Oetinger, Luria's Kabbalah would exercise an indirect influence on German idealism. His familiarity with Kabbalism enabled Oetinger to appreciate what was "Kabbalistic" in Böhme's works and to attempt to effect a synthesis of Böhme and Kabbalism. This tendency is reflected in one of Oetinger's most important works, *Öffentliches Denckmal der Lehrtafel* (1763). This was a commentary on a Kabbalistic painting—commissioned by Princess Antonia of Württemberg—hanging in a small church at Teinach in the Black Forest. Oetinger's account of the Kabbalah in this work is almost entirely Lurianic. Antonia was a follower of a Christian Kabbalist pastor whose Kabbalism had been influenced by Reuchlin. Oetinger also corresponded with Emanuel Swedenborg. In 1765 he published a two-volume work entitled *Swedenborgs und anderer irdische und himmlische Philosophie, zur Prüfung des Bestens* (1765), which was subsequently banned in Württemberg.

Oetinger was also an accomplished scientist, quite learned in the theories of his time. Nevertheless, he was a fierce opponent of both mechanistic materialism and the rationalism of Descartes, Leibniz, and Wolff. In the spirit of Böhmean vitalism he composed a "theology of electricity."[78] Greatly influenced by alchemy, in 1749 he wrote that "Chemistry and theology are for me not two things but one thing."[79] One commentator notes that "Various theosophic currents, including the Hermetic and panvitalistic systems of Giordano Bruno and Paracelsus, the Kabbalah, the Rosicrucian tradition and, most importantly, the obscure speculation of Jakob Böhme, were incorporated into the Swabian Pietistic revival by Oetinger and his school."[80] An enthusiastic chiliast, in the tradition of Joachim de Fiore, he also published a book of inspirational sermons—*Reden nach dem Allgemeinen Wahrheitsgefühl* (1758)—which became quite popular with the laity of Württemberg.

Oetinger holds that "God is an eternal desire for self-revelation" (*eine ewige Begierde sich zu offenbaren*).[81] He writes in one place that "The ancients [*die Alten*] saw God as an eternal process in which He emerges from Himself and returns to Himself; this is the true conception of God and of His Glory; it is the true conception of His infinite life and power which issues in the Blessed Trinity."[82]

Oetinger identifies the fully realized God with *Geist* and treats *Geist* as what he calls an *Intensum*. An *Intensum* is a complex whole, which cannot

78. See Ernst Benz, *The Theology of Electricity*, trans. Wolfgang Taraba (Allison Park, Pa.: Pickwick Publications, 1989).

79. Quoted in Albrecht Ritschl, *Geschichte des Pietismus in der lutherische Kirche des 17. und 18. Jahrhunderts*, vol. 3 (Bonn: Adolph Marcus, 1880–86), 140.

80. Hanratty, "Hegel and the Gnostic Tradition: II," 314.

81. Oetinger, *Biblisches und emblematisches Wörterbuch* (1776; reprinted, Hildesheim: Georg Olms Verlag, 1969), 536. Pagination refers to the original edition.

82. Quoted in Hanratty, "Hegel and the Gnostic Tradition: II," 314; his translation.

be divided into separable pieces. In his *Biblisches und Emblematisches Wörterbuch* (1776), Oetinger defines *Wissen* (to know) as "to see a thing according to all its parts."[83] *Glaube* (belief, faith) is supposed to consist "not in annuling [*aufheben*] the syllogistic order of thought but in enlivening it."[84] Putting the two definitions together, one can see that what Oetinger is after is a kind of thought that proceeds organically, or which aims at the articulation and grasp of organic wholes. Oetinger thus does not reject reason per se; he merely opposes a "living" to a "dead" reason. We come to know the God-process through its manifold aspects, which are not conceived as separable pieces. Oetinger holds, in a manner identical to Hegel, that in the case of an *Intensum* such as *Geist*, the whole is immanent in every part. It is this immanence that enables us to progress from one moment to another in the gradual articulation of the whole.[85]

The "moments" of God represent the "forces" that bring about God's realization in the world, which consists in His corporealization or embodiment in nature and in history. Böhme's claim that no spirit exists "disembodied" is the linchpin of Oetinger's thought. Oetinger writes: "Embodiment is the goal of God's work" (*Leiblichkeit ist das Ende der werke Gottes*).[86] Oetinger departs from the entire earlier philosophical tradition of idealism, by holding that spirit does not exist separate and apart from its embodiment. Rather, spirit comes to progressively more adequate expression through corporeality—what Oetinger calls *Geistleiblichkeit*. A perennial idea in the theosophical tradition, *Geistleiblichkeit* has its probable origins in Caspar Schwenkfeld (1490–1561). As discussed in the last chapter, for Böhme *Leiblichkeit* was the last stage of God's self-unfolding. Still, *Geistleiblichkeit* is a highly obscure conception, perhaps best understood along the lines of an Aristotelian *entelecheia* (actuality): a perfect marriage of (divine) form and matter.

The forces that set in motion this process of cosmic "spiritual corporealization" are antagonistic and mutually determining, and are derived in large measure from Oetinger's studies of the Kabbalah. As was common among Christian Kabbalists, Oetinger identifies the first three *sephiroth* of the Kabbalistic Tree of Life with the Trinity and states that they deal solely with the Godhead. The other seven relate to creation. Like Böhme, Oetinger refers to these as "seven spirits," and like Böhme he favors this way of speaking because it accords with scriptural references to the seven spirits of God (Rev. 4:5). They are the mechanism of God's corporealization or manifestation. He conceives the supernal Trinity as in some degree beyond understanding.

The two fundamental cosmic processes, according to Oetinger, are expansion (*Ausbreitung*), which he identifies with the fourth Kabbalist *sephirah*, Hesed ("mercy," also known by a name which Oetinger also uses, *Gedulah*), and contraction (*Stärke*), which he identifies with the fifth

83. Oetinger, *Biblisches und emblematisches Wörterbuch*, 689.
84. Ibid., 282.
85. See Robert Schneider, *Geistesahnen*, 114.
86. Oetinger, *Biblisches und emblematisches Wörterbuch*, 407.

sephirah, Gevurah (judgment). Creation, and thus God's "embodiment" is set in motion by the primordial conflict of these two forces.

Central to Oetinger's theory of knowledge is his conception of *sensus communis*, which he discusses most fully in *Die Wahrheit des Sensus Communis* (also 1753). *Sensus communis*, Oetinger notes, "is concerned only with things that all men see before them, things that hold an entire society together, things that are concerned as much with truths and statements as with the arrangements and patterns comprised in statements."[87] Oetinger frequently refers to *sensus communis* as an "unmediated cognition" (*unmittelbare Erkenntnis*). Robert Schneider describes *sensus communis* as "the feeling of the deep, total bond [*Verbundenheit*] of man with God and with other beings."[88] *Sensus communis* cannot be defined with full clarity and precision because it in some sense transcends subject and object.[89] *Sensus communis* is understood by Oetinger to lie at the "very center" of our being—it is a state or a faculty that lies beyond the run-of-the-mill distinctions made by consciousness, including the distinction between consciousness and external world.

Oetinger also speaks of a "generative method," which understands both nature and scripture according to their "generative order," as organic systems that unfold as plants do from their seeds.[90] More exalted than *sensus communis* is what Oetinger calls *Zentrallerkenntnis*, an unmediated, synoptic vision in which the mind momentarily sees existence through the eyes of God. Oetinger writes that *Zentrallerkenntnis* leads to the realization that "The truth is a whole [*Die Wahrheit ist ein Ganzes*]; when one finally receives this total, synoptic vision of the truth, it matters not whether one begins by considering this part or that."[91] As Robert Schneider points out, the theme of the truth as a whole (or *the* whole) is a perennial theme of Swabian speculative Pietism. It is for this reason, Schneider suggests, that the sceptical moment of Kant's philosophy was almost universally rejected and reviled in Württemberg.[92] Schneider writes that "there can no longer be any doubt, that in the [Tübingen] *Stift*, spurred on and enriched by the Enlightenment, the original spirit of the [Swabian] *Heimat* was at work, seeking the Truth only in the Whole."[93]

Oetinger reads the entire text of the *Bible* as a "holy emblem book": every detail is in some way significant or symbolic. The Bible is itself an embodiment of God—not a physical embodiment, but an expression of the divine in terms of concrete images, myths, and allegories. Oetinger distinguishes between a "narrow" and a "wide" meaning of scriptural

87. Oetinger, *Die Wahrheit des sensus communis oder des allgemeinen Sinnes, in den nach dem Grundtext erklärten Sprüchen und Prediger Salomo oder das beste Haus- und Sittenbuch für Gelehrte und Ungelehrte* (Tübingen, 1753). Quoted in Gadamer, 27.
88. Robert Schneider, *Geistesahnen*, 124.
89. Stoeffler, *German Pietism*, 115.
90. Priscilla A. Hayden-Roy, "A Foretaste of Heaven": Friedrich Hölderlin in the Context of Württemberg Pietism (Amsterdam: Rodopi, 1994), 42.
91. F. C. Oetinger, *Sämtliche Schriften*, vol. 5, ed. Karl Chr. Eberh. Ehmann (Stuttgart: Steinkopf, 1858–64), 45.
92. Robert Schneider, *Geistesahnen*, 56.
93. Ibid., 54.

terms.[94] The narrow is the literal meaning, the wide the speculative. Because Oetinger holds that both are, in their own way, true, he can claim that his views do not conflict with orthodoxy (though few accepted such a defense in his time). Following Böhme, Oetinger extends this conception to include all of nature, stating that "the natural realm, as well as scripture, is a medium of divine revelation, and . . . therefore the study of one will yield at least some insights into the other."[95] Nature, like the *Bible*, is an emblem-book, where everything is to be read as a sensuous representation of the divine. Since Nature is an emblem book—a sensualization of God in the world progressing toward true spiritual embodiment—scientific experiment or investigation into Nature are for Oetinger a way of "thinking God's thoughts."[96] Oetinger refers to the science that studies these "emblems" as *theologia emblematica* and claims that when fully realized it will unify the sciences and all of human knowledge. One author refers to it as "an eclectic combination of alchemy, Böhme, the cabala, and emblematics."[97]

There are many parallels between Oetinger's thought and Hegel's. The foregoing discussion of Oetinger should have made some of these obvious, but I will offer a brief summary (further parallels will be drawn in later chapters). First there is Oetinger's ideal of an unmediated cognition beyond subject and object; there is his conception of the truth as a "whole"; there is Oetinger's understanding of nature as a self-specification of God and his treatment of natural philosophy as providing insight into "God's mind"; there is Oetinger's *organicism*, his conception of the *intensum* in which the whole is immanent in every part, and his ideal of an organic form of thought; there is the centrality in Oetinger's thought of *Geist* and his ideal of *Geistleiblichkeit*, or spiritual embodiment, which finds its analogue in Hegel's Objective and Absolute Spirit. Hegel states that "Spirit *is* in the most *concrete* sense. The absolute or highest being belongs to it" (LPR 1:142; VPR 1:56). Just as in Oetinger's thought, Hegel's God or the Idea is "embodied" in more or less adequate forms. In nature it exists in inchoate form, but finds more adequate realization in human projects, institutions, art, and religion, finally reaching perfection in an ideal medium: the pure aether of thought realized in speculative philosophy.

Two important followers of Oetinger were Johann Ludwig Fricker (1729–66) and Philipp Matthäus Hahn (1739–90), both of whom studied at Tübingen. Fricker, along with other associates of Oetinger such as G. F. Rösler and Prokop Divisch, developed Oetinger's "theology of electricity" and may have exercised an influence on Franz Anton Mesmer (1734–1815).[98] (Oetinger was, in fact, the first German scholar to take note of Mesmer's theories.)[99] However, perhaps the most influential follower of Oetinger was Hahn, whose theology was similar in most respects to

94. Hayden-Roy, "A Foretaste of Heaven," 43.
95. Stoeffler, *German Pietism*, 110.
96. Ibid., 114.
97. Hayden-Roy, "A Foretaste of Heaven," 46.
98. Faivre, *Access to Western Esotericism*, 77.
99. Benz, *Theology of Electricity*, 69.

Oetinger's. The young Hahn spent half a year at a vicarage in Herrenberg with Oetinger, who was by then quite ill. During his time there, he read Oetinger's voluminous alchemical library.[100] In 1770 Hahn, who had won the favor of Duke Karl Eugen for his design of an astronomical clock, became a pastor in Kornwestheim, north of Stuttgart. In 1781 he moved to Echterdingen and died there nine years later. While at Echterdingen, he made frequent visits in the summer to Nürtingen, where he may have come into contact with the young Schelling and Hölderlin.

Hahn attracted numerous followers from Stuttgart, where he established some conventicles (scriptural "study groups" for lay Pietists), including one exclusively composed of city officials and leading citizens.[101] Hahn was acquainted also with Johann Gottfried Herder (1744–1803), whose own Hermeticism may well have been fueled by this contact with speculative Pietism.[102] In 1774 Herder published Über die älteste Urkunde des Menschgesclechts, in which he devoted considerable space to a serious discussion of Hermes Trismegistus. The work concluded with a chapter dealing with, among other things, the Kabbalah. In 1801, in his journal Adrastea, Herder published a dialogue between "Hermes and Pymander," styled after the dialogues found in the Corpus Hermeticum.[103]

Despite Oetinger's influence, the church and academia remained largely closed to his followers. The Tübingen Stift, for instance, was intolerant of Oetingerites. Nevertheless, even there Oetinger exercised a subterranean influence. The metaphysical writings of Professor Gottfried Ploucquet (1716–90) were strongly influenced by Oetinger's critique of Leibniz. Ploucquet did not, however, dare to cite Oetinger.[104] Hayden-Roy writes that "for pastors hoping for a successful career within the Württemberg church, it was politically expedient to espouse conservative rather than speculative views."[105]

P. M. Hahn is not to be confused with Johann Michael Hahn (1759–1819), an influential disciple of Böhme, whose own life bore a number of parallels to that of the Lusatian cobbler. Hahn founded the Swabian "Hahnisch Fellowship" (Hahnische Gemeinschaft), the members of which were all conventionally religious laity, who just happened to meet every Sunday afternoon to discuss Hahn's brand of Böhmean theosophy.[106]

100. Hayden-Roy, "A Foretaste of Heaven," 55–56.
101. Ibid., 65.
102. Robert Schneider (Geistesahnen, 10) claims that Herder was influenced by Oetinger.
103. Herder was a lifelong Hermeticist. In 1769, when he was only twenty-five years old, Herder wrote two essays in which he treated the universe as the body of God and God as the "idea of the world." He also advanced the micro-cosm-macrocosm thesis, held that human thoughts are a form in which God manifests Himself in the world and claimed that the acquisition of theosophical wisdom gives one "power" over things. Klaus Vondung has discussed Herder's Hermeticism in fascinating detail. See Vondung, "Millenarianism, Hermeticism, and the Search for a Universal Science," in Science, Pseudo-Science, and Utopianism in Early Modern Thought.
104. See Robert Schneider, Geistesahnen, 47.
105. Hayden-Roy, "A Foretaste of Heaven," 69.
106. Stoeffler, German Pietism, 121.

4. Hegel's *Lehrjahre*

In the winter semester of 1788, Hegel began his studies at the Tübingen *Stift*, where J. V. Andreae, Oetinger, J. L. Fricker, and P. M. Hahn had studied. One will search his early writings, including the journal in German and Latin which he began keeping in 1785, in vain for signs of interest in *Naturphilosophie*, idealism, or any of the philosophical concerns of the time. Instead, as Lawrence Dickey claims, "it was the culture of Old-Württemberg, not the principles of German idealism, that furnished what Lucien Febvre would have called the 'mental equipment' of his mind."[107]

We know fairly little about Hegel's religious education. In the gymnasium at Stuttgart, Hegel had been taught J. W. Jager's *Catechism*, which was based on the thought of Bengel and Coccejus. Coccejus interpreted the progress of history in biblical terms, holding that history was the "progressive realization of the divine plan."[108] There is general agreement among scholars that Hegel must have had some degree of exposure to the strain of mysticism in Swabian Pietism. Robert Schneider writes that Hegel and Schelling inhabited an entirely different "conceptual world" (*Begriffswelt*) from that of Enlightenment rationalism and mechanism. Theirs was that of the "ancient categories of chemical (i.e., alchemical)-biological philosophy of nature" (*die uralten Kategorien der chemisch (alchimistisch)-biologischen Naturphilosophie*), stemming from "Oetinger, Böhme, van Helmont, Boyle, Fludd, Paracelsus, Agrippa von Nettesheim, Telesio, and others. . . . This philosophy of nature was still alive in Württemberg during Hegel and Schelling's youth."[109] Wiedmann writes that "Hegel's home, like that of every old, established family in Stuttgart up to the beginning of our century, was marked by Protestant Pietism. And thus Hegel was steeped in its theosophy and mysticism from childhood. His Swabian disposition was never rarefied—not even 'in the element of the universal, the ether of thought and philosophy.' "[110] There was certainly easy access in Württemberg to theosophic literature. Important works by Oetinger and P. M. Hahn were still being brought out in the 1780s and 1790s. Schneider notes that the works of Paracelsus and Böhme, as well as numerous alchemical works, were plentiful in Old Württemberg.[111]

In his publications, manuscripts, and youthful diaries Hegel says nothing about Swabian speculative Pietism and theosophy, and nothing about figures such as Oetinger. This does not, however, constitute a decisive reason for discounting their influence. Robert Schneider's hypothesis is, I think, quite reasonable: "worüber man ständig spricht, schreibt man nichts in sein Tagebuch" ("one does not write in one's diary

---

107. Dickey, *Hegel*, 6.
108. Walsh, *Boehme and Hegel*, 296.
109. Robert Schneider, *Geistesahnen*, 20; my translation.
110. Wiedmann, *Hegel*, 14. See also Karl Lütgert, *Die Religion des deutschen Idealismus und ihr Ende* (Gütersloh: Bertelsmann, 1923).
111. Robert Schneider, *Geistesahnen*, 2.

about that of which one constantly speaks").[112] In other words, the *Begriffswelt* of theosophy and Hermeticism was so prevalent in Württemberg that it did not provoke comment from the young Hegel. Also, the example of Ploucquet (see the preceding section) is enough to show that there was concern among scholars that open alliance with Hermetic philosophy and figures such as Oetinger might provoke censure from their colleagues. Hermeticism was something of a "grass roots" movement in Württemberg—though, as I have shown, it exercised a clandestine influence in academia, the church, and government.

Robert Schneider writes that "Hegel's upbringing can only have been 'Pietist.' "[113] Although there is no record of his parents having been members of any Pietist conventicle, Hegel's own youthful religious orientation seems to have been Pietistic.[114] His "early theological writings" are alive with the sort of issues and questions that were characteristic of Württemberg Pietism. Whatever the exact nature of his parents' Lutheranism may have been, devout Lutherans they were. When Hegel would later come to develop philosophic interests, he saw the philosophies of Kant, Jacobi, and Fichte as outgrowths of Protestantism. Hegel's Protestantism appears to have been sincere and in no way merely "orthopractic."

Some of the earliest entries in Hegel's journal consist in passages from religious and theological texts, laboriously copied out. As H. S. Harris writes, "a fifteen-year-old who . . . spends several days writing out someone else's views on heavenly bliss really does himself believe in heaven."[115] Harris writes that Hegel entered the theological seminary at Tübingen simply because he got his education there for free.[116] However, as far as we know Hegel did not consider studying anything other than theology.[117] The picture that emerges from a study of his early days is that of a pious, almost deliberately conventional and conformist youth, in whom, nevertheless, were planted the mystical Pietist seeds that would later bloom as speculative philosophy.

Pietism exercised a considerable influence on the Tübingen *Stift*.[118] Hegel's instructors there were actively concerned with how Pietism could be reconciled with orthodox Lutheranism. At Tübingen, Hegel read Plato, Kant, Schiller, Jacobi, Hemsterhuis, Montesquieu, and Herder. He declined to join a "Kant Club" formed at the *Stift*, because he

112. Ibid., 17.
113. Robert Schneider, *Geistesahnen*, 16; my translation.
114. There was, of course, much in Pietism that Hegel rebelled against throughout his life, in particular its denigration of knowledge in favor of faith. My contention is merely that Hegel was at the same time influenced by much else in Pietism. Hegel's endorsement, late in life, of the work of Karl Friedrich Göschel (1784–1862), who attempted a kind of synthesis of Hegelianism and Pietism, suggests that Hegel may have been more sympathetic to Pietism than is often thought. See Butler, 537–46.
115. Harris, *Toward the Sunlight*, 23.
116. Ibid., 64.
117. Wiedmann, *Hegel*, 15.
118. Stoeffler, *German Pietism*, 91.

claimed he was too busy reading Rousseau.[119] The later testimony of Magister Leutwein of the *Stift* indicates that Hegel had no interest in Kant or metaphysics while there.[120] Further, Harris has written of Hegel's early "indifference" to theoretical philosophy. This is what one would expect of someone who had been exposed early on to the heady air of theosophy—Schelling, for instance, could only stomach mainstream philosophy in so far as he could read theosophy into it.

Nevertheless, we know that some of Hegel's instructors had been influenced by Kant, particularly Gottlob Christian Storr (1746–1805).[121] Storr—who, according to Robert Schneider, was also influenced by Bengel[122]—appears to have made much of Kant's claim to have "limited reason, in order to make room for faith." Despite the fact that this would have supported the kind of quasi-Pietistic, or simple, natural faith to which Hegel was attracted, he and Schelling (his roommate at the *Stift*, along with Hölderlin, beginning in 1790) appear to have reacted strongly against it. This again suggests that their "Pietist" religious upbringing was anything but conventional. Only a "speculative Pietist" would have been so unmoved by Storr's appropriation of Kant, because speculative Pietism believes in the possibility of wisdom—a knowledge of all things human and divine—and thus must reject sceptical philosophies such as Kant's.

As I mentioned earlier, Hegel's "early theological writings" are alive with the sort of issues and questions that were characteristic of Württemberg Pietism. In the writings from the *Stift* period, Hegel maintains that unreflective "folk religion" is at root identical with the highest, reflective philosophical understanding of the nature of God. As Harris writes of Hegel's early notes on religion, "He is contrasting the healthy, undivided, natural consciousness of the Greeks with the corrupt, divided, artificial consciousness of the moderns; and this, too, is a contrast that he never abandoned."[123] The import of Hegel's position is clear, though he does not say it outright: true religion, true thought about the divine, is somehow already given to man in an unreflective way, in advance of anything like theoretical philosophy. Hegel finds in the Hebrew writings, especially Job, the same sort of simple, unreflective "connectedness" to the divine as he found in the Greeks.[124] Hegel's idolization of Greek culture has been overemphasized by most scholars. It is easy to see that the same "unreflective connectedness to the divine" was to be found also in the Pietist milieu with which Hegel was acquainted from childhood on.

119. Wiedmann, *Hegel*, 19.
120. Johannes Hoffmeister, *Dokumente zu Hegels Entwicklung* (Stuttgart: Frommann, 1936), 430.
121. Interestingly, Storr was the son-in-law of Jeremias Friedrich Reuss (1700–1777), the favorite student of Bengel, and mentor of Philipp Matthäus Hahn. Reuss studied with Oetinger, and was also the mentor of Köstlin, uncle of Schelling.
122. Robert Schneider, *Geistesahnen*, 7.
123. Harris, *Toward the Sunlight*, 76.
124. Harris, *Toward the Sunlight*, 84.

In the so-called "Tübingen fragment" (*Religion ist eine*) (1793), Hegel modifies his stance toward folk religion, and we now see Reason entering the picture, Enlightenment being reconciled with the happy unreflectiveness of the *Volk*. Hegel now holds that religious consciousness must develop, and although the state of the Greeks and Hebrews represents a state of idyllic oneness with God, it is inferior insofar as it is an *unthinking* unity. The development of religious consciousness is a development toward a thoughtful reappropriation of relatedness to the divine. (We are reminded of Böhme's doctrine that the Fall *had* to happen, so that man could achieve a self-conscious unity with God.) Hegel's position, as Harris notes, recognizes the form of consciousness man has come to display over time as being the *mature* or most fully developed standpoint of man.[125] Nevertheless, he does not abandon the idea that in some sense the *realizations* that will come with philosophical insight are already laid up in the mind in an inchoate form—something we appear to possess simply by virtue of being human. (It will be important to keep this idea in mind for the discussion which follows in the next chapter.) Indeed, Hegel maintains in this essay that "the heart" must be followed first, before philosophical consciousness is possible. He maintains that the "subjective religion" of all men is at root identical and cites the line from Lessing's *Nathan the Wise* quoted earlier: "what makes me for you a Christian, makes yourself for me a Jew."[126]

In a letter from Hegel to Schelling dated January 1795, Hegel writes: "Reason and Freedom remain our watchword, and our rallying point the Invisible Church."[127] I have already noted the use of the term *invisible church* by German mystics and Freemasons. H. S. Harris writes: "It seems to me virtually certain that for Hegel, at any rate, the 'invisible Church' originally referred to the cosmopolitan ideal of Freemasonry as envisaged by Lessing in *Ernst und Falk*."[128] However, Robert Schneider holds that Hegel's use of the term *invisible church*, as well as the phrase "Kingdom of God" (which occurs in the same letter), is evidence of the influence of Pietist theology.[129] It may very well be that Hegel and Schelling encountered this terminology in both Masonic and Pietist circles. Harris makes mention of a "secret club" at Tübingen, in which Masonic ideals were discussed (although he thinks that the term *invisible church* was not much used there).[130] Hegel was also influenced early on by the millenarian ideas of two French Masonic *philosophes*, Volney and Rabaut de Saint-Etienne.[131]

In 1793, Hegel graduated from the *Stift* and in October he took a job

---

125. Ibid., 127.
126. The line "truth is not like stamped coin" in the *Phenomenology* (Miller, 22) is from *Nathan*, 4:6.
127. Butler, 32; Hoffmeister #8.
128. Harris, *Toward the Sunlight*, 105.
129. Robert Schneider, *Geistesahnen*, 41. A July 10, 1794 letter from Hölderlin to Hegel refers to "the Kingdom of God" as "our rallying cry" (Butler, 24).
130. Harris, *Toward the Sunlight*, 106.
131. See D'Hondt, *Hegel Secret*, 83–153.

as tutor in the home of C. F. Steiger von Tschugg in Berne. There, in his leisure time, he read Meister Eckhart, as well as Grotius, Hobbes, Hume, Leibniz, Locke, Machiavelli, Montesquieu, Shaftesbury, Spinoza, and Voltaire. He read Kant more seriously, particularly *Religion within the Bounds of Reason Alone*. He also began studying Fichte's works and made preparations for working out a "Philosophy of the Subjective Spirit." In 1795, encouraged by Schelling, Hegel appears to have become deeply immersed in Fichte's idealism. In an April 1795 letter to Schelling, Hegel refers to the Fichtean conception of God as Absolute Ego as a part of "esoteric philosophy."[132] In an August 1795 letter he makes it clear that he accepts this idea.[133]

I have already mentioned that Fichte was a Mason, but his connections with the Hermetic tradition do not end there. There is a very strong similarity between Fichte's dialectic of Absolute Ego, Non-Ego, and Limited Ego and Non-Ego in the *Science of Knowledge* (1794) and the initial tripartite dialectic in Böhme's doctrine of the "seven source spirits." Ernst von Bracken devoted an entire volume to discussing the relation of Fichte to Meister Eckhart.[134] Of this connection, Walsh has written, "Fichte adopted the insights that had been formulated with the greatest difficulty by Eckhart as the union of the soul with God's creative power, to denote the normal condition of man in which the 'I' created the world by the power of thought and realized the action of God."[135]

In Berne, Hegel became part of a family circle that met in the evening for various sorts of entertainment. He kept in touch with them after he went to Frankfurt in 1797.[136] Harris writes that "this association, like all of Hegel's subsequent connections in Frankfurt—as far as these can be traced—has strong overtones of Freemasonry."[137] John Burbidge writes that "Whenever the young tutor arrived in a strange town he soon established contact with people known to be active in the most progressive strands of the Masonic order."[138] Hegel was an enthusiastic reader of the quasi-Masonic journal *Minerva*, which, among other things, disseminated the radical thought of the French Jacobins.[139] Its covers bore curious Masonic and chiliastic inscriptions. For instance, one cover featured the owl of Minerva flying over Greek columns, next to which stands a

132. Butler, 35; Hoffmeister #11.
133. Butler, 41; Hoffmeister #14.
134. Ernst von Bracken, *Meister Eckhart und Fichte* (Würzburg: Konrad Triltsch Verlag, 1943). (Lest anyone think there is little to be said on this subject, it should be noted that Bracken's book is more than 650 pages long!)
135. Walsh, *Boehme and Hegel*, 318.
136. Rosenkranz, *Hegels Leben*, 43.
137. Harris, *Toward the Sunlight*, 156. See also D'Hondt, *Hegel Secret*, 241.
138. Burbidge is summarizing the work of Jacques D'Hondt, in the introduction to his translation of D'Hondt's *Hegel en son temps* (*Hegel in his Time*, trans. John Burbidge [Lewiston, N.Y.: Broadview Press, 1988], viii).
139. Hegel refers to *Minerva* in a letter to Schelling written on Christmas Eve 1794, while Hegel was in Berne. Butler, 28; Hoffmeister #6.

child holding a trowel (an important Masonic symbol). In the shade of a tree stands a woman surrounded by children. Next to her is a shield on which is the head of Medusa and the inscription "The present age is pregnant with the future."[140]

Gerald Hanratty has written that "During his youth Hegel eagerly assimilated Masonic ideas and aspirations which were propagated in Germany by the supporters of the French revolution. Throughout his life he interested himself in the Masonic movement so that its ideas and aspirations were important elements of the matrix from which Hegel's Gnostic system emerged."[141] We have no record of Hegel having ever become a Mason. Although he appears to have been associated exclusively with the "progressive strands" of the order (i.e., the Enlightenment, rationalist strands), he was clearly conversant with its Hermetic or mystical aspects as well, as his poem "Eleusis" illustrates.

In 1796, Hegel learned through Hölderlin in Frankfurt that a more attractive post with the family of the wealthy Jean Noé Gogel might be available for him there. Hegel welcomed the opportunity to be back with Hölderlin, and wrote "Eleusis" for him, in commemoration of their friendship. Jacques D'Hondt has argued that this poem is deliberately laden with Masonic imagery. The Gogels were well-known Masons, and Hegel was apparently hoping that Hölderlin would share "Eleusis" with them, and that it would help to cement their relationship.[142]

The Eleusinian mysteries were very important to the Masons, who traced their initiation back to them.[143] In the poem Hegel refers at one point to "this bond no oath has sealed," which for Harris "suggests a brotherhood inspired by the ideals of Freemasonry but without formal organization."[144] Clark Butler suggests that the "bond" united Schelling, Hegel, and Hölderlin as well as Isaak von Sinclair, another, less famous, friend from the Tübingen *Stift*.[145] Hegel writes:

Your halls have fallen silent, oh Goddess!
Flown is the circle of gods back to Olympus from their consecrated
    altars.
Flown from the grave of a desecrated mankind is
The Genius of innocence that brought them here in thrall.[146]

140. D'Hondt, *Hegel Secret*, 23–24.
141. Hanratty, "Hegel and the Gnostic Tradition: II," 312–13.
142. D'Hondt, *Hegel Secret*, 227–81.
143. See, for example, Schiller, "Die Sendung Moses" in *Sämtliche werke*, vol. 5 (Berlin: Sanssouci-Ausgabe, 1937), 391–414; 399.
144. Harris, *Toward the Sunlight*, 114; D'Hondt, in *Hegel Secret*, like Harris, focuses almost exclusively on the *political* ideals of Masonry.
145. See Butler, 45. Interestingly, Sinclair was descended from a very old Scottish family considered to be the hereditary leaders of the Freemasons. Among other things, they were responsible for the construction, around 1460, of Rosslyn Chapel in Scotland, which is decorated with Templar, Masonic, and Kabbalistic imagery.
146. I am using Butler's translation of the poem, which appears in *Hegel: The Letters*, 46–47. I have altered his translation slightly.

D'Hondt suggests that "the grave of a desecrated mankind" is an allusion to the desecrated grave of Hiram, the central myth of Masonic initiation.[147]

The poem may also contain veiled reference to Swabian speculative Pietism. Hegel writes:

> Sense is lost in contemplation, what I called mine does vanish,
> Unto the Boundless do I myself abandon.
> I am in it, am everything, am only it.

This is remarkably like a description of Oetinger's *Zentrallerkenntnis*, a concept that would have been very familiar to Hölderlin. He writes, further, "Fantasy [*Phantasie*] brings the Eternal closer to sense, wedding it to shape." Again, this is quite reminiscent of the Böhmean-Oetingerite concept of the imagination as the faculty of embodying the ideal.[148] Harris notes that in the original draft Hegel struck out some lines intended to "explain how the imagination achieves the union of finite and infinite spirit which reflective thought breaks down."[149]

A couple of lines later, Hegel writes: "I feel it is the ether of my homeland [*Heimath*] as well, this earnestness, this radiance surrounding you." This strengthens the impression that Hegel may be alluding to the ideas of speculative Pietism, calling Hölderlin's mind back to their common Swabian roots. Hegel refers to himself and Hölderlin as "sons of the Goddess" (Ceres) and remarks that they have not spoken openly of her mysteries ("on their lips you did not live"), but have "preserved them in the sanctuary of their heart."

Whatever Hegel's intentions were in writing "Eleusis," they appear to have paid off, for in mid-January 1797 he arrived in Frankfurt as tutor to the two Gogel boys (actually the sons of Johann David Gogel, brother of Jean Noé, who died in 1793).

5. Pantheism, Hölderlin, and Schelling

The chiliasm of Württemberg Pietism, the subject of much discussion at the Tübingen *Stift*, combined with the drama of the French revolution to create the sense in Hegel and his schoolmates that history was moving toward some ultimate, final act.[150] Alan Olson writes that both Hegel and Hölderlin "were convinced that the future of Germany, especially its political unification, depended on the generation of a common spiritual bond among its people—a *Volksreligion* wholly independent of the alien, imported orientalism of Christianity."[151]

Hölderlin's Tübingen poetry (1788–93) contains few references or allusions to Christian doctrine. Instead, a kind of "pantheistic paganism"

147. D'Hondt, *Hegel Secret*, 263.
148. Faivre argues that Schelling's *Philosophy of Art* was influenced by this idea. See Faivre, *Theosophy, Imagination, Tradition*, 116.
149. Harris, *Toward the Sunlight*, 245.
150. Hayden-Roy, "A Foretaste of Heaven," 216
151. Alan M. Olson, *Hegel and the Spirit: Philosophy as Pneumatology* (Princeton, N.J.: Princeton University Press, 1992), 58.

prevails. He speaks of the "spark" of the "god within us."[152] It is often thought that Hölderlin adopted the Greek phrase *hen kai pan* (One and All) to express his metaphysical outlook while at the *Stift*. As H. S. Harris argues, however, *hen kai pan* should really be seen as the collective motto of Hölderlin, Schelling, and Hegel, though Hölderlin may have been the one who brought it to the group's attention.[153] The phrase *hen kai pan* itself is most likely taken from Jacobi's *Briefe Über die Lehre des Spinoza in Briefen an der Herrn Moses Mendelssohn* (1785), in which Jacobi records Lessing as having said, "The orthodox concepts of the deity are no longer for me. *Hen kai pan*, I know no other." (The context of the comment is a conversation between Jacobi and Lessing about Goethe's poem *Prometheus*.) Jacobi printed Bruno's abstract of his work *On the Cause, the Principles, and the One* as an appendix to his book.

Jacobi's *Über die Lehre des Spinoza* was principally responsible for the Spinoza revival of the late eighteenth century. H. S. Harris refers to the "romantic Spinozism" of Hegel's day.[154] Jacobi's book exercised a profound influence on many thinkers, including Schelling and Hegel. It was not, however, Jacobi's intention to generate a revival of Spinozism. By revealing Lessing's Spinozism, Jacobi hoped to discredit one of the heroes of the *Aufklärung*.[155] To Jacobi, Spinoza's philosophy represented rationalism and determinism in their most extreme and virulent form. (Interestingly, Jacobi also claimed that Spinozism was a form of Kabbalism.)

Friedrich Heinrich Jacobi (1743–1819) was a follower of Johann Georg Hamann (born 1730 in Königsberg, died 1788). Almost forgotten today, Hamann, a Kabbalist and Böhmean who held the familiar thesis of "nature as emblem-book," was extraordinarily influential in his time. Hamann's "Metakritik" essay (published in 1800) stated, in the words of Frederick Beiser, "one of the central goals of all post-Kantian philosophy: the search for the inner unity, the common source of Kant's dualism."[156] Beiser writes that "Herder, Schlegel, and Hegel all accepted Hamann's advice to see reason in its embodiment, in its specific social and historical context."[157] Goethe and Schelling admired Hamann greatly.[158] The already-famous Jacobi met Hamann and, converted to his anti-Enlightenment philosophy, became his most vociferous advocate.[159] It was Jacobi who transmitted Hamann's thought to the Romantics, and to those, like Schelling, engaged in *Naturphilosophie*. (Hegel appears not to have been

152. Hayden-Roy, "A Foretaste of Heaven," 208.
153. Harris, *Toward the Sunlight*, 101–5.
154. Ibid., 295.
155. Some doubted the authenticity of Jacobi's claims about Lessing. But, as Frederick Beiser notes, Lessing's *Nathan the Wise* "is indeed little more than a dramatic presentation of the philosophical doctrine of Spinoza's *Tractatus*" (Frederick C. Beiser, *The Fate of Reason: German Philosophy from Kant to Fichte* [Cambridge, Mass.: Harvard University Press, 1987], 56).
156. Ibid., 43.
157. Ibid., 18.
158. Isaiah Berlin, *The Magus of the North: J. G. Hamann and the Origins of Modern Irrationalism* (New York: Farrar, Straus and Giroux, 1993), 2–3.
159. Ibid., 17.

very directly influenced by Hamann, but in 1828 he published a critical review of Hamann's collected works.[160])

The significance of the *Pantheismusstreit* of the late eighteenth century cannot be overstated. Thanks to Jacobi's revelations, pantheism became, as Heinrich Heine would put it in the next century, "the unofficial religion of Germany."[161] Rheinhold's extremely influential popularization of Kant—*Briefe über die kantische Philosophie* (1786)—aimed at making Kant relevant to the pantheism controversy. Such luminaries as Goethe, Novalis, Herder, Schlegel, and Schleiermacher all dallied with pantheism. There was little difficulty in being both Lutheran and pantheist: as Beiser points out, Lutherans believed in an immediate relationship to God, and pantheism, teaching that all things, including men, are God or are within God, certainly provided that.[162] Hölderlin, in his own journal, copied out the *hen kai pan* passage from Jacobi's book.[163] In a letter to his mother from February 1791 Hölderlin mentions that he has immersed himself in works by and about Spinoza. According to Karl Rosenkranz Hegel, Schelling, and others at the *Stift* all read Jacobi's book.

Hölderlin wrote his only novel, *Hyperion*, in the years 1792–1799. Priscilla A. Hayden-Roy, in her study of the influence of Württemberg Pietism on the poet, claims that the thematic content of *Hyperion* was influenced by Oetinger's doctrine of *sensus communis*.[164] Hayden-Roy is not alone in this thesis. As she notes, Ulrich Gaier and Walter Dierauer have also argued that Hölderlin's poetic theory is based on Württemberg speculative Pietism.[165] Hölderlin may have been indirectly acquainted with P. M. Hahn's work through a poet, C. F. D. Schubart. Hölderlin met Schubart, a follower of Hahn, in the spring of 1789.[166]

Although Hegel was happy to be reunited with Hölderlin in Frankfurt (he had apparently succumbed to depression while in Berne), he was forced to witness Hölderlin's deteriorating mental state. In November 1800, after receiving a small inheritance upon the death of his father, Hegel wrote to Schelling in Jena, appealing for his assistance

160. Hegel, "Hamanns Schriften" in *Werke*, vol. 11, 275–352. Hegel was critical of Hamann, but had studied him carefully. Johann Peter Eckermann reports a dinner conversation between Goethe and Hegel: "A great deal was said about Hamann, with respect to whom Hegel was chief spokesman, displaying a deep insight into this extraordinary mind, such as could only have arisen from a most earnest and scrupulous study of the subject." See Johann Peter Eckermann, *Conversations of Goethe*, trans. John Oxenford (New York: Da Capo Press, 1998), 244.

161. Quoted in Beiser, *German Romantics*, 45.

162. Ibid., 52.

163. Harris, *Toward the Sunlight*, 99.

164. Hayden-Roy, "A Foretaste of Heaven," 227.

165. Ulrich Gaier, *Der gesetzliche Kalkül: Hölderlins Dichtungslehre* (Tübingen: Max Niemeyer, 1962); Walter Dierauer, *Hölderlin und der Spekulative Pietismus Württembergs: Gemeinsame Anschauungshorizonte im Werk Oetingers und Hölderlins* (Zürich: Juris, 1986). Gaier claims that Hölderlin's theory of the "modulation of tones" (*Wechsel der Töne*) is based upon a sevenfold distinction in Oetinger's Kabbalism.

166. Hayden-Roy, "A Foretaste of Heaven," 185.

in relocating there. The two men had not corresponded in five years, and in that time Schelling had become a celebrity, receiving his post at Jena with the backing of Goethe. I shall not enter here into the familiar details of Schelling and Hegel's turbulent friendship. Suffice it to say that Hegel came to Jena in early 1801, sharing quarters with Schelling. After some months, he produced his first philosophical work for publication, *The Difference Between Fichte's and Schelling's Systems of Philosophy* (1801).

What seems to have attracted Hegel to Schelling's early system is Schelling's claim that at the root of all that is real is an *infinite life* (recall Oetinger's *Theologia ex idea vitae deducta*). In Schelling's early "System of Identity," "philosophy of nature" is understood as the story of how Reason, the Absolute Ego, unconsciously produces a tangible world that reaches its consummation with the coming into being of man, who can embody self-conscious Reason or Ego. This is held to be parallel to "transcendental idealism," Reason's actual self-understanding, because in both it is Reason or Ego that is the underlying principle and "result." Thus, the subject-object distinction is transcended: nature, the external world or object, really is Ego expressing or developing itself. This infinite Ego lying behind the subject-object distinction, moving or generating the whole process, was conceived by Schelling as an infinite and primordial life.

Schelling maintained much the same doctrine in the later *Freiheitschrift* (*Philosophical Investigations into the Essence of Human Freedom*; 1809): "Gott ein Leben ist," he writes, "nicht bloss ein Sein" ("God is a life, not merely a being").[167] The influence of Böhme on the *Freiheitschrift*—in which Schelling employs the term *theosophy*—has been remarked on by many,[168] but Robert Schneider argues that the more direct influence is that of Oetinger. According to Schneider, Schelling's use of such terms as *Licht, Finsternis, Abgrund, Band der Kräfte, auflöslich, unauflöslich, bestandhaltend, lebendige Bewegungskräfte* shows the impress of Oetinger's thought.[169] Ernst Benz writes that Schelling's "principal ideas are dependent upon the terminology of Bengel and Oetinger in such a direct and visible way that it is impossible to ignore these fundamental sources of his thought."[170]

167. *Sämtliche Werke*, vol. 7, 403.
168. See Edward Allen Beach, *The Potencies of Gods: Schelling's Philosophy of Mythology* (Albany: State University of New York Press, 1994), and Robert F. Brown, *The Later Philosophy of Schelling: The Influence of Boehme on the Works of 1809–1815* (Lewisburg, Pa.: Bucknell University Press, 1977).
169. Robert Schneider, *Geistesahnen*, 10. Gershom Scholem (*Kabbalah*, 200) finds the influence of Oetinger "discernible" in the works of both Schelling and Hegel. Klaus Vondung notes that "Hermeticism was brought to Schelling's attention by Oetinger, who was an expert in all sorts of esoteric knowledge, although this connection has not yet been investigated satisfactorily." He regards Oetinger as having conveyed to Schelling and Hegel the *pansophic* ideal of a universal "super science" (Vondung, "Millenarianism, Hermeticism," 132, 126).
170. Benz, *Mystical Sources*, 30.

Schelling's connections to Swabian speculative Pietism are much better documented than are Hegel's. We know, for instance, that Schelling's father owned Oetinger's works.[171] Schelling's father and grandfather were both followers of Bengel. Schelling's great uncle Friedrich Philipp von Rieger was a supporter of Oetinger and J. M. Hahn, who expressed his gratitude to Rieger in his autobiography. When Schelling was ten or eleven years old, he lived in Nürtingen with his uncle Nathanael Friedrich Köstlin (1744–1826), a deacon. Köstlin was known to have close ties to the Bengel-Oetinger circle and may have proselytized his nephew.[172] P. M. Hahn's diary reveals that Schelling's father, who taught at the monastery school in Bebenhausen, called on Hahn, with his wife and young Friedrich in tow, on October 6, 1784.[173] Schelling's first published work was a poem that he wrote on the occasion of the death of Hahn. Schelling later wrote of Hahn in a letter: "As a little boy, I beheld this great man with hidden, uncomprehending awe; and strangely enough, the first of the few poems I have written in my life was upon his death. I will never forget his countenance."[174] Schelling was actively interested in Böhme (eventually acquiring three editions of his works), but he remarked to one of his Jena students that Oetinger was "clearer than Böhme."[175]

Oetinger attempted to prove his thesis about the reality of "spirit body" through an actual experiment. He claimed that if crushed balm-mint leaves are boiled their juice will form the pattern of the original leaves on the surface of the water. This was supposed to prove the existence of spirit as something separate from the material body, which it informs. Oetinger coined several words from the Latin *essentia* to describe the unfolding of the potentialities of a thing as made possible by its spirit. He frequently likened the process to the alchemical *opus*.[176] Schelling borrowed Oetinger's language of *essentia*, creating the term *Essentification*. He borrowed the balm-leaf experiment as well. In a lecture, Schelling contrasted two different ideas about death: one which holds that in death soul and body are sundered, and another (Schelling's own) which holds that death is simply an advance to a higher form of existence, in which *both* soul and body are retained, and perfected. Schelling writes:

> This other idea compares the effect of death with the process by which the spirit or the essence of a plant is extracted. Thus one

171. Robert Schneider, *Geistesahnen*, 8. In a September 7, 1806, letter to his father, Schelling states that Franz von Baader asked him if he could obtain for him the writings of Oetinger. Schelling passed the letter along to his friend Pregizer. Pregizer, an Oetingerite, was the founder of "the Joyous Christians," a Pietist sect. According to Pregizer, when he first met Schelling in 1803 they spent almost the entire time talking about Böhme and Oetinger. See Benz, *Mystical Sources*, 13–14.
172. All of these details about Schelling's family are to be found in Robert Schneider, *Geistesahnen*, 7–8.
173. Hayden-Roy, "A Foretaste of Heaven," 54.
174. Schelling, Letter to Heinrich von Schubert, April 4, 1811, in *Sämtliche werke*, vol. 1, 34.
175. See Paola Mayer, *Jena Romanticism and Its Appropriation of Jacob Böhme* (Montreal: McGill-Queen's University Press, 1999), 185.
176. See Robert Schneider, *Geistesahnen*, 123.

imagines that all the power and all the life of a plant pass into the oil extracted from it. . . . Some followers of the doctrine of general regeneration even affirm that the drops of oil-of-balm form the shape of the balm leaves again. I have not seen this personally and therefore will not make a pronouncement on this subject. However, a similar phenomenon observable in etheric liquid oils reveals a strange life within, and proves that it is not a matter of annihilated life but of spiritualized life. Thus, the death of man would not be a separation but rather an "essentification."[177]

(In fact, others were not able to replicate Oetinger's experiment.[178])

Ernst Benz has also shown that several times throughout his work, Schelling employed translations of biblical passages made by Oetinger, without attributing them to him.[179] Schelling betrays his connections with Württemberg Pietism even in the titles of his works. In 1811 he wrote a work entitled *Die Weltalter*, which was also the title of a very well-known book by J. A. Bengel (published in 1746). In Schelling's *Die Weltalter*, the influence of Oetinger is quite apparent. He writes at one point: "The ultimate purpose is that everything, as much as possible, be brought to visible, material form; embodiment [*Leiblichkeit*] is, as the ancients [*Alten*] expressed it, the endpoint of the way of God (*finis viarum Dei*), who wants to reveal Himself as spatial or as temporal."[180]

No sooner had Schelling embraced the Kantian-Fichtean philosophy than he insisted on its supplementation by *Naturphilosophie*, which precipitated his break with Fichte. Robert Schneider argues that Schelling was predisposed to value *Naturphilosophie* due to his early immersion in the thought of Oetinger and his circle. Indeed, Ernst Benz has made the case that it was Schelling's commitment to the principle of *Geistleiblichkeit* that drove him to reject the absolute idealism of Fichte. Schelling writes: "This is the ultimate purpose, that everything will be transformed as far as possible into a visible and corporal form. Corporality is, according to the ancients, the end of the ways of God, who wishes to manifest Himself as much as in space as in place as in time."[181] Accordingly, Schelling had to find Fichte's system merely a "realm of shades" (as Hegel describes his own *Logic*). For Schelling—as for Böhme and Oetinger—the Absolute has to express itself in corporeal form, in nature, or remain an empty abstraction. For exactly the same reasons, Hegel would supplement his Logic with a Philosophy of Nature and Philosophy of Spirit.

Schelling does not, of course, mention Oetinger (I have already discussed the pressures that existed at the time to avoid mentioning him). But the evidence for Oetinger's influence is strong. The authority Schelling actually invokes is Spinoza, who was then becoming a more

177. Schelling, *Sämtliche Werke*, vol. 14, 207. Quoted in Benz, *Mystical Sources*, 53. See Benz's account of this issue, and of other evidence for Oetinger's influence on Schelling, pages 51–55.
178. Walsh, *Boehme and Hegel*, 91.
179. Benz, *Mystical Sources*, 54–56.
180. Schelling, *Sämtliche Werke*, vol. 8, 325.
181. Ibid., vol. 14, 205. Quoted in Benz, *Mystical Sources*, 50–51.

acceptable figure to side with. In his "Exposition of My System of Philosophy" (1801), Schelling makes the claim that the Absolute Ego of Fichte is identical with Spinoza's "God of Nature." He goes on to liken the two parallel parts of his system, transcendental idealism and philosophy of nature, to expositions of Spinoza's twin attributes of thought and extension. He even refers to *Naturphilosophie* as the "Spinozism of physics."[182] Schelling's grand synthesis was extremely appealing to Hegel because it enabled him to reconcile the mystical-Hermetic philosophy to which he, like Schelling, had been exposed in early life, with the mainstream philosophy and theology with which he now, as a university professor, had to publicly align himself. (As H. S. Harris notes, Hölderlin's philosophical fragments show that he was developing something like an "Identity philosophy" as far back as 1795, indicating the same dynamic at work in his own Swabian soul.[183])

Like Böhme, with whom he was acquainted early on, Schelling held that the finite or nature is a mirror (*speculum*) held up to the infinite.[184] Hence, *speculative philosophy*.[185] The speculative activity of the philosopher, which attempts to understand creation in its telos and in all its aspects, is in effect the completion or consummation of the Infinite's self-reflection. Using language that would certainly have reminded some of his readers of Oetinger, Hegel in the *Differenzschrift* refers to the Ego, the "identity point" of philosophy, as the "point of contraction."[186] The Ego is the "indifference point." In the system of the subject (transcendental idealism), the Ego is "contracted" into its primordial self-relation. In the system of the object, or nature, Ego "expands" outward as a real but "frozen" expression of itself to itself.[187] (This brings to mind the doctrine of the "coincidence of opposites" in Eckhart, Cusa, and other mystics.) Schelling even went so far as to interpret laws of nature as laws of Spirit in "unconscious form." His Identity philosophy held out the hope of an experience of the ultimate unity of subject and object, and finite and infinite, in aesthetic consciousness.

H. S. Harris writes of the similarities between Schelling's system of Identity and Böhme's theosophy: "In Böhme's theosophy 'desire' is the *Abgrund* of the 'dark centre' into which self-consciousness 'contracts.' The full realization of the image of God requires that it should 'expand' again into the 'light centre.' The moment of absolute contraction where the transition occurs is a 'flash' (*Schrack*). Thus all the terminology of

---

182. Schelling "Einleitung zu dem Entwurf eines Systems der Naturphilosophie" (1799), in *Werke*, vol. 2, ed. Manfred Schröter (Munich: Beck, 1927), 273.
183. H. S. Harris, "Introduction to the *Difference* Essay," in Hegel, *The Difference Between Fichte's and Schelling's System of Philosophy*, trans. H. S. Harris and Walter Cerf (Albany: State University of New York Press, 1977), 3.
184. Kurt Leeses's dissertation, "Von Jakob Böhme zu Schelling" (University of Erfurt, 1927) deals with the Böhmean influence on Schelling's work.
185. Harris, "Introduction to the *Difference* Essay," 41.
186. *Difference*, 165–67; German ed. of *Differenzschrift*, in *Gesammelte Werke*, vol. 4, ed. Hartmut Buchner and Otto Pöggeler (Hamburg: Felix Meiner Verlag, 1968), 72–73 (henceforth *Differenz*).
187. Schelling, *Erster Entwurf eines Systems der Naturphilosophie* (1799), in *Werke*, vol. 2, 268.

'Schelling's System'... bears the clear impress of Böhme's vision."[188] Like Paracelsus (whom I shall discuss in chapter 6), Schelling held that medicine was the highest of all the natural sciences.[189] (Recall also the emphasis Johann Valentin Andreae placed on medicine.) Antoine Faivre writes of Schelling's system, "The relationship to alchemy is obvious, so much so that Schelling's *Naturphilosophie* appeared from the beginning as an attempt to bring together the traditional givens of pansophy and the spirit of Kantian philosophy."[190] As Robert Brown has shown, in later years Schelling immersed himself even more deeply in Böhme.[191]

In 1802, Schelling published a dialogue, *Bruno*, in which he put his philosophy into the mouth of a character loosely patterned after Giordano Bruno. After reading an advance copy of the dialogue, Goethe wrote to Schiller on March 16, 1802, "Schelling has written a dialogue, *Bruno or On the Divine and Natural Principles of Things*. What I understand of it—or believe I understand—is excellent and agrees with my deepest convictions. But I am doubtful whether it will be possible for others to follow it through all its sections and understand it as a whole."[192]

Goethe could not have known at the time that Schelling was soon to be eclipsed by a thinker even more in agreement with his "deepest convictions," especially where those convictions could be called Hermetic. On April 24, 1825, Hegel wrote to Goethe that "when I look back over the course of my intellectual development, I see you everywhere woven into it, and may call myself one of your sons: what is inward in me has been nourished by you toward resilient strength in the face of abstraction, and has oriented its course by your forms as by beacons."[193]

188. Harris, *Night Thoughts*, 165. Other authors have concentrated almost exclusively on Böhme's influence on Schelling's *later* period. See Beach, *The Potencies of Gods* and Robert F. Brown, *The Later Philosophy of Schelling*.
189. Schelling, "Vorrede zu den Jahrbüchern der Medicin als Wissenschaft," in *Werke*, vol. 4, 65.
190. Faivre, *Access to Western Esotericism*, 83.
191. Schelling also became interested in the visionary mysticism of Emanuel Swedenborg, particularly after the untimely death of his wife Karoline in 1811. See Benz, *Mystical Sources*, 15–16, as well as Friedemann Horn, *Schelling and Swedenborg: Mysticism and German Idealism*, trans. George F. Dole (West Chester, Pa.: The Swedenborg Foundation, 1997).
192. See Xavier Tilliette, *Schelling im Spiegel seiner Zeitgenossen* (Turin: Bottega, d'Erasmo, 1974), 91.
193. Butler, 708; Hoffmeister #489.

The Mythology of Reason

1. The Absolute Religion

In the beginning, Hegel thought that a new religion was needed to unite philosophers and ordinary people, to transcend the Platonic dichotomy between the "wise" and the "vulgar." In their time together in Jena, however, Schelling persuaded Hegel that it is not the philosopher's task to create such a religion. Nevertheless, Hegel continued to insist that a new philosophy could have an effect on religion, making it truer to its own essence. Hegel's view, which remained unchanged throughout his career, was that a completed philosophy would take on a form that would make it accessible in varying degrees to everyone. That form would be a "mythology of reason." This enigmatic phrase appears in a fragment referred to by scholars as "*eine Ethik*" (its first words) and under the title "The Earliest System-Program of German Idealism."

For many years, the authorship of the "System-Program" was in doubt. It was variously attributed to Hegel, Schelling, and Hölderlin. I need not rehearse the various arguments for and against Hegel's authorship here. Most Hegel scholars accept Otto Pöggeler's arguments that Hegel is the author, and I shall follow their lead.[1] Pöggeler dates the fragment to Hegel's Berne period, in late 1796 or early 1797.[2]

The "System-Program" reflects ambivalence about the aim of philosophy. It seems as if Hegel still clings to the idea of a new religion, yet depicts philosophy as an absolute science. In truth, the "System-Program" is Hegel's first attempt to reconcile philosophy and religion. Philosophy can be popular and even religious without becoming religion or giving primacy to religion if its content happens to be the thought forms that underlie all religion and folk consciousness.

Thus, philosophy for Hegel will have as its task the recovery and perfection of these pre-reflective thought forms granted to mankind from time immemorial, a wisdom that has expressed itself partially and imperfectly in all previous art, religion, and philosophy. Genuine philos-

---

1. Otto Pöggeler, "Hegel der Verfasser des ältesten Systemprogramms des deutschen Idealismus," *Hegel-Studien*, Beiheft 4 (1969): 17–32.
2. Gisela Schüler has argued that the "System-Program" was Hegel's last Berne essay in her "Zur Chronologie von Hegels Jugendschriften," *Hegel-Studien* 2 (1963): 111–59.

ophy is uncreative.[3] Instead, it is merely a fully adequate expression of this primordial wisdom. This wisdom belongs not to the consciousness of a people, but to its *unconscious*.[4] In the *Encyclopedia Logic*, Hegel states that "The business of philosophy consists only in bringing into consciousness *explicitly* what people have held to be valid about thought from time immemorial. Thus, philosophy establishes nothing new; what we have brought forth by our reflection here is what everyone already takes for granted without reflection" (EL § 22, Z; Geraets, 55).[5] In a *Zusatz* to the *Encyclopedia Logic*, Hegel remarks that "We usually suppose that the Absolute must lie far beyond; but it is precisely what is wholly present, what we, as thinkers, always carry with us and employ, even though we have no express consciousness of it" (EL § 24 Z: Geraets, 59).[6] In the *Science of Logic*, Hegel states that "The activity of thought which is at work in all our ideas, purposes, interests and actions is . . . unconsciously busy [*bewusstlos geschäftig*] (natural logic [*die natürliche Logik*])." Its basis is "the soul itself" (Miller, 36–37; WL 1:15–16).

The following surreal, macabre, almost unintelligible passage from Hegel's *Realphilosophie* manuscript of 1805–06 reflects his deep immersion in the realm of the unconscious:

The human being is this night, this empty nothing, that contains everything in its simplicity—an unending wealth of many presen-

3. For Hegel's views on mythology and what I shall call "mytho-poetic thought" see the *Lectures on the History of Philosophy*, vol. 1, 81–91 (*Werke* 18:102–13). Hegel was also greatly influenced by the writings of Georg Friedrich Creuzer (1771–1858), a philologist and historian of religion and mythology whom he knew in Heidelberg (Creuzer is mentioned in the passages cited above). Clark Butler writes that "[Hegel] borrowed from Creuzer the idea of a primitive Oriental monism running symbolically through all true religion, expressed in Indian mysticism, preserved in the Greek mysteries, lying behind classical Greek polytheism . . . implicit in classical theism, and coming to self-conscious expression in Hegel's concept of the Absolute as the infinite Incarnation" (Butler, 368). Consider also this passage from a *Zusatz* to the *Encyclopedia Logic*: "Philosophy should not shy away from religion, and adopt the attitude that it must be content if religion simply tolerates it. And on the other hand, we must equally reject the view that myths and religious accounts of this kind are something obsolete, for they have been venerated for millennia by the peoples of the world" (EL § 24 Z3; Geraets, 61).
4. Yates describes Bruno's thought in strikingly similar terms, stating that "it was Bruno's mission to paint and mould within, to teach that the artist, the poet, and the philosopher are all one, for the Mother of the Muses is Memory. Nothing comes out but what has first been formed within, and it is therefore within that the significant work is done" (Yates, *The Art of Memory*, 305).
5. In the *Lectures on the Philosophy of Religion*, Hegel states that "all persons have . . . a consciousness of God, or of the absolute substance, as the truth of everything and so also of themselves, of everything that they are and do" (LPR 1:85; VPR 1:4).
6. Elsewhere, Hegel states: "*Being, Not-Being, One, Many, Quality, Size* and so on are pure essences . . . with which we *keep house* all the time in ordinary life." See "Report of Rosenkranz About Hegel's Philosophy of Spirit in the Early Jena Period," in *System of Ethical Life and First Philosophy of Spirit*, trans. H. S. Harris and T. M. Knox (Albany: State University of New York Press, 1979), 258. See also Rosenkranz, *Hegels Leben*, 183.

tations, images, of which none happens to occur to him—or which are not present. This night, the inner of nature, that exists here—pure self—in phantasmagorical presentations, is night all around it, here shoots a bloody head—there another white shape, suddenly here before it, and just so disappears. One catches sight of this night when one looks human beings in the eye—into a night that becomes awful, it suspends the night of the world here in an opposition. In this night being has returned.[7]

Hegel holds the traditional, Hermetic conception of *philosophia perennis*: all previous systems of thought—religious, mythological, philosophical—aim at and partially unveil the same doctrine.[8] Speculative philosophy is the final, fully adequate, and fully conscious form of the *philosophia perennis*, which can only be accomplished in modern times. In a fragment preserved by Rosenkranz, Hegel writes: "From the true knowledge of [the *principle* of all philosophy], there will arise the conviction that at all times there has been only one and the same philosophy. So not only am I promising nothing new here, but rather am I devoting my philosophical efforts precisely to the restoration of *the oldest of old things*, and on liberating it from the misunderstanding in which the recent times of unphilosophy have buried it."[9] This perennial character of speculation is made quite clear in one of the *Zusätze* to the *Encyclopedia Logic*, where Hegel states that "It should . . . be mentioned here that the meaning of the speculative is to be understood as being the same as what used in earlier times to be called the 'mystical' " (EL § 82, Z; Geraets, 133).[10]

Speculation thus depends on *recollection* (*Erinnerung*), the recollection of the *philosophia perennis*. In another fragment, possibly from the same

---

7. Quoted in Donald Phillip Verene, *Hegel's Recollection* (Albany: State University of New York Press, 1985), 7–8. The translation is Verene's.

8. See H. S. Harris's Introduction to the *System of Ethical Life*, 63–64: "Philosophy is participation in an eternal vision. It is always one and the same, and if one achieves it, the occasion or path by which one does so becomes irrelevant, indifferent. Speculation is the end in and for itself." See also Harris's "Introduction to the *Difference* Essay," 18: "By reasserting the presence of a *philosophia perennis*, Hegel aimed to show that the dialectic of philosophical ideas is subordinate to, and instrumental for, the focal concern of rational speculation, which never varies." Hegel writes in the *Difference* essay that "if the Absolute, like Reason which is its appearance, is eternally one and the same—as indeed it is—then every Reason that is directed toward itself and comes to recognize itself, produces a true philosophy and solves for itself the problem which, like its solution, is at all times the same" (*Difference*, 87; *Differenz*, 11). Hegel is speaking here as an exponent of Schelling's Identity philosophy (and Harris is expounding the views of Hegel the Schellingian), but I am maintaining that on these basic metaphilosophical issues his position did not change.

9. Rosenkranz, *Hegels Leben*, 192.

10. Hegel frequently repeats this observation. In his *Lectures on the Philosophy of Religion* of 1824, Hegel speaks of the Eleusinian mysteries, stating that "The mystical is the speculative, what lies within" (LPR 2:491; VPR 2:391). Later, he states, "The Trinity is called the *mystery* of God; its content is mystical, i.e., speculative" (LPR 3:192; VPR 3:125). In the *Lectures* of 1827, he states that "As a whole the mystical is everything speculative, or whatever is concealed from the understanding" (LPR 1:445; VPR 1:333).

period as the "System-Program," known as "On Mythology, the Spirit of the People, and Art," Hegel speaks of Mnemosyne (Memory) as the "absolute Muse." He writes: "The work of art of mythology propagates itself in living tradition. As peoples grow in *the liberation of their consciousness*, so the *mythological work of art* continuously grows and clarifies and matures. This work of art is a general possession, the work of everyone. Each generation hands it down embellished to the one that follows; each works further toward the liberation of absolute consciousness."[11] Mnemosyne, Memory or Recollection, is the mother of the muse of the poet, the artist, and the philosopher. She is their access to primordial wisdom, knowledge of the whole. All three may hear her voice and express her wisdom in their own ways. Through her voice the philosopher can learn to speak the truly complete and adequate speech, which is speculation, the speech of the Absolute.

The result of Hegel's project was to have been, he hoped, a return to a more "natural" consciousness, like that possessed by the Greeks, but in a form that is fully modern and self-aware (to say nothing of being Protestant and Lutheran). Just as in Böhme, man's fall is necessary because his original unity with God and with his own true nature is an *unthinking* unity. We must be brought back to unity, but this time the unity must be achieved in full self-consciousness. Philosophy will constitute, in effect, a perfected form of living in the world, which will transform religious life, art, and our understanding of history, science, and government—of all aspects of man and his world. As H. S. Harris puts it, "Philosophy is not just a nocturnal study of shadows and reflections; it is the perfected consciousness of human living, or an actual experience of living in the light of the eternal day."[12]

Like Aristotle, Hegel conceives the life of the philosopher as the "highest" form of existence. But the "life" with which his philosophy is concerned will unite all people, the masses and the intellectuals. In the "System-Program" Hegel writes, "in the end enlightened and unenlightened must clasp hands, mythology must become philosophical in order to make the people rational, and philosophy must become mythological in order to make the philosophers sensible. Then reigns eternal unity among us. No more the look of scorn [of the enlightened philosopher looking down on the mob], no more the blind trembling of the people before its wise men and priests."[13]

Philosophy can become accessible to all, it can illuminate the cave with sunlight, if the "mythology of reason" is developed. In the same fragment, Hegel writes, "Here I shall discuss particularly an idea which, as far as I know, has never occurred to anyone else—we must have a new mythology, but this mythology must be in the service of the Ideas, it

11. Translated by Verene, *Hegel's Recollection*, 36; my emphasis.
12. Harris, *Night Thoughts*, 199.
13. I am using H. S. Harris's translation of the "System-Program" in *Toward the Sunlight*, 510–12; 511–12, Harris's interpolations. For a German edition see "Das älteste Systemprogramm des deutschen Idealismus," *Werke* 1 (henceforth, *Systemprogramm*), 234–36.

must be a *mythology of reason*."[14] But what does this mean ? How can speculation be a mythology, if its task is to recover the perennial thought forms *underlying* all mythology, religion, poetry, etc.? Doesn't speculation go deeper than myth?

The phrase "mythology of reason" never occurs again in any of Hegel's other writings or lectures, but it provides a key to understanding Hegel's entire philosophy. To understand this unique conception, something further must be said about the relation of philosophy to recollection.

2. Speculation and Recollection

Accounts of Hegel's view of the history of philosophy tend to overemphasize his claim that all previous philosophy approaches what he ultimately accomplishes in speculative philosophy. What tends not to be emphasized is the necessary presupposition of this account: that thinking man in some sense knew where he was going from the beginning, that the history of philosophy is not the story of the gradual creation of different systems of philosophy, but rather the story of the gradual recollection of the one true "system," of wisdom itself.

If this is the case, one might ask: Why does Hegel insist that his final and adequate recollection of the truth could only have occurred "after history"? When we finally reach the stage at which we make the Absolute our own, when we know that the Absolute, which is God, is the consummation of a universal human consciousness, we fully grasp the "Idea" of philosophy and all philosophical thought reaches closure. Hegel believed that this intellectual achievement could only have been accomplished after history itself was consummated, that is, after human beings have recognized themselves as free and not determined by an Absolute that stands opposed to humanity as an absolute other. The final form of wisdom is necessarily a self-conscious form: the Absolute Idea achieves full realization or disclosure through humanity's explicit recognition of itself as the agent of the Ideas's consummation. Hegelian speculation is not just another expression of the perennial philosophy, but an expression that understands itself *as* an expression of the perennial philosophy. Thus, Hegelian speculation is the in-itself of human consciousness finally made for-itself, made explicit.

If speculation involves recollection then it appears to be a fundamentally passive activity. This is indeed the case, for the term *speculation* comes from *speculum*, or "mirror." What does the speculative philosopher "mirror"? Speculation holds up a mirror to the Idea itself: it allows Idea to comprehend itself. Hegel's concept of speculation harks back to

14. Hegel, *System-Program*, 511; *Systemprogramm*, 236. Friedrich Schlegel claimed that the creation of a "rational mythology" was the literary aim of the Romantic movement. Though Hegel was not exactly sympathetic with Romanticism, he may have been influenced by this idea. See F. Schlegel, *Prosaische Jugendschriften*, 2 vols., ed. J. Minor (Vienna: Konegen, 1906), vol. 2, 357–66. For similar ideas see Schelling, *System of Transcendental Idealism*, trans. Peter Heath (Charlottesville: University Press of Virginia, 1980), 223.

Pythagoras's comparison of the philosophers to spectators at the Olympic games. The philosopher is a vehicle of the muses: an oracle through which Spirit expresses itself, an automatic writer who passively watches the play of the dialectic as it develops on his page.[15]

This talk of "recollection" and of the "perennial philosophy" does not, however, imply that Hegel's project is to recover a wisdom that was once explicit long ago, and which has since been lost. In fact, in the Berlin lectures on the *Philosophy of Nature* (1819–30) Hegel ridicules the idea that in some bygone age, when man was at one with God, he possessed a "consummate science" and that "since our fall from this unity some remnants and distant glimmerings of that spiritual light have remained with us in myths, tradition, and other fragments, on to which the further education of the human race in religion has fastened, and from which all scientific cognition has proceeded. If it were no more difficult than this for consciousness to know truth, but one only had to sit on a tripod and utter oracles, the labour of thought would certainly be spared" (PN § 246, Z; Petry 1:199).[16] What Hegel rejects here, first of all, is the idea that Absolute Science or wisdom was ever, at some earlier time, wholly and self-consciously possessed by man. Second, even if man actually had possessed such wisdom, Hegel rejects the idea that it could be recovered through the use of "pure imagination" or "creativity" in the Romantics' sense. But this does not imply that Hegel rejects the idea of an unconscious wisdom gradually coming to more and more adequate expression through philosophy.

But why should we believe in the existence of this "unconscious wisdom" in the first place? Because all philosophy is implicitly or explicitly dialectical in nature, and the activity of dialectic presupposes that one always already possesses wisdom, but in inchoate form. Dialectic is a recollection and explication of that wisdom. This is true of both Hegelian and Platonic dialectic. The pattern of Platonic dialectic is this: attempts are made to define some universal, all of which prove inadequate, but each of which builds on the previous attempt. For instance, in the *Republic*, Cephalus's definition of justice as "returning what one has borrowed" (331b) is rejected with Socrates's counterexample of the crazed man who demands the return of a weapon. The participants immediately see that this could not be just, that Cephalus's attempt to define Justice is a failure. But they could not make such a judgment—rejecting Cephalus's definition as wrong simply on the basis of Socrates's counterexample—unless they already had some pre-reflective access to the Idea of Justice. The key to the dialectic, then, is that the participants already know, in some sense, the meaning of the terms they aim at defining.

In the same manner, each category of Hegel's *Logic* constitutes a "provisional definition of the Absolute," but each proves partial and inade-

---

15. One is reminded of Jacobi's dictum that it is the task of the philosopher to "disclose existence" (Beiser, *The Fate of Reason*, 67).
16. For a similar passage, see the *Philosophy of Spirit* (PS § 405, Z; Petry 2:231).

quate, forcing us to inquire further, and so the dialectic pushes on. We do not rest content with Being, or with Being-for-self or with the Measureless or with Identity, because we experience a disparity between each category and what we somehow already know the Idea to be. In the *Difference* essay of 1801 Hegel writes:"What the so-called common sense takes to be the rational consists similarly of single items drawn out of the Absolute into consciousness. They are points of light that arise out of the night of totality and aid men to get through life in an intelligent way. . . . In fact, however, men only have this confidence in the truth of these points of light because they have *a feeling of the Absolute* attending these points."[17]

Hegel's muse is Mnemosyne because his dialectic is a recollection of what our finite individual spirit has somehow already glimpsed of Absolute Spirit. In the *Difference* essay, Hegel writes of the "presuppositions" [*Voraussetzungen*] of philosophy. One such presupposition, he says is "the Absolute itself. It is the goal that is being sought; but it is already present, or how otherwise could it be sought?"[18] Jean Hyppolite writes:"In our opinion, if we are to understand Hegel's [dialectic] we must assume that the whole is always immanent in the development of consciousness. Negation is creative because the posited term had been isolated and thus was itself a kind of negation. From this it follows that the negation of that term allows the whole to be recaptured in each of its parts. *Were it not for the immanence of the whole in consciousness, we should be unable to understand how negation can truly engender a content.*"[19] And Hyppolite goes on to say:"We have evidence of the immanence of the whole in consciousness in the teleological nature of the latter's development:'The goal of knowledge is fixed as necessarily as the series of progressions.'"[20]

Dialectic is the "method" by which speculation aims to "recollect" unconscious wisdom and to complete the perennial philosophy. But how can Hegel know that he has brought the perennial philosophy to completion? This seems to involve a further methodological consideration not covered by an account of dialectic alone. In fact, it is precisely Hegel's understanding of speculation as a "Mythology of Reason"—his understanding of speculation as in some sense an aesthetic act—that allows him to demonstrate the completeness of his recollection of the perennial philosophy.

17. Hegel, *Difference*, 98–99, my emphasis; *Differenz*, 20.
18. Hegel, *Difference*, 93; *Differenz*, 16. This may seem to be simply a statement about the Schellingian Absolute, but my contention is that in Hegel's mature philosophy the Absolute is still, in a certain sense, a "goal" to be sought. This will become more clear in my treatment of the *Phenomenology* in the next chapter. Plato, of course, has his own doctrine of recollection, intended to explain exactly the phenomenon described above: how we seem to already know the result we aim at in dialectic, and why we feel at every step as if we are recollecting something we already knew.
19. Jean Hyppolite, *The Genesis and Structure of Hegel's Phenomenology of Spirit*, trans. Samuel Cherniak and John Heckman (Evanston: Northwestern University Press, 1974), 15; my emphasis.
20. Ibid., 15; for the quotation see Miller 51; PG, 62.

3. Speculation as "Mythic"

In the "System-Program" Hegel writes of his Mythology of Reason: "I am now convinced that the highest act of Reason, the one through which it encompasses all Ideas, is an aesthetic act, and that *truth and goodness only become sisters in beauty*—the philosopher must possess just as much aesthetic power as the poet. Men without aesthetic sense is what our literal-minded philosophers [*unsere Buchstabenphilosophen*] are. The philosophy of the spirit is an aesthetic philosophy."[21] During his Jena period, Hegel, like Schelling, claimed that art as well as philosophy gives us access to the Absolute. In the *Difference* essay, Hegel (ostensibly speaking for Schelling) writes: "Both art and speculation are in their essence divine service—both are a living intuition of the absolute life and hence a being at one with it."[22]

At first glance, then, Hegel's "System Program" may seem to be just a repetition of Schelling's ideas about "aesthetic consciousness," but it is not. Unlike Schelling, Hegel does not see *art as such* as our means of experiencing the Absolute. Instead, he speaks of the "highest act *of Reason*" as being an aesthetic act. Somehow, rational or philosophical thought itself must become aesthetic. But how? And how is this related to the conception of a Mythology of Reason? And how is it related to speculation? The second question, at least, seems easily answered: it is clear that Hegel sees mythic thought as sensuous or poetic in form. Later in the "System Program" he writes: "Until we express the Ideas aesthetically, *i.e. mythologically*, they have no interest for the *people*, and conversely until mythology is rational the philosopher must be ashamed of it."[23] Hegel's system, then, as a Mythology of Reason, will somehow meld rational thought with what I shall call "mytho-poetic" thought.

When Hegel claims that philosophy must become aesthetic or mythological, he is *not* recommending that philosophers write poetry, or even that they incorporate poetic elements into their work. Instead, Hegel is setting the stage for an entirely new type of thought, one that unites elements of rational and mytho-poetic thinking at a higher level. Hegel's project is analogous to Oetinger's *theologia emblematica*, which aimed to uncover the "inner spiritual form" of the emblem or image—as opposed, on the one hand, to a purely imaginative grasp of the divine, and, on the other, to the "dead reason," of the abstract concept, which kills the truth the image contains. Like Oetinger, Hegel is advocating a "third position": a completely new form of thought in which the truth is laid bare by transcending and synthesizing the inadequate forms of the pure image and the abstract concept. In the "System-Program" this new form elevates poetic thought to a higher level: "Poetry gains thereby a higher dignity," he writes. "She becomes at the end once more what she was in the beginning: the *teacher of mankind*."[24]

21. Hegel, *System-Program*, 511; *Systemprogramm*, 235. I have altered Harris's translation slightly.
22. Hegel, *Difference*, 172; *Differenz*, 77.
23. Hegel, *System-Program*, 511; *Systemprogramm*, 236.
24. *System-Program*, 511; *Systemprogramm*, 235.

Here an obvious question arises: Doesn't Hegel reject "picture think-ing," and isn't that precisely what "mytho-poetic thinking" is? Hegel does indeed reject picture thinking, but he also rejects its opposite, "abstract" thinking.[25] When Hegel rejects a pair of opposites, however, one can be sure that they have not been rejected: they have been *aufgehoben*; they have been cancelled, but also taken up and preserved. Donald Phillip Verene makes this same point: "The thought of *Vorstellung* must be *aufge-hoben* in absolute knowing. The image of *Vorstellung* . . . must be there in absolute knowing in a transformed sense."[26] Hegel's speculation will be a "sublation" of the truth of *Bild* and the truth of *Begriff*. So how exactly does Hegel's speculation accomplish this? How does it unite the mytho-poetic and the rational?

Unlike "picture-thinking"—poetry, myth, art, etc.—Hegel's specula-tion involves the use of concepts, ideas, or universals. Here, however, the dissimilarity ends, for although the matter of Hegel's philosophy—its employment of concepts rather than images—is substantially different from mytho-poetic thought, its form is strikingly similar.

Hegel's system is a complete conceptual speech about the whole, but it is not merely a network of abstract concepts. Instead it takes the form of a concrete totality. In the introduction to the *Phenomenology*, Hegel defines philosophy as the "actual knowledge of *what truly is*" (Miller, 46; PG, 57).[27] In fact, his philosophical aim is the traditional one: to give an account of Substance, the really real.[28] However, it is the *totality of the sys-*

25. Hegel writes in the preface to the *Phenomenology*: "The habit of picture-thinking, when it is interrupted by the Concept [*Begriff*], finds it just as irk-some as does formalistic thinking that argues back and forth in thoughts that have no actuality" (Miller, 35; PG, 43). Harris, in his Introduction to his and Walter Cerf's translation of *Faith and Knowledge*, writes: "Speculative philoso-phy cannot possibly be 'abstract'. . . because it is a special kind of *remembering* (Hegel plays on the German word *Erinnerung*). The infinite that is within the finite, and reveals itself negatively in the perpetual perishing of the finite, reveals itself positively in the resurrection and perpetuation of the finite as a pattern of 'inwardized' or 'remembered' conceptual significance." See H. S. Harris, Introduction, in G. W. F. Hegel, *Faith and Knowledge*, ed. and trans. H. S. Harris and Walter Cerf (Albany: State University of New York Press, 1977), 39–40.
26. Verene, *Hegel's Recollection*, 12. Hegel explains the meaning of *aufheben* in his *Science of Logic*: "*Aufheben* . . . constitutes one of the most important con-cepts in philosophy. . . . *Aufheben* has a twofold meaning in the language: on the one hand it means to preserve, to maintain, and equally it also means to cause to cease, to put an end to. . . . It is a delight to speculative thought to find in the language words which have in themselves a speculative meaning; the German language has a number of such" (Miller 106–7; WL 1:101).
27. Also: "[Philosophy's] element and content is not the abstract or non-actual, but the actual" (Miller, 47; PG, 34–35).
28. Though, of course, Hegel's Substance reveals itself to be Subject. In the *Phenomenology*, Hegel writes that "the side of reality is itself nothing else but the side of individuality" (*die Seite der Wirklichkeit ist selbst nichts anders als die Seite der Individualität*; Miller, 233; PG, 256). Elsewhere Hegel writes: "Spirit is thus self-supporting, absolute, real being" (Miller, 264; PG, 289). These obser-vations correspond exactly to Aristotle's conception of Substance (*ousia*). In Hegel's 1830 lecture manuscript for the *Lectures on the Philosophy of World His-*

tem that itself gives us this reality.[29] Every "provisional definition of the Absolute" within the system, that is, every category, must fall short because no one category can express *all* of what the Absolute is. Thus, the system does not *describe* the Absolute, it gives form to the Absolute itself. Hegel's philosophy does not tell us what Substance or the Absolute is (in the manner, for instance, of Aristotle's philosophy), *it brings the Absolute into being*. Why? Because it is through speculation that the Idea becomes for-itself, that "God" achieves self-awareness and thus completion. This completed or actualized divine is the Absolute.[30]

Recall the previously quoted fragment preserved by Rosenkranz:

> Every individual is a blind link in the chain of absolute necessity, along which the world develops. Every individual can raise himself to domination over a great length of this chain only if he realizes the goal of this great necessity and, by virtue of this knowledge, learns to speak the *magic words which evoke its shape*. The knowledge of how to simultaneously absorb and elevate oneself beyond the total energy of suffering and antithesis that has dominated the world and all forms of its development for thousands of years— this knowledge can be gathered from philosophy alone.[31]

The magic words are the categories of Hegelian philosophy. The magic power is dialectic guided by recollection. And, as we shall shortly find, our access to this power is through a form of *imagination*. (I discuss the nature of Hegelian imagination in section 5.)

It is important to see the radical difference between Hegelian thought and all other forms of philosophy. Non-Hegelian philosophy answers such questions as "What is God?" or "What is Being?" by equating its subject matter with some property or universal: "God is water" or "God is the Unmoved Mover" or "God is Nature." We can call this mode of thought propositional or predicative. It takes some object as given, and precedes to describe it by attaching one or more predicates to it, usually after lengthy argumentation.

The problem with this form of thought, as Hegel points out in the preface to the *Phenomenology*, is that it draws a rigid distinction between subject and predicate (Miller, 38: PG, 47). One may laboriously demon-

---

tory, he writes that "it is proved in philosophy by speculative knowing that Reason—and we can adopt this expression for the moment without a detailed discussion of its relationship to God—is substance and infinite power. . . . It is substance, i.e. that through which and in which all reality has its being and subsistence. . . . Reason is self-sufficient and contains its end within itself; it brings itself into existence and carries itself into effect" (Nisbet, 27–28; VPR, 20–21). I shall discuss this topic more fully in chapter 5.

29. Hegel writes in the *System of Ethical Life*, "What is truly universal is intuition, while what is truly particular is the absolute concept" (*System of Ethical Life*, 100). German edition: *System der Sittlichkeit*, 2nd ed., ed. G. Lasson (Hamburg: Felix Meiner Verlag, 1923), 415.

30. "God is only God in so far as he knows Himself: this self-knowledge of God, becomes a self-knowledge in man, and man's knowledge of God." (PS § 564; Wallace, 298).

31. Rosenkranz, *Hegels Leben*, 141.

strate that "God is good" but we know that the two terms are connota-
tively different. The predicate does not exhaustively present the subject's
nature to us. We may decide to add other predicates: "God is good," *and*
"just," *and* "all-knowing," etc. But unless we can demonstrate that we
have completely captured the essence of God our knowledge is not
absolute (See LPR 3:271, 277–78; VPR, 196, 203).[32] Thus the predicative or
propositional approach is inherently incapable of giving us what we
want. The predicate of a proposition always places the subject in a *higher,
wider, or more inclusive genus*, for instance, "Man is mortal," "Dogs are
mammals," etc. But Hegel conceives the Absolute as the Whole itself, as
the ultimate category beyond which there is no higher category. Hegel
does not tell us what the Absolute is. Hegel's thought gives form to the
Absolute itself. Yet the dialectic is driven precisely by the supersession of
categories—"provisional definitions of the Absolute"—which purport
to say what the Absolute is, but only say part. Hegel can say that his system is complete because it achieves closure as a *circle* of thought; his
Encyclopedia is exactly what it sounds like, an encirclement. His philosophical "method" (if it can be described as such) is qualitatively different from the *propositional* method of philosophy that I have described.

To borrow a term from the Jungian Erich Neumann, Hegel's speculation is "circumscription." In his book *The Origins and History of Consciousness*, Neumann discusses mytho-poetic thought and its origins in the
unconscious. Contrasting mytho-poetic thought with propositional
thought, he writes:

> The way of the unconscious is different. Symbols gather around
> the thing to be explained, understood, interpreted. The act of
> becoming conscious consists in the concentric grouping of symbols
> around the object, all *circumscribing* and describing the unknown
> from many sides. Each symbol lays bare another essential side of
> the object to be grasped, points to another facet of meaning. Only
> the canon of these symbols congregating about the center in ques-
> tion, the coherent symbol group, can lead to an understanding of
> what the symbols point to and of what they are trying to express.[33]

Myth, in other words, does not attempt to pin down its subject matter by definitively predicating one or more qualities of it. It does not say
"God is just X" or "Nature is just Y." Instead, it "talks around" its object,
describing it in many, sometimes conflicting ways, each of which indicates something true about it. As Neumann says, only the canon of
these symbols congregating about the center in question, only the
whole, is true. The Egyptians, for instance, devised a number of different
and mutually contradictory cosmologies, all of which they seemed to
regard as equally true. As Henri and H. A. Frankfort write:

> The mythopoetic mind, tending toward the concrete, expressed the
> irrational, not in our manner, but by admitting the validity of sev-

---

32. O'Regan discusses this issue in *The Heterodox Hegel*, 76.
33. Erich Neumann, *The Origins and History of Consciousness*, trans. R. F. C.
Hull (Princeton, N.J.: Princeton University Press, 1954), 7; emphasis added.

eral avenues of approach at one and the same time. . . . We should not doubt that mythopoetic thought fully recognizes the unity of each phenomenon which it conceives under so many different guises; the many-sidedness of its images serves to do justice to the complexity of the phenomena.[34]

The form of Hegel's speculation is identical with mytho-poetic circumscription: Hegel rejects propositional thought, which would *define* the Absolute, and instead "talks around" or "thinks around" the Absolute, revealing at each point some aspect or part of it. The totality of Hegel's philosophical speech is the Truth, the Absolute itself. The difference between Hegel's speculation and mytho-poetic thought is that the *points* through which his circle of truth is described are not primarily images, metaphors, or symbols, but *concepts*. Unlike conventional philosophical thought, however, he employs these concepts in a radically different way. The *form* of this thought is identical with mytho-poetic "circumscription." We can see, then, that Hegel has accomplished exactly what I described earlier: the creation of a new form of thought, which takes up and thus in a sense "unites" elements of both abstract, philosophical thought, and mytho-poetic thought. His is truly a mythology of reason: a new myth-form made of ideas, a mytho-poetic creation that is not "concrete" in its elements but only in its totality, as the concrete universal, as the Absolute.[35]

To employ a term that was important in Hegel's early philosophy of nature (and to which I shall return in later chapters), the Absolute is literally embodied in the pure aether of thought. Hegel's philosophical speech is not an account of the Absolute, it is the concrete, "aetherial" realization of the Absolute itself. Oetinger's progressive corporealization of the "spirit body" has become Hegel's "concrete universal." As in Oetinger, God or the Idea is becoming progressively "better embodied." First it exists in inchoate form, in nature, then in human institutions, in art and in religion, and then finally it reaches perfection in the ideal medium: the pure aether of thought realized in speculative philosophy. Hegel's system is the aether body of the Absolute, Oetinger's *Geistleiblichkeit*.

This does not mean that Hegel believed that everything is "idea." The *Logic* has as its result that the Idea is consummated, and becomes Absolute, through its self-reflection. Each category of the *Logic* is a "provisional definition of the Absolute (or of the Idea)." This science constitutes an independent and self-contained totality of thought, forming a circle. But, as I have said, this science is only aetherial, in some sense unreal. The *Philosophy of Nature* and *Philosophy of Spirit* are accounts of the forms in which the Idea embodies itself, "seeking" the self-reflection conceived in the *Logic*. In Absolute Spirit, the Absolute Idea, which is

34. Henri and H.A. Frankfort, "Introduction: Myth and Reality," *The Intellectual Adventure of Ancient Man* (Chicago: University of Chicago Press, 1977), 20.
35. In the 1830 manuscript for the *Lectures on the Philosophy of World History*, Hegel writes that "the universal object is infinitely concrete, all-comprehending and omnipresent, for the Spirit is eternally present to itself; it has no past, and remains forever the same in all its vigour and strength" (Nisbet, 31; *VIG* 33).

merely the *concept* of self-reflection, achieves actual self-reflection. Philosophy, the highest form of Spirit, is a complete account of Idea in-itself (Logic), become for-itself (Nature and Spirit). This does not imply that Nature and Spirit are "really" just logical categories. Instead, the categories do not become fully real until they become Nature and Spirit.

It might be objected that my comparison of Hegel's speculation with mytho-poetic thought leaves out the element of the transcendent—whether cthonic or numinous—that is always present in mytho-poetic thought. Mythic circumscription, unlike propositional thought, does not seek to make its object fully transparent. There is always an element of mystery—and the warning that any attempt to penetrate this mystery is hubris. What could be more unlike Hegel? Hegel rejects a transcendent Absolute and claims to have achieved Absolute Knowing. By Greek standards, Hegel is undeniably guilty of hubris. His Absolute is Spirit or Idea come to consciousness of itself through the activity of speculation: the divine (the Absolute) cannot be without humanity. It is man who "actualizes" God, and thus man becomes, if not God, then certainly a demigod. Hegel can, however, legitimately claim that he has completed or perfected mytho-poetic thought, and that this achievement is true and verifiable, not empty hubris. The aim of mytho-poetic circumscription is to reveal all aspects of a primordial phenomenon through a cluster of images and stories. But there is never any guarantee that the circle is complete, hence there always remains an element of mystery. Hegel, however, believes he can demonstrate that his system closes the circle. Thus, he can claim with some plausibility that he has removed all mystery from the Absolute. He employs mythic circumscription, and uses concepts in a quasi-aesthetic manner, but by closing the circle he turns mytho-poetic circumscription into an absolute science.

4. Further Parallels Between Speculation and Myth

In his *Myth and Philosophy*, Lawrence J. Hatab contrasts mythic thought with conceptual reason on a number of points, allowing us to establish even more clearly the similarity of Hegelian speculation to mytho-poetic thought.[36]

First, Hatab claims that "Myths express what is unique while concepts express what is common." This means that "Myth does not subsume particular occurrences under general laws or abstract classifications."[37] Recall that Hegel conceives the Absolute as the Whole, and there is nothing higher or more inclusive than the Whole. Thus in Hatab's terms, Hegel rejects conceptual reason precisely because his subject matter is unique, the fully concrete Concrete, the true individual.

Second, Hatab claims that "In myth, there is no separation of form and content, thought and sensation."[38] This means that there is no rift in the mytho-poetic consciousness between the form of experience and the meaning-content it imparts: thunder is immediately experienced as the

36. See Lawrence J. Hatab, *Myth and Philosophy: A Contest of Truths* (Lasalle: Open Court, 1990).
37. Ibid., 30–31.
38. Ibid., 30–31.

anger of the gods. Henri and H. A. Frankfort write that modern science "creates an increasingly wide gulf between our perception of the phenomena and the conceptions by which we make them comprehensible. We see the sun rise and set, but we think of the earth as moving around the sun. We see colors, but we describe them as wave-lengths."[39]

Hegel saw the natural sciences as increasingly devaluing or nullifying ordinary experience and alienating the great bulk of humanity. Part of the aim of Hegel's system is to restore something of the "undivided consciousness" of the ancients. Like Rousseau, however, he does not seek to go back to the golden age, but to realize something of it in the modern age. Hegel does not reject modern scientific procedure and its method of explanation, but he does seek to heal the divide between intellectuals—scientists, philosophers—and laymen, the Platonic "wise" and "vulgar." This is the explicit goal of the "mythology of reason," as stated in the "System-Program."

In his system, Hegel incorporates the data of the natural sciences of his time in a Philosophy of Nature. By showing humanity a God who expresses Himself (in part) in nature, he hoped to reconnect science with the experience of the divine, and specifically with the concrete presence of the divine.[40] In the "System-Program" Hegel writes that "we are told so often that the great mob must have a religion of the senses. But not only does the great mob need it, the philosopher needs it too" (Harris, 511; PG, 235).

What Hegel's system promises is a transformed experience of the world, in which we see familiar things in a new light. Science, poetry, art, religion, the state, are all seen to be expressions or embodiments of the Absolute. Ordinary things suddenly take on new meaning. That which had been thought to be a human contrivance, carried out only for finite human ends, devoid of any higher meaning, mystery, or religious significance—that is to say, what had been thought so quintessentially modern—is now suddenly imbued with spiritual significance, the full systematic scope of which can only be experienced by the typical consciousness as sublime. Thus, Hegel attempts to heal the rift in the modern consciousness between thought and sensation, or thought and experience, by giving us a new form of experience. The very modern scientific and philosophical ideas that formerly seemed to cut us off from experience and from our intuitions of the divine are now seen to be moments of a system of experience that constitutes the divine itself.[41] Hegel's system is an attempt to "re-enchant" the world, to re-invest nature with the experience of the numinous lost with the death of the mythical consciousness.

Third, Hatab claims that "Myth is passive and receptive while concep-

39. Frankfort, "Introduction: Myth and Reality," 11.
40. In the preface to the *Phenomenology* Hegel writes: "Let the other sciences try to argue as much as they like without philosophy—without it they can have in them neither life, Spirit, nor truth" (Miller, 41; PG, 50).
41. Hatab also characterizes the modern rift in terms of the "form-content" distinction. As is well known, Hegel explicitly claims in his *Logic* that he has transcended the form-content distinction.

tual reason is active."[42] Hatab characterizes the "activity" of conceptual reason as involving "abstraction, analysis, synthesis, and judgement" which essentially take an object apart in order to get to its "real" nature.[43] Hegel, of course, calls these procedures of conceptual reason "the Understanding" (*Verstand*) and holds that if we are to know truth, we must rise above this level. Speculative philosophy, by contrast, is not creative, it is recollective. Speculative philosophy is not active, it is "essentially receptive, uncritical." The speculative philosopher is not in control of his thoughts. He is "enthralled" by what he is thinking about.

Fourth, Hatab writes that "In myth, language and the world are coextensive."[44] Words are not taken as mere "signs" for things, but are thought of as wedded to the things themselves, even as expressing the nature of things. Knowing an object's name was even thought to give the knower magical powers over it. This understanding of language is characteristic of the Hermetic tradition. For Hegel, words do not carry a literal "magic power"—though, as we have seen, he does speak of the "magic words" that evoke the "shape" of the Absolute. Hegel's completed speech of the Absolute is identical to its object. Hegel's system does not describe the Absolute, it embodies the Absolute. To give it voice is to give it being.[45] Thus it is no stretch of the imagination to call words that call their object into being "magic words."

Fifth, Hatab claims that "In myth there is no conceptual distinction between illusion and truth."[46] For the mythic mentality anything that is experienced may be meaningful. Thus dreams, which to the modern mind are illusory, are deeply significant to the mytho-poetic mind. There is an analogue to this way of thinking in Hegel. The dialectic does not concern itself at each step with truth. In fact it moves by "canceling" false, partial, or illusory positions. Speculation embraces the partial and the fake. All ideas are standpoints of consciousness on the way to Absolute Knowing. This is most obvious in the *Phenomenology of Spirit*, where numerous false and self-deluding standpoints—Sense-Certainty, Stoicism, Scepticism, the Unhappy Consciousness, the Beautiful Soul, etc.—are transcended, but simultaneously incorporated as necessary components in the development of Spirit.

5. Imagination and the Symbolic Forms

Hegel's dialectic functions through recollection of the whole, which it aims to fully articulate. Individual categories, "provisional definitions of the Absolute," prove inadequate, because of their failure to fully express our recollected intuition of what the whole is. They only say part. But

42. Hatab, *Myth and Philosophy*, 33.
43. Ibid., 33.
44. Ibid., 34.
45. Hegel writes in his *Philosophy of Nature* of 1803–4 that "the speaking of the Aether with itself is its reality. . . . What it utters is itself, what speaks is itself, and that to which it speaks is again itself" (quoted in Harris, *Night Thoughts*, 243).
46. Hatab, *Myth and Philosophy*, 35.

what is the mechanism by which a *new*, further category is selected? In other words, how are the transitions made in the dialectic? To answer this question, we must examine the role of imagination in Hegel's system.

The connection between recollection, imagination, and wisdom is found in the Hermetic tradition and its "art of memory."[47] I want to suggest that Hegel's speculative activity be considered along the lines of what has been called "active imagination." Antoine Faivre characterizes active imagination—"the essential component of esotericism"—as "a form of imagination inclined to reveal and use mediations of all kinds, such as rituals, symbolic images, mandalas, intermediary spirits."[48] "Imagination" suggests, of course, the image. It seems straightforwardly to be the faculty that produces images. But this is not its primary significance. Imagination consists fundamentally in a kind of ingenuity for giving form to something, sometimes to the truth.

Verene describes the role of imagination in Hegel's dialectical transitions as follows: "Spirit requires an ingenious act, in which through an immediate act of its own wit it produces a new standpoint. It requires the power of *ingenium*. . . . Spirit must suddenly project a new reality for itself out of a reality in which it finds itself becoming exhausted and dismembered."[49] Ingenium is equivalent to Faivre's active imagination. But Verene argues that Hegel's imagination is fundamentally uncreative, for it depends on recollection. Verene writes that the Hegelian *Erinnerung*—or *Er-innerung*, as Hegel also writes it—strongly implies an "inwardizing of the subject."[50] Faivre, in a commentary on the Rosicrucian *Chemical Wedding*, makes the same observation: *er-innern* means both "to remember" and "to go deeply into one's self."[51] What the philosopher remembers when he goes deeply into himself are *archai*, to use Verene's term. "Archai . . . are drawn forth from consciousness suddenly and without method, that is, without some set procedure. Consciousness turns to itself and suddenly has in its hands something of itself that it did not know was there in any explicit sense. This drawing forth of archai is . . . recollecting in its primordial sense."[52]

The subtext to the transitions in Hegel's dialectic is his use of recollected patterns of thought from the philosophical, religious, and mystical traditions. These include what might be called "symbolic forms," many of which are Hermetic in their origins or associations. Some of these show up as illustrative metaphors or images in Hegel's writing.

47. Faivre writes that "It is partly under the inspiration of the *Corpus Hermeticum* . . . that memory and imagination are associated to the point of becoming identical, part of the teaching of Hermes Trismegistus consisting in 'interiorizing' the world in our *mens*." See Faivre, *Theosophy, Imagination, Tradition*, xxiii.
48. Faivre, *Access to Western Esotericism*, 12.
49. Verene, *Hegel's Recollection*, 22; it should be noted that there is no concept of "method" in the modern sense implied here.
50. Verene, *Hegel's Recollection*, 3.
51. Faivre, *Access to Western Esotericism*, 169.
52. Verene, *Hegel's Recollection*, 24.

Others are explicitly referred to only from time to time, but always seem to be at work beneath the surface, giving form to the system itself. These include the Hermetic-mystical symbolic forms of the triangle (the triad, or trinity), the square, the ennead, and the circle (the alchemical *ouroburos*, which, incidentally, personifies Mercury or Hermes).

Hegel frankly admits that he is drawing on this perennial resource. In fact, he seems to revel in it. In his early *Philosophy of Nature*, Hegel refers reverently to "the Elders," which H. S. Harris has argued refers to both Paracelsus and Böhme.[53] As Harris notes, even where Hegel is drawing from more recent sources he insists "on finding an earlier pedigree . . . in Paracelsus and Böhme."[54] In the preface to the *Phenomenology* he writes that "the *triadic form* must not be regarded as scientific when it is reduced to a lifeless schema, a mere shadow. . . . Kant rediscovered this triadic form by instinct, but in his work it was still lifeless and uncomprehended; since then it has, however, been raised to its absolute significance, and with it the true form in its true content has been presented, so that the Concept of Science has emerged" (Miller, 29; PG, 37).

The reference to Kant having *rediscovered* (*wiedergefundne*) the triadic form indicates that Hegel regards it as a perennial idea. It also indicates that he regards himself as truly reviving and doing justice to the triadic form, as well as raising it to the level of "science" (*Wissenschaft*).[55] In the *Science of Logic* (1812) a similar passage appears: "Kant did not apply the infinitely important form of triplicity—with him it manifested itself at first only as a formal spark of light—to the genera of his categories (quantity, quality, etc.), but only to their species which, too, alone he called categories. Consequently he was unable to hit on the third to quantity and quality" (Miller, 327; WL 1:365).[56] Consider also one of the *Zusätze* to the *Encyclopedia Logic*, in which Hegel remarks that "Any division is to be considered genuine when it is determined by the Concept. So genuine division is, first of all, tripartite; and then, because particularity presents itself as doubled, the division moves on to fourfoldness as well. In the sphere of spirit trichotomy predominates, and it is one of Kant's merits to have drawn attention to this" (EL § 230, Z; Geraets, 298).

53. Harris, *Night Thoughts*, 274fn.
54. Ibid., 278.
55. This passage from the *Phenomenology* is often distorted by well-meaning commentators who see Hegel's apparent obsession with triadic form as an embarrassing superstition. For instance, Gustav Müller treats the passage as follows: "According to the Hegel legend one would expect Hegel to recommend this 'triplicity.' But, after saying that it was derived from Kant, he calls it a 'lifeless schema'. . ." See Müller, "The Hegel Legend of 'Thesis-Antithesis-Synthesis,'" in *The Hegel Myths and Legends*, ed. Jon Stewart (Evanston, Ill.: Northwestern University Press, 1996), 302. Müller, however, completely distorts what Hegel has said. As I have pointed out, Hegel says that Kant *rediscovered* triadic form, not that it *derives* from Kant. Further, Hegel says (in Miller's translation) that triadic form is unscientific "*when* it is reduced to a lifeless schema" (emphasis added). He does not say that it is *always* a "lifeless schema." A cursory glance at the structure of Hegel's system shows that he thought there was some life in this old schema yet.
56. The "third" Hegel refers to is *Measure*.

In the next section, I will discuss Hegel's use of triadicity, by way of a discussion of the "Triangle fragment" and the "triangle diagram." As to the square, the third of the twelve theses composed and defended by Hegel as part of his doctoral exam in Jena in 1801 reads as follows: "The square is the law of nature, the triangle of spirit."[57] In his early philosophy of nature, Hegel conceives nature as containing within itself "resting motion," which involves four dimensions: three spatial, and one temporal. He refers to this as the "squareness" of nature.[58] (Spirit, by contrast, is a triangle composed of the dimensions of time itself: past, present, and future.) As Harris sums up Hegel's early views: "The eternal reality for theoretical contemplation by the mind is a four dimensional spatiotemporal equilibrium. 'Squareness' is the simplest schema for this that we can construct in pure intuition."[59] Heinz Kimmerle has suggested that Hegel attempted to "map" the parts of his early, quadripartite system onto the four moments of "resting motion."[60] In the next section we will see how the square works into Hegel's discussion of the "Divine Triangle." I will have more to say about Hegel's endorsement of the doctrine of the four elements later.

As to the ennead, Hegel's system as a whole is a triad, each element of which is a separate science, divided according to three chief moments, which are analyzed in turn into three constitutive moments, which are themselves analyzed into their three constitutive moments. This means that each major subdivision of each science is a triad of enneads, "nines" (meaning that each science is an ennead of enneads). The "Doctrine of Being" in the *Logic* is subdivided into Quality, Quantity, and Measure. Quality is subdivided into Being, Determinate Being, and Being-for-self. Being is subdivided into Being, Nothing, and Becoming. And so on. The system is a triad of triads of triads of triads of triads.

Hegel describes his system in the *Encyclopedia Logic*, however, as a "circle of circles": "The whole . . . presents itself as a circle of circles, each of which is a necessary moment, so that the system of its peculiar elements

---

57. G. W. F. Hegel, *Philosophical Dissertation on the Orbits of the Planets (1801) Preceded by the 12 Theses Defended on August 27, 1801*, trans. Pierre Adler, *Graduate Faculty Philosophy Journal* 1 (1987): 269–309; 276. Adler is employing Georg Lasson's edition of the *Dissertation*, which has his German translation and the original Latin on facing pages. See Hegel, *Sämtliche Werke*, vol. 1, *Erste Druckschriften* (Leipzig: Felix Meiner Verlag, 1928). Hegel does not waver from this proposition in later years. In the lectures on the *Philosophy of Nature* given in the Berlin period (in the years 1819–30), Hegel states that "in Spirit the fundamental form of necessity is the triad" (PN § 248, Z; Petry 1:211). The triangle and square represent, of course, threeness and fourness. Seven, the sum of three and four, is a powerful number in the Hermetic tradition. Julius Evola writes: "Metaphysically, Seven expresses the Three added to the Four. . . . Seven is the manifestation of the creative principles (triad) in relation to the world made up of the four elements; the full expression of nature creating nature (*natura naturans*) in action" (Evola, *The Hermetic Tradition*, 52).
58. Harris, *Night Thoughts*, 86–87, 90–91.
59. Ibid., 90.
60. Heinz Kimmerle, "Dokumente zu Hegels Jenaer Dozententätigkeit (1801–1807)," *Hegel-Studien* 4 (1967): 21–100.

constitutes the whole Idea—which equally appears in each single one of them" (EL § 15; Geraets, 39). Circularity is a perennial image associated with Hermetic and mystical thought. Interestingly, the phrase *hen kai pan* or *hen to pan* is associated with the alchemical symbol of the *ouroburos*. The Greek phrase is often written inside or around the serpent.[61] Erich Neumann, in *The Origins and History of Consciousness*, suggests that the *ouroburos* is not just an alchemical symbol but an archetype of the collective unconscious symbolizing the original unity of all things and the return to that unity.[62]

Notice, however, that the *archai* that Hegel adopts as imaginative "guides" to speculation (i.e, at the level of "meta-speculation") are all mathematical or geometrical. To be sure, other sorts of "images" occur in Hegel, but only as illustrations of his concepts. In an "aphorism" from the "Wastebook" (written between 1803 and 1806), Hegel states: "In philosophizing there is nothing to be represented. Now and then there is an image. Men cling to this. The *tabula rasa* of Aristotle is accidental and used as a makeshift. Everyone is familiar with this. However, it does not express the essence of Aristotle's concept of the soul."[63] In short, metaphors or images are a bonus, an aid to understanding only. In order to be understood, from time to time, Hegel must write, as Jacob Böhme would put it, "according to a creaturely way and manner, otherwise you could not understand." Many of Hegel's images or archetypes are drawn from the Hermetic-alchemical and mystical traditions, as I will show in later chapters. (These include *caput mortuum*, aether, and the four elements.) But in terms of Hegel's "metaphilosophy" his guiding images are mathematical-geometrical alone. (In the next section I will explore the image of the triangle.)

What are we to make, then, of the following remark from Hegel's 1805 *Lectures on the History of Philosophy*?

> [There is a] method of representing the universal content by means of numbers, lines and geometric figures. These are figurative, but not concretely so, as in the case of myths. Thus it may be said that eternity is a circle, the snake that bites its own tail [i.e., the *ouroburos*; see above]. This is only an image, but Spirit does not require such a symbol. There are people who value such methods

61. See Coudert, *Alchemy: The Philosopher's Stone*, 142. *Hen kai pan* is also sometimes symbolized by a cosmic egg. See also Coudert, *Leibniz and the Kabbalah*, 95.
62. See Neumann, *Origins and History*, 5–38. Evola in *The Hermetic Tradition* traces the phrase "hen to pan" and its connection to the *ouroburos* to the alchemical *Chrysopoeia of Cleopatra* (Marciano codex [Venice], ms. 2325. fol. 188b; and ms. 2327, fol. 196). He writes (pp. 20–21), "The alchemical ideogram of 'One the All,' is 0, the circle: a line or movement that encloses within itself and contains in itself both its end and beginning. In Hermetism this symbol expresses the universe and, at the same time, the Great Work [i.e. the preparation of the Philosopher's Stone]."
63. G. W. F. Hegel, "Aphorisms from the Wastebook," trans. Susanne Klein, David L. Roochnik, and George Elliott Tucker, *Independent Journal of Philosophy* 3 (1979): 1–6; 5. Werke 1:562.

of representation, but these forms do not go far. (LHP 1:88; *Werke* 18:109–10)[64]

This sounds as if Hegel is rejecting the use of symbolic forms altogether, but that is not the case. He is simply saying that the use of geometrical images, like all images, is limited and not fully adequate for the presentation of philosophical wisdom; images cannot replace the "conceptual" language of philosophy. But my claim about Hegel's "symbolic forms" is not that they are forms which occur *in* the text, but that they are forms that lie beneath the text, structuring it, although to be sure, we do find Hegel sometimes explicitly reflecting on these forms—as in the famous "circle of circles" passage.

Hegel's speculation, as I have characterized it, is a sophisticated, post-Kantian reappropriation of the memory magic and "active imagination" of Hermetic thinkers such as Bruno and Böhme. The doctrine of a perennial philosophy or of a "collective unconscious" was an Hermetic commonplace. It now becomes clear why and how Hegel could take alchemy and the Kabbalah, and the thought of such men as Böhme, seriously. He saw them as expressions of the unconscious wisdom of Spirit-in-itself, of the perennial philosophy. In this respect, Hegel was very much in tune with the spirit of his time, in which, "There persisted a strong sense of the possibility that embedded in the accretions of alchemical literature lay important truths expressed in symbolic form."[65]

Hegel's attitude toward the Hermetic tradition was cautious, but cautiously approving. Hegel saw the Hermetic tradition as a manifestation of unconscious wisdom, of the perennial philosophy, struggling to transcend its purely sensuous form. This explains his strongly positive attitude to Böhme, even though Böhme grossly violates Hegel's prohibition on "picture-thinking." Hegel's claim is that Böhme comes close to the truth, even though he is caught in "the hard, knotty oak of the senses." What accounts for Böhme's inspiration? My contention is that Hegel would have to admit that eternal truth simply happens to "well up" in certain special individuals, in the form of certain archetypal forms of expression. Hegel refers to religions as "sprouting up fortuitously, like the flowers and creations of nature, as foreshadowings, images, representations, without [our] knowing where they come from or where they

---

64. Hegel makes similar remarks in the *Science of Logic*: "To take numbers and geometrical figures (as the circle, triangle, etc. have often been taken), simply as symbols (the circle, for example, as a symbol for eternity, the triangle, of the Trinity), is so far harmless enough; but, on the other hand, it is foolish to fancy that in this way more is expressed than can be grasped and expressed by thought. Whatever profound wisdom may be supposed to lie in such meagre symbols or in those richer products of fantasy in the mythology of peoples and in poetry generally, it is properly for thought alone to make explicit for consciousness the wisdom that lies only *in* them; and not in symbols, but in nature and in mind. In symbols the truth is dimmed and veiled by the sensuous element; only in the form of thought is it fully revealed to consciousness: the meaning is only the thought itself" (Miller, 215; WL 1:228–29).
65. Charles Webster, *From Paracelsus to Newton: Magic and the Making of Modern Science* (Cambridge: Cambridge University Press, 1982), 10.

are going to" (LPR 1:196; VPR 1:106). Hegel states that "Religion is a begetting of the divine spirit, not an invention of human beings but an effect of the divine at work, of the divine productive process within humanity" (LPR 1:130; VPR 1:46). Recall the *Zusatz* to the *Encyclopedia Logic* quoted earlier: "It should . . . be mentioned here that the meaning of the speculative is to be understood as being the same as what used in earlier times to be called the 'mystical.' "[66]

6. The "Divine Triangle" and the Triangle Diagram

I turn now to what can be regarded as an early, fascinating, but abortive attempt on Hegel's part to realize the Mythology of Reason: the so-called "Divine Triangle" fragment. The "Divine Triangle" shows Hegel's conscious reappropriation of Hermetic thought, as well as his "return" to Christianity. In Hegel's early musings on the "new religion" there was something vaguely anti-Christian about the whole project, a charge that Christianity is somehow "unnatural." Certainly there is nothing "Christian" about the "System-Program" fragment, no suggestion that its Mythology of Reason is to involve a revivification of Christian myth. With the Divine Triangle, however, Hegel seems to make his peace with Christianity. Part of the project of the Mythology of Reason now seems to be a reconciliation between philosophical reason and a specifically Christian revelation.

The Divine Triangle fragment no longer survives. A description of it, as well as some quotations, were preserved by Rosenkranz. Scholars disagree about when it was written. Rosenkranz says in the winter of 1804–05. More recently, Heinz Kimmerle has argued for the spring of

---

66. The passage reads more fully as follows: "It should . . . be mentioned here that the meaning of the speculative is to be understood as being the same as what used in earlier times to be called 'mystical'. . . . When we speak of the 'mystical' nowadays, it is taken to be synonymous with what is mysterious and incomprehensible; and, depending on the ways their culture and mentality vary in other respects, some people treat the mysterious and incomprehensible as what is authentic and genuine, whilst others regard it as belonging to the domain of superstition and deception. About this we must remark first that 'the mystical' is certainly something mysterious, *but only for the understanding*, and then only because abstract identity is the principle of the understanding. But when it is regarded as synonymous with the speculative, the mystical is the concrete unity of just those determinations that count as true for the understanding only in their separation and opposition. So if those who recognise the mystical as what is genuine say that it is something utterly mysterious, and just leave it at that, they are only declaring that for them, too, thinking has only the significance of an abstract positing of identity, and that in order to attain the truth we must renounce thinking, or, as they frequently put it, that we must 'take reason captive.' As we have seen, however, the abstract thinking of the understanding is so far from being something firm and ultimate that it proves itself, on the contrary, to be a constant sublating of itself and an overturning into its opposite, whereas the rational as such is rational precisely because it contains both of the opposites as ideal moments within itself. *Thus, everything rational can equally be called 'mystical'*; but this only amounts to saying that it transcends the *understanding*. It does not at all imply that what is so spoken of must be considered inaccessible to thinking and incomprehensible" (EL § 82, Z; Geraets, 133; emphasis added).

1804.[67] The manuscript may have been accompanied by diagrams, none of which survive. (Hegel's triangle diagram, to be discussed shortly, does not correspond to the remarks in the Divine Triangle fragment.)

In his discussion of the fragment, Rosenkranz asserts that it belongs to a "theosophical" phase in Hegel's development.[68] In fact, Rosenkranz claims that the "theosophical" phase begins in the Frankfurt period. (This is interesting, for one thing, because, as noted in the last chapter, Hegel's time in Frankfurt was marked by an association with Freemasonry.) Rosenkranz claims that Hegel abandoned the approach of the Triangle fragment because "the lack of correspondence between the image-form and the form of pure thinking became too great."[69] This view is wrongheaded. As we shall see, the Triangle fragment is heavily laden with mytho-poetic language and preoccupied with what Rosenkranz calls "geometrizing," but this is all to be found in the later writings, especially the *Phenomenology of Spirit*, the *Logic* and the *Philosophy of Nature*.

Rosenkranz suggests that Hegel may have been inspired in part by the works of Franz von Baader. As was discussed in chapter 1, Hegel tried for many years to curry Baader's favor. This must be regarded as quite peculiar, as Baader was the leading occultist of his era, dismissed by many as a crank. In particular, Rosenkranz suggests that it was Baader's 1798 essay, *On the Pythagorean Square in Nature or the Four Regions of the World*, that served as Hegel's source for the Triangle fragment. H. S. Harris (drawing on the research of Helmut Schneider) summarizes this essay as follows:

> In Baader's essay the 3 domains of natural history (animal, vegetable, mineral) and the 3 types of matter (combustible, salty, earthy) are subordinated under 3 "basic forces" or "principles" (fire, water, earth). These elements would remain inert, however, were it not for the 4th principle (air) which enlivens them. The relation of the 4 elements is symbolically portrayed as a triangle with a point in the middle (representing air). This symbol (triangle with a point) Baader calls Quaternarius or Pythagorean Square.[70]

The alchemical, and specifically Paracelsian, influence on Baader's triads and his symbolism is clear. As Harris points out, the triangle with central point was also used by Böhme.[71] Rosenkranz suggests a Böhmean influence on the Hegelian Triangle fragment. As we shall see, it is

---

67. See Heinz Kimmerle, "Zur Chronologie von Hegels Jenaer Schriften," *Hegel Studien* 4: 125–76; 144, 161–62. Walter Jaeschke is convinced that this dating refutes Rosenkranz's thesis of a "mystical-theosophical phase" in Hegel's development. This has no bearing on my claims. In effect, I am arguing that Hegel's "mystical-theosophical phase" never ended. See Jaeschke, *Reason in Religion*, 126.
68. Karl Rosenkranz, "Hegels ursprüngliches System 1798–1806," *Literarhistorisches Taschenbuch* 2 (1844): 157–64; 157. Trans. in Harris, *Night Thoughts*, 184.
69. Ibid., 159 (Harris, 184).
70. Ibid., 159 (Harris, 184).
71. Harris, *Night Thoughts*, 185, n.

Böhme's influence (and perhaps also that of Oetinger) that is indeed decisive.[72]

Rosenkranz's summary of the Triangle fragment is as follows:

> To express the life of the Idea, [Hegel] constructed a *triangle of triangles*, which he suffered *to move through one another* in such a way that each one was not only at one time *extreme* and at another time *middle* generally, but also it had to go through this process internally with each of its *sides*. And then, in order to maintain the ideal plasticity of unity amid this rigidity and crudity of intuition, to maintain the fluidity of the distinctions represented as triangle and sides, he went on consistently to the further barbarity of expressing the totality as [a] *square resting* over the triangles and their process. But he seems to have got tired in the following out of his labour; at any rate he broke off at the construction of the *animal* [*Thier*].[73]

H. S. Harris has offered an ingenious reconstruction of the geometrical theosophy of the Triangle fragment, but as we cannot be sure that it expresses what Hegel actually had in mind, I will not go through the details of Harris's reconstruction here.[74]

As Rosenkranz points out, Hegel's preoccupation with triadicity does not simply reflect an infatuation with Böhmean symbolism, but also a conscious attempt to embrace the Christian Trinity, to bring it into philosophical speculation. Rosenkranz writes: "He wanted now to grasp the *Trinity* in the triangle of triangles. He wanted at this date, not to banish this image from himself as irrational, in which the faith had for centuries reverenced its highest possession."[75] Rosenkranz goes on to point to Hegel's interest (starting, it seems, in his Berne period) in Christian mystics such as Eckhart and Tauler.

72. Harris writes: "Hegel's attitude to Böhme in 1804 to 1806 is critically appreciative, but he consistently attacks the direct acceptance of Böhme's metaphors and symbols as the simple truth. See esp. the *Wastebook*, items 45 and 48 (Rosenkranz, [*Hegels Leben*] pp. 546, 547, and 199). So if we project this attitude back to an earlier period when Hegel was less discontented with pictorial modes of expression generally, we might fairly take the triangle fragment as an attempt to *develop* what Hegel took to be Böhme's meaning in Böhme's own mode" (*Night Thoughts*, 185, n). My one quarrel with Harris here is that Hegel never becomes fully dissatisfied with the sort of "pictorial modes of expression" discussed in the preceding section: the meta-dialectical "symbolic forms" of the triangle, circle, etc.
73. Rosenkranz, "Hegels ursprüngliches System," 160 (in Harris, *Night Thoughts*, 185). It is worth noting here the similarity to Hegel's treatment of the "circle of circles" in the *Encyclopedia Logic* of 1817: "Each of the parts of philosophy is a philosophical whole, a circle that closes upon itself; but in each of them the philosophical Idea is in a particular determinacy or element. Every single circle also breaks through the restriction of its element as well, precisely because it is inwardly [the] totality, and it grounds a further sphere. The whole presents itself therefore as a circle of circles, each of which is a necessary moment, so that the system of its peculiar elements constitutes the whole idea—which equally appears in each single one of them" (EL § 15; Geraets, 39).
74. See also Helmut Schneider's attempted reconstruction in his "Anfänge der Systementwicklung Hegels in Jena," *Hegel-Studien* 10 (1975): 133–71.
75. Rosenkranz, "Hegels ursprüngliches System," 161 (in Harris, *Night Thoughts*, 185).

The influence of the doctrine of the Trinity shows itself in Hegel's claim in the Triangle fragment that "A more intelligible expression for the notion of God as the universal life [*Allebens*] is the term *Love*, but a deeper one is *Spirit*."[76] Insofar as it is possible to penetrate the obscurity of the lines Rosenkranz quotes from the Triangle fragment, it appears that the triangles represent the process of God's coming to consciousness of Himself. This is what is meant by Spirit (what Hegel will later call "Absolute Spirit"). There appear to be three triangles in all, with the "triangle of triangles" being the figure made up by the set of the three.

The first triangle is described by Hegel as follows: "In this First, which is at the same time only One side of the absolutely unique Triangle, there is only the Godhead in reciprocal intuition and cognition with Himself." This cannot help but remind us of Böhme's description of God "in Himself." Recall that Böhme's first three spirits—Sour, Sweet, and Bitter—form a primordial Trinity of conflict within the Godhead, preceding its manifestation. They are a triad of the unmanifest God or God-in-Himself. David Walsh writes: "Hegel suggested, as Böhme also did, that the first Trinity of God in himself is not sufficient for the divine self-revelation."[77] In fact, Hegel's account of the Trinity here is quite similar to his account of Böhme's Trinity in the *Lectures on the History of Philosophy* (LHP 3:197–214; *Werke* 20:99–116).

Hegel continues: "[The Idea of the Godhead is that] in which the pure light of unity is the middle, and whose sides are likewise the pure raying outwards, and the pure refraction of the ray back into itself."[78] Light, for Böhme, is the pure principle of openness, of manifestation without any hiddenness. Fire, for Böhme, is the kindling of light within the darkness that is God in Himself. This seems to be something like what Hegel is aiming at here: light comes to be within the Idea that is the triangle of God in Himself. It "rays" outwards. This is "God the Father." The second triangle is "God the Son." Hegel writes: "In the Son, God is cognizant of Himself *as* God. He says to Himself: I am God. The within-itself ceases to be a negative."[79] The triangle of the Son is the consummation of the light that is kindled in the triangle of the Father (or the Idea). "The within-itself ceases to be negative" means something

---

76. Harris writes that "'Spirit is deeper' as a name of God because it names a self-cognitive experience" (Harris, *Night Thoughts*, 163). Rosenkranz paraphrases this line in his account. The line, as I have given it, appears as a direct quotation from the fragment in R. Haym's *Hegel und seine Zeit* (1857; reprint, Hildesheim: Georg Olms, 1962), 101. Oetinger also gave Love a central place in his thought, as Robert Schneider notes: "Love is thus the highest knowledge-form [*Erkenntnisform*], because in it the beloved [*Geliebte*] is entirely contained within the soul, because you [*du*] and I become identical" (*Geistesahnen*, 84).

77. See Walsh, *Boehme and Hegel*, 321.

78. Rosenkranz, "Hegels ursprüngliches System," 163 (Harris, *Night Thoughts*, 187).

79. Obviously with the *Logos* in mind, Harris writes of this passage: "The Absolute Being, the Father, utters himself as the son. He *says* what he is in order that he may himself know what he is. The *Universe* as a totality is this 'saying'" (*Night Thoughts*, 164). It is interesting in this context to recall what Böhme says about *Ton* (see chapter 1).

analogous to Böhme's transformation of the "in-Himself" of God (Sour-Sweet-Bitter) into God become for-Himself through Heat, Love, Tone, and Body.

Hegel continues:

> The distinction and the wealth of God's self-consciousness is reconciled [in the triangle of the Son] with His simplicity, and the realm of the Son of God is also the realm of the Father. The self-consciousness of God is not a withdrawal back within Himself and an otherness of the Son, just as it is not an otherness of His withdrawal back within Himself as simple God, but His intuition in the Son is the intuiting of the simple God as His own self, but in such a way that the Son remains Son, or as not distinguished and at the same time distinguished; or the farspread Realm of the Universe, which has no longer any being-for-self over against itself, but rather its being-for-self is a returning back within God, or is God's returning back within Himself, a joy over the majesty of the Son whom He intuits as Himself.[80]

Here Hegel is expressing the identity-in-difference of the Father and Son. The Son is a distinct moment from the Father, yet the Son is God, insofar as it is only in the Son that the Father actually becomes God.

Hegel writes further of this triangle of the Son: "In the Second [Triangle] God's intuiting has stepped over to one side. He has come into connection with Evil and the middle is the bad[ness] of the mixing of both. But this triangle becomes a Square, in that the pure Godhead floats above it." I have little to say about how the "square" figures in here (Harris has his own conjectures). The "geometrical" aspects to this fragment are difficult to understand completely. What is more important here is the role played by Evil. Walsh writes of this section of the fragment that "creation separated from God is the evil reality."[81] With the Son, difference is introduced into the Godhead. It provides for God's actualization as God, but it is difference, division, opposition nonetheless. Taken on its own, this opposition is evil. Evil is the part attempting to stand on its own, to stand in for the whole. In Böhme, as I noted in chapter 1, Lucifer represents the will to isolation, cutting-off, a selfishness that all things exhibit. (I will discuss the role of evil in Hegel's philosophy much more extensively in the following chapter.)

The separated moment that stands opposed to the Godhead must be "transfigured" and brought into unity within God. Hegel writes that "the Son must go right through the Earth, must overcome Evil, and in that he steps over to one side as the victor, must awaken the other, the self-cognition of God, as a new cognition that is one with God, or as the Spirit of God: whereby the middle becomes a beautiful, free, divine middle, the Universe of God."[82] This heralds the arrival of a new

---

80. Rosenkranz, "Hegels ursprüngliches System," 162 (Harris, *Night Thoughts,* 186–87).

81. Walsh, *Boehme and Hegel,* 320.

82. Rosenkranz, "Hegels ursprüngliches System," 163 (in Harris, *Night Thoughts,* 187–88).

triangle, presumably of the Holy Spirit (though Hegel is not clear about this).

That the Son must pass over into a third stage of the Spirit is, however, obvious. Consider the following, which occurs earlier in what Rosenkranz has preserved for us: "What stands over against the Son in his majesty as He intuits the Earth, is the majesty of God Himself, the looking back and returning home to Him. And for the consecrated Earth this self-consciousness of God is the Spirit, which proceeds from God, and in which the Earth is one with Him and with the Son."[83]

Hegel writes further of Spirit in the following:

This Spirit is here the eternal mediator between the Son returned unto the Father, who is now wholly and only one, and between the being of the son within himself, or of the majesty of the Universe. The simplicity of the all-embracing Spirit has now stepped into the middle and there is now no distinction any more. For the Earth as the self-consciousness of God is now the Spirit, yet it is also the eternal son whom God intuits as Himself. Thus has the holy triangle of triangles closed itself. The First [triangle] is the Idea of God which is carried out in the other triangles, and returns into itself by passing through them.[84]

If what Rosenkranz has preserved of the Triangle fragment is examined carefully, it becomes clear that it is the blueprint of Hegel's entire system. The nature of his *Logic* is expressed here very clearly: the first "triad" of the system (in the later *Logic*, Being-Essence-Concept) is the "Idea of God." In the *Science of Logic*, in a well-known passage, Hegel declares that his aim is "the exposition of God as he is in his eternal essence before the creation of nature and a finite Spirit" (Miller, 50; WL 1:33–34). This Idea is expressed (made real) in the triads of the Son, that is, the Philosophy of Nature (Mechanics, Physics, Organics)[85] and the Philosophy of Spirit (Subjective, Objective, and Absolute Spirit). Toward the end of what Rosenkranz quotes of the Triangle manuscript, Hegel even employs emanation imagery to describe the relation of the first triad of the Idea of God to the others: "through the second triangle of the Son, the Third has immediately formed itself, the return of all into God Himself, or the having-been-poured-out [*das Ausgegossensein*] of the Idea overall."[86] In the transition to Nature at the end of the *Science of Logic*, Hegel writes that "the Idea freely releases itself in its absolute self-sufficiency and stasis" (*die Idee sich selbst frei entlässt, ihrer absolut sicher und in sich ruhend*; Miller, 843; WL 3:305). The "Idea of God" becomes the "Universe of God" (see above): the Idea becomes concrete, embodied. Here again we see the influence of Böhme and Oetinger.

83. Ibid., 162 (Harris, 187); italics in original.
84. Ibid., 162–63 (Harris, 187).
85. In a *Zusatz* to the *Philosophy of Nature* (Berlin period, 1819–30), Hegel remarks that "Nature is the Son of God . . . " (PN § 247, Z; Petry I, 206).
86. Rosenkranz, "Hegels ursprüngliches System," 164 (Harris, *Night Thoughts*, 188).

It might be claimed that a major difference between the doctrine of the Triangle fragment and Hegel's mature philosophy is that the former describes the Earth as "the self-consciousness of God." On closer examination, however, there is no disparity. As we have seen, Hegel claims that "the Earth as the self-consciousness of God is now the Spirit." Nature itself (excluding man) is one form in which the Idea of God finds concrete expression. But God's self-consciousness is achieved only through a natural (terrestrial) being that simultaneously rises above nature to the ideal: mankind or Spirit.

Writing of the transfigured Earth as the "Universe of God," Hegel says: "This Second Triangle is (*qua* being in the separation) herewith itself a *twofold* Triangle, or its two sides are each a triangle, the one the converse of the other, and the middle is in this movement of history the all-effecting force of the absolute unity that floats above the first, and takes this up into itself and changes it into another within itself. But what is visible, that is the two triangles, but the middle is only the invisible might at work in the inward [soul]."[87] This passage is exceedingly obscure, but we can immediately glean from it that even in this early manuscript Hegel is speaking of God's achievement of self-consciousness as an historical process. Could the "invisible might at work in the inward [soul]" be equivalent to the "cunning of Reason"?

This manuscript was obviously not intended by Hegel for publication. It constitutes notes to himself. Its baffling, frenzied style indicates that Hegel was rushing to get his inspirations onto paper, to give himself a rough outline of his system, a roadmap for where he was going. This is the earliest such fragment to indicate the entirety of the system in its outlines. What is so striking is how indebted Hegel obviously is to Hermeticism. The chief debt is clearly to Böhme. But there is also evidence of the influence of Baader, Oetinger, and Eckhart. Even more striking is the way in which the entire text is ruled by a concern for an exact fit between speculative truth and geometric form.

As noted above, the triangle diagram does not appear to be an illustration of the ideas of the Triangle *fragment*. H. S. Harris concurs in this judgment, stating, rather enigmatically, that the diagram "belongs in the context of *magical* speculation."[88] We do not know when Hegel made this diagram. We do not even know with certainty that he made it. Nevertheless, it was found in Hegel's papers and has always been attributed

87. Ibid., 163–64 (in Harris, 188); Harris interpolates "soul."
88. Harris, *Night Thoughts*, 157. Harris writes that the "philosophical background to the symbolism is Neo-Pythagorean, rather than Christian." I do not see what would incline one to this judgment, as opposed, for instance, to the judgment that the symbolism is "Neo-Paracelsian" or "Neo-Aggripian" or "Neo-Böhmean." Helmut Schneider also holds that the diagram does not illustrate the fragment, for obvious reasons: "The text describes a triangle *of* triangles, whereas the drawing shows a triangle *with* triangles." See Helmut Schneider, "Zur Dreiecks-Symbolik bei Hegel," *Hegel-Studien* 8 (1973): 55–77; 57 (my translation). This is one of the very few discussions of this drawing in print.

1. Hegel's triangle diagram. Reprinted by permission of
Felix Meiner Verlag, Hamburg.

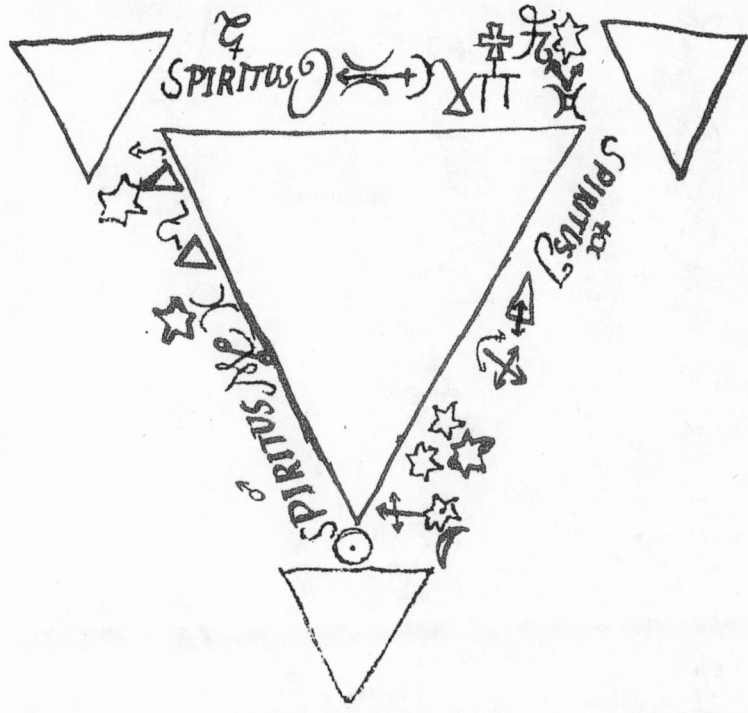

to him. It was first published in 1937 in G. Stuhlfauth's *Das Dreick* and
has since been very seldom reprinted.[89]

I have reproduced the diagram as figure 1. It is drawn partly in pen,
partly in a ruddy pencil, on cheap, gray-brown paper. The drawing's
major components are four triangles: one large central triangle and three
others at each of its points. They are all pointing in the same direction,
but it is uncertain whether the drawing is to be positioned so that the
triangles point up or down, or to one side or the other. Helmut Schneider prints it with the triangles pointed down, as does Häussermann.
Around the sides of the large triangle is a collection of bizarre symbols.
The word *Spiritus* appears three times, each time at the left end of one of
the sides (the "S" at the beginning of the word is also written in pencil,
whereas the rest of the word is in pen). A few of the symbols are easily
identified (see the key I have provided in figure 2). They include the traditional symbols for the sun, the moon, Mars, Mercury, Jupiter, and Sat-

89. See G. Stuhlfauth, *Das Dreieck: Die Geschichte eines religiösen Symbols*
(Stuttgart, 1937), Abbildung 16. In 1939 it was reprinted by Friedrich
Häussermann in his "Das 'gottliche Dreieck' und seine Bedeutung für die
Philosophie Hegels," *Zentrallblatt für Psychotherapie* 11 (1939): 359–79. Häusser-
mann's article is, in fact, a Jungian discussion of the Triangle *fragment*.

2. Key to triangle diagram

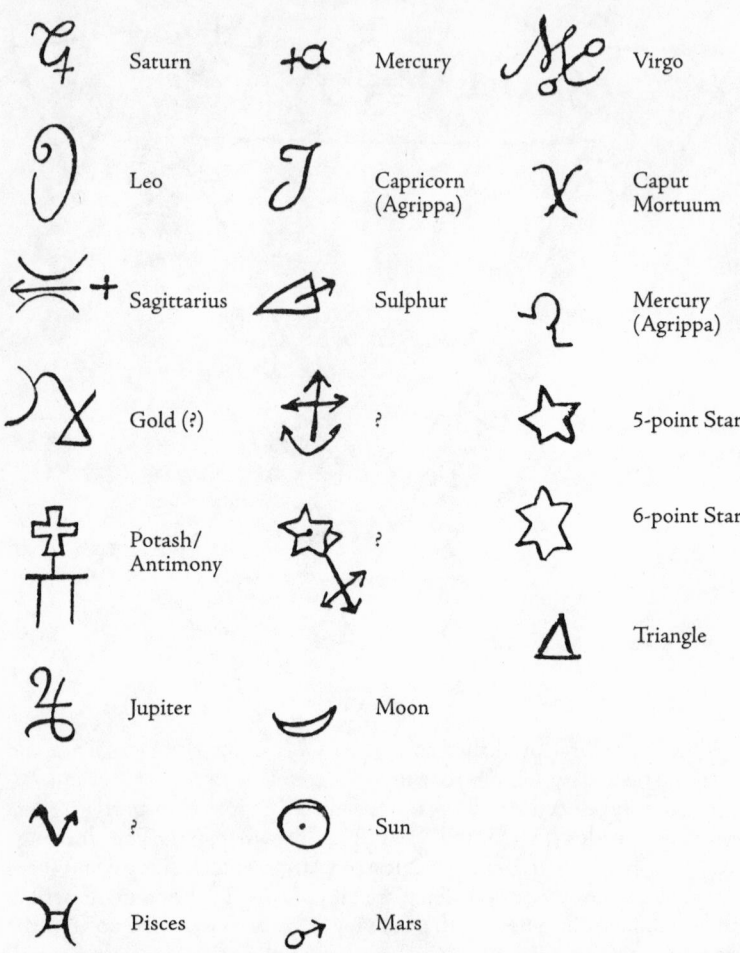

Saturn	Mercury	Virgo
Leo	Capricorn (Agrippa)	Caput Mortuum
Sagittarius	Sulphur	Mercury (Agrippa)
Gold (?)	?	5-point Star
Potash/ Antimony	?	6-point Star
Jupiter	Moon	Triangle
?	Sun	
Pisces	Mars	

urn. There is a certain symmetry to the symbols, as Schneider points out, insofar as a planetary symbol appears over each occurrence of "Spiritus."[90] Others are harder to identify. One appears to be an alternate, older symbol for Mercury. Another might be Pisces. Some of the other symbols could possibly be chemical or alchemical. One appears to be a symbol for sulphur, another alum or potash, still another *caput mortuum* (see chapter 5 for my discussion of Hegel's use of this alchemical term). The other symbols, which include seven stars (some with five points, others with six) and two smaller triangles, are of very uncertain origin.

90. Helmut Schneider, "Zur Dreiecks-Symbolik bei Hegel," 58.

Hegel regularly employed astrological, chemical, and alchemical symbols in his manuscripts, as abbreviations. These include the symbols for Sun, Moon, Earth, Mars, Venus, Jupiter, Saturn, Mercury, water, fire, acid, salt, salpeter, and sulphur.[91]

If this drawing is a copy no one has yet succeeded in locating the original. It does bear a striking resemblance to many alchemical and magical drawings in books that Hegel could have perused. For instance, as Helmut Schneider points out, many alchemical or magical diagrams were printed in more than one color of ink—typically black and red—and it could be that Hegel substituted pencil for the parts printed in red.[92] In truth, although Hegel's diagram looks superficially like many "Hermetic" illustrations, it is unusual in a number of respects, as I shall discuss shortly. I have printed two examples of genuine magical diagrams that contain elements similar to Hegel's as figures 3 and 4.

In 1810, Hegel began a correspondence with Karl Joseph Hieronymous Windischmann (1775–1839). In 1809, Windischmann had published a review of the *Phenomenology of Spirit* in the *Jenaische Allgemeine Literatur-Zeitung*.[93] Windischmann's review, which was positive, was one of the most significant to be published in Hegel's early career. Windischmann had studied philosophy and medicine at the universities of Mainz, Würzburg, and Vienna. In 1797 he began practicing medicine, but in 1803 he was made a professor of natural philosophy at Aschaffenburg. Windischmann was a Freemason (a fact of some significance, to which I will return in the following chapter), and during the period of his correspondence with Hegel he was engaged in a study of magic. In 1813 he would publish *Untersuchungen über Astrologie, Alchemie und Magie*.[94] Windischmann considered magic to be a special kind of controlling influence exerted by one individual on another (Hegel accepts this account completely—see chapter 6). However, he also attributed this power to natural forces, thus committing himself to a panpsychist phi-

91. See editorial matter in Hegel, *Gesammelte Werke*, ed. Klaus Düsing and Heinz Kimmerle, vol. 6 (Hamburg: Felix Meiner Verlag, 1975), 339.

92. Helmut Schneider, "Zur Dreiecks-Symbolik bei Hegel," 60. It could also be, as Schneider suggests, that this indicates that Hegel copied the diagram, substituting pencil for red. As I have said, however, no one has found the original and there are enough idiosyncrasies in the drawing—for instance the triple "Spiritus" rather than the usual "Spiritus-Anima-Corpus"—to indicate that it represents Hegel's appropriation of some occult symbols for his own purposes.

93. K. J. H. Windischmann, *Rezension, Phänomenologie des Geistes, Jenaische Allgemeine Literatur-Zeitung*, 31–34 (1809) columns 241–72.

94. In 1818 Windischmann was made professor of the history of philosophy at Bonn. Windischmann was a Roman Catholic and became increasingly orthodox as the years went on. This appears to have been partly the cause of a parting of the ways between Windischmann and Hegel (whose sentiments were decidedly anti-Catholic). The real break came in the 1820s when Hegel, lecturing on the *Philosophy of World History*, publicly accused Windischmann of having stolen his interpretation of Chinese philosophy. See Petry, *Philosophy of Subjective Spirit*, vol. 2, 573–75.

3. From an eighteenth-cenury manuscript known to Goethe. Reprinted in J. Scheible, *Doktor Johannes Fausts Magia naturalis et inaturalis oder Dreifacher Höllenswang, letztes Testament and Siegelkunst* (Stuttgart, 1849). Reprinted by permission of the Robert W. Woodruff Library, Special Collections and Archives, Emory University, Atlanta, Georgia.

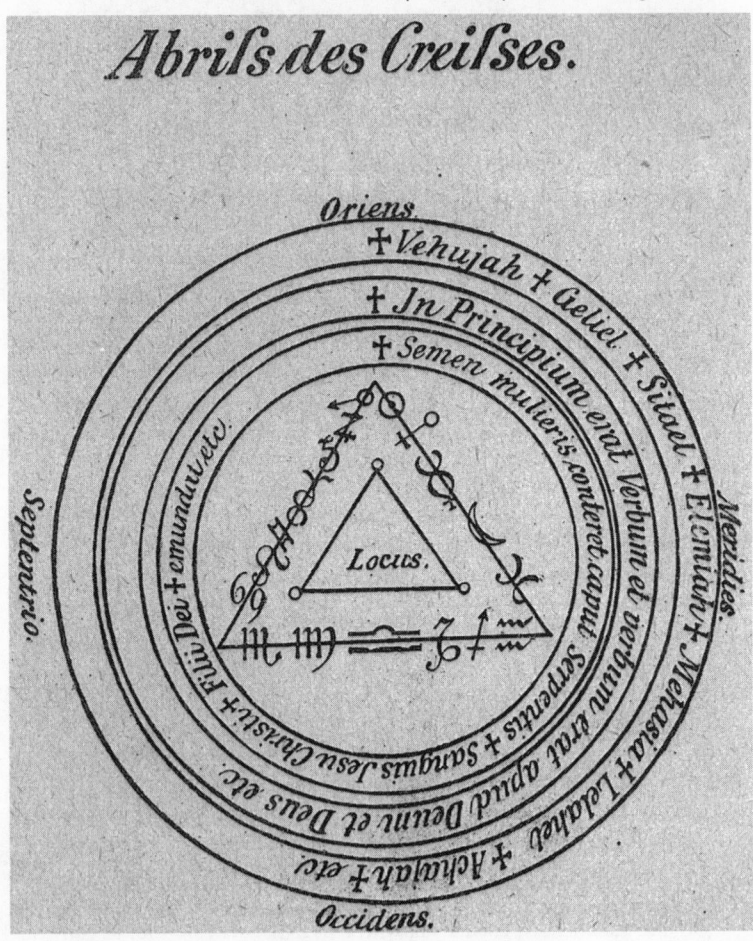

losophy of nature.[95] Windischmann wrote the following lines to Hegel concerning his research into magic:

> Everything rests on the fundamental thought that what is temporal, finite, in a state of becoming . . . is the eternal itself comprehended in its evolution, development, and self-knowledge, and that the impenetrable Spirit must of necessity individualize itself and take form in the infinity and infinite diversity of moments, which in themselves can nonetheless be most sharply grasped. In this way equally numerous forms of one-sidedness and of incantation are

95. See Butler, 559.

4. Illustration from Samuel Norton, *Mercurius redivivus* (1630).
Reprinted by permission of the estate of C. G. Jung.

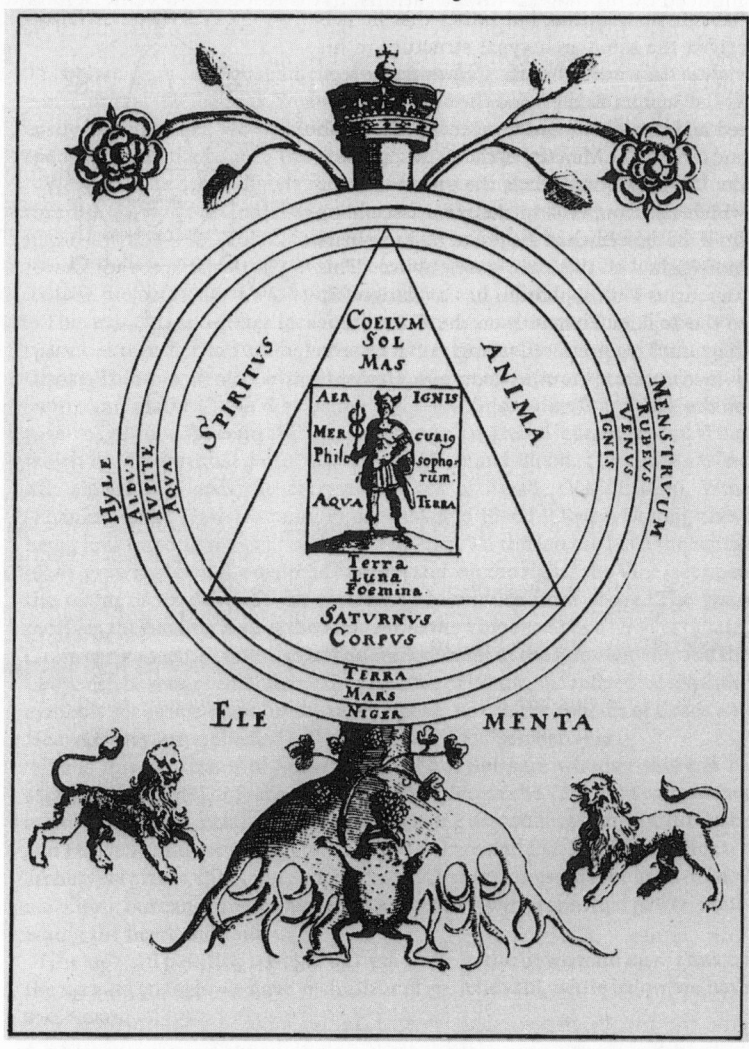

possible and effective, each along the path of Spirit's development.
All such forms must find their explication in this investigation,
beginning with the first and full magical power of the Impenetrable—and of Nature surging forth everywhere—over man, proceeding through the isolation and interlocking of moments, and
ending with the penetration, illumination, and complete magical
power of Spirit itself, which dissipates all magical incantation and
constitutes the clarity and freedom of life itself.[96]

96. Quoted in ibid., 559.

Windischmann goes on to complain of the terrible mental state induced by his magical investigations. In his response to Windischmann (May 27, 1810), Hegel offers his sympathy: "I am very curious to have your work on magic in hand. I confess I would not dare tackle this dark side and mode of spiritual nature or natural spirit, and am all the happier that you will both illuminate it for us and take up many a neglected and scorned subject, *restoring it to the honor it deserves*."[97]

It seems that Hegel is saying here that he has never deliberately delved into the area of the occult or of esoteric philosophy. But Hegel goes on to suggest—in a passage I shall quote at length—that he has at some point in the past undergone Windischmann's torments himself:

> Consider yourself convinced that the frame of mind you depict to me is partly due to this present work of yours, to this descent into dark regions where nothing is revealed as fixed, definite, and certain. . . . From my own experience I know this mood of the soul, or rather of reason, which arises when it has finally made its way with interest and hunches into a chaos of phenomena but, though inwardly certain of the goal, has not yet worked its way through them to clarity and to a detailed account of the whole. For a few years I suffered from this hypochondria to the point of exhaustion. Everybody probably has such a turning point in his life, the nocturnal point of the contraction of his essence in which he is forced through a narrow passage by which his confidence in himself and everyday life grows in strength and assurance. . . . Continue onward with confidence. It is science [*Wissenschaft*] which has led you into this labyrinth of the soul, and science alone is capable of leading you out again and healing you.[98]

It seems likely, as others have suggested, that Hegel is drawing here from his own experience in the Berne-Frankfurt period.[99] Recall that Rosenkranz places the beginning of Hegel's "theosophical phase" in Frankfurt. It is likely that Rosenkranz uses "theosophical" to refer to occult or Hermetic philosophy, rather than "mere" mysticism, for Rosenkranz knew that in Berne Hegel became interested in Eckhart and Tauler. (In other words, by characterizing the Frankfurt period alone, and not the Berne-Frankfurt periods together, as Hegel's "theosophical stage" Rosenkranz implies that the "theosophy" in question was not the mysticism of Eckhart and Tauler.) Helmut Schneider writes: "Hegel had connections [*Beziehungen*] to alchemy, gnosticism, Rosicrucianism, Freemasonry, and astrology. The drawing is perfectly locatable within this horizon [*Horizont*]."[100] My hypothesis is that the triangle diagram represents, to use Hegel's own words, "a turning point," a "nocturnal point of the contraction of his essence." It represents Hegel's initial synthesis of theosophy—such as he was exposed to in his Swabian *Heimat*, as well as whatever else he encountered in Frankfurt—with the

97. Ibid., 561; Hoffmeister #158; my italics.
98. Butler, 561; Hoffmeister #158.
99. See Butler, 560.
100. Ibid., 73.

idealism of Kant and Fichte, which, as we have seen, he studied in earnest during the same period.[101]

The word *Spiritus* occurs three times in the midst of astrological and (possibly) alchemical symbols, on each of the sides of the central triangle. This could represent Hegel's philosophical realization that all reality—whether celestial (the planets) or terrestrial (the elements)—must be understood in terms of the development of Spirit.[102] Around the probable time of the Triangle fragment Hegel begins using the term *Geist* to speak of the divine: "A more intelligible expression for the notion of God as the universal life [*Allebens*] is the term *Love*, but a deeper one is *Spirit*."[103] Nature is to be seen as an expression of the divine Idea, and mankind (*Spirit*) as the highest expression of nature, and the consummation or completion of the divine. *Spiritus* is the "magic word" that evokes the "shape" of the Absolute, which allows us to comprehend the Absolute in its totality.

Hegel's early presentation of his system (ca. 1802–3) consisted of four parts: Logic and Metaphysics, Philosophy of Nature, System of Ethical Life, and theory of the Absolute Idea (art, religion, and philosophy).[104] The later Hegel, of course, collapsed the third and fourth parts into Philosophy of Spirit, turning the System of Ethical Life into Objective Spirit. (The triangle and the square thus seem to vie with one another in the Jena period for the honor of being Hegel's central symbolic form.) If the diagram is from this period, the large triangle might possibly represent Absolute Spirit, and the smaller triangles the other parts of the system.

It is also possible that the four triangles represent the four elements. In his mature *Philosophy of Nature* (1819–1830), Hegel identifies the "Mineral Kingdom" with Earth, the "Plant Kingdom" with water and the "Animal Kingdom" with fire. Hegel suggests that fire gives way to "etheriality" (*das Aetherische*) but never explicitly identifies man with air, the fourth element. This is, of course, the obvious move to make, for

---

101. Helmut Schneider, "Zur Dreiecks-Symbolik bei Hegel," 76, states that it is probably impossible to date the drawing with any certainty.

102. The term *Spiritus* is quite common in alchemical and magical diagrams. It is generally part of a triad: *Spiritus*, *Anima* (Soul), *Corpus* (Body). The fact that Hegel includes only *Spiritus* and writes it three times ("taking the place" of *Anima* and *Corpus*) could indicate that Spirit is being *absolutized* vis-à-vis Body (materiality: the four elements) and Soul (this is a possible reading of the *Philosophy of Spirit*, in which "soul" [*Seele*] appears at the lowest level, before Spirit proper; Sean Kelly notes that "soul" is the mediating, common term between Spirit and nature). See Kelly, *Individuation and the Absolute* (New York: Paulist Press, 1993), 38. In his *Lectures on the History of Philosophy*, in the exposition of Böhme's thought, Hegel refers to Böhme's "three kinds of powers or *Spiritus* in different *Centris*, but in one *Corpore*" (LHP 3:214; *Werke* 20:116). However, the description which follows does not appear to shed any light on the diagram.

103. As noted above, Rosenkranz paraphrases this line in his account. The line, as I have given it, appears as a direct quotation from the fragment in Haym's *Hegel und seine Zeit*, 101.

104. Harris, *Night Thoughts*, xlix; see also Harris's Introduction to the *System of Ethical Life*, 6.

air = *pneuma* = *Spiritus*. Thus, in our diagram, the central triangle could represent man/air, and the other triangles nonliving matter/Earth, plants/water, animals/fire.

But why is the *Spiritus* triangle surrounded by astronomical and other symbols? This can be explained if we remember the connection Aristotle draws between *pneuma* and *aether*. In the *Generation of Animals* he writes, "Now it is true that the faculty of all kinds of soul seems to have a connection with a matter different from and more divine than the so-called elements. . . . All have in their semen that which causes it to be productive. I mean what is called *thermon*. This is not the fire or any such [sublunary] force, but it is the *pneuma* included in the semen and the foam-like, and the natural principle in the pneuma [is] like the element in the stars" (736b29–737a1). The element in the stars is, of course, aether. Insofar as we humans are knowers (i.e., receivers of form), we contain something of this astral substance. (Plotinus takes the doctrine a step further, claiming that we possess an astral or aetherial *body*, which was to become a major tenet of the later Hermetic philosophy and of the contemporary "New Age.")

Thus, to follow out this chain of equivalences and connections, if man = *Spiritus* = *pneuma*, and the *pneuma* or life-force of man contains *aether*, and *aether* is the substance of the heavenly bodies, then there is an identity between man and the heavenly bodies. Thus, Hegel blends *Spiritus* with the planets and stars. If Hegel is drawing on all of this, it is a way for him to state what I said earlier: that all reality—whether celestial or terrestrial is to be understood in terms of Spirit as its telos. (As I have already mentioned and will discuss much more fully in chapter 6, the aether is an important concept for Hegel.)

But this is by no means the only possible interpretation of the diagram. If we take the central triangle as representing the Trinity, each point stands for a person of the Trinity: Father (divine *Logos*), Son (created Nature), and Holy Spirit. *Spiritus* is written on each side, perhaps, because the first two "moments" of the Trinity are comprehended by the third. The Father and the Son are *aufgehoben* in the Spirit. As this is not a temporal sequence but a logical one, Father and Son are always already within the whole that is Spirit. The sides of the triangle unite and, in fact, create the points, the "moments" of the divine whole. Father and Son are what they are through Spirit. Thus, the sides of the triangle are identified with *Spiritus*, which is both an individual point of the triangle and that which permeates and bonds together the whole. (Here we see the fundamental inadequacy of pictorial expressions of speculative philosophy: what can only be understood through Reason is expressed in a mode suited to the Understanding, which is quite literally "two-dimensional" thinking.)

It is also, of course, possible that the central triangle represents Spirit alone, and the three smaller triangles, Father, Son, and Holy Spirit. If this is the case, a similar analysis applies: Hegel draws a large, central triangle of Spirit, pointing to the other three, to indicate how Spirit is not simply a moment of the Trinity, but the "final" moment that comprehends and binds together the Trinity itself. If, however, we take the central triangle to represent the Trinity, then perhaps the three smaller triangles represent the individual "sciences" of the Trinity: Logic, Philosophy of Nature, and Philosophy of Spirit.

I have suggested that the diagram represents a synthesis of theosophy with the Fichtean-Kantian idealism because the diagram, amidst much arcane "Hermetic" symbolism, seems to represent the absolutization of human Spirit or Ego. Recall Schelling's 1795 letter to Hegel, quoted in the last chapter: "For Spinoza the world, the object by itself in opposition to the subject, was *everything*. For me it is the *self*."[105] My suggestion is that Hegel's diagram represents a stage (or a step) in Hegel's thought parallel to Schelling's: the modification of a Spinozistic-Kabbalistic-pantheistic nature mysticism with an absolutization of Spirit or Ego as *Ziel* and *Quelle* of nature itself. (It is also possible, of course, that Hegel realized that this "synthesis" was in fact similar to the Böhmean-Oetingerite brand of theosophy.)

Earlier in this chapter I spoke of the historicity of Hegel's speculation and stated that it could only have been accomplished after history itself was consummated, after human beings have recognized themselves as free and self-determining, not determined by an Absolute which stands opposed to humanity as an absolute other. If the composition of the triangle diagram represents Hegel's realization of the centrality of Spirit or Ego, then the diagram constitutes, in effect, a kind of marker point at the end of history.

It certainly seems plausible to suggest, then, that the diagram represents the inspiration that led Hegel to "convert" to a form of Schellingian idealism. What is significant here is that the conversion, contrary to what is usually maintained, appears not to have been the result of Hegel's moving in a straight line from Kant to Fichte and finally to Schelling, as the latest and most adequate exponent of idealism. Rather, the conversion was more likely effected through Hegel's realization that Schelling's Identity philosophy represented a revision of the Kantian-Fichtean philosophy in accord with the "deep truth" revealed through Proclus, Eckhart, Böhme, Oetinger, and the alchemists.

7. Summary of the Argument Thus Far

The present chapter has been largely "programmatic": laying out an account of how Hegel's overall project can be understood as a reappropriation of Hermetic ideals, themes, and symbols. In the next four chapters, I will develop an interpretation of Hegel's mature philosophical writings and lectures in terms of my understanding of their debts to and affinity with the Hermetic tradition. I will continue to introduce sources that may have influenced Hegel and continue to spell out in what way I regard his work as itself belonging to the Hermetic tradition. Before moving on to that account, a brief summary of the argument thus far seems in order.

105. Quoted in Butler, 32.

Hegel's thought is not a part of the history of philosophy. It represents an altogether different standpoint, one that represents *completed wisdom*, not the search for wisdom. Hegel is a wise man offering not *Philosophie* but *Wissenschaft, scientia, episteme*. He calls this science of wisdom"speculation" and opposes it to reflection (*Reflexion*). Recall that "speculation" comes from *speculum*, mirror. Reflection is not the "mirroring" Hegel advocates, because it is a mere "duplication"—observation or phenomenological description, such as we find in Kant's Transcendental Aesthetic and Analytic or later in Husserl's phenomenology.

Hegel in the *Encyclopedia Logic* states that "the term 'reflection' is primarily used of light, when, propagated rectilinearly, it strikes a mirrored surface and is thrown back by it" (EL § 112, Z; Geraets, 176). Reflection or understanding thinks within a straitjacket of false dichotomies, thus it receives back from its contemplation only what it has put into it: its "rays of thought" are merely reflected back to it. By contrast, dialectical thinking does not involve projections from the thinker: instead, it allows the medium within which the thinker thinks to itself "shine forth" truth (see figure 5). Speculation's *speculum* does not merely reflect the surface appearance *of the individual*. It is, instead, a "magic mirror," reflecting the deepest essence *of Spirit*. According to Kabbalistic tradition, Moses alone among prophets or wise men "gazed through a speculum that shines."[106] Hegel is the modern Moses receiving the new Word and Covenant of God, not on Sinai but on the Golgotha of Absolute Spirit, not at the beginning of history but at its end.[107]

Like Moses (according to legend), Hegel is the recipient of Kabbalistic wisdom, only it is a Christian Kabbalah, and it is received not directly from God but from Böhme, Oetinger, and the tradition of speculative Pietism. Hegel's "Kabbalah" is a revelation of eternal truth through the self-unfolding of Absolute Knowledge, the self-grounding display of an organic thought-form that is itself the actualization of God in the world. This revelation of God is at the same time the complete speech of the Whole. It is a reconciliation of faith and scientific knowledge, without following the Kantian route of limiting knowledge to make room for faith. Hegel's system, furthermore, represents the overcoming of the distinction between the "wise" and the "vulgar," and the achievement of the classical philosophical ideal of self-knowledge.[108]

106. See Elliot R. Wolfson, *Through a Speculum that Shines: Vision and Imagination in Medieval Jewish Mysticism* (Princeton, N.J.: Princeton University Press, 1994), 147.

107. Kojève remarks that "The Wise Man . . . entrusts himself without reserve to Being and opens himself entirely to the Real without resisting it. His role is that of a perfectly flat and indefinitely extended mirror: he does not reflect on the Real; it is the Real that reflects on him, is reflected in his consciousness, and is revealed in its own dialectical structure by the discourse of the Wise Man who describes it without deforming it." See Alexandre Kojève, *Introduction to the Reading of Hegel*, trans. James H. Nichols, Jr. (Ithaca, N.Y.: Cornell University Press, 1969), 176.

108. The "wise-vulgar" distinction *is* overcome in Hegel, but certainly not in the sense that his philosophy is fully intelligible to everyone. In the *Lectures on*

5. "Speculation" graphically depicted. Frontispiece to Johann Joachim
Becher, *Psychosophia oder Seelan-Weisheit* (Lauenberg, 1707). Reprinted
by permission of the J. R. Ritman Library, Bibliotheca Philosophica
Hermetica, Amsterdam.

Hegel's science further distinguishes itself from philosophy by containing nothing that could conventionally be called "proof" or argumentation. It is a self-grounding speech. It is, furthermore, a realization of

the Philosophy of Religion (1:180; VPR, 88), Hegel states that "Religion is for
everyone. It is not philosophy, which is not for everyone." He overcomes the
distinction primarily by showing that the content of philosophy is identical
to that of religion, which is accessible to the common man. Also, Hegel's philosophy provides an intellectual framework which can be taught to everyone
to a certain degree (as Hegel thought he had proved at the Gymnasium in
Nuremberg).

Oetinger's quest for a "third" form of thought, cutting a middle course between a purely figurative or imaginative approach to the divine and a purely "abstract" one. Hegel's new form of thought resolves the quarrel between philosophy and mytho-poetic thought. Hegel adopts the Hermetic ideal of a perennial philosophy, treating his dialectic, the "method" of speculation, as a "recollection" of the inchoate wisdom of mankind that has been expressed in art, religion, mythology, and philosophy in imperfect form.

The real power behind dialectic, the power that makes recollection possible, is imagination. Hegel recognizes perennial symbolic forms (recall the *Phenomenology*; Miller, 29) and draws them, in effect, from what Oetinger called *sensus communis*.[109] His use of them in the architectonic of his system is strikingly similar to the Hermetic "memory magic" of Bruno and others (in particular, as we shall see in chapter 5, that of Ramon Lull). Hegel also engages in a form of analogical reasoning suspiciously like the Hermetic "science of correspondences." Recall his attempt to map the forms of the terrestrial world onto the four elements, as well as, most strikingly, the ubiquitous Trinitarian structure. Recall that Oetinger opposed his science of "emblematics" (another variation on the *ars memoria*) to the modern geometrical, quantitative method. In Hegel we find the two, as might be expected, *aufgehoben*: the symbolic forms, the "emblems" that animate speculation are themselves "quantitative" (or "quantifiable") forms. A numerology pervades Hegel's system, in particular a fascination with Proclean triads.

Hegel conceives the whole articulated through dialectic exactly along the lines of Oetinger's *intensum*. Recall that an *intensum* is an organic whole that cannot be divided into pieces, but only articulated into inseparable, noetic "moments." Principal among the moments articulated in Hegel's science is a triad equivalent to the Christian Trinity. Exactly as Böhme and some versions of Kabbalism do, Hegel conceives the first moment, the Christian "Father," as God "in-Himself," *in potentia*. God is the eternal *Logos*; hence, Logic. Exactly as do Eckhart, Cusa, Böhme, and Goethe, Hegel conceives the second moment, the "Son," as Nature. Through the third moment, Spirit, God achieves full actuality as "objective" and "absolute" Spirit, the Hegelian analogues to Oetinger's *Geistleiblichkeit*. Spirit is the most adequate "embodiment" of God.

As we have seen, Hegel employs the language of "magic" to describe his system. Recall the fragment quoted by Rosenkranz in which Hegel bids us to learn "to speak the magic words" which evoke the "shape" of the Absolute.[110] Further, in a passage also quoted earlier, Hegel writes in the *Phenomenology*: "Spirit is this power only by looking the negative in the face and tarrying with it. This tarrying with the negative is the

109. The truth which speculation finds within poetry (or myth) and rational (philosophical) thought, and which it takes up and preserves, is none other than the perennial philosophy. Hegel held that the philosopher is not sufficient unto himself. Like Socrates in the *Crito*, he held that the people and its *nomoi* give birth to the philosopher.

110. Rosenkranz, *Hegels Leben*, 141.

magical power that converts it into being" (Miller, 32). And Hegel's remarks about "real" magic often express a respectful, if cautious, curiosity. I have already quoted Hegel's letter to Windischmann, in which he writes, "I am very curious to have your work on magic in hand," and expresses his hope that Windishmann will restore his subject "to the honor it deserves." I will discuss Hegel's interest in magic and the paranormal in chapter 6.

Hegel's attitude toward alchemy is similar. Also in chapter 6, I will deal in detail with Hegel's indebtedness to alchemy. For now, I will simply mention that in Hegel's *Naturphilosophie* lectures of 1803 he connects the division "metals-combustibles-neutrals-earths" with Paracelsus's distinction "mercury-sulphur-salt."[111] Earlier I noted how in his early philosophy of nature, Hegel reverently refers to Paracelsus and Böhme as "the Elders." And, to repeat, even where Hegel draws on more recent sources he insists, as Harris puts it, "on finding an earlier pedigree . . . in Paracelsus and Böhme."[112] Harris speaks of Hegel's "evident desire to show that the older alchemical tradition of Paracelsus (and probably Böhme himself) contained symbolic expressions of important speculative truths."[113]

In the introduction, I briefly mentioned one aspect of Hermeticism that, so far, I have not discussed extensively: initiation. If Hegel believed that the reception of the system of science could be accomplished simply by reading about it in a book, he would not have first written the *Phenomenology of Spirit*. As I said of Hermetic initiation in the introduction, one must be led up to illumination carefully; one must actually explore the blind alleys that promise illumination but do not deliver, and one must be purified of false presuppositions. Only in this way will the true doctrine mean anything; only in this way will the initiate's life actually change. As I have said, Hegel's system is not simply a "theory" about the world; it is meant to *transfigure* our experience and effect a new way of being in the world. The *Phenomenology of Spirit* is Hegel's initiatory experience. It is Hegel's Eleusis, it is his Bacchanalian revel.

111. See Harris, *Night Thoughts*, 274; G. W. F. Hegel, *Gesammelte Werke* 6:114, 4–17.
112. Harris, *Night Thoughts*, 278.
113. Ibid., 399.

Part 2. Magnum Opus

Hegel's Initiation Rite:
The Phenomenology of Spirit

1. Initiation

The Phenomenology of Spirit was conceived by Hegel in 1806 as an intro-duction or propaedeutic to the tripartite system of Logic-Nature-Spirit. It is therefore quite reasonable to ask if the Phenomenology is really a nec-essary part of the system, or merely something "tacked on."

Hegel's Absolute, unlike Schelling's, cannot be expressed in a simple formula, like "the indifference point," or "the coincidence of opposites." According to Hegel, to grasp the Absolute we must go through the Sci-ence, go through every moment of the Absolute, and remake it for our-selves. Furthermore, a preparatory exercise is necessary before we can reach this point. A few lines down from the passage just quoted, Hegel writes that "truth is not a minted coin that can be given and pocketed ready-made" (Miller, 22; PG, 29).[1] Hegel believed that the consummation of the love of wisdom in Absolute Knowing was not equally possible in every historical epoch. Instead, he held that his achievement was pos-sible only at a particular point in history, the end of history, when the philosophical, cultural and religious achievements of the ages were spread out before his gaze, when the accumulated substance of history was converted to an account on which he could draw. Furthermore, he could not have acquired Wisdom without the consciousness of this ground. Thus, it is not enough to stand with Hegel at the end of history and read his books: one must work through the system in full con-sciousness of what has made it possible, and one must overcome all false or partial standpoints that would make assimilation of the system impossible.

If the Phenomenology is intended in part to acquaint readers with the intellectual and cultural strata on which the system stands, then is it a work of history? In a way, yes. In the final paragraph of the Phenomenol-ogy, Hegel writes that the totality of the forms of Spirit "regarded from the side of their free existence appearing in the form of contingency, is History; but regarded from the side of their [intellectually] compre-hended organization, it is the Science of Knowing in the sphere of appearance." (Miller, 493; PG, 531). The Phenomenology of Spirit displays the forms in which Spirit has appeared in time. We may think of each as

---

1. This is an allusion to Lessing's Nathan the Wise, 4:6.

a "mode" of consciousness or mind. Hegel shows how each "mode" is an approximation of what he calls at the end of the book "Absolute Knowing."[2] The *Phenomenology* stands in the same relation to history as the *Philosophy of Nature* stands to nature. The *Philosophy of Nature* is an account of the fundamental moments, the eidetic divisions, which nature exhibits to scientific consciousness. It is not a history of nature, in the sense that Hegel thought that natural beings appeared in the order of his chapter headings and divisions. (Hegel rejected biological evolution.) Similarly, the object of the *Phenomenology* is not to present a history of mind, but a "natural history" of its fundamental forms in their logical relationship.

As is often pointed out by confused readers, however, Hegel covers much the same ground again in the *Philosophy of Spirit* (which even includes a section titled "Phenomenology"). This is true, but the context and purpose of the *Philosophy of Spirit* are completely different from those of the *Phenomenology*. The *Phenomenology of Spirit* shows that all forms of consciousness or mind aim at Absolute Knowing. This includes cultural or social forms in which mind "embodies" itself, such as natural science, art, and religion. However, none of these forms actually achieves Absolute Knowing. Hegel's purpose in the *Phenomenology* is to give his readers a total theory of psychology, science, society, culture, and history in terms of their telos, Absolute Knowing. The *Phenomenology* is an Aristotelian Science, understanding all of its objects in terms of their "striving" after the knowledge of God.

The *Phenomenology* merely describes Absolute Knowing; it does not achieve Absolute Knowing itself. This is the task primarily of the *Logic*, for in working out the categories of the *Logic* the self-reflection of Idea is realized. The categories of the *Logic* are never explicitly discussed in the *Phenomenology*, but they are there beneath the surface. The *Logic* is the recollection of the categorial structures underlying Spirit. The *Logic* is the unconscious in-itself of Spirit become for-itself. In the *Philosophy of Nature* we understand nature as an "other" to Idea, striving to *express* Idea. The *Philosophy of Spirit* repeats much of the ground of the *Phenomenology*, this time in the full context of an understanding of Idea and its imperfect embodiment in nature. Spirit must be covered again, for once we have glimpsed Idea, and understood the antecedents of Spirit in nature, our understanding of Spirit will of necessity be transformed.

The *Phenomenology* shows why every standpoint other than Absolute Knowing is partial or false and must be abandoned. The *Phenomenology* is the tool by which Hegel puts his readers in the "frame of mind" necessary to work through the pure determinations of the Idea in-itself. This is not the purpose of the *Philosophy of Spirit*. But why work through the *Phenomenology* and the rest of the system? Why achieve Absolute Knowing? In effect, I answered this question in the preceding chapter when I

2. Hegel writes in the preface: "It is this coming-to-be of Science as such or of knowledge that is described in the Phenomenology of Spirit" (Miller, 15; PG, 21).

said that Hegelian philosophy will constitute a perfected form of living in the world; in the words of H. S. Harris, "an actual experience of living in the light of the eternal day."[3] This is the attraction. All philosophy, including Hegel's, presupposes that at least some men yearn to know themselves and the world fully.[4] Just as the magicians of old—men such as Agrippa and Bruno—believed that knowledge of the right incantations could give one tremendous power, so Hegel believes that knowledge of the "magic words" that evoke the Absolute can empower the individual by reconciling him with the world. Kojève defines the Hegelian wise man as the man of both perfect self-consciousness and perfect self-satisfaction.[5] Wisdom and self-satisfaction do not consist, however, in ego-aggrandizement, but in the transcendence of ego and identification with Spirit as such. Kojève writes: "For Self-consciousness to exist, for philosophy to exist, there must be *transcendence* of self with respect to self as given."[6] H. S. Harris notes that "In [Hegel's] view we have to annihilate our own selfhood in order to enter the sphere where Philosophy herself speaks."[7] Here again we see a clear affinity with mysticism.

If it is the task of the *Phenomenology* to achieve this transcendence of the self, then the *Phenomenology* begins to look like a mystical initiation. It is a work that "purifies" the reader for the reception of Divine Wisdom. Traditionally, Hermes, the guide of souls, presided over the initiation rites of the mystery religions.[8] Garth Fowden writes of the Hermetic initiation that "it is not envisaged as a form or symbol, or something that one just reads about, but as a real experience, stretching all the capacities of those who embark upon it: 'for it is an extremely tortuous way, to abandon what one is used to and possesses now, and to retrace one's steps towards the old primordial things.'"[9] (Anyone who has ever attempted to read the *Phenomenology* knows how it can stretch all of one's capacities and be a "tortuous way," indeed, a highway of despair!)

Fowden writes in the same context that "the [Hermetic] initiation falls into two phases, the former emphasizing self-knowledge, the latter knowledge of God."[10] Again, there is an interesting parallel to Hegelian philosophy. The *Phenomenology* can be thought of as a voyage of self-discovery, whereas the rest of the system (also a tortuous way) is a dis-

3. H. S. Harris, *Night Thoughts*, 199.
4. "Hegelian Wisdom is a necessary ideal only for a definite type of human being, namely, for the man who puts the supreme value in Self-consciousness; and only this man can realize this ideal. . . . In other words: the Platonic-Hegelian ideal of Wisdom is valid only for the Philosopher" (Kojève, *Introduction to the Reading of Hegel*, 84).
5. Ibid., 76–77. Kojève's third definition is that the wise man is the "morally perfect man" (Kojève, *Introduction to the Reading of Hegel*, 78).
6. Ibid., 39.
7. Harris, *Night Thoughts*, 51.
8. Joseph Campbell, *The Hero with a Thousand Faces* (Princeton, N.J.: Princeton University Press, 1968), 73.
9. Fowden, *The Egyptian Hermes: A Historical Approach to the Late Pagan Mind* (Princeton, N.J.: Princeton University Press, 1993), 106. Fowden is quoting *Corpus Hermeticum*, treatise iv, § 9.
10. Ibid.

covery of the Absolute or God. Of course, as I have already indicated, the entire Hegelian philosophy is both a knowledge of the Whole and of the self. In a discussion of Oriental mysteries that is applicable to the Hermetic tradition, Joseph Campbell writes: "In the sacred books of the Orient, the ultimate mystery of being is said to be transcendent, in the sense that it 'transcends'. . . human knowledge, thought, sight, and speech. However, since it is explicitly identified with the mystery of our own being, and of all being whatsoever, it is declared to be immanent as well: in fact, that is the main point of most Oriental, as well as of most pagan, primitive, and mystical initiations."[11]

Jacques d'Hondt and others have claimed that the *Phenomenology*'s "initiation" was inspired by the Masons. John Burbidge writes that the *Phenomenology*, "with its lengthy and arduous process of initiation, came at a time when Hegel was frequenting the company of known Masons, some of them graduates of the banned *Illuminati*."[12] K. J. H. Windischmann, a Mason discussed in the last chapter, took the *Phenomenology of Spirit* as a Masonic manifesto in the tradition of Lessing. He refers to this elliptically in an 1810 letter to Hegel: "The study of your system of Science has convinced me that this work will some day, when the time of understanding arrives, become the primer [*Elementarbuch*] of the liberation of mankind, as foretold by Lessing. You understand, of course, what I am trying to say, and you also recognize what this work is to me (not merely as *writing* [*Schrift*], but as *work* [*Werk*])."[13] It is significant that a Mason—on the basis of a few cues—could so easily take the *Phenomenology* as a Masonic document.[14]

In chapter 2, I discussed the Masonic character of Hegel's 1796 poem "Eleusis." Significantly, the *Phenomenology* makes several references to the Eleusinian initiation mysteries. The most famous occurs in the preface: "Appearance is the arising and passing away which itself does not arise or pass away, but is in-itself [*an sich*], and constitutes the actuality and movement of the life of truth. The True is thus the Bacchanalian revel [*bacchantische Taumel*] in which no member is not drunk; yet because each member collapses as soon as he drops out, the revel is just as much transparent and simple repose" (Miller, 27; PG, 35). The Eleusinian mysteries and the cult of Dionysus (Bacchus) were associated with each other starting around the late fifth century and early fourth century.[15] Later in the *Phenomenology*, Hegel refers to the "Eleusinian mysteries of Ceres and Bacchus" (Miller, 65; PG, 77; the poem "Eleusis" also refers to Ceres, or Demeter).

Another allusion to Bacchus/Dionysus appears in the preface in Hegel's discussion of the essential moment of negativity in the path to

11. Joseph Campbell, *The Masks of God*, vol. 3, *Occidental Mythology* (New York: Penguin Books, 1964), 109.

12. See Burbidge's introduction to D'Hondt's *Hegel in his Time*, xi.

13. April 27, 1810; Hoffmeister #155.

14. D'Hondt, *Hegel Secret*, 299–300.

15. Martin P. Nilsson, *Greek Folk Religion* (Philadelphia: University of Pennsylvania Press, 1978), 48.

Absolute Knowing:"But the life of Spirit is not the life that shrinks from death and keeps itself untouched by devastation, but rather the life that endures it and maintains itself in it. It wins its truth only when, in utter dismemberment, it finds itself" (Miller, 19; PG, 26). Like the Egyptian Osiris, Dionysus was, of course, torn to pieces and then resurrected. To a Mason, these lines would have been highly significant. The central legend in Masonry is that of Hiram, the master builder, who was murdered, buried, resurrected, dismembered, put together again, and then reburied. Each Master Mason is supposed to identify himself in his initiation with Hiram. As Alexander Piatigorsky writes, "All Master Masons are raised from a Figurative Death."[16] What dies in them is ignorance. They are "torn apart" and then led to enlightenment. "The candidate moves from total ignorance to the knowledge of the Word, or from the total darkness to the light which would enable him to 'leaven the death.'"[17]

In *Bruno*, Schelling has "Anselm" remark that in the Eleusinian rites, "men first learned that there is something unchanging, uniform, and indivisible beyond the things that ceaselessly change and slide from shape to shape."[18] Anselm then invites Bruno to describe the kind of philosophy imparted by the mysteries. Hegel accepts Schelling's description of the mysteries completely. In the *Phenomenology*, he writes that

> we can tell those who assert the truth and certainty of the reality of sense-objects that they should go back to the most elementary school of wisdom, viz. the ancient Eleusinian mysteries of Ceres and Bacchus, and that they have still to learn the secret meaning of the eating of bread and the drinking of wine. For he who is initiated into these Mysteries not only comes to doubt the being of sensuous things, but to despair of it; in part he brings about the nothingness of such things himself in his dealings with them, and in part he sees them reduce themselves to nothingness. (Miller, 65; PG, 77)

Schelling remarks that the purpose of "all the mystery rites is none other than to show men the archetypes of all that they are accustomed to seeing in images."[19] Hegel's *Phenomenology* is an initiation into the knowledge of those "archetypes" (the categories of the *Logic*) via a transcendence of the understanding, with its penchant for the particular and for the image.

Martin P. Nilsson writes that the Eleusinian rites consisted "in the seeing by the mystae of something which was shown to them."[20] The

---

16. Alexander Piatigorsky, *Who's Afraid of Freemasons? The Phenomenon of Freemasonry* (London: The Harvill Press, 1997), 376.
17. Ibid., 273. Italics in original.
18. F. W. J. Schelling, *Bruno: Or on the Natural and Divine Principle of Things*, in *Werke*, 3:233 (pagination corresponds to *Sämtliche Werke*). English translation: Michael G. Vater (Albany: State University of New York Press, 1984), 134.
19. Ibid., 233; 134.
20. Nilsson, *Greek Folk Religion*, 43.

Phenomenology is just such a showing. It is a "gallery of images" (Miller, 492; PG, 530).[21] It is the self-display of the phenomena of Spirit. (Heidegger writes: "*phainomenon* [in Greek] means that which shows itself, the manifest."[22])

2. Hermetic influences

a) Jena

The *Phenomenology of Spirit* was conceived and written in Jena, where Hegel lived for about six years. We know that during this period Hegel was actively interested in theosophy, a holdover from his time in Frankfurt (see chapter 3). It is likely that both the Triangle fragment and diagram date from the Jena period, though the diagram may have been drawn just prior.

Hegel's lectures on the Philosophy of Nature during this time reflect an ongoing interest in alchemy. In the lectures of 1803 the division "metals-combustibles-neutrals-earths" is connected with Paracelsus's distinction "mercury-sulphur-salt."[23] To repeat H. S. Harris's observation, this reflects Hegel's peculiar insistence on "finding an earlier pedigree [for his observations] . . . in Paracelsus and Böhme."[24] Hegel also speaks of the "virgin earth," an old alchemical conception, possibly originating with Böhme, which we first encountered in chapter 2 in connection with Goethe's alchemical experiments. The 1803 lectures also contain discussions of "noble" and "base" metals, as well as a hierarchical structure of metals (though Hegel is somewhat sceptical of the latter).[25] As noted in the preceding chapter, Hegel sometimes referred ideas to "the elders" whom Harris takes to be "the alchemists."[26]

It was in Jena as well that Hegel became deeply immersed in Böhme. H. S. Harris is "inclined to believe in Böhme's influence upon Hegel from 1801 onwards."[27] Harris contends that Hegel initially viewed Böhme with uncritical enthusiasm. In 1804–5, however, Hegel gained some critical distance, while remaining sympathetic. Recall that Hegel's account of Böhme in his 1805 *Lectures on the History of Philosophy* is strikingly detailed and positive.[28]

Hegel's interest in, and sympathy for, Böhme must have been widely known. In 1811, one of Hegel's former Jena students, Peter Gabriel van

21. In the *Lectures on the Philosophy of Religion*, Hegel declares that the idea that the mysteries imparted a special wisdom is "stupid" and "absurd" (LPR 2:181–82; VPR 2:87–88). Eleusis was significant for Hegel as a *symbol*, but he did not believe that the true and final philosophy was taught there.
22. Martin Heidegger, *Being and Time*, trans. John Macquarrie and Edward Robinson (New York: Harper and Row, 1962), 51.
23. Harris, *Night Thoughts*, 274; *Differenz*, 114, 4–17. Harris also notes that in the same manuscript Hegel links his use of "earth" with Böhme.
24. Harris, *Night Thoughts*, 278.
25. Ibid., 274.
26. Ibid., 274, n.
27. Ibid., 85; as Harris notes there are indications of Böhme's influence in the manuscripts of 1801–3 (161).
28. LHP 3:288; not present in *Werke*, see *Sämtliche Werke*, vol. 19, ed. Hermann Glockner (Stuttgart: Fromann, 1928), 377.

Ghert (1782–1852), a Dutchman, sent him Böhme's collected works as a gift. Van Ghert would not have done this unless it was plain to those who knew Hegel in Jena how important Böhme was to him. Hegel thanked van Ghert in a letter of July 29, 1811: "Now I can study Jakob Böhme much more closely than before, since I was not myself in possession of his writings. His theosophy will always be one of the most remarkable attempts of a penetrating yet uncultivated man to comprehend the innermost essential nature of the absolute being. For Germany, he has the special interest of being really the first German philosopher."[29] This shows not only that Hegel intended to continue his study of Böhme, but also that he regarded Böhme as a genuine philosopher.

Hegel writes further in the same letter that Böhme's endeavor "constitutes the most arduous struggle both to bring the deep speculative [content], which he holds in his intuition, into representation and so to master the element of representational [thinking] in order that the speculative content might be expressed in it."[30] Certainly, Böhme's thought is paradigmatic "picture-thinking," but given the limits of his medium his thought comes amazingly close, in this inadequate form, to capturing the Concept. Furthermore, Hegel thinks that Böhme realized this inadequacy and struggled against it. Hegel continues: "There remains so little that is constant and fixed in his work, because he feels everywhere the inadequacy of representation to what he is trying to achieve, and feels representation again overturned."[31]

Hegel's social contacts in Jena must have encouraged his enthusiasm for Böhme and theosophy in general. David Walsh writes that Jena in Hegel's day

> had become the focal point of the German Romantic movement, and many of its greatest figures were assembled there, including Tieck, Novalis, Schelling, F. Schlegel, and A. W. Schlegel. Within that company an intense center of interest was formed by their rediscovery of the German mystical tradition. For the first time the works of the great medieval and Reformation mystics were becoming widely available within their native land. The appearance of Eckhart and Böhme in particular was heralded as a liberating release from the deadness of Enlightenment rationalism. They read, too, the major eighteenth-century commentators of Böhme . . . and the Swabian Pietist theologian Friedrich Christoph Oetinger, in whom they found a more contemporary application of the great mystical insights of the past.[32]

Novalis immersed himself in the study of Böhme during the winter of 1799–1800. He came to espouse the Paracelsian view that man is

---

29. Butler, 573; Hoffmeister #192. The fact that Hegel did not own Böhme's works in Jena should not suggest half-hearted interest in them. It was difficult in those days for a young associate professor, with an annual salary of only 100 thalers, to afford a well-stocked library.

30. Butler, 573–74.

31. Ibid., 574.

32. David Walsh, "The Historical Dialectic of Spirit," 22–23.

charged with the task of redeeming nature and spoke of a "magic idealism." Friedrich Schlegel called Böhme's work "the greatest, most profound, most individual, most admirable work of idealism."[33] He believed he saw a correspondence between Böhme's thought and Fichte's. Paola Mayer conjectures that Böhme was probably read aloud at meetings of the Jena circle in 1799–1800.[34]

Schelling was, of course, an enthusiastic reader of Böhme and Oetinger and likely encouraged Hegel's interest in theosophy. In speaking about his time in Jena, Ludwig Tieck (1773–1853) reported that he found Schelling very receptive to Böhme's theosophy.[35] Tieck had left Jena by the time Hegel arrived there, but Hegel was unquestionably familiar with his work. The "Force and the Understanding" section of the *Phenomenology* includes a discussion of what Hegel calls "the topsy-turvy world," *die verkehrte Welt*, the title of a play Tieck published in 1799.[36] The first reference to Böhme by a member of the Jena circle occurs in a letter from Schlegel to Novalis, dated December 2, 1798, in which Schlegel mentions that Tieck has been studying Böhme. One of Tieck's biographers states, "None of his works written between 1799 and 1801 is free of Böhme."[37] It was Tieck who introduced Novalis to Böhme. In commemoration of this, Novalis later wrote his poem "An Tieck," in which he called Tieck "der Verkündiger der Morgenröte" ("Herald of Morning Glow").[38] In Munich in 1804, Tieck established a close relationship with Franz von Baader.

b) The Hermetic Subtext to Hegel's Preface

What we know about the intellectual milieu of Jena can shed a great deal of light on some of the mysteries surrounding the composition of the *Phenomenology*. It is often difficult for interpreters to understand who Hegel is attacking in the *Phenomenology*—especially in the preface—and why he describes his own project in the peculiar way that he does. I have already suggested "initiation" as one possible framework for understanding the project of the *Phenomenology*. I wish now to suggest something even more radical: the background against which we must understand Hegel's programmatic remarks in the preface is his own critical appreciation of Hermetic theosophy.

Hegel's attitude toward the Hermeticism of Böhme and others is sim-

---

33. Quoted in Paola Mayer, *Jena Romanticism and Its Appropriation of Jacob Böhme* (Montreal: McGill-Queen's University Press, 1999), 140.
34. Ibid., 182.
35. Edwin H. Zeydel, *Ludwig Tieck, the German Romanticist: A Critical Study* (Princeton, N.J.: Princeton University Press, 1935), 130.
36. Donald Phillip Verene was the first commentator to point out the possible connection between Hegel's "*verkehrte Welt*" and Tieck's (Verene, *Hegel's Recollection*, 39–58).
37. Roger Paulin, *Ludwig Tieck: A Literary Biography* (Oxford: Clarendon Press, 1985), 100. Paola Mayer has recently challenged this assessment of Böhme's influence on Tieck and the other Romantics. See Mayer, *Jena Romanticism*.
38. Zeydel, *Ludwig Tieck*, 127.

ilar to his attitude toward mainstream religion: he believes that it approaches the truth very closely, but is hindered by its "sensuous" mode of expression. Hegel opposes the school of Romantic intuitionism, often inspired by Hermeticism, which believes that truth is to be felt or intuited. Hegel makes his feeling about the Romantics very plain early on in the preface: "Such minds, when they give themselves up to the uncontrolled ferment of [the divine] substance, imagine that, by drawing a veil over self-consciousness and surrendering understanding they become the beloved of God to whom He gives His wisdom in sleep; and hence what they in fact receive, and bring forth to birth in their sleep, is nothing but dreams" (Miller, 6; PG, 9).

Just a few passages later occurs the famous paragraph in which Hegel attacks a certain conception of the Absolute as "the night in which . . . all cows are black" (Miller, 9; PG, 13). Commentators usually take this as a reference to Schelling. Indeed, in a letter to Schelling of May 1, 1807, Hegel seems to try to "soften the blow" of the preface, which was about to be printed. He writes that "In the Preface you will not find that I have been too hard on the shallowness that makes so much mischief with your forms in particular and degrades your science into mere formalism."[39] But there is more than one passage in the preface that can be taken as addressing itself to Schelling or his followers.

Let us look more closely, then, at the passage in question. A few lines up from the "cows" simile we read the following: "Dealing with something from the perspective of the Absolute [according to Hegel's opponents] consists merely in declaring that, although one has been speaking of it just now as something definite, yet in the Absolute, the A = A, there is nothing of the kind, for therein all is one" (Miller, 9; PG, 13). To be sure, this sounds like a criticism of Schelling's view of the Absolute as the "indifference point" (the language of "A = A" was used by Schelling, who appropriated it from Fichte). However, it sounds even more like the mystical doctrine of the "coincidence of opposites," found in Cusa and others.[40] Further, Hegel uses the phrase "therein all is one" (*darin sei alles Eins*). Writing this, how could Hegel not have recalled the youthful motto he shared with Schelling and Hölderlin: *hen kai pan*? In his preface to the second edition (1827) of the *Encyclopedia Logic*, Hegel equates the philosophy of *alles eins*, "All is one" with the "Identity-System" (Geraets 7; *Werke* 8:18). Furthermore, in the *Lectures on the Philosophy of Religion* of 1827, Hegel entertains the suggestion that the Identity philosophy of Schelling is equivalent to pantheism (LPR 1:374–75; VPR 1:272).

The passage from the *Phenomenology* continues: "To pit this single

---

39. Butler, 80; Hoffmeister #95.
40. Klaus Düsing argues that this doctrine was transmitted to Schelling via Jacobi's *Über die Lehre des Spinoza*. Jacobi printed extracts from Bruno's *De la Causa* as an appendix to his book, in which Bruno repeats arguments from Cusa. See Klaus Düsing, "Absolut Identität und Formen der Endlichkeit: Interpretationen zu Schellings and Hegels erster absoluter Metaphysik," in *Schellings und Hegels erste absolute Metaphysik (1801–1802)*, ed. Klaus Düsing (Köln: Jürgen Dinter, 1988), 114, 151.

insight, that in the Absolute everything is the same, against the full body of articulated cognition, which at least seeks and demands such fulfillment, to palm off its Absolute as the night in which, as the saying goes, all cows are black—this is cognition naively reduced to vacuity."[41] Hegel is attacking Schelling here, but he is attacking Schelling as the latest exponent of a type of mysticism which he believes is inadequate: a mysticism that stops short in the face of contradiction and declares that God is inconceivable.[42] (Hegel, of course, was well aware of Schelling's ties to mysticism and theosophy, and Schelling's willingness to publicly ally himself with these currents.)

In effect, Hegel rejects this kind of mysticism in favor of the theosophy of Böhme. Consider Hegel's remarks about Spinoza's pantheism in his lectures of 1805: "His [Spinoza's] philosophy is only fixed substance, not yet Spirit; in it we do not confront ourselves. God is not Spirit here because he is not the triune. Substance remains rigid and petrified, without Böhme's sources [Quellen]. The particular determinations in the form of thought-determinations are not Böhme's source-spirits which work and unfold in one another."[43] Hegel accepts the Schellingian doctrine of the Absolute as the Whole that transcends the distinction between subject and object. He merely contends that without a developmental account of how this Absolute becomes actual—which constitutes, at the same time, a description of its internal moments—"the Absolute" is merely an empty phrase. As far as Hegel and his contemporaries knew, this "developmental" approach was Böhme's innovation—and it is, of course, precisely the respect in which Böhme's brand of "mysticism" is different from that of Cusa, Eckhart, and others.

A couple of paragraphs later in the preface Hegel speaks of Substance becoming Subject, claiming that the Absolute is "the process of its own becoming, the circle that presupposes its end as its goal, having its end also as its beginning; and only by being worked out to its end, is it actual" (Miller, 10; PG, 14). Hegel, in the next passage, then immediately makes the quasi-mystical observation that "the life of God and divine cognition may well be spoken of as a disporting of Love with itself; but this idea sinks into mere edification, and even insipidity, if it lacks the seriousness, the suffering, the patience, and the labour of the negative" (Miller, 10; PG, 4–15). Hegel is saying that thinking which draws inspiration from such mystical metaphors is fine, and much can be learned from it, but it is empty unless supplemented by the careful, painstaking working out of the moments of the "life of God." Hegel ends this passage with the admonition that the Absolute must be conceived in "the whole

41. Geraets 7; Werke 8:18.
42. In the Lectures on the Philosophy of Religion of 1827, Hegel states that "a mystery is called inconceivable, but what appears inconceivable is precisely the Concept itself, the speculative element or the fact that the rational is thought. . . . Now when the Understanding comes to this point it says, 'this is a contradiction,' and stands still at this point. . . . Thus the nature of God is inconceivable [for it]" (LPR 3:282–83; VPR 3:207–8).
43. LHP 3:288; not present in Werke, see Sämtliche Werke, vol. 19, ed. Hermann Glockner (Stuttgart: Fromann, 1928), 377.

wealth of the developed form. Only then is it conceived and expressed as an actuality" (Miller, 11; PG, 15).

The next paragraph provides the key that explains all. It begins: "The true is the whole" (*Das Wahre ist das Ganze*). Recall that Oetinger, developing the ideas of Böhme, held that "The truth is a whole [*Die Wahrheit ist ein Ganzes*]; when one finally receives this total, synoptic vision of the truth, it matters not whether one begins by considering this part or that."[44] Oetinger also sometimes spoke of his *Ganze* as equivalent to *Geist* and treated it as an *intensum*: a thing that cannot be divided into literal pieces, only into noetic moments. In an intensum such as *Geist*, the whole is immanent in every part. It is this immanence that enables us to progress from one moment to another in the gradual articulation of the whole.[45] As noted in chapter 2, the theme of the truth as a whole (or *the* whole) is a perennial theme of Swabian speculative Pietism.[46]

Considering the context of Hegel's "True is the whole" passage—his response to Schelling and to the mystics of the *coincidentia oppositorum* school—it seems that Hegel is rebuking his fellow Swabian by deliberately invoking the authority of Oetinger and Württemberg theosophy. *He is exhorting Schelling to become more Böhmean.*[47] Coupling this with Hegel's approving attitude toward Böhme, we can see that there is a hidden subtext to the preface. Although nothing in it is completely transparent, the surface of the preface involves Hegel opposing himself to all previous philosophy (as, for instance, in his odd critique of philosophical prefaces). The subtext, however, involves a response to all previous mysticism as well.

The reasons why such material would be consigned to the "esoteric" dimension of the text should be clear. We have seen that intolerance against admirers of Oetinger existed in Hegel's time. Also, it must be kept in mind that the *Phenomenology* belongs, in truth, to an older tradition of literary work in which reference to one's predecessors was largely indirect.

Just as Hegel wants philosophers to "lay aside the title 'love of knowing [*Wissen*],'" and achieve actual knowing, so he wants to raise "mysticism" to the level of *theosophy*, to knowing the wisdom of God. Mysticism is inadequate because it lets mystery remain. Like Aristotle, Hegel wants to remove wonder; he wants to penetrate into the Absolute and let the light of truth shine where before there was darkness, absence, hiddenness. None of this is inconsistent with Hegel's critique of Böhmean-style theosophy. Hegel sees religion in all its forms, and particularly Christianity, as a sort of halfway house to Absolute Knowing, and

44. F. C. Oetinger, *Sämtliche Schriften*, vol. 5, ed. Karl Chr. Eberh. Ehmann (Stuttgart, 1858–64), 45.
45. Schneider, *Geistesahnen*, 114.
46. Ibid., 56.
47. Böhme's *Ungrund*, though itself indeterminate, is supposed to contain all determinations. This sounds, of course, rather like Schelling's "indifference point," which could be the reason why Hegel never mentions Böhme's *Ungrund*, apparently considering it a dispensable part of Böhme's philosophy.

his own philosophy is animated by religious categories and symbolic forms.

In effect, Hegel is saying that mysticism (including Schellingian "philosophical mysticism") is a clue to the nature of the Absolute. In its highest form, Böhmean-Oetingerite theosophy, mysticism comes strikingly close to the philosophical grasp of the Absolute. In a gesture of philosophical syncretism, Hegel opens the doors of his temple of Absolute Spirit to the Böhmean theosophists, saying, "Your God is my God, but if you wish to go a further step and truly know God, you must submit yourselves to the seriousness, the suffering, the patience, and the labour of my initiation." (We shall shortly see this demonstrated even more clearly in the *Phenomenology*'s account of "revealed religion"— Christianity—which is strikingly Böhmean.)

If it seems implausible that Hegel would so closely identify his own philosophical approach with any sort of mysticism at all—consider again the following lines from one of the *Zusätze* to the *Encyclopedia Logic*:"It should . . . be mentioned here that the meaning of the speculative is to be understood as being the same as what used in earlier times to be called 'mystical.' " (EL § 82, Z; Geraets, 133).

c) Böhmean Elements in the *Phenomenology*

David Walsh has argued that Hegel's use in the *Phenomenology* of such terms as *element, aether, light, expansion,* and *contraction* has its roots in his acquaintance with the Böhmean-Oetingerite tradition, as well as with Paracelsus.[48] (I will discuss Hegel's concept of aether much more extensively in chapter 6.) It is in Hegel's section on "Self-Consciousness," however, that the influence of Böhme becomes evident in its most substantive form. In the spirit of the *Hermetica*, Böhme recognized that selfhood develops in opposition to the not-self. (Fichte and Hegel are merely Böhme's followers in this regard, as are Sartre, Piaget, and others.) But Böhme even had the audacity to claim that this must apply to God as well.[49] In his remarks in the *Lectures* of 1805, Hegel includes the following quote from Böhme:"Nothing can be revealed to itself without opposition [*Wiederwärtigkeit*]: For if there is nothing that opposes it, then it always goes out of itself and never returns to itself again. If it does not return into itself, as into that from which it originated, then it knows nothing of its origin."[50]

Hegel's account of selfhood involves the claim that at some level the self relates to its other by willing its *cancellation*. At the root of all the forms of Spirit that unfold in the *Phenomenology* is a primal, demonic

48. Walsh, "The Historical Dialectic of Spirit," 28.
49. David Walsh writes that "At the core of his construction was Böhme's discovery that conflict and opposition were necessary to the self-revelation of God. It was an extrapolation from what is required for the self-realization of man to what is required for the self-realization of God" ("A Mythology of Reason," 153).
50. See Jakob Böhme, *Der Weg zu Christo*, Sixth Book, "Von Göttlicher Beschaulichkeit," in *Sämtliche Schriften*, vol. 4, chap. 1, § 8. Hegel quotes this passage in his *Lectures on the History of Philosophy* 3:203; *Werke* 20:106.

drive for complete possession or mastery of the object, for, in effect, the annihilation of otherness. By implication, this drive is simultaneously a will to remove the divide between subject and object, for by canceling "otherness" it seeks to exalt the self (this implication is crucial for understanding the section on "Self-Consciousness"). This drive, this complete and utter negativity that ultimately issues in a complete and exalted positivity, also has its equivalent in Böhme—but in order to fully explain this I must elaborate further on the nature of this negativity and how it operates in the *Phenomenology*.

In discussing this "primal drive" to annul otherness—which is exhibited at all levels of Spirit—Hegel speaks again of the Eleusinian mysteries, in a passage I have quoted earlier. He writes of how the mysteries cause one to "doubt the being of sensuous things" (Miller, 65; PG, 77). By this, he does not mean what modern philosophers mean when they speak of doubting the "external world." A world of sensible objects really is "out there," but metaphysically speaking, it is made *insubstantial* by the activity of the subject. The aggrandizement of the subject = the "withdrawal" of substance from the world and "into" the subject. The subject becomes substance—that which persists, the unmoving pivot around which the world of objects is set awhirl as it is conquered and transformed according to the plans and desires of the subject. When Hegel says that the initiate "brings about" the nihilation of sensible things himself he is stating the principle of his *Idealism*: it is the vocation of mankind, or Spirit, to transform the given world, to make it conform to Idea, to remove the distinction between real and ideal, subject and object.

"Transformation" can mean two things. It can be a literal, noticeable change, whether of trees into dwellings or of children into educated men, or it can be a transformation of the unknown into the known, the grasped. In both cases what is involved is the annihilation of the *resistance* of things, an annihilation of their otherness, their hiddenness. The first sense of transformation is only an approximation to the true unity of subject and object, ideal and real—which is achieved only through the full development of the second kind of transformation: the total, thoughtful grasp of the Whole through a system of Science. For Hegel, it is not enough for Spirit to change the world; it must interpret it. It is ultimately through this urge to cancel or "master" otherness that the true individual, true substance, true self, and true God are simultaneously actualized.

In the *Lectures on the Philosophy of Religion* of 1827, Hegel states, "Ideality means that this being [that is] external (i.e., its spatiality, temporality, materiality, and mutual externality) is sublated. Inasmuch as I know this being, its contents are not represented things, being outside one another; rather they are within me in a simple manner. Though a tree has many parts, it nevertheless is merely simple in my representation. Spirit is knowledge. For it to be knowledge, the content of what it knows must have attained this ideal form, it must have been negated in this manner" (LPR 1:184; VPR 1:92). In the *Encyclopedia Logic*, Hegel states that "In cognition what has to be done is all a matter of stripping away the alien character of the objective world that confronts us" (EL § 194 Z-1; Geraets, 273). In the *Philosophy of Spirit* Hegel writes: "All the activities of Spirit are nothing but the various modes in which that which is external is led back into the internality, to what is Spirit itself, and it is only by means of this leading back, this idealizing or assimilation of that which is external, that Spirit becomes and is Spirit" (PS § 381, Z; Petry 1:37). "All the activities of Spirit"—all modes of consciousness—Hegel says, are forms in which we strive to overcome otherness.[51]

Furthermore, freedom is only possible through overcoming otherness. "Freedom," Hegel states, "is only present where there is no other for me that is not myself" (EL § 24 Z-2; Geraets, 58). Elsewhere, he writes that "A freedom for which something is genuinely external and alien is no freedom at all; freedom's essence and its formal definition is that nothing is absolutely external."[52] As I have said, Spirit's triumph over the other is only fully actualized in Science. Hegel states that "the purpose of all true science is just this, that Spirit shall recognize itself in everything in heaven and on earth" (PS § 377, Z; Petry 1:5). At the very end of the *Philosophy of Nature*, Hegel remarks that Spirit "wants to liberate itself by fashioning nature from within itself; this action of Spirit is called philosophy. . . . The aim of these lectures is to convey an image of nature, in order to subdue this Proteus: to find in this externality only the mirror of ourselves, to see in nature a free reflection of Spirit" (PN § 376 Z; Petry 3:213). "Spirit [when contemplating nature] has the certainty which Adam had when he beheld Eve, 'This is flesh of my flesh, this is bone of my bone'" (PN § 247 Z; Petry 1:204).

The will to overcome otherness is seen in all of nature. Faced with the opposition of the external world the animal gobbles it up.[53] The difference between man and animal, however, is that man can "master" nature and "absorb" the external without *literally* annihilating it. In his early *Philosophy of Nature* of 1805–6, Hegel writes, "eating and drinking make inorganic things into what they are in themselves, in truth, it is the unconscious comprehending of them—they become thus sublated thereby, because they are in themselves [this fire essence]."[54] Eating and drinking annihilate sensible things and reduce them to their elements, to what they are "in-themselves." Thus, eating and drinking prefigure Science,

---

51. "An out-and-out other simply does not exist for Spirit" (PS § 377 Z; Petry 1:5).

52. Hegel, *Naturrecht*, in *Gesammelte Werke*, vol. 4, ed. Harmut Buchner and Otto Pöggeler (Hamburg: Felix Meiner Verlag, 1968), 446.

53. For a treatment similar to that of the *Phenomenology*, see the *Philosophy of Spirit*, 381 Z; Petry 1:33; also see *Philosophy Of Nature*, 357 Z; Petry 3:136: "The organism must . . . posit the subjectivity of externality, appropriate it, and identify it with its own self; this constitutes *assimilation*." And *Philosophy of Nature*, 359 Z; Petry 3:144: "Animal appetite is the idealism of objectivity, whereby this objectivity loses its alien character."

54. Quoted in Harris, *Night Thoughts*, 448. Harris writes that animal nutrition is "the self-intro-reflection of the inorganic."

the *true*"reduction" of things to their essence, which is their relationship to the Absolute.[55]

"Sense-Certainty"—the initial division of the *Phenomenology*—is the most basic, primitive form in which the urge to cancel or master the other manifests itself *in consciousness*. Spirit in Sense-Certainty believes— tacitly—that the object in its real, concrete particularity can be adequately"grasped" through bare sensory experience alone. In short, Sense-Certainty believes that intuition can make the object fully present, fully transparent in its concreteness, and thus no longer "other." Sense-Certainty thinks it can grasp the singularity of the object as a "this," in its pure immediacy. But, Hegel writes, "An actual sense-certainty is not merely this pure immediacy, but an *instance* of it" (Miller, 59; PG, 70). In other words, the gesture or the "this" through which we think we can grasp and thus"master" the particularity of the object is really a *universal*, applicable not just to *this* "this" but to all "thises." Consciousness had wanted to grasp the other in its individuality (which is really the same thing as annihilating the other's individuality) but it eludes our grasp.

We can now already glimpse the end of the Hegelian philosophy in its beginning. In Absolute Knowing the drive to totally grasp the object, and to annul the subject-object distinction, will be realized. Absolute Knowing will be the total grasp of an individual in its uniqueness. In fact, it will be the total grasp of the only true, unique individual there is: the Absolute—again, the analog to Aristotelian *ousia* is very clear.[56] However, in Hegel's thought substance has become subject:"what seems to happen outside of [the self], to be an activity directed against it, is really its own doing, and Substance shows itself to be essentially Subject" (Miller, 21; PG, 28). Knowledge of this individual is simultaneously self-knowledge. Otherness still exists, but it is now understood in terms of its place within the Whole, which is the Absolute = Substance = Subject. Substantive otherness, however, has passed away, because what is substantive has become subjective. In short, Absolute Knowing achieves exactly what is desired, covertly, by Sense-Certainty (and the other forms of Spirit).

In introducing"Self-Consciousness," Hegel introduces the term *Desire* (*Begierde*) to describe the primal urge for the cancellation of otherness and the individuation-absolutization of subject.[57] But Spirit is not just

---

55. Also in the 1805–6 *Philosophy of Nature*, Hegel states that"The animal organism creates its own internal environment. . . . [The] animal organism feeds all its other functions—all the functions of its'inner organism'—upon the energy produced by its nutritive system" (quoted in Harris, *Night Thoughts*, 448). Again, there is a close analogy here between the system of Science and the"internal environment" of the animal: Science comprehends ("digests") things by locating them in the system of Science, which is conceived by Hegel as an organic unity.

56. The Absolute is the individual, which subsumes universals as its particular manifestations. See Richard Dien Winfield,"On Individuality," in *Freedom and Modernity* (Albany: State University of New York Press, 1991).

57. Kojève asks, what is Desire but the will to"*transform* the contemplated thing by an action, to overcome it in its being that is unrelated to mine and independent of me, to negate it in its independence, and to assimilate it to

this desire to absolutize itself. All human desires aim at the same telos, from the base desire simply to negate and destroy otherness, to the more sophisticated forms of "negating" otherness through transformation. This telos is *self-consciousness* (which is not just the topic of this one section, but of the entire work).[58] Hegel shows that when the subject transforms objects according to its will, or rages at and destroys that which resists its desires, it is really being moved by the desire to confront itself. The desire of the subject to annul the other and absolutize itself is just the same thing as the desire to be confronted by the self *and no other*. But as Böhme said, "No thing can be revealed to itself without opposition." This means that if the goal of consciousness is self-knowledge, it cannot achieve this by annihilating all objectivity, but only by making objectivity reflective, by transforming objects into a mirror of consciousness.

This entire account of the positive role of destructive Desire in the ultimate realization of the self and of the Absolute is Böhmean. For Böhme, what Hegel calls Desire—the urge to annihilate the other and absolutize self—is Evil. Since a true human self is possible only through interaction with otherness, the "self" that this nihilating impulse creates, if left to its own devices, does not raise itself above the animalistic concerns of pleasure, comfort, and satisfaction. This is the "criminal type," the man who stands in opposition to all else, "looking out for number one."[59] The paradox of this "selfishness" is that it involves no real self at all. Böhme designates this way of being as "the Sour"—an indrawing, a pulling away, a shutting off and negation of all else. He regards it as a necessary moment of the being of God and all creation.[60] Hegel writes of this doctrine that "Böhme has really here penetrated into the utmost depths of divine essence; evil, matter, or whatever it has been called, is the I = I, the Being-for-self, the true negativity" (LHP 3:206; *Werke* 20:109). Everything good that subsequently comes to be, *is* only through having overcome this negative moment.

Böhme's position is Hegel's. This negativity in human nature is a "tool" used by the Cunning of Reason to actualize all that is good: religion, morality, society, justice, and ultimately God Himself. This is

---

myself, to make it mine, to absorb it in and by my I ?" (Kojève, *Introduction to the Reading of Hegel*, 37–38).

58. Hegel, like Böhme, regards self-knowledge not simply as what *ought* to be achieved, but rather as what all men (and reality itself) are directed toward by a primal will.

59. Just before the "Böhme myth" in the *Phenomenology* (see below), Hegel writes: "Evil [*Böse*] appears as the primary existence of the inwardly-turned consciousness . . ." (Miller, 468; PG, 504). Hegel writes in the *Philosophy of Spirit* that "evil is nothing else than Spirit which puts its separate individuality before all else" (PS § 382 Z; Petry 1:51).

60. Speaking of Hegel's account of plant life in the 1805–6 *Philosophy of Nature*, H. S. Harris writes, "Every 'part' of 'life' as the plant displays it for us, is a satanic urge to be the whole kind 'for itself' or on its own account. We have to conceive of life as an absolute tension of imperialism and anarchy in order to comprehend what its most elementary form . . . can do and will do, once planted in the earth" (*Night Thoughts*, 447).

Hegel's transformation of the Christian doctrine of Original Sin. Hegel holds that Spirit is by nature evil. But this evil can be utilized in such a way that it brings good into the world. Robert Schneider states that Oetinger, like Hegel, sees knowledge as developing through the negative force of Desire (*Begierde*). He writes that "the stuff of Concrete Spirit begins in Hegel as in Oetinger with drive [*Trieb*] and Desire [*Begierde*]."[61]

During 1804–5, Hegel wrote out and then criticized a "myth" concerning the fall of Lucifer. Hegel portrays nature in its separation from God as evil. He writes,

> God, having turned toward nature and expressed Himself in the pomp and dull repetition of its forms, became aware of His expansion . . . and became angry over it. Wrath [*Zorn*] is this formation, this contraction into an empty point. He finds Himself in this way, with His being poured out into the unending, restless infinity, where there is no present but an empty transcendence of limit, which always remains even as it is transcended.[62]

God's "Wrath" here invites comparison, of course, to Böhme's "sour" (*Herb*), though the parallel is not exact. In his *Lectures on the History of Philosophy*, Hegel employs the term *Zorn* to speak of Böhme's theosophy, identifying the "first *Principium*" of Böhme's thought with *Gott in Zorn* (LHP 3:192; *Werke* 20:95).[63]

Hegel continues: "The anger of God, here fixed outside Himself in His otherness, the fallen Lucifer, rose up against God and his beauty made him arrogant. Nature, through consciousness of its own form, brought it to completion and flattered itself over it."[64] God's wrath, then, according to Hegel, becomes the spirit of Lucifer, who is at home with the finite and ephemeral. Again, there is a clear parallel to Böhme's idea that evil or the demonic is a moment of God, a *moment "broken off" from the divine life. This is exactly what human Spirit is, before its consummation: a moment broken off from the whole. Self-consciousness "is wrath itself, the ignition [*Entzündung*], of wrath within it which burns itself out and consumes its arrogant pomp."[65]

However, as one might expect, through the finite realm of nature Spirit rises up and can transcend this evil. It does so in this "myth" through understanding and making peace with its own finitude. Hegel writes,

> The consumed nature rises up in a newer, more ideal form, like a realm of shadows which has lost its first life, the appearance of its spirit after the death of its life. But this new form [Spirit] is the overcoming of the evil, the enduring of the glowing fire [*Glut*] of pain in the center point, where as purified it leaves all the flakes behind in the crucible [*Tiegel*], a residuum, which is the pure noth-

61. Robert Schneider, *Geistesahnen*, 126.
62. Johannes Hoffmeister, ed., *Dokumente zu Hegels Entwicklung* (Stuttgart: Fromann, 1936), 364–65.
63. See also LHP 3:206; *Werke* 20:109.
64. *Dokumente*, 365.
65. Ibid.

ing. It raises itself up as a freer spirit, which sees its radiance only in nature.[66]

(Note the use of the alchemical imagery of "purification.")

Hegel then immediately goes on to criticize this account—which he refers to as "the intuitions of Barbarians" (die Anschauungen der Barbarei)—because in it Spirit remains unconscious of the fact that it itself is the source of this process of the divine self-alienation and return. Hegel appears to think that this further, higher realization is necessary to "complete" Böhmean theosophy. Despite his objection to the "barbarism" of the Böhmean conception (which is repeated in the 1805 lectures), Hegel is clearly so close in spirit to Böhme that he can generate Böhmean-style "myths" with ease.

Furthermore, much of the language and spirit of Hegel's "Böhme myth" recur in the "Revealed Religion" section of the Phenomenology, and there his attitude toward Böhme is more positive.[67] David Walsh writes that Hegel's account is "from start to finish identical with the theosophic Christianity of Böhme."[68] In "Revealed Religion" Hegel presents speculative readings of various Christian dogmas. In his treatment of the fall from paradise the Böhme myth reappears. Paradise for Hegel represents the innocence of immersion in "pure immediacy," such as we find in Sense-Certainty. The withdrawal into "thought" is the loss of innocence. Having turned inward, consciousness now represents "Evil." This is Böhme's "Sour." But, Hegel says, "Evil" requires a "Good," and indeed we find that consciousness has split into "Evil" and "Good." (Hegel is not very clear, however, about what moment of consciousness corresponds to the "Good.")

Hegel then states, "It can therefore be said that it is the very first-born Son of Light [Lucifer] himself who fell because he withdrew into himself or became self-centered, but that in his place another was at once created" (Miller, 468; PG, 504). Just as in the "myth" of 1804–5, Hegel immediately distances himself from this way of conceiving things: "Such a form of expression as 'fallen' which, like the expression 'Son,' belongs to representation [Vorstellen; "picture-thinking"] and not to the Concept, reduces [herabsetzten] the moments of the Concept to the level of representation, or carries representation over into the realm of thought" (Miller, 468; PG, 504).

Commentators, again, take Hegel as roundly rejecting Böhme here, but he goes on to pay Böhme indirect tribute two paragraphs later. Still speaking of the "myth" of Lucifer, Hegel remarks that picture-thinking cannot conceive of evil, of the negative, as a "moment" of God: "Representation takes the other aspect, evil, to be a happening alien to the divine being; to grasp it in the divine being as the wrath of God, this demands from representation, struggling against its limitations, its

---

66. Ibid.
67. The Böhme-Lucifer issue reappears in the Philosophy of Nature, 248 Z; Petry 1:211. Böhme's Lucifer doctrine, and the "wrath" of God are explicitly discussed in the Böhme chapter of LHP 3:205–6; Werke 20:108–10.
68. Walsh, "The Historical Dialectic of Spirit," 28.

supreme and most strenuous effort, an effort which, since it lacks the Concept, remains fruitless" (Miller, 470; PG, 506). Böhme, of course, saw evil as a moment of God, and Hegel knew this. Though Böhme's thought could not ultimately become Absolute Knowing because of its picture-thinking, it comes as close to Absolute Knowing as picture-thinking can.

d) Alchemical Elements
That Hegel was familiar with alchemy and was ready and willing to employ its "thought patterns" is evident from the "Böhme myth" of 1804–5, which states that Spirit "is the overcoming of the evil, the enduring of the glowing fire [Glut] of pain in the center point, where as purified it leaves all the flakes behind in the crucible [Tiegel], a residuum, which is the pure nothing. It raises itself up as a freer spirit, which sees its radiance only in nature."[69] Alchemical metaphors were common in the writings of Württemberg Pietists. August Langen writes that alchemical language constitutes one of the most important sources for Pietist writers.[70] (I will offer a much more extensive discussion of Hegel's knowledge of, and indebtedness to, alchemy in chapter 6.)

The concept of the negative as a moment in the positive is an old Hermetic theme. In alchemy, making gold involves breaking base metals down into their primal elements and then "raising them up" to the perfected metal-form of gold. Each metal was said to contain a "seed of gold" that could be made to sprout and blossom. At the same time, the alchemist was expected to purify himself, or the process would not work. In this we can see an analogy to the function of the Phenomenology itself. In the phenomenological crucible, Spirit is separated from its impurities and, literally, perfected. The "seed" of Absolute Spirit is present in every flawed, imperfect form that Spirit takes. The work of this purification has happened, in part, through the historical process. But Hegel provides the final, secret ingredient necessary to synthesize Absolute Spirit. He has placed the historical forms of Spirit into his alembic and, through the fire of dialectic, has caused them to reorganize into a form that reveals the necessity within their apparent contingency.

Hegel closes the Phenomenology with the image of Golgotha, of the Schädelstätte, the "Place of the Skull."[71] This image is found in some alchemical texts. The crucifixion is an image of the nigredo, the initial alchemical stage of putrefaction or death, from which comes (eventually) the philosopher's stone. Caput mortuum—"death's head"—was the

---

69. Dokumente, 365.
70. August Langen, Der Wortschatz des deutschen Pietismus (Tübingen: Max Niemeyer Verlag, 1968), 71.
71. Hegel counterposes the Schädelstätte to the Schädellehre, phrenology. Phrenology enjoyed something of a revival in the eighteenth century due to the writings of Johann Kasper Lavater (1741–1801), a Swiss preacher with mystical tendencies. Aside from this, there is nothing "Hermetic" about phrenology. It is an example of the reductive materialism most Hermeticists vehemently opposed. (Hegel's critique of phrenology occurs in PG, 206–33; Miller, 185–210).

term used by alchemists to denote the substance remaining after putrefaction or purification by fire has taken place, and it was symbolized by a skull. *Caput mortuum* is a term actually employed by Hegel, as I shall discuss in the following chapter. The skull (with crossbones) also figures as an important image in Masonic initiation.

Alchemists like Heinrich Khunrath (1560–1605) identified Christ Himself with the philosopher's stone. In truth, the image of Golgotha at the end of the *Phenomenology* is a continuation of the "Bacchanalian revel" imagery that occurs early on in the text. Aside from the "Bacchanalian revel" passage itself, another passage contains an oblique reference to Dionysus: "the life of Spirit is not the life that shrinks from death and keeps itself untouched by devastation, but rather the life that endures it and maintains itself in it. It wins its truth only when, in utter dismemberment, it finds itself" (Miller, 19; PG, 26).

In *Faith and Knowledge* (1802) Hegel writes that the "pure Concept" must "re-establish for philosophy the Idea of absolute freedom and along with it the absolute Passion, the speculative Good Friday in place of the historic Good Friday."[72] Mythically, Christ is equivalent to Dionysus (and Osiris), the God who benefits mankind through being sacrificed. Spirit must die, it must be dismembered, in order to attain Absolute Knowing and become Absolute Spirit. Karin Figala writes that the crucifixion is an "*Ursymbol* of the alchemical process, of the 'whitening of the *nigredo*.' A primordial symbol of pre-Christian gnosis for the transformation of *nigredo* into *albedo* is the saga of Osiris's death and resurrection."[73]

Hegel's *Phenomenology* is a rite of initiation and an alchemical transmutation: the material (mundane mind or spirit) must be broken apart or sacrificed, in order to be transmuted into a higher form.

e) The Foaming Chalice

The final image of the *Phenomenology* is the "foaming chalice." Spirit as displayed in the *Phenomenology*'s "way of despair" constitutes "the recollection and the Golgotha [*die Schädelstätte*] of Absolute Spirit, the actuality, truth, and certainty of his throne, without which he would be lifeless and alone; only, 'from the chalice of this realm of spirits, foams for Him his own infinity'" (Miller, 493; PG, 531).[74] Hegel has paraphrased Schiller's poem "Die Freundschaft" ("Friendship"; 1782). The last two lines of which read: "Aus dem Kelch des ganzen Seelenreiches, / Schäumt *ihm*—die Unendlichkeit."[75] Hegel has revised these lines to read "Aus

72. *Faith and Knowledge*, trans. Walter Cerf and H. S. Harris (Albany: State University of New York Press, 1977), 191. German edition: *Gesammelte Werke*, 4:414.

73. See Karin Figala, "Der alchemische Begriff des Caput Mortuum in der symbolischen Terminologie Hegels," in *Stuttgarter Hegel-Tage 1970*, ed. H. G. Gadamer (Bonn: Bouvier, 1974), 143–44. See chapter 5 on *caput mortuum*.

74. The "way of despair" (*Weg der Verzweiflung*) is mentioned at Miller, 49; PG, 60. It is a clear reference to the *via dolorosa*.

dem Kelche dieses Geisterreiches, / schäumt ihm seine Unendlichkeit."
To understand the significance of the changes, one must look at the final stanza of Schiller's poem in its entirety:

> Freundlos war der grosse Weltenmeister,
> Fühlte *Mangel*—darum schuf er Geister,
>   Selge Spiegel seiner Seligkeit!—
> Fand das höchste Wesen schon kein gleiches,
> Aus dem Kelch des ganzen Seelenreiches
>   Schäumt *ihm*—die Unendlichkeit.

This might be translated:

> Friendless was the great World Master
> Felt a lack—thus he created spirits,
>   Blessed mirrors of his bliss—
> Still found the highest being no likeness,
> From out of the chalice of the whole realm of the soul
>   Foams for Him—infinity.[76]

The imagery of the World Master creating "spirits" as a "mirror" calls to mind Böhme's doctrine of God's wisdom, which he depicts as a mirror and analyzes into the seven "source-spirits" (*Quellgeister*). Hegel's claim, as we have seen in connection with the "myth" of 1804–5, is that any developmental account of the "life of God" must understand Spirit as its origin and object. Hegel contends that this is the crucial component missing from Böhmean theosophy. Encountering a similar "myth" in Schiller's *Die Freundschaft*, Hegel thus identifies Schiller's created *Geist* (or, literally, *Geister*) with the soul of the World Master: "Seelenreiches" becomes "Geisterreiches."

There is a further irony in Hegel's use of Schiller's poem. Hegel must also reject Schiller's claim that "Still found the highest being no likeness." In a *Zusatz* to the *Encyclopedia Logic* Hegel states that "the original calling of man, to be an image of God, can be realised only through cognition [*Erkennen*]" (EL § 24 Z-3; Geraets, 63). For Hegel, the "world master" *must* find an adequate likeness.

Finally, Schiller writes that out of this "realm of the soul foams for Him—infinity," implying that infinity unfolds before God, as an external show. Hegel revises the last line of the poem to read "foams to him, his infinity [*seine Unendlichkeit*]." Spirit is now to be identified with the infinite. This must be understood in contrast to what Hegel calls "bad infinity" (*Schlechte Unendlichkeit*), which is an infinity that stands opposed to what is finite as something external. Such opposition limits infinity, thus making it not infinite but finite. "Good infinity" *comprehends* finitude.

---

75. Friedrich Schiller, *Sämtliche Werke*, 4 vols., ed. Gerhard Fricke and Herbert G. Göpfert with Herbert Stubenrauch, 6th ed. (Munich: Hanser, 1974–80), 1:93.
76. Translated in Verene, *Hegel's Recollection*, 6.

Thus, Spirit does not face an infinity "foaming" out away from it; it *is* the infinite. This, its true nature, has revealed itself through the *Geisterreich* that is the *Phenomenology*.[77]

There is a yet another, still more interesting implication to Hegel's use of this passage. Consider the context in which it occurs. Hegel speaks of "the recollection and the Golgotha of Absolute Spirit, the actuality, truth, and certainty of his throne, without which he would be lifeless and alone." The meaning of this imagery seems to be obvious: the way of Spirit to Absolute Knowing is likened to Christ's passion. But Hegel then immediately introduces his paraphrase of Schiller. In this context, the reference to the "Kelche" can only call to mind the image of the Holy Grail, the cup in which Christ's blood was captured during his crucifixion.

The Holy Grail was also the cup of the last supper, from which the disciples drank wine transubstantiated into Christ's blood. The Grail is represented to this day by a communion chalice. Hegel's use of the image of the "Kelch" extends the comparison of his doctrine to Christianity. It also circles back to his discussion of the Eleusinian mysteries, in which he spoke of the Eleusinian "communion": "the secret meaning of the eating of bread and the drinking of wine" (Miller, 65; PG, 77). In drinking from the communion cup we become one with God. Hegel believes that he has actually realized this oneness in his *Phenomenology*. For a philosopher like Hegel, who believes that at the end of time we rend and devour our God like the Titans did Dionysus, the cup of Christ's blood is a useful symbol for a dangerous idea.[78]

The image of the Holy Grail was appropriated by Hermeticists, particularly alchemists. In Wolfram von Eschenbach's *Parzival* (c. 1170–1230), the version of the Grail story with which Hegel was most likely familiar, the Grail appears not as a cup but as a stone. In the story, the hermit Trevrizent tells Parzival that the name of the Grail is *Lapsit exillis*.[79] Although this looks like Latin, it literally means nothing. Most scholars have thought it a mistake on Wolfram's part. It is generally agreed that *lapsit* is supposed to be *lapis*, stone. Julius Evola argues for *lapis elixir*, making an obvious connection with alchemy.[80] I find Emma Jung's suggestion of "*lapis exilis*" more plausible, however, for the philosopher's stone was explicitly named *lapis exilis* in some works of Arnold of Villanova, born 1220. The term may be much older.[81] *Exilis* means "poor" or

---

77. My interpretation of these lines is based in part on that of Verene, *Hegel's Recollection*, 6–7.

78. Oetinger believed that the spilling of Christ's blood in the crucifixion was highly significant. For instance, he seems to have held that our "participation" in the life of Christ through holy communion is emblematic of the "taking up" of the true doctrine, transmitted through Christ, through which we may nurture our spiritual body and so work to actualize the divine spiritual concretion which is God. See Robert Schneider, *Geistesahnen*, 123.

79. Wolfram von Eschenbach, *Parzival*, IX. 469:7.

80. Julius Evola, *The Mystery of the Grail*, trans. Guido Stucco (Rochester, Vt.: Inner Traditions, 1994), 153.

81. Ibid., 149.

"mean." Emma Jung notes that traditionally the philosopher's stone is at once priceless, as well as the most common thing there is, "trodden underfoot in the street."[82] She writes that the philosopher's stone is "a particle of God concealed in nature, an analogy to the God who, in Christ, came down to earth in a human body, subject to suffering. On the other hand, the 'cheapness' of the stone . . . alludes to the fact that every human being is its potential bearer, even its begetter."[83]

Hegel finished the *Phenomenology* in great haste, according to legend, on the eve of the battle of Jena. When he looked for an image to end the book, what came to him was the crucifixion of Jesus on Golgotha—and then a chalice, the foaming chalice of Schiller. Perhaps Hegel's inspiration to use Schiller's chalice in the context of the image of the crucifixion can only have seemed right to him because of its association with the Holy Grail, perhaps even the *un-Chalice* of Wolfram—the Grail as stone, the *Stein der Weisen*. The *Phenomenology* has been called a *Bildungsroman*, but perhaps a better description would be Grail quest, where the Grail represents what all other philosophers have sought, but none before Hegel has attained: Absolute Knowing.

---

82. Emma Jung and Marie-Louise von Franz, *The Grail Legend*, trans. Andrea Dykes (Boston: Sigo Press, 1986), 153.
83. Ibid., 157.

The Kabbalistic Tree

The Science of Logic

> Once you have entered the magic circle the sorcerer has drawn
> around himself, you are lost.
> —Eric Voegelin, "On Hegel: A Study in Sorcery"

1. The Project of Hegel's *Logic*

Hegel's second book, the *Science of Logic* (*Wissenschaft der Logik*) was published 1812–16. In 1817, Hegel published another version of his "Logic": the so-called *Encyclopedia Logic*, the first book of his *Encyclopedia of the Philosophical Sciences in Outline* (*Enzyklopädie der Philosophischen Wissenschaften im Grundrisse*). The *Science of Logic* is verbose and obscure. The *Encyclopedia Logic* is terse and obscure. The latter is a collection of numbered paragraphs that served as a lecture outline for Hegel's classes in the Gymnasium in Nuremberg, and later in the universities of Heidelberg and Berlin. These paragraphs are extremely difficult to understand in isolation and require Hegel's amplifying lecture remarks. Fortunately, many of these remarks were written down verbatim by Hegel's students and have been printed in subsequent editions of the *Encyclopedia* as the *Zusätze*. Except where I have indicated otherwise, I will use the term *Logic* to refer to both texts in general, and neither in particular.

Heidegger held that virtually all philosophers before him have "forgotten Being." Metaphysicians think that talking about Being means talking about some particular (if exalted) being, such as God. Hegel's *Logic* is very much a part of this "onto-theo-logical" tradition of metaphysics. The *Logic* is simultaneously an account of what it means to be and an account of the highest individual being. In Aristotelian terms, the *Logic* is an account of substance as such, but it is also an account of the highest individual substance.[1]

On the initial page of the preface to the first edition of the *Science of Logic*, Hegel implies that he intends to provide Germany with its own metaphysics: "If it is remarkable when a nation has become indifferent

---

1. H. S. Harris writes that "The logic presents the divine life as an absolute Substance in which the essence (being, activity) is identical with the existence (becoming, passive product or expression). The substance *is* eternally as a process of coming-to-be" (*Night Thoughts*, 300).

to its constitutional theory, to its national sentiments, its ethical customs and virtues, it is certainly no less remarkable when a nation loses
its metaphysics, when the spirit which contemplates its own pure
essence is no longer a present reality in the life of the nation" (Miller,
25; WL 1:3). In the introduction to the *Science of Logic*, Hegel contrasts
his book to "former metaphysics" (Miller, 64; WL 1:50). In the introduction to the *Encyclopedia Logic*, Hegel writes that "Speculative Logic contains the older logic and metaphysics; it preserves the same forms of
thought, laws, objects, but it develops and transforms them with further categories" (EL § 9; Geraets, 33).

So why did Hegel call this metaphysics *Logic*? In fact, commentators
rarely ask why Hegel selected the title that he did. The answer lies in
the derivation of the term *logic* from the Greek *logos*. Rosenkranz
reports that Hegel in his Jena years "loved . . . to present the creation of
the universe as the utterance of the absolute *Word*, and the return of
the universe into itself as the understanding of the Word, so that
nature and history become the medium between the speaking and the
understanding of the Word—a medium which itself vanishes qua
other-being."[2]

But I shall let Hegel speak for himself, in a series of quotations that
will enable us to piece together an accurate account of the subject matter
of the *Logic*.

In the preface to the second edition (1832) of the *Science of Logic*, Hegel
discusses the consummating idea of his *Logic*, the "Concept" (*der Begriff*):
"This Concept is not sensuously intuited or represented; it is solely an
object, a product and content of thinking, and is the absolute, self-
subsistent thing [*Sache*], the *logos*, the reason of that which is, the truth
of what we call things; it is least of all the *logos* which should be left outside the science of logic" (Miller, 39; WL 1:19). This passage implies that
Hegel's "Doctrine of the Concept" will satisfy the claim of the science
itself to be both metaphysics and ontology: it will give us the *Logos* both
as "absolute, self-subsistent object" and as the "reason of that which is,
the truth of what we call things." Hegel's Absolute Idea (*absolute Idee*) is
this *Logos*.[3] Hegel writes in the *Encyclopedia Logic* that "ideas are not just
to be found in our heads, and the Idea is not at all something so impo-
tent that whether it is realised or not depends upon our own sweet will;
on the contrary, it is at once what is quite simply effective and actual as
well" (EL § 142, Z; Geraets, 214). Hegel writes, further, that "It is not *we*
who 'form' concepts, and in general the Concept should not be considered as something that has come to be at all" (EL § 163, Z; Geraets, 241).

Lecturing on one of the early paragraphs of the *Encyclopedia Logic*,
Hegel remarks that the subject matter of the *Logic* is *truth* (EL § 19 Z-1;
Geraets, 46). Hegel amplifies this remark by adding that what thought
thinks in the *Logic* is "what is eternal" (EL § 19 Z-2; Geraets, 47). This is

---

2. Rosenkranz, *Hegels Leben*, 193. Hegel, *System of Ethical Life*, 265.
3. In the *Philosophy of Nature* Hegel states at one point, "the idea, i.e. the
logos . . . " (PN 1:247, Z; Petry 1:205).

then explained as being "the supersensible world" (EL § 19 Z-2, Geraets, 48). In the *Lectures on the Philosophy of Religion*, Hegel states that "Philosophy is no worldly wisdom, as it used to be called. . . . It is not in fact a wisdom of the world but instead a cognitive knowledge of the non-worldly; it is not a cognition of external existence, of empirical determinate being and life, or of the formal universe, but rather cognition of all that is eternal—of what God is and of what God's nature is as it manifests and develops itself" (LPR 1:117; VPR 1:33–34). In the *Science of Logic*, Hegel identifies the eternal with God (Miller, 78; WL 1:68). In the *Encyclopedia Logic*, Hegel avers that both philosophy and religion hold that "God and God alone is the truth" (EL § 1; Geraets, 24). In his manuscript for the *Lectures on the Philosophy of Religion* (1824), Hegel writes that "God is the one and only object of philosophy" and that "philosophy *is* theology" (LPR 1:84; VPR 1:3–4). In a famous passage of the *Science of Logic*, Hegel states that the *Logic* "is to be understood as the system of pure reason, as the realm of pure thought. This realm is truth as it is without veil and in its own absolute nature. It can therefore be said that this content is the exposition of God as He is in his eternal essence before the creation of nature and a finite Spirit" (Miller, 50; WL 1:33–34).

On the basis of all of the foregoing, then, we are entitled to conclude that, for Hegel, The Eternal = Truth = *Logos* = Absolute Idea = God, and that this is the subject matter to be *recollected* in the *Logic*. Just exactly *how* Hegel can make this series of identifications constitutes the argument of the *Logic*. Against the tradition of "negative theology," as well as the tradition that claims in general that the human intellect is finite and frail, Hegel holds that the Infinite and Eternal *must* be knowable. Hegel even claims, surprisingly, that stressing man's finitude and God's unknowability is contrary to the Christian faith. In his *Lectures on the Philosophy of Religion*, he states, "I declare such a point of view to be directly opposed to the whole nature of the Christian religion, according to which we should *know* God *cognitively*, God's nature and essence, and should esteem this cognition above all else" (LPR 1:88; VPR 1:7).

In the same manuscript, after Hegel claims that philosophy is occupied with God alone—"philosophy *is* theology"—he goes on to say that *everyone* already has a consciousness of God (LPR 1:85; VPR 1:4; again, we see that Hegel's philosophical method involves recollection). This is another theme of Hegel's *Logic*. In the preface to the second edition of the *Encyclopedia Logic*, Hegel writes that "Religion is the mode, the type of consciousness, in which the truth is present for all men," but philosophy is something only a few take up and comprehend (Geraets, 11; *Werke* 8:23). This does not mean that philosophers leave behind the concept of God: as we have seen, Hegel claims in the *Logic* that *both* religion *and* philosophy hold that God alone is the Truth. It simply means that religion—ritual, worship, devotional literature, etc.—is for all men, whereas philosophy is only for a few.

In the very next sentence of the preface, however, Hegel alludes to Homer and says that certain things, such as Truth, have two names, "one in the language of Gods, and the other on the tongues of us men" (Geraets, II; *Werke* 8, 23). The structure of Hegel's sentences suggests that he is saying that religion is to philosophy as the language of Gods is to the language of men. But this is not his meaning. It is philosophy that is the language of Gods. Indeed, in a *Zusatz* to a later section of the *Encyclopedia Logic*, Hegel states that "the original calling of man, to be an image of God, can be realised only through cognition [*Erkennen*]" (EL § 24 Z-3; Geraets, 63). This is no innocent scriptural allusion. In the *Lectures on the Philosophy of Religion*, Hegel states that "God *is* only in and for thought" (LPR 1:209; VPR 1:118).

In making such claims, Hegel is not simply attacking longstanding religious views about man's relationship to God, he is also opposing the Kantian philosophy. Hegel's claim that we *can* know the thing-in-itself is the major reason why so many "tough-minded" philosophers seem to regard him as slightly mad. In fact, Hegel's claim—for which the entire *Logic* serves as an argument—is tightly reasoned and built on Kant's own premises. In the *Science of Logic*, Hegel writes that the critical philosophy holds that "we place our thoughts as a medium between ourselves and the objects, and that this medium instead of connecting us with the objects rather cuts us off from them" (Miller, 36; WL 1:15). Much later in the *Logic*, Hegel infers—as he does in many other places—that Kant's claim that the thing-in-itself is unknowable is equivalent to the claim that "*reality* lies absolutely outside the Concept" (Miller, 593; WL 3:24).

Hegel fastens on to Kant's occasional identification of the thing-in-itself with "the Unconditioned." For Hegel, only the Absolute is unconditioned, for it cannot be subsumed by any higher or wider category. Nor can it be made present in intuition. In the *Logic* he presents a system which articulates the conceptual moments of the Absolute, employing a method Kant to some degree anticipated but never fully appreciated: dialectic. The moments of the Absolute are simultaneously categories of the real and categories of human thought. In fact, a superficial glance at the divisions of Hegel's *Logic* reveals that it is partly a reworking of Kant's Table of Judgments and Table of Categories. Kant's categories are the conditions for the possibility of knowledge and conditions for the possibility of objects as such. Once this is understood, the reasoning behind Hegel's claim to know the thing-in-itself becomes clear. For Hegel, the *totality of conditions* is itself the Unconditioned. These conditions form an organic totality, which can be known as a whole. Therefore, if the totality of these conditions is the Unconditioned, and the Unconditioned is the thing-in-itself, then we can know the thing-in-itself.

Furthermore, this Unconditioned—as an organic totality—is an *individual*. It is a unique, self-sufficient individual determined by nothing, but whose moments determine everything else. Thus, another name for the Unconditioned is *God*. Because its moments account for *all being*, it also constitutes the system of the *World*, or Reality as a whole. Finally, because the categories that make up the Unconditioned are, as I have said, also categories of human thought in all its forms, an account of the Unconditioned is equivalent to an account of the Mind or *Soul*. Thus, Hegel believes that he has, through a radically new method of thought, made Kant's noumenal realm present: what things-in-themselves *are* is the Absolute or Unconditioned, which is World, Soul, and God together.

However, the well-known "dual aspect" reading of Kant's phenomena-noumena distinction might lead one to ask if Hegel's claim to know the thing in itself means that he thinks we can know or experience things *as they are when they are not appearing to us*. The answer to this question is, *yes and no*. We can know things as they are in themselves because the finite things that appear to us are themselves appearances of that infinite, eminently knowable being which is the Absolute or the Unconditioned. In other words, what individual things are in themselves is the Absolute—which we come to know through Hegel's philosophy. However, we cannot know the Absolute in the sense of making it intuitively or sensuously given. It is this kind of knowledge that Kant has in mind when he denies knowledge of things-in-themselves. But Kant's claim that genuine knowledge must always involve intuition is simply arbitrary; it is the chink in Kant's critical armor.

Hegel believes that through the "purificatory initiation" of the *Phenomenology*, he has, in effect, put himself in an altered state of consciousness, beyond the distinction between subject and object, whereupon the dialectic of the *Logic* simply flows from nothing.[4] As I said in chapter 3, the philosopher is a vehicle of the muses: an oracle through which Spirit expresses itself, an automatic writer who passively watches the play of the dialectic as it develops on his page.

Some further discussion of the nature of this process is in order here. As is well-known, Hegel claims that there is a necessity to his dialectical transitions and a completeness to the system. What makes these features possible is Hegel's use—described in chapter 3—of the triangle and the circle as symbolic forms governing the fundamental architectonic of his system. The necessity of Hegel's dialectical transitions is displayed in their triadic structure. It is frequently pointed out that this structure is often inadequately portrayed as a process of "thesis-antithesis-synthesis."[5] Some have even suggested that the "triadic form" of the dialectic is a mere Hegel "myth" and should be discarded. As we have seen, however, Hegel placed special emphasis on the triad as an element out of the *philosophia perennis* (recall his remark about Kant and the triadic form in the preface to the *Phenomenology*).

The triadic structure of dialectic may be described as follows: first there is an initial idea, which when thoroughly thought through suggests its opposite, or, at least, an opposing or contradictory idea; a third term then appears that "reconciles" these two. This reconciliation is

---

4. Arthur Versluis writes of the transformation in the soul of the Böhmean theosopher that "when the soul gives itself up to the nothingness, then it becomes dead to its own will, and the nothing, pure God's will, makes the soul alive according to its own nature." Versluis, *Wisdom's Children*, 149.
5. See Müller, "The Hegel Legend of 'Thesis-Antithesis-Synthesis.'" As is always pointed out, Hegel himself never uses these terms.

accomplished in various ways, but frequently it involves a discovery of an underlying identity or commonality between the two terms initially thought to be different. The real problem with the formula thesis-antithesis-synthesis is with the characterization of the third term as synthesis. Nevertheless, there *are* some Hegelian third terms that do look like syntheses. For instance, in the *Philosophy of Right*, the third term to Family-Civil Society-State appears to take up and *combine* elements of the first two: the state, like Civil Society, is an association of autonomous individuals, but it cancels the external relation of those individuals in Civil Society and, like the family, relates them internally through a shared foundation of values and interests.

The completeness of Hegel's system—especially the *Logic*—is achieved through its circularity. If the final category of the *Logic* (or of the system as a whole) leads back to the beginning, then everything that could be said has been said: nothing has been left out. H. S. Harris writes that "The ideal of philosophy as a self-justifying circle is definitive for Hegel's concept of system from the beginning."[6] Speaking of the dialectic, Hegel says in the *Phenomenology* that "It is the process of its own becoming, the circle that presupposes its end as its goal, having its end also as its beginning; and only by being worked out to its end, is it actual" (Miller, 10; PG, 14). Early in the *Science of Logic*, Hegel writes that "The essential requirement for the science of logic is . . . that the whole of the science be within itself a circle in which the first is also the last and the last is also the first" (Miller, 71; WL 1:60). In the *Encyclopedia Logic*, Hegel writes:

> Each of the parts of philosophy is a philosophical whole, a circle that closes upon itself; but in each of them the philosophical Idea is in a particular determinacy or element. Every single circle also breaks through the restriction of its element as well, precisely because it is inwardly [the] totality, and it grounds a further sphere. The whole presents itself therefore as a circle of circles, each of which is a necessary moment, so that the system of its peculiar elements constitutes the whole idea—which equally appears in each single one of them. (EL § 15; Geraets, 39)

The system is a circle of circles, and the *Logic* is one such circle.

An important question must be asked about Hegel's metaphor, however. If the *Logic* on reaching its "final" category gives way to the *Philosophy of Nature*, then how can it be said to return to its beginning? The answer is that each part of the system—Logic-Nature-Spirit—constitutes a separate "domain." Each separate Hegelian science gives a complete speech about one of these domains. It is not "Absolute Idea" that *leads to* the *Philosophy of Nature*. Rather, it is the *Logic* as a whole that requires supplementation by the categories of Nature. Hegel writes in the *Encyclopedia Logic* that "The Logic is the science of the pure Idea, that is, of the Idea in the abstract element of thinking" (EL § 19; Geraets, 45). As abstract, the

---

6. Harris, *Night Thoughts*, 235; Kojève also makes the point that it is the circularity of the system that proves its completeness (Kojève, *Introduction to the Reading of Hegel*, 93).

Idea is without full *realization* or *expression*, although it is fully *intelligible* in the "abstract element of thinking." The Absolute Idea is presupposed in the beginning of the *Logic*—Being—and Absolute Idea is a return, of sorts, to Being. Hegel's circle of circles might best be understood as a *chain*: each link is a whole, and although one link touches another, it is not fastened to that other or permanently connected with it.[7]

In one of the *Zusätze* to an early paragraph in the *Encyclopedia Logic*, Hegel states: "When . . . we consider the Logic as the system of *pure* thought-determinations [*reinen Denkbestimmungen*], the other philosophical sciences—the Philosophy of Nature, and the Philosophy of Spirit—appear, in contrast, as applied logic, so to speak, for the Logic is their animating soul. Thus, the concern of those other sciences is only to [re]cognise the logical forms in the shapes of nature and spirit, shapes that are only a particular mode of expression of the forms of pure thinking" (EL § 24 Z-2; Geraets, 58). Hegel continues these remarks, in a manner that will shortly emerge as very important: "In this way the Logic is the all-animating spirit of all sciences, and the thought-determinations contained in the Logic are the pure spirits; they are what is most inward, but, at the same time, they are always on our lips, and consequently they seem to be something thoroughly well-known" (EL § 24 Z-2; Geraets, 59). Hegel is here referring to the idea, explored already in chapter 3, that we always already know—implicitly—the content of philosophy.

Something further must be said, though, about the relation of the *Logic* to the whole system. At the end of his introduction to the *Encyclopedia Logic*, Hegel gives the structure of his system as follows:

I. The *Logic*, the science of the Idea in and for itself.

II. The *Philosophy of Nature*, as the science of the Idea in its otherness.

III. The *Philosophy of Spirit*, as the Idea that returns into itself out of its otherness. (EL § 18; Geraets, 42)

Much later in the *Encyclopedia Logic*, Hegel states that "The Idea is what is true in and for itself, the absolute unity of Concept and objectivity" (EL § 213; Geraets, 286). The "in itself" refers to the parts of the *Logic* that Hegel calls "objective logic"—Being and Essence—whereas the truth "for itself" is "subjective logic," the Concept (Miller, 63–64; WL 1:50–51). In the *Logic*, all the eidetic determinations of *objects* are explicated and are shown to lead to an idea that reflects on itself or is self-referential—this is what Hegel means by the Idea being "for itself" or "subjective."

Absolute Idea is the *abstract conception* of self-thinking thought. Through nature and man it "seeks" worldly realization and finds it only in the embodied self-thinking thought of the philosopher.

7. I owe this metaphor of the chain to Donald Phillip Verene (seminar on the *Phenomenology of Spirit*, Emory University, fall 1996). The metaphor of the chain (*Kette*) also occurs in Oetinger: "Die Welt ist eine Kette." See Robert Schneider, *Geistesahnen*, 127.

2. Böhmean Influences on the *Logic*

In 1816 Hegel received invitations to teach at Heidelberg and Berlin. His chances in Berlin, however, were sabotaged by the powerful Berlin theologian Wilhelm Martin Leberecht de Wette (1780–1849), who, as Wiedmann notes, denounced Hegel's *Logic* as an obscure "occultism" (*Geheimwissenschaft*).[8] Earlier, in an 1815 letter to Hegel's archenemy Jakob Friedrich Fries (1773–1843), de Wette wrote that "Mysticism reigns here mightily, and how deep we have sunk is shown in the thought of Hegel."[9]

At times, Hegel seems to have positively encouraged the impression that he is a mystic. In the 1805 *Lectures on the History of Philosophy*, Hegel stated that "The philosophers are closer to the Lord than those who live by the crumbs of the Spirit; they read, or write, the cabinet orders of God in the original; it is their duty to write them down. The philosophers are the *mystai* who have been present at the decision in the innermost sanctuary."[10] In the preface to the second edition of the *Encyclopedia*, Hegel writes that "what was revealed as a mystery in earlier times should now be revealed for thinking itself" (Geraets, 17; *Werke* 8:31).

The preface to the second edition of the *Encyclopedia* (1827) provides ample evidence of Hegel's willingness to be grouped with the mystics. Introducing some of his basic ideas, Hegel mentions Böhme more than once. He writes, "The spirit is essentially consciousness, and hence [consciousness] of the content made into an object. As feeling, the spirit is just the not yet objective content itself (only a *quale*, to use an expression of Jakob Böhme); it is just the lowest stage of consciousness, in the form of the soul, which we have in common with the lower animals" (Geraets, 12; *Werke* 8:24). Hegel goes on to write of Böhme:

> The name "Teutonic Philosopher" has rightly been conferred upon this mighty spirit. On the one hand, he has enlarged the basic import of religion, [taken] on its own account, to the universal Idea; within that basic import he formulated the highest problems of reason and tried to grasp spirit and nature in their determinate spheres and configurations. [All this was possible] because he took as his foundation [the thesis] that the spirit of man and all things else are created in the image of God—and, of course, of God as the Trinity; their life is just the process of their reintegration into that original image after the loss of it. On the other hand (and conversely), he forcibly misappropriated the forms of natural things (sulphur, saltpeter, etc.; the sharp, the bitter, etc.) as spiritual forms and forms of thought. (Geraets, 15; *Werke* 8:28–29)

In the same text Hegel also makes several admiring references to the arch-theosophist and occultist of his day, Franz von Baader. In support

8. Wiedmann, *Hegel*, 53.
9. Nicolin, *Hegel in Berichten seiner Zeitgenossen*, 117.
10. Hegel, *Geschichte der Philosophie*, ed. Hermann Glockner, *Jubiläumsausgabe*, vol. 3 (Stuttgart: Fromann, 1927–1940), 96.

of his own attempt to "rationalize" religious doctrine, Hegel quotes volume 5 of Baader's *Fermenta Cognitionis* (1824). Baader claims there that the idea that religion is only a "matter of the heart" is a view dear to atheists, who know that to undermine religion they must undermine the notion that a rational theory of religion is possible.[11] After quoting Baader, Hegel goes on to state that

> What is most sublime, most profound, and most inward has been called forth into the light of day in the religions, philosophies, and works of art, in more or less pure, in clearer or more obscure shapes, often in very repulsive ones. We can count it as a particular merit of Franz von Baader that he not only goes on bringing such forms to our recollection, but also with a profoundly speculative spirit he brings their basic import expressly into scientific honour because on that basis he expounds and confirms the philosophical Idea. (Geraets, 15)

In an extraordinary footnote, Hegel writes that "I am certainly delighted to learn that Herr von Baader agrees with many of my propositions—as is evident both from the content of several of his more recent writings and from his references to me by name. About most of what he contests—and even quite easily about everything—it would not be difficult for me to come to an understanding with him, that is to say, to show that there is, in fact, no departure from his views in it" (Geraets, 15; *Werke* 8:29). Hegel then goes on to take issue with a criticism Baader made of one aspect of his *Philosophy of Nature*.[12]

Although Baader does make some favorable remarks about Hegel in the first volume of *Fermenta Cognitionis*, Hegel's assessment of his relationship with Baader seems to have been highly unrealistic. Baader, for his part, appears to have been simply puzzled by Hegel's attention and insistence on their ability to "come to an understanding." It is not unusual for one prominent scholar to "court" another, for career advancement, or often simply to establish an intellectual friendship. Baader, however, was a decidedly strange and marginal figure for Hegel to court—unless, of course, Hegel saw himself as somehow belonging on the margins with Baader.

To return to Böhme, in the 1812 Doctrine of Being of the *Science of Logic*, Hegel offers the following in a remark concerning "quality" in the section on *Dasein*:

> *Qualierung* or *Inqualierung*, [which are terms from out of] a philosophy which goes deep but into a turbid depth, refers to Determinacy as in itself, but at the same time is another in itself; or it refers to the familiar nature of opposition, as it is in its essence. In this respect opposition constitutes the inner nature of quality and is essentially its self-movement in itself. *Qualierung* means therefore, in the afore-

11. Baader, *Fermenta Cognitionis* (Berlin, 1824), preface, ixff (quoted in Geraets, 14; *Werke*, 27).
12. Baader replied to Hegel's defense of himself here in an 1824 essay entitled "Hegel on My Doctrine in the Preface to the Second Edition of the Encyclopedia." See his *Sämtliche Werke*, ed. F. Hoffmann et al. (Leipzig, 1851–60), Folge I, 10:306–9.

mentioned philosophy, the movement of a determinacy in itself, in which respect it situates and fastens itself in its negative nature (in its *Qual*) from out of another, signifying in general the quality's own internal unrest by which it produces and maintains itself only in conflict.[13]

Qualierung or *Inqualierung*—which might be rendered "qualification" or "inqualification"—refer to Böhme's dynamic conception of quality. In *Aurora* he states that "A quality is the mobility, boiling, springing and driving of a thing."[14] Hegel quotes this line in his remarks on Böhme in the *Lectures on the History of Philosophy* (LHP 3:199; *Werke* 20:103).

In the 1832 edition of the Doctrine of Being (the only segment of the *Logic* Hegel finished revising before his death), the above passage has been significantly altered. It now reads as follows: "*Qualierung* or *Inqualierung*, an expression of Jakob Böhme's, whose philosophy goes deep, but into a turbid depth, signifies the movement of a quality (of sourness, bitterness, fieriness, etc.) within itself in so far as it situates and fastens itself in its negative nature (in its *Qual*) from out of an other—signifies in general the quality's own internal unrest by which it produces and maintains itself only in conflict" (Miller, 114; WL 1:[1832], 109). Aside from cutting some of the more opaque lines from the original, Hegel has now explicitly attributed *Qualierung* and *Inqualierung* to Böhme, and included reference to Böhme's categories sour, bitter and "fire" (heat?).

For some reason, Hegel decided against referring to Böhme by name in the first edition of the Doctrine of Being. In fact, Hegel makes no reference to Böhme in any of his published writings until the *Encyclopedia* in 1817 (in which a very brief reference to Böhme occurs in paragraph 472 of the *Philosophy of Spirit*). In the 1832 edition of the Doctrine of Being—as well as in the preface to the 1827 *Encyclopedia* quoted above—Hegel seems to be deliberately correcting this omission and more openly acknowledging his indebtedness to Böhme. This very likely indicates that since 1805 Hegel continued to study Böhme closely, no doubt making use of van Ghert's kind gift of the Böhme edition (see chapter 4). Thus, we are faced with exactly the opposite of what many commentators on Hegel's relationship to Böhme would have us expect: instead of moving away from Böhme in his mature period, Hegel actually seems to be moving, in a very public manner, *toward* him. Hegel's attempt to ally himself with Baader, who was widely known at the time as *Böhmius redivivus*, only reinforces this impression.

I now proceed to what is specifically Böhmean in the *Logic*. In the *Encyclopedia Logic* Hegel states that "the Logic is the all-animating spirit of all sciences, and the thought-determinations contained in the Logic are the pure spirits [*die reinen Geister*]" (EL § 24 Z-2; Geraets, 59). In the *Science of Logic* Hegel refers to Logic as a "realm of shades [*Schatten*]."[15] These passages make sense only if we suppose that Hegel thinks of the

13. WL (1812 ed.), 82. Since Miller bases his translation on the 1832 edition, he does not include this passage.

14. *Aurora*, chap. 1, § 3; Sparrow, 40.

15. Hegel, *Wissenschaft der Logik*, 3 vols., ed. L. von Henning, (Berlin: Duncker and Humblot, 1840–1847), vol. 3, 47.

categories or ideas of the *Logic* as being in some sense *minds*. The identification of *eide* with minds is a perennial idea in the philosophic tradition. It appears in Aristotle when he says of the soul that it "must be a substance as the form of a natural body potential with life, and [such] substance is an actuality [*entelecheia*]. So the soul is the actuality of such a body."[16] It is also a theme of Spinoza's thought.

The place of this idea in Hegel's *Logic* should be fairly obvious: if Absolute Idea is, in effect, the "pure *eidos*"—or, in Aristotelian terms, the *actuality*—of self-thinking thought, then Absolute Idea is a kind of *pure mind*, or *formal mind*. In the preface to the *Phenomenology*, Hegel states that when Being becomes "absolutely mediated," it becomes "the Concept," which, he says, is "self-like" (*selbstisch*; Miller, 21; PG, 29). Since all preceding categories of the *Logic* are approximations to Absolute Idea, each is, in effect, an approximation to mind. They are ghostly (*geisterhaft*) "shades" because they are only partially real. Even the Absolute Idea, the Pluto of this "Reich der Schatten," is ultimately only the shadow cast by embodied self-thinking thought.

We might ask what the relation is between the spirit-shades of the *Logic* and the Spirit of the *Phenomenology* and *Philosophy of Spirit*. Quite simply, the Spirit realized in mankind is Holy Spirit, Holy Ghost (*heilige Geist*). In themselves, the *eide* of the *Logic* are, as I have already said, merely formal and empty. In the living Spirit of mankind, however, these *eide*-spirits have trod the Via Dolorosa of the *Phenomenology* and, so to speak, "earned their wings." They have become fully concrete, fully expressed. There is more than a mere analogy to Christian doctrine here, however. Hegel's spirits and his Spirit *really are supernatural*. In the 1831 preface to the second edition of the *Science of Logic* Hegel writes, "If nature as such, as the physical world, is contrasted with the natural sphere, then logic must certainly be said to be the *supernatural* [*übernatürliche*], which permeates every relationship of man to nature, his sensation, intuition, desire, need, instinct, and simply by doing so transforms it into something human, even though only formally human, into ideas and purposes" (Miller, 32; WL 1:10; my emphasis). The spirits of the *Logic* are logically prior to the natural world, and the Holy Spirit only appears in the world through the activity of men who have raised themselves above the level of nature or the animal.

Böhme, of course, analyzes God and the process of coming-to-be into seven "source spirits" (*Quellgeister*), which he also calls "forms" (*Gestalten*), "properties" (*Eigenschaften*), and "qualities" (*Qualitäten*). Hegel's *Logic* and its "moments" are analogous to Böhme's source spirits or forms. Hegel's categories, like Böhme's, inform all of reality and are the *Grundbegriffe* for all the sciences. Further, Böhme introduces his discussion of the seven source-spirits as a discussion "of the corpus of an angelical kingdom."[17] Hegel does not treat his Logic-spirits as angels,

---

16. Aristotle, *De Anima*, B, 412a20–22, in *Aristotle: Selected Works*, trans. Hippocrates G. Apostle (Grinnell: Peripatetic Press, 1982), 266.
17. *Aurora*, chap. 8, heading; Sparrow, 147.

but rather as shades like those in Hades or Limbo. Nevertheless, the parallel is clear.

Further, Böhme's account of the interrelationships of his seven source-spirits is strikingly like Hegel's treatment of his system of logical moments. In *Aurora*, Böhme writes, "All the seven spirits are generated one in another, the one continually generates the other, not one of them is the first, nor is any one of them the last; for the last generates as well the first as the second, third, fourth, and so on to the last."[18] In Böhme's *Clavis*, he writes that "the first and seventh properties are always to be reckoned as one, and also the second and sixth as one, as well as the third and fifth as one, the fourth alone is the separating limit [*Scheide-Ziel*], since there are only three properties of nature, according to the revelation of the Holy Trinity of God."[19]

What these quotations call to mind, of course, is the famous circularity of the *Logic*. Böhme claims that his first and final spirits are one, just as Hegel claims that the end of the *Logic* returns to the beginning. In the *Phenomenology* Hegel says that the dialectic "is the process of its own becoming, the circle that presupposes its end as its goal, having its end also as its beginning; and only by being worked out to its end, is it actual" (Miller, 10; PG, 14). Of course, Böhme also says that his second and sixth and third and fifth spirits are one, but there is even an analogue for this in Hegel. Each of the triadic subdivisions Being, Essence, and Concept in the *Logic* "correspond" with one another, so that, for instance, "Quality" in Being is analogous to "Intro-reflection" (*Reflexion in ihm selbst*) in Essence, just as the major triad of Being-Essence-Concept corresponds to the major, triadic divisions of the other Hegelian sciences.

Whereas Hegel employs the image of the circle to describe the structure of the *Logic* and the system as a whole, Böhme employs the image of the *wheel*. Böhme writes in *Aurora*,

> But if I should describe the Deity in its birth in a small, round circle, in the highest depth, then it is thus: Suppose a wheel standing before you, with seven wheels one so made in the other that it could go on all sides, forward, backward and cross ways, without need of turning back. In its going, that always-one wheel, in its turning about, generates the others, and yet none of them vanishes out of sight, but all seven are visible. . . . The seven wheels are the seven spirits of God. They are always generating one another, and are like the turning of a wheel . . . and the seven wheels are hooped round with fellies, like a round globe.[20]

Böhme goes on to liken the seven wheels or spirits to "God the Father," the nave of the wheel of wheels ("there are not seven naves, but one only") to the "Son of God," and the spokes to the "Holy Spirit." Of course, it is Hegel's entire "developmental" account of God, and not just this or that detail, which seems so strikingly like Böhme. (Interestingly,

18. *Aurora*, chap. 10, § 2; Sparrow, 207–8.
19. Quoted in Walsh, *The Mysticism of Innerworldly Fulfillment*, 82.
20. *Aurora*, chap. 13, §§ 71–72; Sparrow, 328–29.

Oetinger also makes prominent use of the circle metaphor. In his *Philosophie der Alten* (1762) he writes, "Nature is a circle, it has many beginnings and endings."[21])

In *Mysterium Magnum*, Böhme refers to God before his "development," God as *Ungrund*, as "the dark nature" and states that "in the dark nature he is not called God."[22] The concept of *Ungrund* bears some similarity to Hegel's aether, which I shall discuss more extensively in the following chapter. Like the aether, it is an ultimate, dynamic ground of all being. Walsh refers to *Ungrund* as a "dark inchoate will for self-revelation."[23] All of the spirits are "contained" within God as *Ungrund*, *in potentia*. Böhme refers to the *Ungrund* as both *Alles* and *Nichts*.[24] God as *Ungrund* cannot achieve self-revelation unless He takes some determinate form, unless, as Walsh puts it, He generates "a spiritual corporeality."[25] This is, in effect, Böhme's Logic: the "system" of seven spirits, represented as a wheel of wheels, existing eternally, from which nature or extension will be "projected."

Böhme expresses the ideality of this system by calling it "eternal nature." The coming-into-being of this spiritual corporeality is a process of *specifying* or determining the will of the *Ungrund*. The *Ungrund* is an "out-going" will—a will for self-revelation—which Böhme calls *Nichts*. To achieve this revelation, however, the out-going will must fall within the gravitational attraction of an "in-going" will, which is a "contracting" and individuating force. It is the in-going will that gives *Nichts* determinate being. In fact, Böhme calls this will *Etwas*. Böhme writes in *Mysterium Magnum* that "the eternal free will has introduced itself into darkness, pain, and source; and so also through the darkness into the fire and light, even into a kingdom of joy; so that the Nothing might be known in the Something."[26] Böhme writes that "the nothing is a craving after something."[27]

The parallels to Hegel scarcely require comment. *Ungrund* corresponds to the pure indeterminacy with which Hegel begins the *Logic*. Böhme calls *Ungrund Alles* and *Nichts*, just as Hegel calls his indeterminacy *Reines Sein* and *Nichts*. Further, Böhme conceives the *Alles-Nichts* as an active will, just as Hegel sees *Sein-Nichts* as a kind of conceptual dynamism, and so dubs it *Werden* (Becoming). For Böhme, the out-going will of *Alles-Nichts* must enter into or become (he is not too clear on this point) the

---

21. Oetinger, *Die Philosophie der Alten, wiederkommend in der güldenen Zeit* (Frankfurt and Leipzig, 1762), vol. 1, 182. Some of Hegel's programmatic remarks in the *Logic* also seem to bear the impress of Oetinger. In the *Science of Logic*, in a passage concerning the nature of "logical forms" (*logischen Formen*), Hegel writes, "When they are taken as fixed determinations and consequently in their separation from each other and not as held together in an organic unity, then they are dead forms and the spirit which is their living, concrete unity does not dwell in them" (Miller 48; WL 1:31).
22. *Mysterium Magnum*, chap. 7, § 14.
23. David Walsh, "A Mythology of Reason," 154.
24. Böhme, *Von der Gnaden-Wahl*, in *Sämtliche Schriften*, vol. 6, chap. 1, § 3.
25. Walsh, *The Mysticism of Innerworldly Fulfillment*, 78.
26. *Mysterium Magnum*, chap. 26, § 37.
27. Böhme goes on to say that this is "the eternal origin of magic." Quoted in Nicolescu, *Science, Meaning, and Evolution*, 211.

more determinate will of *Etwas*. In the *Logic*, Becoming gives rise to Being-there (*Dasein*), which is translated by many commentators as "Determinate Being." This is obviously analogous to Böhme's *Etwas*. In fact, in the *Science of Logic*, in a passage immediately following the discussion of Böhme's *Qualierung*, Hegel writes that, "Being-there is *a being-there, Something*" (*das Dasein ist Daseiendes, Etwas*; Miller, 115; WL 1;110).

In one of the *Zusätze* to the *Encyclopedia Logic*, Hegel describes the dialectical "overcoming" of Becoming in language that immediately calls to mind Böhme: "becoming proves itself to be what is thoroughly restless, but unable to maintain itself in this abstract restlessness; for, insofar as being and nothing vanish in becoming—and just this is its concept—becoming is thereby itself something that vanishes, like a fire that dies out within itself by consuming its material." *Dasein* or *Etwas* is the ashes left behind by the fire: the energy of *Werden* (= *Sein/Nichts* = *Nichts/Sein*) "coagulates" as *Dasein*, as Determinate Being.

Böhme frequently talks about God "in Himself." He often uses this expression to refer to the "contracted being" of God within the first of the source-spirits, Sour. However, it is God's nature to become "for Himself" (an expression Böhme does not use). In the *Lectures on the Philosophy of Religion* of 1827 Hegel states that "God can be known or cognized, for it is God's nature to reveal Himself, to be manifest" (LPR 1:382; VPR 1:278). Hegel claims that to say otherwise is contrary to the Christian faith. The above quote continues as follows: "Those who say that God is not revelatory do not speak from the [standpoint of the] Christian religion at any rate, for the Christian religion is called the revealed religion. Its content is that God is revealed to human beings, that they know what God is. Previously they did not know this; but in the Christian religion there is no longer any secret—a mystery, certainly, but not in the sense that it is not known."

Hegel criticizes Spinoza in his *Lectures on the History of Philosophy* on the grounds that his God or substance remains "in Himself." Recall that these lectures were delivered in 1805, during Hegel's initial period of Böhme-enthusiasm in Jena. Hegel refers to Spinoza's God as *der Abgrund der Substanz* (the abyss of substance). *Abgrund* is first used in a philosophical context by Eckhart. It seems to be the conceptual ancestor of Böhme's *Ungrund* (and Böhme also sometimes uses *Abgrund*). The sense in which Hegel uses *Abgrund* here makes it very clear that he is thinking of Spinoza's God as equivalent to the unmanifest, undeveloped, *potentia* of Böhme's *Ungrund*.

This impression is confirmed by the following passage from the *Lectures*:

> [Spinoza's] philosophy has only a rigid and unyielding substance, and not yet Spirit; in it we are not at home with ourselves [*man ist nicht bei sich*]. God is not Spirit here, because he is not the triune [*der Dreieinige*]. Substance remains rigid and petrified, without Böhme's sources [*Quellen*; i.e. source-spirits]; for the individual determinations in the form of determinations of the understanding are not Böhme's source-spirits [*Quellgeister*], which energize and expand in one another. (LHP 3:288; *Werke* 20:166)

This passage is extraordinary because Hegel is criticizing a major "canonical" philosopher for failing to come up to the standard of Böhme, a marginal figure widely considered even in Hegel's day not to be a philosopher at all. It is also extraordinary because it shows how deeply immersed Hegel was in Böhme's way of thinking, how in discussing a thinker very different from Böhme, Hegel was still operating with the terms and distinctions and thought-patterns of Böhme uppermost in his mind.

In the Appearance (*Erscheinung*) section of the Doctrine of Essence in the *Logic*, Hegel discusses the category of "Force and its Utterance" (*Kraft und ihre Äusserung*). He claims that in Force, the opposition of "Whole and Parts" is reconciled. In a *Zusatz* to the *Encyclopedia Logic* Hegel states, "Although it consists implicitly of parts, the whole does cease to be a whole when it is divided; a force, on the other hand, only proves itself to be a force by uttering itself. It returns to itself in its utterance, for the utterance is itself a force once more" (EL § 136 Z-1; Geraets, 206–7). One is reminded here of Böhme's *Ton* (Sound or Tone). At a certain point, the primal will toward self-manifestation gives rise to the source-spirit *Love*, which is a seeking after illumination or self-completion. As I said in chapter 1, this seeking issues in Tone, a phenomenon which is a kind of "eject" of the seeking—a kind of significant epiphenomenon. As separate from Love, but as a product of Love, Tone makes Love manifest to itself. With Tone, the life of God is ready for fulfillment: having given rise to a "speech" or "expression" of itself (Tone), the process becomes a thing definite to itself.

Böhme's seventh spirit, of course, is Body (*Corpus*), which encompasses the other six. It represents the "concretization" of the process through its self-expression. This concretization is the completion of the cycle, but as involving the cycle's self-awareness it includes the cycle as well. Böhme states that God's "hunger and desire is after substance."[28] For Böhme, all things strive to become fully specified and concrete, including God. In a striking parallel to Böhme's thought, Hegel characterizes his Concept as a fully concrete being, and treats it as substance, as a kind of spiritual body. Of course, for both Böhme and Hegel this eidetic process must realize itself in the world and become truly embodied in order for it to be fully actual. Thus, Hegel speaks in the *Philosophy of Spirit* of "Objective Spirit," in which the Idea is embodied in law and morality, as well as of "Absolute Spirit," in which the Idea finds its highest expression in art, religion, and philosophy.

Finally, although its relevance to Böhme is slight, the occurrence of alchemical terminology in the *Logic* is worth mentioning. Three times in the *Encyclopedia Logic* Hegel employs the term *caput mortuum*.[29] Geraets and his coeditors explain this as "the alchemist's term for the 'dead' precipitate that remained when all the 'living spirit' had been extracted or given off" (Geraets, 316 n.45). Cyril O'Regan writes that *caput mortuum*

---

28. *Six Theosophic Points*, chap. 1, § 27.
29. For a discussion of Hegel's use of this term, see Figala's "Der alchemische Begriff des Caput Mortuum in der symbolischen Terminologie Hegels."

is the "precipitate that remains after spirit has been extracted."[30] C. J. S. Thompson seems to concur, describing *caput mortuum* as "the term given to the residue that was left in the bulb of a retort after an operation."[31] Hegel first applies the term to the Kantian thing-in-itself (EL § 44; Geraets, 87). Later, he refers to Essence taken abstractly as "the *caput mortuum* of abstraction" (EL § 112; Geraets, 175). Finally, he applies the term to the transcendent conception of God: "As the abstract essence in the Beyond, outside of which all distinction and determinacy must fall, God is in fact a mere name, a mere *caput mortuum* of the abstractive understanding" (EL § 112, Z; Geraets, 177). It is apparent that Hegel would regard Böhme's *Ungrund* as a *caput mortuum*.

Hegel's use of *caput mortuum* to describe Essence is the most interesting occurrence of the term. Essence, of course, is a stepping-stone on the way to Concept and Absolute Idea. Essence itself is indeed a *caput mortuum* insofar as it is a *negated* provisional definition for the Absolute Idea. It "dies" or falls away, yet it is at the same time "material" used in the process of dialectic that presses on to Absolute Idea. Hegel's use of *caput mortuum* to describe Essence taken abstractly (i.e., taken on its own, in isolation from the other categories) indicates that he recognized the parallel between dialectic and alchemical transmutation: determinate negation is the *nigredo* that precedes the synthesis of *rubedo*, the philosopher's stone, or the Absolute (see the following chapter for a more detailed treatment of alchemy in relation to Hegel).

3. The Kabbalah

a) The Kabbalistic Writings

"Kabbalah" means "tradition." The Kabbalah is thought to have been a teaching handed down from God to Moses, although the earliest textual evidence of a Jewish mystical tradition dates from about the first century B.C. Kabbalism is a fusion of early Jewish mysticism with Gnosticism, Neoplatonism, and possibly Hermetic Gnosis.[32] Some have argued that Kabbalism definitely begins in the twelfth to thirteenth centuries in Spain. Others maintain that it goes back much farther. Far from being one unitary doctrine or movement, there are various schools and strains of Kabbalism. Some may be considered to be fairly traditional in concurring ultimately with the teachings of orthodox, nonmystical Judaism; others are quite radical in their departure from tradition.

As to the major texts of the Kabbalah, three must be mentioned. Gershom Scholem calls the *Sefer Yezirah* or *Book of the Creation* the "earliest extant Hebrew text of systematic, speculative thought."[33] Its date of composition is uncertain, but we know that versions of the *Sefer Yezirah* existed in the tenth century. It was first printed in Mantua in 1562. Composed of less than two thousand words, the *Sefer Yezirah* dealt with the

30. See O'Regan, *The Heterodox Hegel*, 384, n61.

31. C. J. S. Thompson, *The Lure and Romance of Alchemy* (New York: Bell Publishing, 1990), 116.

32. M. H. Abrams, *Natural Supernaturalism* (New York: W. W. Norton, 1971), 157–58.

33. Gershom Scholem, *Kabbalah*, 23.

thirty-two "secret paths of wisdom," the mystical significance of the twenty-two elemental letters of the Hebrew alphabet, and the ten *Sephiroth*, which will be discussed shortly. The *Bahir* ("brilliance" or "illumination"), a collection of Kabbalistic writings, some new and some very old, was assembled in Provence in the twelfth century. Many Kabbalists ascribe parts of the *Bahir* to Rabbi Nehuniah ben HaKana, who flourished in the first century A.D. The *Bahir* is noteworthy for its highly imaginative usage of symbolism and metaphor. The classic text of speculative Kabbalism, however, is the *Sefer Ha Zohar*, or *Book of Splendor*, a text of almost a thousand pages now thought to have been composed by Moses de Leon of Castille in the late thirteenth century, though attributed by him to earlier sources.

b) Hegel's Knowledge of Kabbalism

Hegel studied several histories of philosophy in putting together his *Lectures* of 1805. One of these was Johann Jacob Brucker's *Historia Critica Philosophiae*, which appeared in five Latin volumes in Leipzig from 1742 to 1744 (a second edition came out in 1766–67). Faivre writes that Brucker's work represents the "first really systematic description of the Western esoteric currents.... Although a work of little objectivity, marked by the rationalism of the Enlightenment, its importance should not be underestimated, because for several generations it acted as a point of reference for philosophy in general and esotericism in particular." Faivre notes that the entry on "Theosophie" in Diderot's *Encyclopédie* was largely plagiarized from Brucker.[34] Brucker's attitude toward Hermeticism is predominantly hostile.

Brucker devotes considerable attention to the Hermetic tradition. His discussion of "Egyptian philosophy" includes an account of Hermes Trismegistus. He discusses figures like Bruno, Lull, and Campanella. In volume 4, part 1, he includes a chapter entitled "The Restoration of Pythagorean-Platonic-Kabbalistic Philosophy," which includes accounts of the work of Reuchlin, Agrippa, and the Cambridge Platonists Cudworth and More. A later chapter in the same volume, titled "The Theosophists," discusses Fludd, Böhme, and Francis Mercury van Helmont. Most significant, however, is the more than 150 pages devoted to the Kabbalah in volume 2. In introducing his *Lectures*, Hegel states that Brucker's work "is so much useless ballast" (LHP 1:112; *Werke* 18:134). The substance of Hegel's criticism is that many of Brucker's accounts are inaccurate and deformed by his commitment to Wolffian metaphysics.[35] Nevertheless, Hegel read these volumes carefully.

In his *Lectures on the History of Philosophy*, Hegel boils down Brucker's extensive remarks on the Kabbalah to about two pages. Though the brevity of Hegel's treatment might suggest that he shared Brucker's hostility, there is no evidence for this in what Hegel actually says. He does mention that Kabbalistic writers sometimes "sink into the fantastic" (LHP

---

34. Faivre, *Theosophy, Imagination, Tradition*, xviii; 18–19.
35. See also the preface to the second edition of the *Encyclopedia Logic*, in which similar criticisms are leveled against Brucker (Geraets, 10; *Werke* 8:22).

2:395; *Werke* 19:426), but he says similar things about Böhme and yet takes Böhme's thought very seriously.[36] I will not discuss Hegel's account of the Kabbalah here, for it is from start to finish identical with a particular form of Kabbalah, that of Isaac Luria (1534–72), which I shall discuss at length in chapter 7.[37] In the present section, I will be concerned simply with an account of the basic concepts of the Kabbalah. Whether or not Hegel consciously recognized his indebtedness to the Kabbalah is irrelevant. His thought is similar to it in an extraordinary number of ways.

If there was an influence of the Kabbalah on Hegel, how did it take place? One source was undoubtedly Brucker. Another, more indirect source was Böhme, whose indebtedness to the Kabbalah is almost universally acknowledged (Brucker even remarks on it). When Oetinger asked a rabbi in Frankfurt am Main how he might better understand the Kabbalah, the rabbi directed him to Böhme's works. A seventeenth-century follower of Böhme, Johann Jacob Späth, was so astounded on learning of the roots of Böhme's thought in the Kabbalah that he converted to Judaism.[38] Lurianic Kabbalism was a major influence on Böhme. Cyril O'Regan maintains that Oetinger provides the key to understanding the influence of the Kabbalah on Hegel.[39]

It is unlikely that Hegel read any Kabbalist works in the original Hebrew. However, it is highly probable that he did read at least some Latin translations, published as part of Knorr von Rosenroth's two-volume compendium of Kabbalistic literature, the *Kabbala Denudata* (*Kabbalah Unveiled*) (1677, 1684). Rosenroth, a Pietist nobleman, included large excerpts from the Lurianic Kabbalah, as well as a long essay by Francis Mercury van Helmont, an alchemist and friend of Leibniz. The *Kabbala Denudata* made Kabbalism accessible to every educated person and affected attitudes to and interpretations of Kabbalah until the end of the nineteenth century.[40] It contains many errors of translation, but does not seriously distort Kabbalism.[41]

I now turn to some of the details of the Kabbalist metaphysics and cosmology.

---

36. In the preface to the second edition of the *Encyclopedia Logic* Hegel makes a brief swipe at "gnostic and Kabbalistic phantasmagorias" (Geraets, 17; *Werke* 8:31). But "kabbalistische" was a common epithet in Hegel's day for what the Germans call *Schwärmerei*, ecstatic, visionary mysticism or enthusiasm of a particularly mindless sort. It does not necessarily refer to the real Kabbalah, any more than our term "cabal" refers to actual Kabbalistic sects.

37. Cyril O'Regan also identifies Hegel's presentation of the Kabbalah as Lurianic. See O'Regan, "Hegel and Anti-Judaism," *The Owl of Minerva* 28 (1997): 141–82; 162.

38. Both anecdotes are recounted in Scholem, *Major Trends*, 238.

39. Cyril O'Regan, "Hegel and Anti-Judaism," 160. O'Regan further states (p. 166) that "The historical fact that the linkage of the Kabbalah with Böhme was available to Hegel through the mystical Pietism of the previous generation leads one to emphasize its value for characterizing Hegelian ontotheological narrative."

40. There had been earlier translations of some Kabbalist works. For instance, Guillaume Postel (1510–81) translated the *Sefer Yezirah* and *Zohar* into Latin.

41. Scholem, *Kabbalah*, 416.

c) *Bereshith* . . .

The root of the Hebrew word *Yahveh* means "to become." Scholem writes that "The essence of the Kabbalistic idea of God . . . lies in its resolutely dynamic conception of the Godhead."[42] Though God is understood as a *process*, and this process is knowable, most Kabbalists could not accept the idea of a God made wholly manifest and so they held onto the idea that God possesses a transcendent *aspect*. This was given a name by the early Kabbalists of Spain and Provence: *Ein-Sof* ("the Infinite"). Some Kabbalists, like Moses Cordovero (1522–70), the teacher of Isaac Luria, maintained that the transcendent *Ein-Sof* alone is truly God.

In the works of other Kabbalists, such as Luria, *Ein-Sof* plays a role virtually identical to Böhme's *Ungrund*. The *Zohar* of Moses de Leon (1240–1305)—which Scholem characterizes as "Jewish theosophy"[43]—announces that "From the mystery of *Ein-Sof* a flame is kindled and inside the flame a hidden well comes into being. The primordial point shines forth in being when the well breaks through the aether."[44] Just as Böhme holds that nature is an unfolding of the dynamic "eternal nature" contained within God, so the *Zohar*, in Scholem's words, holds that "The creation of the world, that is to say, the creation of something out of nothing, is itself but the external aspect of something which takes place in God Himself."[45]

The first stage in the manifestation of *Ein-Sof* is sometimes conceived as *Ayin*, or "Nothing." *Ein-Sof*, as the Infinite, is supposed to be Absolute All, whereas *Ayin* is Absolute Nothing. According to Halevi, these two are really identical.[46] (In Böhme's formulation, *Alles = Nichts*; in Hegel's, *Sein = Nichts*.) Scholem maintains that *Ayin* is a kind of primal unity that transcends the subject-object distinction.[47] Nevertheless, although *Ein-Sof/Ayin* is neither subject nor object, its telos is to develop into a true or absolute subject. *Ayin* is said to become *Ani*, "I" (*Ayin le-Ani*, "Nothing changes into I")[48] According to the Kabbalists, "God willed to see God," to become fully manifest to Himself; to achieve perfect self-knowledge or self-relation.[49]

In the *Encyclopedia Logic*, Hegel uses "I" to express the self-relation of Idea or God through man, stating that "only man reduplicates himself in such a way that he is the universal that is *for* the universal. This is the case for the first time when man knows himself to be an 'I'" (EL § 24 Z-1; Geraets, 57). Of course, Hegel holds that it is through man that God "achieves" self-knowledge. According to traditional Judeo-Christian

42. Scholem, *On The Mystical Shape of the Godhead: Basic Concepts in the Kabbalah*, trans. Joachim Neugroschel (New York: Schocken Books, 1991), 158.
43. Scholem, *Major Trends*, 205.
44. *Zohar* 1:15a; quoted in Scholem, *Kabbalah*, 109–10.
45. Scholem, *Major Trends*, 217. See also p. 223: "Creation is nothing but an external development of those forces which are active in God Himself."
46. Z'ev ben Shimon Halevi, *A Kabbalistic Universe* (York Beach: Samuel Weiser, 1977), 7.
47. Scholem, *Major Trends*, 221.
48. Ibid., 218.
49. Halevi, *A Kabbalistic Universe*, 7.

belief, making God somehow dependent on man is heretical. The Kabbalah, however, is not traditional Judaism. Scholem writes that "the *Zohar* identifies the highest development of God's personality with precisely that stage of His unfolding which is nearest to human experience, indeed which is immanent and mysteriously present in every one of us."[50]

The "I" of God is identified by many Kabbalists with *Malkhut* or "Kingdom." This is the tenth and "final" of the famous Kabbalistic *Sephiroth*, which are almost always depicted as circles and often shown grouped and interconnected in a diagram known as the "Tree of Life." The term *Sephiroth* first occurs in the *Sefer Yezirah*, which is the earliest known Kabbalistic text. *Sephiroth* (singular: *Sephirah*) means "numbers." The *Sephiroth* are also sometimes called *mekorot*, "sources." The role of the *Sephiroth* in Kabbalism is strikingly similar to the role of the *Quellgeister* in Böhme's theosophy: they in some sense delineate the stages of God's progressive self-manifestation.

However, as Cordovero recognized, the crucial question is whether the *Sephiroth* are aspects of God, or merely instruments by which God expresses Himself. Cordovero argued that the *Sephiroth* are "organs" of God, which makes them parts of God in essence, but not identical with Him, in the same way that my heart is a part of me, but not identical with me. Of course, the *Sephiroth* are not physical organs, so Cordovero tried to interpret them as "stages of the divine mind."[51] Cordovero also conceives the *Sephiroth* as expressing the underlying structure of nature itself and of every created being. Scholem writes that "this tree of God [the Tree of Life] is also, as it were, the skeleton of the universe; it grows throughout the whole of creation and spreads its branches through all its ramifications. All mundane and created things exist only because something of the power of the *Sephiroth* lives and acts in them."[52] This idea is essentially identical to Böhme's conception of the "eternal nature" of the source-spirits as the essence of nature, as well as to Hegel's claim that the Logic constitutes the "animating soul" of nature (EL § 24 Z-2; Geraets, 58).

Other Kabbalists were more radical than Cordovero. In the thirteenth century, many held the view that the *Sephiroth* were moments of God's essence itself, and not something distinct from God. According to Scholem, the author of the *Ma'arekhet ha-Elohut* (a very early Kabbalist treatise), "was led to the daring conclusion that only the revealed God can in reality be called 'God,' and not the hidden deus absconditus, who cannot be an object of religious thought."[53] Even the *Zohar* does not make the Sephiroth "outside" God, but instead conceives the "emanation" of the *Sephiroth* as occurring within God.

As to the *Sephiroth* themselves and their structure, they are always presented in an hierarchical order that almost never varies in the works of the Kabbalists. Despite this hierarchy, each *Sephirah* is conceived of as

50. Scholem, *Major Trends*, 216–17.
51. Ibid., 252; cf. Scholem, *Kabbalah*, 102.
52. Scholem, *Major Trends*, 214–15.
53. Scholem, *Kabbalah*, 89.

being equally close to its "source" in *Ein-Sof* or *Ayin*. Thus the hierarchy is artificial. Again, Böhme comes to mind:

> These seven generatings in all are none of them the first, the second, or the third, or last, but they are all seven, every one of them, both the first, second, third, fourth, and last. Yet I must set them down one after another, according to a *creaturely way* and manner, otherwise you could not understand it: For the Deity is as a wheel with seven wheels made one in another, wherein a man sees neither beginning nor end.[54]

Oddly enough, instead of the familiar tree diagram, the *Sephiroth* are sometimes depicted as concentric circles, just like Böhme's wheels. Scholem says the following about the doctrine of the *Sefer Yezirah*: "it is emphasized that the ten *Sephiroth* constitute a closed unit, for 'their end is in their beginning and their beginning in their end' and they revolve in each other; i.e., these ten basic principles constitute a unity."[55] Luria depicted the *Sephiroth* as concentric circles and, as I have said, it is Lurianic Kabbalah that influenced Böhme most strongly. (In fact, Lurianic Kabbalah incorporated both the linear and circular arrangement of *Sephiroth*, as we will see in chapter 7.) Scholem notes that "From the 13th century onward we find the idea that each *Sephirah* comprises all others successively in an infinite reflection of the *Sephiroth* within themselves."[56]

The *Sephiroth* and their arrangement as the "Tree of Life" are shown in figure 6.

The *Sefer Yezirah* refers to *Keter* as *ru'ah*, which can be translated as "aether" or "spirit." This is the point at which God in Himself, *Ein-Sof*, bursts into manifestation. This manifestation is thought of as a circuit running through the ten *Sephiroth*, and it is symbolized as a jagged flash of lightning, touching or "activating" each *Sephirah*, pictured as a circle or a bowl (recall Böhme's *Schrack* or "Flash"). *Keter* or "crown" is on some accounts *Ayin* or Nothing, on other accounts the One, or God's Supernal Will. In fact, it is perhaps all of these: it is blank Oneness, which is yet indeterminate and without character. In this tension between unity and indeterminacy is born a drive or a *conatus* toward a plurality of determinations. This is represented by the second Sephirah, *Hohkmah* or Wisdom, which is the "thought" of creation: the idea of all that is or can be.

Like everything in the Kabbalah, the doctrine of the *Sephiroth* is expressed in figurative language that is often difficult to interpret. Thus any interpretation is necessarily speculative. We can say with some assurance, however, that as a movement away from blank Oneness and toward determination, *Hohkmah* is a determination *of Oneness*.[57] I suggest that it represents *the Universal* as such: Hohkmah is the One-Nothing of *Keter* become a *determinate nothingness*. A universal is precisely a determinate nothingness: it is *no thing* at all, but rather an empty—yet

---

54. *Aurora*, chap. 23, § 18; Sparrow, 615–16.
55. Scholem, *Kabbalah*, 24.
56. Ibid., 113.
57. See Aryeh Kaplan, editorial remark in his translation of *The Bahir* (York Beach, Maine: Samuel Weiser, 1979), 97.

6. The "Tree of Life" as rendered by Brucker, *Historia Critica Philosophiae*, vol. 1, 1742. We can be virtually certain that Hegel studied this diagram in preparing his remarks on the Kabbalah in the *Lectures on the History of Philosophy*. Reprinted by permission of the Robert W. Woodruff Library, Special Collections and Archives, Emory University, Atlanta, Georgia.

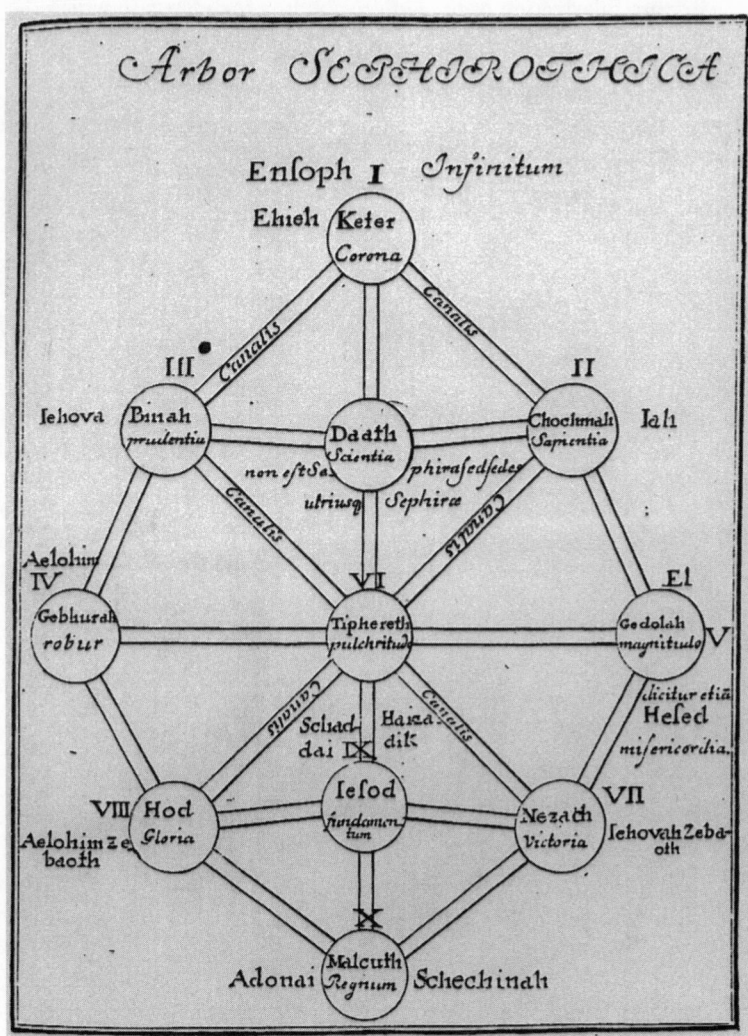

determinate—form. Scholem writes that *Hokhmah* "represents the ideal thought of Creation, conceived as the ideal point which itself springs from the impulse of the abysmal will."[58] Thus, *Hohkmah* is a further determination of *Keter*, the Nothing that is at the same time Unity.

58. Scholem, *Major Trends*, 219.

Recall from chapter 1 that for Böhme, Wisdom is the first stage of God's "othering" Himself, and it takes the form of the seven source-spirits. The further determination of *Hohkmah* is *Binah*, or "Understanding," sometimes referred to as the "Womb." *Hohkmah* is the Universal contracted into an undifferentiated whole. *Binah* represents the specification or particularization of the Universal.[59] It is the matrix in which the Wisdom of God, or the Idea of the Universal, becomes fully specified as a system of universals. It can easily be seen that these three *Sephiroth* are similar to the Plotinian trio of the One, *Nous*, and World Soul. *Keter*, *Hohkmah*, and *Binah* are thought by the Kabbalists to be the three most important and ultimate of the *Sephiroth* (thus tempting Christian Kabbalists to identify them with the persons of the Trinity).

The seven remaining *Sephiroth* are conceived as representing the seven days of creation, and deal with aspects, in effect, of the created world born from the womb of *Binah* (some Kabbalists thus make a sharp distinction between the first three and the last seven Sephiroth, but as we have seen others identify all seven with the essence of God). Before passing on to the first of the seven, however, the lightning flash of manifestation passes through an anti-*Sephirah* or phantom *Sephirah* called *Da'at*. *Da'at* does not appear in Kabbalism until the thirteenth century. Scholem conjectures that "This addition arose from the desire to see each group of three *Sephiroth* as a unit comprising opposing attributes and as a synthesis which finally resolved them."[60] In other words, *Da'at* was intended to be a third to *Hokhmah* and *Binah*, just as *Tiferet* is a third to *Gevurah* and *Hesed*, and *Yesod* is a third to *Hod* and *Nezah*. Meaning literally "Knowledge," according to Scholem *Da'at* is supposed to represent the "external aspect of *Keter*," which is directly above *Da'at* on the Tree of Life.[61] What could this mean? *Keter*, we have seen, is a will or a drive that is constituted by the tension of Nothing and Unity, or Indeterminacy and Determinacy. *Da'at* is sometimes referred to as the "temporal present," and *Keter* as "eternal now." I want to suggest that *Da'at* is time itself, conceived in opposition to *Keter's* "eternal now," which is, of course, outside of time. (One is reminded of Hegel's description of Time as "the Concept itself that is there" [Miller, 487; PG, 524]). *Da'at* is not a real part of the Tree of Life because the system of the *Sephiroth* is outside of time. *Da'at* is knowledge because it represents the "contact point" of the Kabbalist with the *Sephiroth*: our knowledge of God and the cosmos is a unity of Wisdom (*Hokhmah*) and Understanding (*Binah*), a knowledge of Wisdom through Understanding; we know the eternal in a sensuous way, and our knowledge is in time. Significantly, *Da'at* is also sometimes referred to as "Holy Spirit."

From *Da'at* we pass on to *Hesed* or *Gedullah*, which is generally translated as "Mercy," and then across (on the Tree of Life) to *Din* or *Gevurah* ("Stern Judgment"). These represent the forces of expansion and con-

59. Kaplan notes that *Binah* represents differentiation (*Bahir*, 97).
60. Scholem, *Kabbalah*, 107.
61. Ibid., 107.

traction. The further specification of being takes place in the tension of expansion and contraction. As we saw in chapter 2, Oetinger speaks of expansion (*Ausbreitung*) and contraction (*Stärke*) and identifies them explicitly with *Hesed* and *Gevurah*.[62] Goethe also makes use of these concepts. In the last chapter, I discussed how in 1804–5, Hegel wrote out and then criticized a "myth" concerning the fall of Lucifer. He writes, "God, having turned toward nature and expressed Himself [*hat sich ausgebreitet*] in the pomp and dull repetition of its forms, became aware of His expansion [*Expansion*]. . . and became angry over it. Wrath [*Zorn*] is this formation, this contraction [*Zusammennehmen*] into an empty point. He finds Himself in this way, with His being poured out into the unending, restless infinity, where there is no present but an empty transcendence of limit, which always remains even as it is transcended."[63] Hegel identifies Wrath with contraction here. Similarly, the Kabbalah identifies *Gevurah/Din* with "fire," "wrath," and "severity."[64]

According to the Kabbalah, *Din* is the origin of evil. Ordinarily, *Din* and *Hesed* balance each other: severity of judgment is balanced by mercy; sharp distinction, cutting-off, or closedness is balanced by unity, embrace, or openness. However, as Scholem notes, "When [*Din*] ceases to be tempered, when in its measureless hypertrophical outbreak it tears itself loose from the quality of mercy, then it breaks away from God altogether and is transformed into the radically evil, into Gehenna and the dark world of Satan."[65] Hegel, in his "myth" of 1804–5, writes that "The anger of God, here fixed outside Himself in His otherness, the fallen Lucifer, rose up against God and his beauty made him arrogant. Nature, through consciousness of its own form, brought it to completion and flattered itself over it."[66] God's wrath, then, according to Hegel, becomes the spirit of Lucifer, who is at home with the finite and ephemeral. The same Kabbalistic conception of evil, as we have seen, is to be found in Böhme. Evil has its origin as a moment of God—negativity is sublated within the whole—but it is a moment "broken off," as it were, from the divine life.

Applied to human life, *Din* would represent what Hegel calls Desire—the urge to annihilate the other and absolutize the self. Böhme designates this way of being as "the Sour"—it is an indrawing, a pulling away, a shutting off and negation of all else. Both Böhme and the Kabbalah regard this as a necessary moment of the being of God and all creation. Everything good that subsequently comes to be, *is* only through having overcome this negative moment. This is, of course, Hegel's own position, as I discussed in the preceding chapter.

62. "Durch die vierte [*Sephirah*], Gedulah, breitet Er seine Kräften aus in sich selbst (Ps. 150, 1: *Lobet ihn in der Ausbreitung seiner Kraft*). Durch die fünfte, Gebhurah, intendirt und verfasst Er sie wieder zusammen, dass wir ign in seinem [sic] *Gebhurot*, 'Kräften,' loben (Ps. 150, 1)" (Friedrich Christoph Oetinger, *Die Lehrtafel der Prinzessin Antonia*, ed. Reinhard Breymayer and Friedrich Häusserman [Berlin, 1977], 1:93).
63. Hoffmeister, *Dokumente*, 364–65.
64. Scholem, *Major Trends*, 237.
65. Ibid., 237.
66. Ibid., 365.

From *Din*, we proceed to *Tiferet*, which stands in the center of the Tree of Life, directly below *Keter* and *Da'at*. This center line is known as the "Pillar of Equilibrium." The *Sephiroth* standing in this pillar have a "reconciling function": *Da'at* in some sense reconciles *Hokhmah* and *Binah*, and *Tiferet* reconciles *Hesed* and *Din* (only *Keter* and *Malkhut* stand "outside" this pattern, as will shortly be accounted for). As the reconciliation of *Hesed* and *Din*, *Tiferet* is sometimes (especially in the *Zohar*) called *Rahamim*, which means "compassion." *Tiferet* is usually translated as "Beauty" or "Adornment." It is also called "the King," and is masculine in character. Tiferet is also conceived as the "son" of *Malkhut* and *Binah* (in most diagrams of the Tree of Life, *Tiferet* is directly connected with *Malkhut* and *Binah*). *Tiferet* represents the Idea of the Universe: the self-expression of the infinite through sameness and difference, brought forth in expansion and contraction. But the process is not fully realized with *Tiferet*, however.

Nezah and *Hod*, the last two dyadic *Sephiroth*, both represent revelation or prophecy. Unfortunately, here Kabbalists become extremely obscure, making these two very hard to interpret. Their names are frequently translated as "Eternity" and "Reverberation" (often "Majesty"). *Nezah* and *Hod* appear to be the utterance or expression of the plan of God, a "reflection" back upon what has gone before, and a projection forward: the eternal structure of the first seven *Sephiroth* (including the phantom *Sephirah Da'at*) echoing forward through time. *Nezah* and *Hod* represent God as eternal, yet as unfolding in time. *Yesod* or "Foundation" contains all the preceding *Sephiroth*. It is depicted as the male sexual organ because it is supposed to be the channel through which all preceding *Sephiroth* "flow into" the final *Sephirah*, *Malkhut*.[67]

Malkhut or "Kingdom" (sometimes "Glory") is conceived of as feminine—in contrast to the "male" *Tiferet* and *Yesod* (the "organ" of *Tiferet*)—and is often referred to under the alternate name of *Shekhinah* or "Divine Presence." If one looks at a drawing of the Tree of Life, *Malkhut* and *Keter* seem to stand apart from the others. *Yesod* and *Malkhut* are the only *Sephiroth* in the Pillar of Equilibrium that are not separated by dyadic *Sephiroth*, making *Malkhut* seem almost like an extension of the Tree, a sort of appendage. This is not accidental, for *Malkhut* represents the divine presence *in the world*: with *Malkhut* the *Sephiroth* have reached down into the world of space and time. I will discuss the Kabbalist concept of *Malkhut* or *Shekhinah* more fully in chapter 7, for it relates to Hegel's *Philosophy of Spirit*: *Shekhinah* is conceived as God embodied in the *Keneset Yisrael*, the "community of Israel," a doctrine remarkably like Hegel's theory of Objective Spirit.

In addition to the doctrine of the *Sephiroth*, traditional Kabbalah also teaches a doctrine of "four worlds": *Atsiluth*, *Beriah*, *Yezirah*, and *Asiyah*. The first of these is, in effect, the world of God "in Himself," the eternal, unchanging world of the *Sephiroth*. The others, however, are worlds "emanated" from the *Sephiroth*. In his discussion of Kabbalah in the

67. Ibid., 227–28.

Lectures, Hegel includes a brief account of the "four worlds," which is entirely accurate:

> In the first place there came forth ten of such emanations, *Sephiroth*, forming the pure world of *Azilut* [*die reine, azilutische Welt*], which exists in itself and does not change. The second is the world of *Briah* [*die briatische Welt*], which does change. The third is the formed world of *Jezirah* [*die geformte, jeziratische Welt*], the world of pure spirits set in matter, the souls of the stars—that is, further distinctions into which this dark wisdom proceeds. In the fourth place comes the created world, the *Asiah* [*viertens die gemachte Welt, die asiahtische*]: it is the lowest, the vegetative and sensible world. (LHP 2:396; *Werke* 19:427–28)

d) Language and Method in the Kabbalah

Scholem discusses how Kabbalist thought can be considered a form of Gnosticism, and then remarks, "at the same time, side by side with this Gnostic outlook, we find a most astonishing tendency to a mode of contemplative thought that can be called 'dialectic' in the strictest sense of the term as used by Hegel."[68] Scholem writes, further, that "The process of emanation of the *Sephiroth* is described by Cordovero as dialectical. In order to be revealed, God has to conceal Himself. This concealment is in itself the coming into being of the *Sephiroth*. Only the *Sephiroth* reveal God, and that is why 'revealing is the cause of concealment and concealment is the cause of revealing.' "[69] Scholem refers to the structure of the *Sephiroth* as being "built out of triangles."[70] Aryeh Kaplan, in his commentary on the *Bahir*, quotes the last of the "Thirteen Principles of Exegesis" of Rabbi Ishmael: "Two verses oppose one another until a third verse is brought to reconcile them." Kaplan comments: "It is this dialectic that results in the basic triplet structure so often found in Kabbalah."[71] We have already seen examples of this, in the triadic structure of the transitions in the *Sephiroth*: how *Hokhmah* and *Binah* are reconciled by *Da'at*, *Hesed* and *Din* by *Tiferet*, etc. The *Bahir* itself echoes this: "A third verse comes and reconciles the two. It is written (*Psalm* 139:12), 'Even darkness is not dark to you. Night shines like day—light and darkness are the same.' "[72]

The Kabbalists believe that by manipulating the language of Adam they are recovering the wisdom he possessed and then lost in the Fall. Scholem writes that "Man, as he was before his fall, is conceived as a cosmic being which contains the whole world in itself and whose station is superior even to that of Metatron, the first of the angels."[73] The *Sephiroth Tiferet* and *Malkhut* are identified with, respectively, the Tree of Life and Tree of the Knowledge of Good and Evil from the Garden of Eden.

68. Scholem, *Kabbalah*, 143.
69. Ibid., 402.
70. Ibid., 107.
71. Kaplan, editorial remark in *Bahir*, 87.
72. Ibid., § 1; Kaplan, 1.
73. Scholem, *Major Trends*, 279.

Adam's sin consisted in "separating" the two trees and choosing to "worship" only the Tree of the Knowledge of Good and Evil. Here again, there is a remarkable similarity to Böhme. We saw in chapter 1 how for Böhme the Tree of Good and Evil represents disharmony, a separation of the spirits of nature into units under the sway of the "Eternal No," withdrawn into themselves, spurning unity. Thinking that it would provide him with the wisdom he sought, Adam naively ate of this tree.[74] Adam's action constituted a turning away from divine unity.

Like the Kabbalists, Böhme holds the view that before his fall, Adam was privy to the Wisdom of God, "But yet when he fell, and was set into the outward birth or geniture, he knew it no more, but kept it in remembrance only as a dark and veiled story; and this he left to his posterity." Böhme also ascribes supernatural powers to Adam. For instance, Adam, who was originally androgynous, could procreate at will by the power of imagination, could exist without eating or sleeping, and could alter the essences of objects through magic words.[75] The Kabbalist view of Adam is very similar although somewhat more complicated, as we will see in chapter 7.

Although there is a Böhmean influence on the *Logic* and on Hegel's conception of system, the deeper influence is that of the Kabbalah. Böhme is a Christian Kabbalist, and so there is an indirect influence of the Kabbalah on Hegel, by way of Böhme. Also, Hegel read Brucker's extensive account of the Kabbalah and probably Rosenroth's *Kabbala Denudata* as well. There are other possible channels of influence, however: the writings of Reuchlin, whom Hegel discusses very briefly in the lectures, as well as those of Baader, and of course, the tradition of Christian Kabbalism in Württemberg as represented preeminently by Oetinger.

Let the following serve as a summary of some of the more significant doctrinal correspondences between Kabbalism and Hegel's system:

> 1. God is conceived in various forms of Kabbalism, as well as in Hegel, as *dynamic*, as a God somehow "in process."
> 2. The "God process" is delineated into separate *Sephiroth*, which are conceived of as "moments" of God's being (according to some Kabbalists)—just as the categories of the *Logic* are moments of an organic totality constituting "the exposition of God as He is in his eternal essence before the creation of nature and a finite Spirit" (Miller, 50; WL 1:33–34).[76]
> 3. In Kabbalism, *Ein-Sof* or the "Absolute All" is made equivalent to *Ayin*, "Nothing." In Hegel: Being = Nothing.
> 4. *Ayin* (or *Ayin = Ein-Sof*), the point at which Kabbalist discussions of God's nature begin, is held to transcend the distinction between subject and object.[77] It's telos is to develop into an "absolute subject."

74. *Mysterium Magnum*, chap. 18, § 33.
75. Ibid., chap. 17, § 43.
76. Cyril O'Regan points to a general "symmetry" between the first three *Sephiroth* (Keter-Hokhmah-Binah) and Hegel's Being-Essence-Concept. See O'Regan, "Hegel and Anti-Judaism," 161.
77. In the text of the *Science of Logic*, Hegel actually draws on the mystical traditions of India to explain "Pure Being": "With this wholly abstract purity of

In Hegel's *Logic*, Being-Nothing, which transcends the subject-object distinction, develops into Absolute Idea, which is a kind of "abstract conception" of the self-thinking thought of Spirit.

5. In Kabbalism, the highest development of God's "personality" is identified, according to Gershom Scholem, "with precisely that stage of His unfolding which is nearest to human experience, indeed which is immanent and mysteriously present in every one of us."[78] The same could be said of Hegel's theology.

6. All the *Sephiroth* are immanent as a totality within the final *Sephirah*—just as all the categories of Hegel's *Logic* are immanent within, or constitute the "definition" of, Absolute Idea.

7. The *Sephiroth* are seen as penetrating and informing all levels of being, constituting the "skeleton" of nature. Hegel claims that the moments of his *Logic* constitute the "animating soul" of nature (EL § 24 Z-2; Geraets, 58).

8. Such commentators as Scholem and Kaplan have pointed out the triadic, dialectical structure of the thought-forms in Kabbalah.

9. The Kabbalist treatment of *Din*, or evil, as a moment of God's being corresponds to Hegel's sublation of the negativity of Desire within his system.

4. Ramon Lull and the Tradition of *Pansophia*

In this final section I will discuss a wholly different strand of Hermetic influence discernable in the *Logic*, that of Ramon Lull and the tradition of *pansophia* or *encyclopedism*. As we shall see, at a certain point Lullism crosses paths with Christian Kabbalah.

Lull was born in Majorca in 1235 and, after many travels and adventures, died there in 1316. In his early life, Lull was a courtier with no formal training as a scholar. He lived a hedonistic life until 1272, when he had a mystical vision on Mount Randa in Majorca. His vision revealed to him the "attributes of God" in all their glory, radiating out into creation. Lull was inspired to create an art based on these attributes that would allow one to know God and achieve total understanding of all that exists.

Lull believed that his Art was based on ideas common to the three great religions of the West, Christianity, Judaism, and Islam.[79] At the same time, the Art is supposed to constitute a "science of sciences," a superscience

---

continuity, that is, indeterminateness and vacuity of conception, it is indifferent whether this abstraction is called space, pure intuiting, or pure thinking; it is altogether the same as what the Indian calls Brahma, when for years on end, physically motionless and equally unmoved in sensation, conception, fantasy, desire and so on, looking only at the tip of his nose, he says inwardly only *Om, Om, Om,* or else nothing at all. This dull, empty consciousness, understood as consciousness, is—*being*" (Miller, 97; WL 1:89).

78. Scholem, *Major Trends*, 216–17.

79. Lull was influenced by Muhyi al-Din Ibn al-'Arabi (1165–1240), who was one of the founders of "theosophical Sufism." He believed that reality is a progressive realization of God's self-knowledge. See Dan Merkur, *Gnosis: An Esoteric Tradition of Mystical Visions and Unions* (Albany: State University of New York Press, 1993), 246. Merkur writes: "Lull's debts to Ibn al-'Arabi were so extensive as to amount occasionally to plagiarism" (ibid.).

consisting of the ultimate truths of reality, which can be used to order all existing knowledge.[80] Likewise Hegel believed his *Logic* could "order" all the scientific knowledge of his day and reveal its place in the divine whole.

The attributes or Names of God are, according to Lull, *Bonitas, Magnitudo, Eternitas, Potestas, Sapientia, Voluntas, Virtus, Veritas,* and *Gloria* (Goodness, Greatness, Eternity, Power, Wisdom, Will, Virtue, Truth, and Glory). These he designated with the letters B, C, D, E, F, G, H, I, and K (Yates notes that "the unmentioned A is the ineffable Absolute").[81] Lull employed these letters in diagrams, usually around the edge of circles. These circles function as "wheels": by turning the wheels, each inscribed with the letters, new combinations of the letters could be arrived at, each of which bore some ontological or cosmological significance. This procedure generally involved the manipulation of three wheels—or some other such device—yielding triadic combinations of letters: BBB, BBC, CFG, GDC, etc.

Lull placed great emphasis on the Trinity and trinitarian structure.[82] Anthony Bonner writes that "it was Lull's idea to show that the Christian mysteries were part of the very structure of the universe, which would therefore be incomplete or imperfect without them."[83] Lull believed that through the contemplation of triadic combinations of the divine Names, we can ascend in thought to the Trinity of Father-Son-Holy Spirit itself. Hegel's system is pervaded by triadic structures that are all "modeled on" or reflect the primary triad of Logic-Nature-Spirit, which in turn is patterned after the Christian Trinity.

Lull was a prolific author who wrote on a very wide variety of subjects, including the natural sciences. No matter what subject he took up, however, Lull always laid out its central parts in terms of the attributes B to K. Lull was employing an analogical method in his "complete speech," involving appeal to fundamental correspondences or, as Bonner puts it, "arguments of congruence."[84] Here too is a clear parallel to Hegel. In Hegel's system each major subdivision reflects the triadic structure of the whole, in which there are detailed conceptual analogues and correspondences between the parts of the different "sciences" (e.g., the correspondence between "Consciousness" in the *Phenomenology* and the "Doctrine of Being" in the *Logic*). Like Hegel's *Logic*, it is *both*: a means to order and understand all our other knowledge, and at the same time the most fundamental kind of knowledge.

80. See Paolo Rossi, "The Legacy of Ramon Lull in Sixteenth-Century Thought," *Mediaeval and Renaissance Studies*, 5 (1961): 181–213, 185.
81. Yates, *The Occult Philosophy*, 11.
82. See ibid., 178–9; see also R. D. F. Pring-Mill, "The Trinitarian World Picture of Ramon Lull," *Romantisches Jahrbuch* 7 (1955–56): 229–56.
83. Anthony Bonner, editor's introduction in *Doctor Illuminatus: A Ramon Llull Reader* (Princeton, N.J.: Princeton University Press, 1985), 51. Recall J. N. Findlay's observation that "[Hegel's] whole system may in fact be regarded as an attempt to see the Christian mysteries in everything whatever, every natural process, every form of human activity, and every logical transition" (Findlay, *Hegel: A Re-Examination*, 131).
84. Ibid., 51.

Lull does not just employ circles or wheels to represent combinations of the divine names. He also uses the triangle and the square. The circle represents the heavens (no doubt because of the "spheres" and the circular movements of the planets); the triangle represents divinity (the trinity), and the square represents the four elements. As an example of Lull's fusion of logic and metaphysics, he attempts to map the four elements onto the four categorical propositions of the traditional "Square of Opposition." His most common image, however, combines the circle with the triangle. Lull's most famous diagram shows a circle ringed round with B to K, joined in myriad triadic combinations by triangles drawn within the circle. Yates describes this as, "a mystical figure in which we meditate on the complex relations of the Names with one another as they are in the Godhead, before extension into the creation, and as aspects of the Trinity."[85] Apparently, Lull and his followers actually made "wheels" of his concentric circles so that they could turn the circles and produce new revelations about the nature of God and the cosmos.

Lull is often placed in the tradition of Christian Kabbalah. Many Lull scholars hotly dispute this. I agree with Yates, however, that an influence of Kabbalism on Lull was certainly possible. As Yates points out, the concept of the "Names of God" is fundamental to Jewish mysticism. The *Zohar* was, of course, written in Spain during Lull's lifetime. Lull's practice of combining and recombining B to K and contemplating these combinations is similar to the meditative practices of Abraham Abulafia.[86] Pico della Mirandola himself pointed this out.[87] Scholem speaks of Abulafia's method as a "mystical logic" and writes that "From the motion of the letters of thought result the truths of reason."[88]

Hegel devotes about two pages to Lull in his *Lectures*, grouping him with John Charlier, Ramon of Sabunde, and Roger Bacon as *Mystiker* of the scholastic variety (Lull receives the most extensive treatment).[89] Hegel writes that

> The chief object aimed at in this man's 'Art' was an enumeration and arrangement of the various concepts under which all objects fall, or of the pure categories according to which they can be determined, so that it may be possible in regard to every object to indicate with ease the conceptions applicable to it. Lullus is so systematic that he becomes at times mechanical. He constructed a diagram in circles, on which were marked triangles through which the circles pass. (LHP 3:93; *Werke* 19:586)

85. Yates, *The Art of Memory*, 181.
86. According to Dan Merkur, Abulafia had his followers visualize the letter combinations on a rotating wheel (Merkur, *Gnosis*, 249).
87. Yates, *The Art of Memory*, 177, 188–89.
88. Scholem, *Major Trends*, 134–35. Arthur Edward Waite, in his eccentric but ambitious study of the Kabbalah, disputes any influence of Kabbalism on Lull. See A. E. Waite, *The Holy Kabbalah* (New York: Citadel Press, 1992), 440, 442.
89. Hegel states in general of the group, "Among them genuine philosophy is to be found—termed also Mysticism; it tends to inwardness and bears a great resemblance to Spinozism" (LHP 3:91; *Werke* 19:584).

In the *Science of Logic*, in the "Doctrine of the Concept," Hegel states that the "Leibnizian application of the calculus of combinations and permutations to the syllogism and to the combination of other notions, differed from the notorious Art of Lull [*der verrufenen Lullianischn Kunst*] solely in being more methodical on the arithmetical side, but for the rest, they were both equally meaningless" (Miller, 685; WL 3:128).

This remark must be understood in the context of the *Science of Logic*, in which Hegel is rejecting all "abstract" conceptions of philosophy that oppose method to subject matter, a defect present in Lull. Elsewhere, Hegel is more positive. In his discussion of Bruno, Hegel anticipates Yates's connection of Bruno with Lull: "The main endeavour of Bruno was . . . to represent the All and One [*das All und Eine*], after the method of Lullus, as a system of classes of regular determinations" (LHP 3:134–35; *Werke* 20:36).

Earlier in his remarks on Bruno, Hegel glosses the Lullian art as "the art of finding differences in the Idea" (LHP 3:123; *Werke* 20:31). This is highly significant, for Hegel's *Logic* is precisely an articulation of the different moments of Absolute Idea. Hegel cannot have simply dismissed Lull's thought if he regarded it as a precursor to his own in this significant respect.[90] In his remarks on Spinoza, Hegel states that "Lullus and Bruno attempted to draw up a system of form, which should embrace and comprehend the one substance which organizes itself into the universe; this attempt Spinoza did not make" (LHP 3:287; *Werke* 20:194).

Yates devotes a chapter in her *The Art of Memory* to Lull and attempts to locate him within the tradition of *ars memoria*. However, she notes that Lull's art is devoid of the dramatic images of the classical *ars memoria*. Instead, it employs an abstract letter notation.[91] Nevertheless, Lull does belong to the tradition of *ars memoria* because he conceives his Art as a means of recollecting Truth.[92] We have seen that for Hegel Mnemosyne is the "absolute muse" because by hearing her voice the philosopher comes to speak the complete speech.

Verene has drawn a parallel between the traditional *ars memoria* and the *Phenomenology of Spirit*, exploiting the famous line at the end of the *Phenomenology* where Hegel speaks of the work as a "gallery of images" (*Galerie von Bildern*; Miller, 492; PG, 530).[93] The traditional *ars memoria* employed striking images arranged in systematic order to cause the onlooker to "recollect" the wisdom already latent in him. The best example of this is the "memory theater" of Giulio Camillo (c. 1480–1544), which appears to have been a small, walk-in amphitheater decorated with various combinations of archetypal images, underneath which were small drawers contain-

90. Hegel states that God "posits determinations within Himself" (LPR 1:307; VPR 1:212).
91. Yates, *The Art of Memory*, 176
92. See Frances Yates, "The Art of Ramon Lull: An Approach to it Through Lull's Theory of the Elements," *Journal of the Warburg and Courtauld Institutes*, 17 (1964): 115–73, 162. Cf. Yates, *The Art of Memory*, 174.
93. Donald Phillip Verene, "Two Sources of Philosophical Memory: Vico Versus Hegel," in *Philosophical Imagination and Cultural Memory*, ed. Patricia Cook (Durham, N.C.: Duke University Press, 1993), 41.

ing scrolls covered in further images or, perhaps, aphorisms or "abstracts" of the works of great thinkers. In the words of a sceptical contemporary of Camillo, working one's way through the entire theater was supposed to produce a transformation of the mind, "in such a way that the beholder may at once perceive with his eyes everything that is otherwise hidden in the depths of the human mind."[94] Camillo's ideal was basically the same as that later championed by Descartes and the rationalists: knowledge unified and organized around certain fundamental ideas.

Verene has Camillo in mind when he compares the *Phenomenology* to a "theater of memory," but he does not extend the parallel to apply to the entire Hegelian system. In fact, the *ars memoria* that the system Logic-Nature-Spirit most resembles is not that of Camillo but that of Lull. Insofar as speculative philosophy may be located within the *ars memoria* tradition, Lull's can be seen as a kind of "bridge position." Whereas the traditional *ars memoria* is bound up with sensuous images, Lull's Art is "abstract," employing a quasi-algebraic notation and a "method." As I argued in chapter 3, Hegel sublates "picture thinking" and "abstract reason," producing a new type of philosophy that employs what are normally termed "abstract concepts" in an organic system of thought governed by the *Urbilder* of the circle, triangle, and square. Lull comes very close to this Hegelian position. He rejects, in the main, the sensuous images of the *ars memoria*, but retains its ideal of universal knowledge and knowledge of God. He produces a new system of thought that is both logic and metaphysics, which aims—as Hegel himself saw—at knowing the "moments" of God, and which is structured according to the circle, the triangle, and the square. But he separates form and content, and in practice his Art degenerates into an extreme formalism in which an external "method" is imposed on a pregiven subject matter.

As to Lull's influence on the tradition, for some time those who expressed an interest in his work were subject to persecution. Nicholas of Cusa was very much interested in the Art, but could not say so publicly.[95] Lull had a tremendous impact during the Renaissance on figures such as Pico, who expressly stated his desire to fuse Lull's Art with Kabbalism. It was thus during this period, as Yates notes, that Lullism became "assimilated to various aspects of the Hermetic-Cabalist tradition."[96] A very large number of pseudo-Lullian alchemical works were published after Lull's death, beginning in about 1332. As a result, by the fifteenth century, Lull was almost universally regarded as a great alchemist. Hegel himself reports on Lull's "strong inclination toward alchemy" (LHP 3:192; *Werke* 19:585)—but there is not the slightest evidence for this. The first man to teach Lull's Art publicly was Bernard de Lavinheta (d. c. 1530), at the University of Paris. Bernard's *Explanatio*

94. The writer is Viglius Zuichemus, in a 1532 letter to Erasmus, quoted in ibid., 132.

95. Bonner, introduction to *Doctor Illuminatus*, 58. Merkur notes that Cusa's library contained more works by Lull than any other author (Merkur, *Gnosis*, 250).

96. Yates, *The Art of Memory*, 188.

compendiosaque applicatio artis Raymundi Lulli (1523) melded Lull with *pansophia*, alchemy, and the *ars memoria*.[97] The first German commentator on Lull was Agrippa, who wrote *In Artem brevem Raymundi Lulli Commentaria* (first published in 1531). Bruno, as has already been mentioned, was greatly influenced by Lull and wrote seven books on the Art. Interestingly, he first took up Lull after his time in Germany (1586–88). Leibniz was also apparently interested in Lull.

Lull's Art belongs to the tradition of the search for *pansophia*, "universal wisdom." As we saw in the introduction, the ideal of the "complete speech" or "perfect discourse" (*teleeis logos*) is a fundamental tenet of Hermeticism. *Pansophia*, encyclopedism, and Rosicrucianism were intimately entwined throughout the seventeenth century. It was a time of grand plans for encyclopedias synthesizing all human knowledge. Consider the case of Sir Francis Bacon (1561–1626). Bacon has long been revered by modern Hermeticists, who have attributed an almost universal wisdom to him—along with the works of Shakespeare and Robert Burton, not to mention the King James *Bible*.[98] Paolo Rossi and Frances Yates have, however, argued soberly and convincingly that Bacon's thought must be understood in the context of Renaissance Hermeticism.[99] Yates even spies Rosicrucian imagery in Bacon's *New Atlantis*.[100]

In the *Novum Organum* (1622), Bacon, like Lull, called for a radically new logic, one which would deal with "the particulars themselves, and their series and order," and rejected the sterile formalism of the schoolmen. Bacon's projected reform of science not only influenced such seventeenth-century Rosicrucian pansophists as Comenius, Hartlib, and Dury, it also influenced the standard-bearer of the eighteenth-century Enlightenment, the great *Encyclopédie ou Dictionnaire raisonné, des sciences, des arts et des métiers* of Diderot and d'Alembert, published between 1751 and 1772 in thirty-five volumes.[101]

Robert Fludd (1574–1637) was a Paracelsian physician, a Christian Kabbalist, a would-be Rosicrucian, and the author of an immense, unfinished multivolume work, the *History of the Macrocosm and the Microcosm* (1617–26), which Joscelyn Godwin describes as "more of an encyclopedia than a history in the modern sense," insofar as it aimed at nothing less than a total synthesis of all human knowledge of man, the cosmos, and the correspondences between them.[102]

97. Bonner, introduction to *Doctor Illuminatus*, 65.

98. See, for example, Manly P. Hall, *An Encyclopedic Outline of Masonic, Hermetic, Quabbalistic and Rosicrucian Symbolical Philosophy, Being an Interpretation of the Secret Teachings concealed within the Rituals, Allegories and Mysteries of all Ages* (Los Angeles: The Philosophical Research Society, 1988).

99. Paolo Rossi, *Francis Bacon: From Magic to Science* (London: Routledge, 1968).

100. See Yates, *The Rosicrucian Enlightenment*, 127–29.

101. Bacon's influence on the French *Encyclopédie* is made clear in Jean Le Rond d'Alembert, *Preliminary Discourse to the Encyclopedia of Diderot* (1751), trans. Richard N. Schwab (Chicago: University of Chicago Press, 1995).

102. Joscelyn Godwin, *Robert Fludd: Hermetic Philosopher and Surveyor of Two Worlds* (Grand Rapids: Phanes Press, 1991), 7–8.

Another typical and influential pansophist is Jan Amos Komensky, called Comenius (1592–1670). A native of Moravia, Comenius considered himself a Rosicrucian. He was greatly influenced by Andreae's manifestos, and associated himself openly with Rosicrucian circles. Comenius was also influenced by Cusa, Paracelsus, Patrizzi, Campanella, and Fludd.[103] He received his education at Heidelberg University, from which he graduated in 1613. Yates conjectures that Comenius might have met Andreae while in Heidelberg. The development of a pansophic encyclopedia of universal knowledge was Comenius's goal in life. He called his first attempt, begun in 1614, an "amphitheater" of all existence.[104] Comenius's writings deal with philosophy, science, theology, politics, education, and other subjects. In 1623 he produced *The Labyrinth of the World and the Paradise of the Heart*. One of the classics of Czech literature, it contains passages lifted from Andreae's Rosicrucian writings, as well as a chapter devoted to Rosicrucianism.[105] The book is similar to Campanella's *City of the Sun* in its description of a utopian city representing all the departments of learning.

Comenius believed he had discovered a means to achieve knowledge of all things. He developed an ontology and cosmology grounded in the threefold distinction of Divine Word, Nature, and Man. According to Dagmar Capková, this ontology "promised to reveal the common principles, relationships and differences concerning everything, on the basis of which people would learn the truth and how to act in accordance with it."[106] His pansophic encyclopedia was supposed to harmonize microcosm and macrocosm and unite man with God. He attempted to combine a transcendent with an immanent view of God, holding that while God is present in Nature, He also possesses a transcendent dimension. Comenius's thought can to some extent be called dialectical. He attempted to show how apparently incompatible concepts can be reconciled and stressed that a proper understanding of the relations between whole and parts, universal and particular, and individual and society is a central feature of wisdom, and a prerequisite for reform.

Comenius was associated with two other pansophists, Samuel Hartlib (1595–1662), and John Dury (1595–1680). Hartlib, a Pole, translated two works by Andreae into English (*Christianae societas imago*—see chapter 2—and *Christiani amoris dextera porrecta*) and in 1641 composed a utopia, *A Description of the Famous Kingdom of Macaria*. Dury, a Scotsman who corresponded with Andreae, had made Hartlib's acquaintance when the latter was still in Elbing. All three men were given to millenarianism. Millenarian tendencies, in fact, flourished among the German

103. See Dagmar Capková, "Comenius and His Ideals: Escape from the Labyrinth" in *Samuel Hartlib and Universal Reformation*, ed. Mark Greengrass et. al. (Cambridge, U.K.: Cambridge University Press, 1994), 76.
104. Yates, *The Rosicrucian Enlightenment*, 157.
105. John Comenius, *The Labyrinth of the World and the Paradise of the Heart*, trans. Howard Louthan and Andrea Stark (New York: Paulist Press, 1998), chap. 13.
106. Capková, "Comenius and His Ideals," 83.

"systematics" of the period (Clucas names Alsted, Polanus, and Bister-field) who attempted to marry rationalism with *ars memoria, pansophia,* and *mathesis universalis.*[107] German proponents of *mathesis universalis* such as Jungius believed that their new superscience would restore the wisdom lost with Adam's fall.[108] As we have seen, this is a key tenet of Kabbalism.

G. W. F. Leibniz (1646–1716) also belongs squarely in the tradition of *pansophia* and encyclopedism. In his "Introduction to a Secret Encyclopedia" (*Introductio ad Encyclopaediam arcanum,* c. 1679), Leibniz's description of "General Science" is strikingly pansophic:

> [The General Science] includes not only what has hitherto been regarded as logic, but also the art of discovery, together with method or the means of arrangement, synthesis and analysis, didactics, or the science of teaching, Gnostologia (the so-called Noologia), the art of memory or mnemonics, the Art of Combination, the *Art of Subtlety,* and philosophical grammar; the Art of Lull, the Cabala of the wise, and natural magic. Perhaps it also includes Ontology, or the science of something and nothing, being and not being, the thing and its mode, and substance and accident. It does not make much difference how you divide the sciences, for they are one continuous body, like the ocean.[109]

There is, furthermore, ample evidence of Leibniz's interests in Rosicrucianism, alchemy, and Kabbalah. Yates mentions that "There is a persistent rumour that Leibniz joined a Rosicrucian society at Nuremberg in 1666," and she speculates that this society may have been founded in 1628 by Andrae himself.[110] She also notes that the precepts of Leibniz's proposed "Order of Charity" are "practically a quotation from the *Fama.*"[111]

Allison Coudert's *Leibniz and the Kabbalah* makes a strong case for the influence of Lurianic Kabbalah on Leibniz.[112] She discusses in detail Leibniz's relationship to two leading Kabbalist-Alchemist-Hermeticists of the time: Francis Mercury van Helmont (1614–1698), and the aforementioned Knorr von Rosenroth (1636–1689), editor of the *Kabbalah Denudata.* Helmont was the son of John Baptist van Helmont, a renowned alchemist who claimed to have seen and touched the philosopher's stone. (Hegel praises Helmont in his *Lectures on the History of Philosophy* as having "many profound thoughts," but gets his dates wrong [LHP 3:113; *Werke* 20:15].) Bruno is frequently cited as the source of Leibniz's monadology, but Coudert argues instead for the influence of von Rosenroth and van Helmont. Indeed, it appears that Leibniz's relationship with van Helmont was particularly close. Leibniz kept a detailed

107. Stephan Clucas, "In Search of 'The True Logick': Methodological Eclecticism Among the Baconian Reformers," in *Samuel Hartlib and Universal Reformation,* 54.

108. Ibid., 63.

109. G. W. Leibniz, "Introduction to a Secret Science," in *Philosophical Writings,* ed. G. H. R. Parkinson, trans. Marry Morris and G. H. R. Parkinson (London: Everyman, 1973), 5–6.

110. Yates, *Rosicrucian Enlightenment,* 154.

111. Ibid., 154.

112. I discuss Luria's Kabbalah in chapter 7.

record of his conversations with van Helmont, including their discussions of Kabbalah. Leibniz first met him in Mainz in 1671, where they discussed alchemy at length. Leibniz's interest in alchemy was no secret: some years after his meeting with van Helmont he was elected secretary of an alchemical society in Nuremburg, a fact to which Hegel himself alludes (LHP 3:326; Werke 20:234). Leibniz's final words on his death bed are reported to have concerned the transmutation of iron nails into gold "through the action of a certain spring."[113]

Coudert, drawing on the work of Anne Becco, argues that Leibniz actually wrote van Helmont's last book, a Christian Kabbalist work entitled Some Premeditate and Considerate Thoughts upon the Four First Chapters of the First Book of Moses Called Genesis (published 1697). In this work, van Helmont/Leibniz describes creation as the articulation of divine thought. Beresith, the first word of Genesis is interpreted as meaning not "in the beginning" but "in the head" (a reading still supported by some scholars). This would make the first sentence of Genesis, "In the head, God [Elohim] created the heavens and the earth"—calling to mind the Egyptian creation myths, as well as gnostic Hermeticism and, of course, modern idealism.

Hegel invited his contemporaries to place him in the traditions of pansophia and encyclopedism by entitling his third book Enzyklopädie der Philosophischen Wissenschaften im Grundrisse. (As we shall see in chapter 7, he also invited his readers to identify him with a latter-day incarnation of Rosicrucianism.) These traditions were still very much alive in Hegel's Württemberg.

In the introduction to his Encyclopedia, Hegel writes, "The philosophical encyclopedia distinguishes itself from the other, ordinary encyclopedia [such as the French Encyclopédie] because the latter has to be some sort of aggregate of sciences, which are taken up contingently and empirically; and among them there are also some 'sciences' only in name, since they are themselves no more than a mere collection of bits of information" (EL § 16; Geraets, 39–40). (Hegel offers heraldry as one example of a pseudoscience.) His Encyclopedia differs from the ordinary sort not only in being an integrated, internally related body of knowledge, but also in eschewing everything that has the status of mere observation, mere empirical data. The Encyclopedia does, of course, deal with empirical data—in the philosophies of Nature and Spirit—but only such data as illustrate the fundamental eidetic moments of these subjects (Hegel writes in the same paragraph that the Encyclopedia "has to be restricted to the beginnings and the fundamental concepts of the particular sciences" [EL § 16; Geraets, 39]).

Hegel's Encyclopedia is exactly what its title promises: an "encirclement" of the whole of Being. It is thus the true encyclopedia. It is the true pansophia Patrizzi, Comenius, Hartlib, and Dury only dreamt of, setting the stage for the coming of the Age of the Holy Spirit and the end of history. It is Comenius's teaching of Divine Word, Nature, and Man become Logic, Nature, and Spirit. It is Leibniz's "innocent magia,"

---

113. Coudert, Leibniz and the Kabbalah, 7.

and *mathesis universalis*; his "Gnostologia" and his "ontology"—"the science of something and nothing, being and not-being"—all presented as "one continuous body, like the ocean." It is the science of sciences and the true teaching of the "names" (provisional definitions, moments) of God. It is the absolute art of memory. It is the recovery of the Wisdom of Adam—the intimate knowledge Adam had of God "in Himself," "in His eternal essence"—and thus the vindication of the nostalgia of the Kabbalists, of Agrippa, Böhme, Bacon, Jungius, Leibniz, Helmont, and others. It is the *true logic* Bacon sought. It is the Kabbalah of the Absolute Religion, Leibniz's "Cabala of the wise," the teachings of Böhme, and Oetinger become *Wissenschaft*.

The Alchemist's Laboratory:
The Philosophy of Nature and Philosophy of Subjective Spirit

1. Introduction

If Eric Voegelin could describe the *Phenomenology of Spirit* as a grimoire, one could equally well describe the "scientific" portions of the *Encyclopedia*—the *Philosophy of Nature* and *Philosophy of Subjective Spirit*—as an alchemical manual, an Emerald Tablet for the modern age.

My intention is not, however, to give comfort to those who dismiss Hegel's scientific writings as charlatanry and pseudoscience. Attacks on the *Philosophy of Nature* are seldom made by informed critics. It is simply assumed that Hegel's science is a product of armchair, a priori theorizing. But in the *Encyclopedia Logic*, Hegel writes that "the relationship of speculative science to the other sciences is simply the following: speculative science does not leave the empirical content of the other sciences aside, but recognises and uses it, and in the same way recognizes and employs what is universal in these sciences, [i.e.,] the laws, classifications, etc., for its own content; but it also introduces other categories into these universals and gives them currency" (EL § 9; Geraets, 33). Hegel makes an even more striking assertion in the *Philosophy of Nature* that "philosophy must accord with the experience nature gives rise to; in its formation and in its development, philosophic science presupposes and is conditioned by empirical physics" (PN § 246; Petry 1:197).

Hegel's *Philosophy of Nature* is not, of course, a mere catalogue of empirical data culled from the science of his day.[1] Instead Hegel organizes and explains that data according to the categories of the *Logic*. Hegel is entirely aware of the "open-ended" nature of scientific investigation. He knows that the science he is dealing with is not "final." Nevertheless, he regards the logical framework into which he has fitted science as final, because it is a reflection of the eternal Idea. In the *Dissertation* Hegel writes that "the study and knowledge of the laws of nature rest on nothing other than our believing that nature has been formed by reason [*ratio*] and our being convinced of the identity of all laws of nature."[2] This is a

---

1. In the interest of brevity, I will sometimes refer simply to *Philosophy of Nature* where I have in mind Hegel's entire treatment of empirical science, including Subjective Spirit, the Dissertation, the early lectures on philosophy of nature, etc. The context will make it clear when I am referring exclusively to the *Encyclopedia Philosophy of Nature*.

2. Hegel, *Philosophical Dissertation on the Orbits of the Planets*, trans. Pierre Adler, *Graduate Faculty Philosophy Journal* 11 (1987): 301.

statement with which even the most empirically oriented scientist could not disagree. All science assumes that nature is rational, that it possesses a definite order and behaves regularly, and that we can therefore use our own rationality to comprehend it. Hegel claims nothing more than this. Because he believes that his *Logic* maps out the eternal, objective order, he expects that nature can be shown, with a little insight and imagination, to conform to it.

It is generally conceded that Hegel's grasp of science was superior to Schelling's and that his *Philosophy of Nature* was much less fanciful and more solidly grounded than Schelling's scientific works. Hegel was critical of the Schellingians' propensity to speak in terms of "correspondences" (an "error" which, as I will discuss later, Hegel committed with abandon!). In the preface to the *Phenomenology of Spirit*, Hegel writes that "Formalism in the Philosophy of Nature takes the form of teaching that understanding is electricity, animals are nitrogen, or equivalent to the South or North pole, and so on" (Miller, 30; PG, 37). In an 1814 letter to Paulus, Hegel states that "You know that I have occupied myself too much not only with ancient literature but also with mathematics and recently with higher analysis, differential calculus, physics, natural history, [and] chemistry to be affected by that humbug in natural philosophy which consists in philosophizing without knowledge by the power of imagination, and in regarding empty brainstorms born of conceit as thoughts."[3] The low repute in which Hegel's *Philosophy of Nature* is held is due almost entirely to the confusion of its content with the content of the writings of Schelling on the same subject—an ignorant error made even by contemporaries of the two men.

Nevertheless, Hegel and Schelling had much in common, no matter how much Hegel sought to distinguish himself from the Schellingian school. For instance, both regarded Newtonian science as a depiction of a dead, mechanical system of externally related entities. Instead, Hegel and Schelling saw the world as a cosmos: an internally related organic whole.[4] In his later *Philosophy of Nature*, Hegel speaks of the "whole organism of the Earth" and writes that "The entire condition of the atmosphere, including the trade-winds is . . . a vast, living whole" (PN § 288, Z; Petry 2:51–52). For both Schelling and Hegel, Newtonianism is the physics of the Understanding, which thinks that even organic nature can be understood mechanistically. Both Schelling and Hegel hold that Newton misapplies his mechanical model to such subjects as light, color, and gravity, which cannot be understood mechanically. Both, however, hold that there is a delimited place for mechanism in their philosophies of nature. Mechanics cannot, however, explain what Hegel calls Physics (*Physik*) or Organics (*Organische Physik*). Schelling and Hegel both champion the science of Kepler, their fellow Swabian, as superior to that of Newton.

Hegel's *Philosophy of Nature* is in large measure a revival of an older,

3. Butler, 309; Hoffmeister #235.
4. Harris, introduction to *System of Ethical Life and First Philosophy of Spirit*, 19.

specifically Aristotelian way of thinking about nature, which the scientists of Hegel's day considered completely worthless and dead. In particular, the *Philosophy of Nature* incorporates a modernized version of the classical "great chain of being."[5] On Hegel's account, nature is seen to "give way" to Spirit, which "constitutes the truth and ultimate purpose of nature, and the true actuality of Idea" (PN § 251; Petry 1:216).[6] Hegel understands each "level" or "moment" of nature in very Aristotelian terms: as constituting an approach to—one might even say imitation of—Absolute Idea's actualization as Spirit. Just as in Aristotle, each level of nature "strives" to be an independent, self-sufficient "system," like the Absolute Idea.[7]

Before passing on to the Hermetic influences on the *Philosophy of Nature* and *Philosophy of Spirit*, something must be said here about the notorious transition from *Logic* to *Nature*. Hegel writes in the *Science of Logic* that "the Idea freely releases itself in its absolute self-sufficiency and stasis" (*die Idee sich selbst frei entlässt, ihrer absolut sicher und in sich ruhend*; Miller, 843; WL 3:305). The *Encyclopedia Logic* is only slightly more helpful: "The absolute *freedom* of the Idea . . . is not that it merely *passes over* into *life*, nor that it lets life *shine* within itself as finite cognition, but that, in the absolute truth of itself, it *resolves to release out of itself* into freedom the moment of its particularity or of the initial determining and otherness, [i.e.,] the *immediate Idea* as its reflexion, or itself as *Nature*" (EL § 244; Geraets, 307).

This concept of "free release" is patterned on the traditional Christian idea that God creates the world as an unnecessitated act of generosity. (It also calls to mind Neoplatonic emanation.) However, Hegel is a heretic because he holds the view that an abstract and transcendent God is deficient. Thus, Idea *must* "give rise to" nature. Because the categories of the *Logic* are complete, and thus a "category" of nature is not required to *supplement* Absolute Idea, and because no physical mechanism acts on Idea to "produce" nature, Idea must be said to "freely" release itself. But does this make sense? Exactly what work does Idea do in bringing about or sustaining nature? What is the "itself" that is freely released? Are we to understand Hegel's language of "free release" as purely metaphorical? Is he simply saying that the *Logic* is the *eidetic* "subtext" of nature, a set of categories in which nature is to be understood? As is frequently claimed by interpreters, the relationship between *Logic*

5. See Harris, *Night Thoughts*, 374.
6. See Oetinger's position on Spirit and Nature, as summarized by Robert Schneider: nature "is . . . only the threshold for spirit, it is the signature, the cipher for the spirit of man and for divine transcendence" (*Geistesahnen*, 91).
7. The difference between Hegel and Aristotle, however, is that the Unmoved Mover, which is perfectly independent and self-sufficient, is no "system" in the sense of a unity of parts, because it has no parts. Aristotle regards organic being as the most perfect form of being in nature, because of the integrity of the organism's parts. Therefore, it could be said that Hegel transplants Aristotle's criterion for "natural substance" into the "heavens," and conceives the Unmoved Mover (Absolute Idea) on the model of organic being. This should not be surprising, for Hegel would regard Aristotle's transcendent Unmoved Mover as an unrealized abstraction.

and nature is not a *temporal* one. Hegel's language of "free release" would certainly seem to be figurative, then.

In section 3, I will discuss the difficulties with treating Hegel's language as merely figurative. For the moment, however, let us try to understand the relation of Logic to nature in purely conceptual terms. Like Böhme and Oetinger, Hegel believes that for Absolute Idea to become truly *Absolute*, it cannot abide simply in the transcendent realm of ideas: it must be "embodied." This occurs when Absolute Idea enters the world and becomes an embodied thought that reflects on itself.[8] Such thought is *philosophy*. We have seen in our examination of the *Phenomenology* and *Logic* that Hegel has generated his system through reflection on the nature of consciousness in all its forms. He has realized the ancient imperative of philosophy, "Know Thyself." This attainment of self-knowledge by individual human thinkers is the realization of the Absolute Idea in the world. Hegel writes in an 1819 letter to Hinrichs that "Comprehension of the Absolute is thus the Absolute's comprehension of itself, just as theology—admittedly theology more as it once was than as it now is—has always expressed this same self-comprehension."[9]

For Hegel the object of philosophy is God. Hegel identifies God with the Absolute Idea, just as Aristotle identified God with self-thinking thought. However, if God is identical with Absolute Idea, it follows that Hegel must hold that God is *merely formal* and *irreal*. Earlier I quoted Hegel stating that the *Logic* is "the exposition of God as he is in his eternal essence before the creation of nature and a finite Spirit" (Miller, 50; WL 1:33–34). God "in his eternal essence," then, is deficient. Hegel states in the *Philosophy of Nature*, "God as an abstraction is not the true God; His truth is the positing of His other, the living process, the world, which is his Son when it is comprehended in its divine form" (PN § 246, Z; Petry 1:204).

In other words, The Absolute Idea does represent a system of pure ideas, complete unto itself. It requires no other *category* or *concept* to complete it. However, the system *as a whole* is deficient because logical or eidetic being is itself deficient. On its own, logic (or the logos) is formal and one-dimensional. To be fully realized, the Idea must "express itself" in the world of space and time. Thus, the *Logic* must be supplemented by the *Philosophy of Nature*. But if Idea comes to actual self-consciousness through a self-thinking thought, through a human activity, then why does Hegel write a *Philosophy of Nature* instead of just going straight to the *Philosophy of Spirit*?

The answer, in part, is that much of the *Philosophy of Nature* pertains to human beings insofar as they are physical, organic systems. A complete account of Spirit must therefore include these elements. But this is not Hegel's primary consideration. Hegel's aim is to work out a developmental account of reality as a whole, in terms of which everything is made significant or intelligible. The telos of the universe is the Absolute

---

8. Hegel states in the *Philosophy of Spirit* that with Spirit we are concerned "with the most concrete and developed form attained in the self-actualization of the Idea" (PS § 377, Z; Petry 1:3). And later: "Spirit is the actualized Concept which is for itself and has itself for object" (PS § 382, Z; Petry 1:49).
9. Butler, 478; Hoffmeister #357.

Idea's realization in the world through the speculative activity of the philosopher, which is achieved through a long historical process. The non-human cannot, however, drop out of this picture as unintelligible. To explain why non-human physical reality exists at all, Hegel adopts a quasi-Aristotelian standpoint and claims that in some sense all physical and organic reality is intelligible in terms of its "approximation" to the self-related self-sufficiency of the Absolute Idea, or self-thinking thought.

As to the transition from nature to Spirit, the second topic of this chapter, in the introduction to the *Philosophy of Nature* Hegel alludes to Schelling's description of nature as "petrified intelligence" (*versteinerte Intelligenz*), and states that "God does not remain petrified and moribund however, the stones cry out and lift themselves up to spirit" (PN § 247; Petry, 206). He is alluding, of course, to the *necessity* of the move from nature to Spirit. For Hegel, Spirit is both antecedent and consequent of nature. In one of his many Aristotelian moments, Hegel states that "It is precisely because Spirit constitutes the end of nature, that it is antecedent to it" (PN § 376; Petry 3:212). In other words, Spirit is the telos of nature. Spirit presupposes nature, *and* nature presupposes Spirit. Hegel writes that "The purpose of nature is to extinguish itself, and to break through its rind of immediate and sensuous being, to consume itself like a Phoenix in order to emerge from this externality rejuvenated as Spirit" (ibid.).

Spirit is characterized by its drive to overcome the subject-object distinction, to eliminate the "otherness" of the other. What Spirit achieves is an experience of a world that is "merely an apprehension of itself" (PS § 377; Petry 1:5). Hegel writes that "the aim of all genuine science is just this, that Spirit shall recognize itself in everything in heaven and on earth. An out-and-out other simply does not exist for Spirit" (ibid.).

Hegel divides the *Philosophy of Spirit* into Subjective Spirit, Objective Spirit, and Absolute Spirit. I am only concerned in this chapter with the *Philosophy of Subjective Spirit*.

2. The Four Elements

Ernst Benz writes that "We must not overlook or even negate the fact that the language of modern natural science and cosmology has its roots in mystical natural philosophy; we must be aware that knowledge and mystery are of necessity interrelated."[10] Such authors as Allen G. Debus, P. O. Kristeller, Stephen A. McKnight, D. P. Walker, and Frances Yates, among others, argue for the influence of alchemy, Kabbalism, magic, and Hermeticism in general on modern science. In Hegel's time it was not unusual for a serious man of science to be interested in these subjects.[11] To be sure, the prevailing opinion was that these "sciences" were worth-

10. Benz, *The Theology of Electricity*, 74.
11. One of the most famous such cases, of course, is that of Isaac Newton. Ernst Benz notes that the terms *attraction* and *repulsion* made their way into Newton's science via his teacher, the Cambridge Platonist and theosophist Henry More. More got them from an English translation of Böhme's *Mysterium Magnum*. See Benz, ibid.

less, but there were holdouts. Hegel and the Schelling brothers, as well as Goethe, Oetinger, Baader, Herder, Steffens, Ritter, and others, are to be numbered among them.

Given the Hermetic influences on Hegel's *Logic*, his application of its categories to scientific data results in a philosophy of nature amounting to a sophisticated synthesis of modern science and Hermeticism. As David Walsh puts it: "What Hegel set out to do was to integrate the rationality of modern science with the penumbra of larger spiritual expectations which have also been an abiding feature of the modern world. It is perhaps the most impressive attempt at reconciling science with pseudo-science."[12] In keeping with this aim there is an influence of alchemy on the *Philosophy of Nature*.

Central to alchemy is the ancient Greek doctrine of the four elements: Earth, Air, Fire, and Water. When Hegel speaks of "the square" he generally has in mind the four elements. In chapter 3, I discussed how squareness as a symbolic form figures prominently in Hegel's early Philosophy of Nature. Recall also that in the Triangle fragment the "triangle of triangles" is made to become at one point a square. The triangle diagram may also refer to the four elements in its use of four triangles.

As we have seen, the triadic form dominates Hegel's system, but in his early philosophy he apparently held that although the triangle predominates as a symbolic form in the realm of Spirit, the square is the key to the realm of nature. Consider the third of Hegel's twelve doctoral examination theses from 1801: "The square is the law of nature, the triangle of mind [*mens*]." This view is still to be found in the mature *Philosophy of Nature*. Hegel does not, to be sure, organize that work in a quadratic form—it is triadic like all the others—but the quadratic form does crop up within a number of different divisions. Before looking at the *Philosophy of Nature* and the occurrence of the four elements there, let us look back at some of the earlier works.

In Hegel's so-called "First Philosophy of Spirit" (1803–4), he treats consciousness as the "ideality of nature" and then offers the following opaque observations:

> The elements in which [consciousness] exists as middle are just the elements of air and earth, as the indifferent self-identical elements, not the unrest of fire and water[13]; for consciousness only is qua absolutely self-identical, and qua existing middle it is posited as a quiescent indifferent middle. As concept of consciousness this middle is in that element which is the simple self-

12. David Walsh, "A Mythology of Reason," 159. J. M. Petry writes that "For Hegel . . . the Idea of Nature involves a combination of the Baconian and Böhmean attitudes to natural phenomena." See Petry, introduction to *Hegel's Philosophy of Nature*, vol. 1, 114.

13. Oetinger held that fire and water are a dynamic pair, which gives rise to all beings. See Schneider, *Schellings und Hegels schwabische Geistesahnen*, 95. This position is stated outright by Hegel in the *Realphilosophie* of 1803–4: "Feur und Wasser [sind] die Grund-Anfänge und Elemente aller Dinge." He also refers to them as "tätig," active. *Jenenser Realphilosophie*, ed. Johannes Hoffmeister, vol. 1 (Leipzig: Meiner, 1931), 47, 44.

identical one among the elements; its external middle [medium] is the air.[14]

In the *Phenomenology* Hegel writes:

Air is the enduring, purely universal, and transparent element; Water, the element that is perpetually sacrificed; Fire, the unity which energizes them into opposition while at the same time it perpetually resolves the opposition; lastly, Earth, which is the firm and solid knot of this articulated whole, the subject of these elements and of their process, that from which they start and to which they return; so in the same way, the inner essence or simple Spirit of self-conscious actuality displays itself in similar such universal—but here spiritual—masses or spheres, displays itself in a world. (Miller, 300; PG, 326)

All these ideas are present in the mature *Philosophy of Nature*. In one of the *Zusätze* from 1819–30, he refers to polarity, saying that "there is also a positing of the return out of the opposition into unity, and it is this third term which constitutes the necessity of the Concept, a necessity which is not found in polarity" (PN § 248, Z; Petry 1:211). Here again we find the claim that a full account of the real must consist of a triad of moments. Hegel goes on, however, to say that "In nature taken as otherness, the square or tetrad also belongs to the whole form of necessity, as in the four elements, the four colors, etc.; the pentad may also be found, in the five fingers and the five senses for example; but in Spirit the fundamental form of necessity is the triad" (ibid.). This particular aspect of Hegel—the obsession with dyads, triads, tetrads, pentads, mathematico-geometrical constructions of all kinds—is typical of thinkers influenced by Hermetic philosophy.

Section 281 of the *Philosophy of Nature* is entitled "The Elements" (*Die Elemente*). This and the following sections, including the *Zusätze* from 1819–30, must be taken as representing his mature understanding of the four elements. Hegel states that "The air corresponds to light, for it is passive light which has sunk to the level of a moment" (PN § 281, Z; Petry 2:34). Like Hegel's other remarks on the four elements this is hardly clear. Perhaps he means that air, like light, permeates everything, and air is to be thought of as "extinguished light" (later Hegel states, in language that is strikingly Böhmean, that air "is a slumbering fire" [PN § 282, Z; Petry 2:38]). Hegel refers to fire and water as the "elements of opposition." He says that fire corresponds to the lunar plane, and water to the cometary. He has little to say on the subject of earth in this initial treatment.

Some paragraphs later, we find Hegel saying that air "constitutes the universal ideality of everything akin to it; that it is the universal in relation to its other, and that it effaces all opposing particularity" (PN § 284, Z; Petry 2:41). Fire "is the same universality, but it appears as such, and

---

14. Hegel, *System of Ethical Life*, 215; *System der Sittlichkeit*, 277. There is much more to this passage that is quite interesting, particularly in its treatment of the aether, but I cannot deal with it here.

therefore has the form being-for-self, it is existent ideality therefore, or the nature of air which has passed into existence; by appearing, it reduces its other to an appearance." Water, on the other hand, is "passive neutrality" (ibid.). Hegel refers to earth as "the individual element" (*individuelles Element*). It is the element "of developed difference . . . In its distinctness from the other moments, this element is as yet indeterminate; as the totality which holds together the variety of these moments in individual unity, however, it is the power which stimulates and sustains their process" (PN § 285; Petry 2:41).

At the beginning of his remarks on Organics, Hegel refers to the terrestrial, vegetable, and animal organisms as belonging to the "Kingdom of Earth," "Kingdom of Water," and "Kingdom of Fire," respectively (PN § 337, Z; Petry 3:12–14). What is omitted, of course, is the "Kingdom of Air"—*pneuma*, *spiritus*—which Hegel could not consider here, for this Kingdom stands outside nature. Under his treatment of the Animal Organism, Hegel suggests correspondences between the senses and the elements: touch is the sense of the "mechanical sphere" and thus corresponds to earth and fire (which seems to mean density and temperature). Touch is "the sense of the earthy element." Smell and taste, the "senses of opposition," correspond to air and water. Sight corresponds to light, and hearing doesn't seem to correspond to anything, but is simply the reception of "the manifestations of internal being, which reveals itself as such in its expression" (PN § 358; Petry 3:138–39).

So Hegel makes extensive use of the four elements—but how is this evidence of alchemical influence? After all, the doctrine originates with Empedocles and was developed systematically by Aristotle. Isn't this just evidence of *Greek* influence? Certainly Hegel and his contemporaries knew of the history of this doctrine (Hegel even mentions Empedocles in connection with it [PN § 281, Z; Petry 2:34]). Nevertheless, by Hegel's time the doctrine of the four elements was so closely associated with alchemy that his use of it could not have failed to have a strong alchemical connotation not only for his listeners and readers, but for himself as well. As I discussed in chapter 2, alchemy was still very much on the scene in Hegel's day. Thus Hegel's use of the four elements would have "pegged" him in the minds of his audience as someone who still saw some truth in the "Hermetic art." After introducing the four elements in the *Philosophy of Nature*, Hegel remarks ruefully that "No educated person, and certainly no physicist or chemist is now permitted, under any circumstances, to mention the four elements" (PN § 281, Z; Petry 2:34). Thus Hegel is deliberately and boldly risking ridicule in order to hold fast to what he regards as an important truth.

H. S. Harris writes that "Hegel's continual appeals to the four elements of this mortal world are not poetic or metaphorical."[15] He literally believes in the elemental nature of fire, air, water, and earth (or fieriness, airiness, liquidity, earthiness). The analogies Hegel draws between the elements and the five senses and the levels of Spirit, the heavenly bodies,

---

15. Harris, introduction to *System of Ethical Life*, 203, n.

as well as other types of being, are correspondences in the old-fashioned, Hermetico-magical sense. It was common for practitioners of magic and alchemy to devise elaborate tables of correspondences between the elements of one sphere of being and another. According to Agrippa, the four elements of fire, air, water, and earth correspond to the four angels ruling over the corners of the earth (Seraph, Cherub, Tharsis, Ariel), the four evangelists (Mark, John, Matthew, and Luke), the four seasons, the four humors (choleric, sanguine, phlegmatic, melancholic), the four princes of devils (Samael, Azazel, Azael, Mahazael), etc.[16] Should all this seem totally remote from Hegel's enterprise, it should also be noted that Agrippa holds that the four elements correspond to the senses: fire to sight, air to hearing, water to taste and smell, and earth to touch. The four elements also correspond to the "four elements of man": fire to the mind, air to spirit (recall *Spiritus* and my discussion of the elements from chapter 3), water to the soul, and earth to body.[17]

Despite Hegel's own use of correspondences, he nonetheless criticizes the practice in others, especially the Schellingian school. In the *Philosophy of Nature*, we find the following:

> Schelling and Steffens have drawn a parallel between the planetary series and that of metals. This is an ingenious and pregnant comparison, but it is not a new idea, for the representation of Venus by copper, Mercury by quicksilver, the Earth by iron, Jupiter by tin, and Saturn by lead, is a commonplace, just as it is to call the Sun golden and the Moon silver. There is something completely natural about this, for metals are the most compact and independent bodies to be found on Earth. The planets do not belong to the same field as the metals and the chemical process, however. Cross-references [*Anspielungen*] of this kind are external comparisons and decide nothing. They merely sparkle before the imagination without furthering the scope of knowledge. (PN § 280, Z; Petry 2:31–32)[18]

Hegel also attacks correspondences in the *Phenomenology*. Despite such attacks, Hegel frequently engaged in analogical "correspondence-thinking." H. S. Harris lists some of the correspondences to be found in Hegel's early philosophy: "Solar System/*Volk*; Earth with mineral—or, meteorological—process/human organism with mind process; vegetable and animal kingdom/system of need and system of justice."[19] Perhaps the most famous—or infamous—example is the *Dissertation* of 1801, in which Hegel suggests that if we are to believe that nature conforms to a rational pattern, then we might do well to consider the ubiquitousness in nature and human thought of the number *seven*. The

immediate inspiration for this idea comes from Plato's *Timaeus*.[20] Hegel
suggests that there may be a reason why the men of his day had identified only seven planets. He hypothesizes that seven may be the necessary and correct number of planets.[21] Nor is this pattern of thought
confined to Hegel's youth, for he organized his entire mature system in
terms of corresponding levels of nested triangles.

3. Aether

Hegel does not confine his *Naturphilosophie* to the four mundane elements. He also deals with the fifth element, the aether, the stuff of the
stars. Hegel refers to the aether throughout his writings, but in his early
Philosophy of Nature it played a much more significant role.[22] Although the
concept of aether was part of mainstream science in Hegel's time, its origins are ancient. It figures prominently in the philosophies of Anaxagoras, Democritus, Aristotle, and the Stoics. Aristotle makes aether the
fifth element, but holds that it is different from the other four in being
indestructible and unchanging. Aether moves in a circle, which is the perfect form of motion for Aristotle. (The importance of circularity to
Hegel is likely a reason why he hit on the aether as a significant concept.)
All the heavenly bodies and their spheres are composed of this incorruptible substance. The Stoics identified the aether with *pneuma* or spirit
and held that aether-pneuma is found not only in the heavens but in
earthly matter as well. The Stoics make use of the aether in their physical
theory in order to explain, among other things, the transmission of light.
In these early Aristotelian and Stoic accounts of aether, we can already
see much of Hegel's doctrine.

Oddly enough, given its status as a fifth element, aether did not enter
into alchemical speculation until the middle of the fourteenth century.
John of Rupescissa's *Consideration of the Fifth Essence* may have been the
first alchemical text to popularize the idea that there are five elements.[23]
In alchemy, aether is frequently referred to as the fifth essence. Marsillio Ficino identified *spiritus* with the fifth element in his magical theory.
In magic, the "astral plane" on which spirits are encountered and on

20. Harris writes that "What impressed Hegel about this ancient example, is
that with seven moving bodies to organize in his World-Soul 'Timaeus' was
already working with a series based on the powers of two and three. *In this
instinct of Reason* Hegel saw a confirmation of his thesis that 'at all times there
has been only one and the same philosophy'" (ibid., 93; my italics).
21. Hegel, *Orbits of the Planets*, 302. Hegel does not "deduce" that there are
seven and can be only seven planets, as is often claimed. His argument is, in
fact, hypothetical. See Hegel, *Dissertatio Philosophica de Orbitis Planetarum.
Philosophische Erörterung über die Planetenbahnen*, trans. with introduction and
commentary, by Wolfgang Neuser (Weinheim: Acta humaniora d. VHC,
1986), 51. Robert Schneider has argued for the influence of the Oetingerite
and "electrical theologian" J. L. Fricker on Hegel's Dissertation (*Geistesahnen*,
48).
22. Like Harris, I employ the "ae" diphthong and write "aether" to emphasize
that we are dealing with a use of the term wholly different from the ordinary
one, which refers to a gas. See Harris, introduction to *System of Ethical Life*,
202–3, n. (Harris, however, is not consistent in using "ae.")
23. Merkur, *Gnosis*, 74.

which the magician can travel is also called aetherial. Magic itself is often conceived as a manipulation of the aether.[24] Paracelsus referred to aether as a "fifth element," as the substance of stars and souls, and spoke of an "aether Body."

In the modern period, conceptions of aether played roles in the scientific theories of Descartes and Newton. Klaus Vondung writes that Newton presented his theory of aether "as a hermetic cosmogony in the language of science."[25] Newton held that aether was a plenum, permeating all space. Aether is elastic for Newton and can condense and rarify. Vondung writes, further, that "Newton even put forward the hypothesis that aether, in its different degrees of condensation, is the substance of all bodies, and that it produces, by means of perpetual condensation and vaporization, the cycle of becoming and vanishing. . . . In Newton's early theory aether assumed the role of a divine creative *quinta essencia*."[26] These elements in Newton's theory are seldom discussed.

Aether was still a living idea for scientists in Hegel's time, indeed well into the nineteenth century. Herder, who was deeply immersed in the Hermetic tradition, took up Newton's esoteric aether theory in its entirety and incorporated it into his own Hermetic cosmology.[27] Aether also figured in Schelling's philosophy of nature, which was probably the most direct influence on Hegel's doctrine. Unfortunately, Hegel's "aether doctrine" has come down to us only in fragments—and the fragments are among the most enigmatic in Hegel.

For Hegel the aether is metaphysical bedrock. It is an ultimate plastic medium that is nothing in particular, but has the potentiality to become everything. H. S. Harris writes, "The aether is characterized objectively as 'absolute elasticity' and further as 'uncloudable transparency.' Unlike Aristotle's prime matter, it is an active potentiality. It is the unity of intellect and thing, not 'prime' but 'absolute' matter, matter that can give itself form." And: "The aether, as that which abides unchanged in all the changes which express its dynamic essence, is the 'Idea' of God."[28] The aether lies at the basis of everything in experience.[29] It is to be conceived as boundlessly active and fertile. The aether is pure thought, pure mat-

24. Ibid., 72.
25. Vondung, "Millenarianism," 138. See also Richard S. Westfall, "Newton and the Hermetic Tradition," in *Science, Medicine and Society in the Renaissance*, ed. Allen G. Debus (New York: Science History Publications, 1972), 2:183–98.
26. Vondung, "Millenarianism," 139.
27. Ibid., 138–39.
28. Harris, *Night Thoughts*, 420; cf. 305. Harris's discussions of aether, in *Night Thoughts* and elsewhere, are the best survey of Hegel's "aether doctrine" in English.
29. Harris writes, "[Hegel] is trying to find the most abstractly general description of the unformed element or medium, which takes on different shapes and patterns in every human language and in every other aspect of communal life and experience" (introduction to *System of Ethical Life*, 193). And "The aether is the *energy* that is absolutely conserved, the continuum at the basis of all experience" (editorial note in Hegel, *The Jena System, 1804–5: Logic and Metaphysics*, trans. and ed. John W. Burbidge and George di Giovanni, introduction and notes by H.S. Harris [Kingston: McGill-Queen's University Press, 1986], 172).

ter, pure space, and pure manifestation all at once. It can be all of these things because these represent the nature of the aether expressed in wholly different layers or levels of reality. Aether expresses itself in the eternal thought-world of the *Logic*, and then as empty space,[30] the pure possibility of extension, then in extension itself (the absolute other to thought) or absolute matter,[31] then in the world of matter as revealed, as light.[32] From these there follows an entire world of nature, including man.[33] Hegel also seems to conceive the aether as the "life-force" inhabiting the Earth; it is a "World-Soul."[34]

Hegel's first transition from Idea to nature is significant as an initial exposition of the aether doctrine.[35]

> As determinate being which has returned to Concept, the Idea may now be called absolute matter or aether. It is apparent that this has the same meaning as Pure Spirit, for this absolute matter is in no way sensuously given, but is the Concept as pure Concept in itself. As such it is Existent Spirit. . . . aether in its simplicity and self-sameness is therefore the indeterminate soul of Spirit; it is motionless quiescence or the being which is perpetually returning into itself from otherness. It is the substance and being of all things, that which is absolutely elastic and abhors every form, but which is likewise absolutely plastic, giving itself and expressing every form. Aether is therefore Being . . . it constitutes everything. In so far as it is said to be aether or absolute matter, it is in itself, or pure self-consciousness. . . . However, this determinateness of non-determinate being passes over into determinate being, and the element of

---

30. *Difference*, 4; *Differenz*, 14.

31. *Gesammelte Werke*, vol. 7, 178, 1–2, and 188, 5–5; 280, 14–15. Harris writes: "Matter as gravity is the self-positing of the *aether* which is the indifferent identity of the divine life, the creative power that expresses itself in all forms of real existence, whether conscious or unconscious, extended or intelligent" (*Night Thoughts*, 76).

32. Hegel, *Gesammelte Werke*, vol. 7, 218, 11; vol. 8, 34, 17–36, 2. Harris, on Hegel's early *Philosophy of Nature*, writes: "Hegel regards light as the showing forth of 'free force.' It is the 'totality' of the aether (which is polarized into the existing bodily units of the system)" (*Night Thoughts*, 425).

33. *Gesammelte Werke*, vol. 4, 467. Harris comments: "In the [early] Philosophy of Nature Hegel traces the evolution of the 'ether' (which he calls 'the Idea of God' but says is *not* 'the living God') from its primary positing as light and darkness, through the dynamic space-time equilibrium of the solar system, to the physical equilibrium of the earth-process, which sets the stage for organic life" (editorial note in *The Jena System*, 186). As Böhme claims, "the world's existence is nothing else than coagulated smoke from the eternal aether, which thus has a fulfillment like the eternal" (*Six Theosophical Points*, Point 1, chap. 2, § 19).

34. Harris writes, "The 'absolute life-force' which exists in the Earth, but which has thus achieved independent existence, is the *aether* which is the ultimate source of things" (*Night Thoughts*, 286). And: "The aether is a world-soul in the Greek sense, i.e. it is a life principle" (ibid., 242).

35. Hegel mentions the aether as early as "Eleusis," his 1796 poem addressed to Hölderlin: "It is the ether of my homeland as well" (Butler, 46; Hoffmeister #18).

reality is the universal determinateness in which spirit has its being as nature.[36]

In Hegel's *Philosophy of Nature* of 1803–4 he writes that "the speaking of the aether with itself is its reality. . . . What it utters is itself, what speaks is itself, and that to which it speaks is again itself."[37] In the so-called "First Philosophy of Spirit" of 1803–4, Hegel writes that in the "second part" of philosophy, "Idea fell absolutely apart in the Philosophy of Nature; absolute Being, the aether, sundered itself from its becoming or Infinity, and the union of the two was the inner aspect, the buried [essence] which lifted itself out in the organism and exists in the form of singularity, that is, as a numerical unit."[38] Then, in the same text: "In the Spirit the absolutely simple aether has returned to itself by way of the infinity of the Earth; in the Earth as such this union of the absolute simplicity of aether and infinity exists; it spreads into the universal fluidity, but its spreading fragments itself as singular things."[39] Elsewhere, Hegel states that "In the indifference of light, the aether has scattered its absolute indifference into a multiplicity; in the blooms of the solar system it has born its inner Reason and totality out into expansion."[40] Later in the same essay: "the aether, which permeates nature, is the inseparable essence of the *Gestalten* of nature."[41]

Nor is aether confined simply to the early manuscripts. In the preface to the *Phenomenology* Hegel writes, "Pure self-recognition in absolute otherness, this aether as such, is the ground and soil of Science or knowledge in general. The beginning of philosophy presupposes or requires that consciousness should dwell in this element" (Miller, 14). Aether begins appearing in Hegel's manuscripts around 1803 and continues to be prominent until about 1806, sometime after the *Phenomenology of Spirit* was composed, that is, well after the detailed outlines of his system had been established. However, after the Jena period, the aether is deemphasized. It is no longer a major category of the *Philosophy of Nature*, although it occasionally puts in a very minor appearance, for instance, in Organics in the *Philosophy of Nature*: "This constitutes the initiation of the living subject, soul, aetheriality, the essential process of articulation into members and expansion" (PN § 337, Z; Petry 3:13).

Hegel's aether doctrine was richly imaginative and speculative. But what is the question to which aether is the answer? The solution to this problem might tell us why Hegel dropped the concept of aether. Since the Pre-Socratics, philosophers have tried to identify what persists through change, or what lies at the root of all things. This is the question of *ousia*, substance. For the Greeks, *ousia* was not only that which persisted through change, but also, because of its persistence and unchangingness, that which truly could be said *to be*. The aether is

36. Hegel, *Jenenser Realphilosophie*, vol. 1, vol. 2, 3–4.
37. Quoted in Harris, *Night Thoughts*, 243.
38. *System of Ethical Life*, 205–6; *System der Sittlichkeit*, 268.
39. *System of Ethical Life*, 206; *System der Sittlichkeit*, 265–66.
40. Hegel, *Gesammelte Werke*, vol. 4, 464.
41. Ibid., 467.

Hegel's initial answer to the question of substance. The aether is the ultimate stuff of nature. As Harris puts it, "The ether is the *energy* that is absolutely conserved, the continuum at the basis of all experience."[42]

However, as *ousia*, aether is a substratum, a *hypokeimenon*. In the *Metaphysics*, Aristotle considers the possibility that *ousia* is a *hypokeimenon* and rejects it, identifying *ousia* not with some indefinite underlying stuff, but instead with the most definite and self-sufficient individual in existence: God. Hegel's system closely resembles Aristotle's in putting at its apex a concept of God or the Absolute, which is conceived as the one, true individual and as a self-thinking thought. This quasi-Aristotelian substance, the Absolute, is the moving principle, the telos of all of reality for Hegel. The aether thus emerges as a superfluous, "second *ousia*," in the mold of the more naive and simplistic *ousia* of the Pre-Socratics. Once we have understand all of nature and history as progressively realizing the Absolute, there is no need for a "dynamic aether" propelling change or giving rise to different spheres of being. As to the ultimate physical constituents of matter, that is an issue that may be left to science.

It seems likely that in his treatment of the aether, Hegel was drawing inspiration, in roughly equal proportions, from both "hard science" and alchemical-Hermetic speculation. There is a suspiciously close fit between the Hermetic magus as aetherial voyager and Hegel's conception of the philosopher who, from the standpoint of Absolute Knowing, moves within the plane of Logic and brings aetherial Idea to full actualization in self-thinking thought. Furthermore, since Hegel says that the aether is not the living God but only the "Idea of God,"[43] it must be inferred that in the transformation effected by Spirit at its highest level—its realization of the "speaking of the aether with itself"[44]—it has *created* God, using the aether as a medium. This is indeed High Magic.

4. The Alchemical Opus

Aether plus the four elements does not entirely sum up Hegel's debt to alchemy. The most interesting connection between Hegel and alchemy does not consist in his explicit references to alchemical terms or doctrine, but in the parallelism between his philosophical project and the alchemical opus. Seeing this parallelism requires reading alchemical doctrines as symbolic expressions of an esoteric philosophy.

C. C. Jung popularized the treatment of alchemical language as figurative. However, Jung's approach is to view alchemy as an unconscious expression of something that actually goes on in the psyche of the "alchemist." My approach is closer to that of Julius Evola, who regards alchemical works as deliberate instances of esoteric writing. It is significant that this latter kind of reading is actually encouraged by some alchemists, as I shall show. In order to see the esoteric meaning of alchemy and its parallelism to Hegel, we must take a look at its exoteric shell, so what follows is a brief overview of traditional alchemical doctrine.

42. H. S. Harris, editorial note in *The Jena System*, 172.
43. Hegel, *Gesammelte Werke*, vol. 7, 188, 10–13.
44. Ibid., vol. 4, 463–64.

Alchemy is often referred to simply as hermeticism, or as the "hermetic art" (Evola titles his book on alchemy *The Hermetic Tradition, La tradizione ermetica*). Alchemists prided themselves on being called "hermeticists." Like the *Emerald Tablet*, many alchemical texts were attributed to Hermes Trismegistus. Indeed, alchemy appears to have come to conceptual fruition contemporaneously with the *Hermetica*. Bolos of Mendes in the second century B.C. is generally regarded as the first true alchemist, that is, the first to write of a science of alchemy that had spiritual overtones and did not look simply like metallurgy. Twenty-eight books of the alchemist Zosimos of Panopolis (late third or early fourth century A.D.) have been preserved. Other early names in the history of alchemy include Synesius (fourth century), Olympiodorus (sixth century) and Stephanos of Alexandria (seventh century).

David Walsh, drawing on the work of Mircea Eliade, argues that alchemy developed out of the metallurgical myths of the Iron Age, as well as the Egyptian skilled crafts.[45] It was believed by ancient miners that metals were generated by a living Earth Spirit, a conception not unlike Hegel's Natural or Earth Soul.[46] The ancient smiths believed that they played a role in the "gestation" of metals in the earth. Similarly, the alchemist believed it was his task to bring metals to their natural perfection: gold. The aim here was not the production of wealth, but the knowledge and perfection of nature. A perennial Hermetic theme, as we have seen, is the idea that the purpose of human existence is to "complete" or perfect the cosmos (or even God). The means for the perfection of nature is, according to most alchemists, the distillation of the Philosopher's Stone. Just what exactly was the Philosopher's Stone? Also termed "the Essence," "the Stone of the Wise," "the Magisterium," "Magnum Opus," "the Quintessence," and the "universal Essence,"[47] descriptions of the stone vary:

> It is described as being of various colors, sometimes as a red, white, or black powder, or it may be yellow, blue, or green. Raymond Lully calls it "carbunculus," while Paracelsus declares it to be a solid body like a ruby, transparent and flexible. Beregard says it is "the colour of a wild poppy, with the smell of heated sea-salt," and van Helmont describes it as being "yellow, the colour of saffron, in the form of a heavy powder, with a brilliancy like glass." Helvetius likewise describes it as being yellow and the colour of sulphur, but it is most frequently referred to as the red or white stone.[48]

The Philosopher's Stone was thought to be at one and the same time priceless and as common as dung.[49] Emma Jung writes that the philosopher's stone is "a particle of God concealed in nature, an analogy to the God who, in Christ, came down to earth in a human body, subject to suffering. On the other hand, the 'cheapness' of the stone . . .

---

45. Walsh, *Boehme and Hegel*, 44–46.
46. See C. G. Jung's discussion of Basilius Valentinus on the Earth-Spirit in *Psychology and Alchemy*, trans. R. F. C. Hull (Princeton, N.J.: Princeton University Press, 1968), 342–43.
47. C. J. S. Thompson, *Lure and Romance of Alchemy*, 69.
48. Ibid., 71.
49. Emma Jung and von Franz, *Grail Legend*, 153.

alludes to the fact that every human being is its potential bearer, even its begetter."[50]

Descriptions of the function of the philosopher's stone vary as well. By it, claims one anonymous alchemical author, "all infirmities might be cured, human life prolonged to its utmost limits, and mankind preserved in health and strength of body and mind, clearness and vigour."[51] This seems to make the stone identical to the fabled "elixir of life," but it was generally conceived as much more than this. The stone was also held to be capable of isolating the literal essence of any object it was exposed to, and of transmuting substances one into another.

The philosopher's stone was supposed to possess the characteristics of both sulphur and mercury, which were thought by alchemists to be the dual *materia prima* of all things. The four elements of Earth, Air, Fire, and Water—which are the ground of the active qualities of dry, cold, heat, and wet—are often thought to proceed from the aether, the *materia prima* in its first or most pristine form. These elements make up all of physical reality, and each "contains" all the others (as represented in the theory that each can change into the others through an alteration in the degrees or balance of dry, cold, heat, and wet). Heat is conceived as the most basic of the qualities, and Fire the most basic of the elements.

This theory of the elements and their relationships constitutes the basic alchemical "theory of matter." There is more, however, and it is intimately bound up with the perennial Hermetic theory of the correspondence of the macrocosm and the microcosm. In alchemy, the metals (formed through the interaction of the elements) are related to the planets (we have already encountered Hegel referring to this doctrine in connection with Schelling and Steffens). As David Walsh explains it, "The seven planets are ordered in the tension between the two poles of the active and spiritual powers of the sun, gold, and the passive receptive powers of the moon, silver. They are all represented by variations on the three basic symbols . . . for the sun, for the moon, and for the cross [representing] the elements. The only planet that contains all three [of the symbols] is Mercury, which signifies the predominance of the passive lunar power over the solarian formation of the four elements."[52]

Mercury, as the intersection of the physical elements and the active and passive forces, represents the isolation of *materia prima*, the aether lying at the basis of all forms. It is conceived as the androgyne. As we have seen, the Philosopher's Stone is the unity of sulphur and mercury, a dual *materia prima*. We can see, then, that the Philosopher's Stone is something like a corporealization or "solidification" of the aether, which is "decomposable" into the twin properties of sulphur and mercury. In fact, the Philosopher's Stone was sometimes referred to as the lapis aethereus, and both the Philosopher's Stone and the aether are commonly referred to as the "fifth essence."[53] The alchemical operation that achieves this is often represented by two serpents coiling together around a rod (symbolizing, perhaps, the

50. Ibid., 157.
51. Quoted in Thompson, *Lure and Romance of Alchemy*, 70.
52. Walsh, *Boehme and Hegel*, 49.
53. Jung, *Psychology and Alchemy*, 243.

aether). This image is, of course, the cadeucus, the staff of Hermes or Mercury. The Philosopher's Stone is also sometimes symbolized by the *ouroburos*, a snake biting its tail—symbol of the *hen to pan* or *hen kai pan*.

The stages of the alchemical opus—the creation of the Philosopher's Stone—were usually given as three, but sometimes as four. First comes the *nigredo*, or black stage. This is the *caput mortuum*, in which the substance with which the alchemist begins is burned or cooked until it is reduced to a dark powder. Then comes the *albedo*, or white stage, in which the material is further purified. Third is *citrinatis*, the yellow stage, and fourth is *rubedo*, the red stage. It is impossible to describe these processes in detail, for in alchemical texts they are cloaked in layer upon layer of allegory and image, and the texts differ widely. Around the fifteenth or sixteenth century, the yellow stage was dropped and thereafter we meet almost always with only the black, white, and red stages, the red symbolizing the Philosopher's Stone. Jung notes that there is a vacillation and tension in alchemy between the numbers three and four:

> In alchemy there are three as well as four *regimina* or procedures, three as well as four colors. There are always four elements, often three of them are grouped together, with the fourth in a special position—sometimes earth, sometimes fire. Mercurius is of course *quadratus* but he is also a three-headed snake or simply a triune. This uncertainty has a duplex character—in other words, the central ideas are ternary as well as quaternary.[54]

Although most of the details regarding the stages of the alchemical opus are unclear, the initial stage is well-understood: it involves a principle of putrefaction or death. As Evola puts it, in order for the "new life" of the Philosopher's Stone to come to be, "it is the unanimous opinion of all the hermetic philosophers that a 'mortification' must intervene."[55] Ronald Gray writes that "It was for long believed that in order for growth to take place in an organism, that organism must first die."[56] In short, negation or cancellation is a necessary moment in the emergence of the Stone, and life itself is conceived as a perpetual dynamic involving affirmation and negation, yes and no.

The most famous German representative of the alchemical teaching was, of course, Paracelsus. Paracelsus was supposed to have been taught alchemy by Solomon Trismosin (whom he met in Constantinople in 1520), who himself learned alchemy (and possibly Kabbalah) from a Jew.[57] Paracelsus, not generally given to modesty, was not shy about claiming to have discovered the Philosopher's Stone.[58] Born in 1492 or 1493 in Switzerland, he was the son of a Swabian physician. In Paracelsus's lifetime, only sixteen writings appeared under his name, but his influence was immense. The major work of his maturity, *Astronomia Magna oder die Ganze Philosophia Sagus der Grossen und Kleinen Welt*,

54. Ibid., 26.
55. Evola, *The Hermetic Tradition*, 72.
56. Gray, *Goethe the Alchemist*, 12–13.
57. Raphael Patai, *The Jewish Alchemists* (Princeton, N.J.: Princeton University Press, 1994), 268–70.
58. Ibid., 29.

appeared in 1537–38. No less a figure than Erasmus of Rotterdam was one of Paracelsus's admirers. A letter from Erasmus to Paracelsus, thanking him for medical advice, is still extant: "I recognize the deep truth of your mysterious words," Erasmus writes, "not by any knowledge of medicine, which I have never studied, but by my simple feeling."[59]

David Walsh writes that Paracelsus "greatly expanded the significance of the principles of alchemy, from a limited psycho-material technique to the illuminative center for an understanding of nature as a whole, by integrating them with the dominant Hermetic-Neoplatonic philosophy."[60] According to Paracelsus, the world is an emanation of the One, the *Mysterium Magnum*, produced via the force of *separatio*. Paracelsus accepted the traditional alchemical four elements, but supplemented them with a second elemental system, that of sulphur-mercury-salt. Paracelsus does not hold that these three are literally present in all things. Allen Debus writes that he illustrated their meaning by burning a twig: "the vaporous fumes denote mercury, the flame was sulphur, and the final ashes were salt."[61] (Hegel well understood that Paracelsus's doctrine could not be taken literally, as will shortly become apparent.) Paracelsus identified his three principles with the persons of the Trinity. The philosopher's stone was conceived as the union of the three: in effect, God. Mercury was identified with the Holy Spirit. Paracelsus writes that "in this manner, in three things, all has been created . . . namely, in salt, in sulphur, and in liquid. In these three things all things are contained, whether sensate or insensate. . . . So too you understand that in the same manner that man is created [in the image of the triune God], so too all creatures are created in the number of the Trinity, in the number three."[62]

Man is at the center of Paracelsus's cosmos. Man is the *quinta essentia* who contains the spirits or essences of all other things. Thus, man, as the microcosm, can achieve knowledge of the whole by looking within himself. Thus, in true Hermetic fashion, Paracelsus identifies self-knowledge and knowledge of the world: to know nature is to know it in terms of the being which is its telos, man. Man is not, however, merely a passive product of God's will, for Paracelsus holds that God created the world in an imperfect state. It is man's role to bring the world to perfection: "The created world has been given over to man in order that he may fulfill it. More than that: man's original and specific mission is to lead it to perfection: he has been placed in the world solely for this purpose."[63] For Paracelsus, man has been "excreted" from the world as its savior, like a healing tincture drawn out from an herb.[64] Not surprisingly,

59. Quoted in Jolande Jacobi, *Paracelsus: Selected Writings*, trans. Norbert Guterman (Princeton, N.J.: Bollingen, 1951), lii–liii.

60. Walsh, *Boehme and Hegel*, 54.

61. Debus, *The Chemical Philosophy*, vol. 1, 57.

62. Paracelsus, *Theologische und religionsphilosophische Schriften*, ed. Kurt Goldammer. (Wiesbaden and Stuttgart: Steiner, 1955), 63.

63. Jacobi, *Paracelsus*, xlvi.

64. Heinrich Schipperges, "Paracelsus and his Followers," *Modern Esoteric Spirituality*, 156.

Paracelsus, like Eckhart and Cusa and the Hermeticists, held an organic view of the created world: everything is related to everything else in one organic whole ordered by God. He frequently employed the Hermetic microcosm-macrocosm principle. Andrew Weeks has written that the microcosm-macrocosm correlation is a staple of German mysticism: "from Hildegard on . . . German mysticism is preoccupied with large and small 'worlds,' ranging from the absolute world of divinity to the microworlds encompassed by the smallest organism, space, or discrete thing."[65]

The two theses of man's role as "perfecter" of nature, and of the interrelatedness of all things, are the twin pillars of Paracelsus's philosophy and his medical theory. Medicine is the chief science for Paracelsus (a position later maintained by Schelling), as it deals with the righting of imbalances in nature, and thus with nature's improvement. Medical practice is, in turn, based on the organic view of creation, for Paracelsus's medicine depends on the standard Hermetic theory of correspondences and occult sympathies. Symptoms of disease are "signatures" of imbalances or disharmonies in nature. The practitioner of the medical art is supposed to correct the imbalance and restore harmony.[66]

In keeping with others in the Hermetic tradition, Paracelsus held that behind the visible world lies an invisible world of spirits or "astral" or "aetherial" bodies. What unites all the different levels of reality is the *will* moved by *imagination*, through which God generates the astral bodies, "images" of the Ideas in the divine mind. The astral bodies in turn produce earthly bodies as images of themselves, and they communicate their influences to earthly things, producing health or disease. Paracelsus reinterpreted the traditional alchemical concept of *materia prima* to identify it with the logos become flesh, holding within it the "seeds" for everything else (the influence of the Stoics on Paracelsus's doctrine is clear).

In *Septem Defensiones* (*Seven Defenses*), Paracelsus analyzes the origin of disease into five *entia* or causes: *ens astrale, ens venale, ens naturale, ens spiritale,* and *ens deale.* Heinrich Schipperges writes: "These five *entia* confront us with no less than the closed circle of human life with all its crises, and thus with the anthropological conception of an all-embracing order and way of life in days of health as well as days of sickness."[67]

Ens venale, "toxic situation," refers to the mystery of poison. Everything, Paracelsus claims, is poison, if it is present in certain quantities. The proportion determines what is poisonous and what is not. Thus, Paracelsus holds, poison is an integral part of nature. According to him, it is the task of the *alchemist* to distinguish in practice what is poisonous from what is not. Paracelsus's treatment of alchemy makes it seem more or less indistinguishable from his theory of medicine: alchemy has as its task the chemical perfection of nature.[68] Paracelsus holds an "alchemical" view of the structure of the universe, claiming that everything was cre-

65. Weeks, *German Mysticism,* 9.
66. Beck, *Early German Philosophy,* 144.
67. Schipperges, "Paracelsus and his Followers," 157.
68. Ibid., 159.

ated by God in a "chemical" manner and must be perfected "chemically."[69] *Ens venale* can be seen as a first step, consummated with Böhme and Hegel, toward an account of creation that makes room for the *negative*. Paracelsus's conception of alchemy as a healing art, and his triad of salt-sulphur-mercury found their way into Böhme's writings, along with many other Paracelsian concepts.

Many of the alchemical terms and conceptions of Paracelsus and the alchemists have a dual significance. On the one hand, they are meant literally, as referring to actual substances. At the same time, however, they have a symbolic and mystical significance. This latter does not appear to have been a late development, but rather something accepted by many alchemists all along. The literal-minded laboratory alchemists seeking only to change lead into gold were derisively referred to by the genuine adepts as "puffers," in reference to their constant use of bellows. In the minds of the true alchemists, transmutation was not just something that happened in a vessel, but "a process which transformed the individual from an ordinary mortal immersed in the physical world to a superior being fully conscious of the mystery of life and death."[70] The Philosopher's Stone was held to represent the *hen kai pan*, and the quest for the Stone the knowledge of all things, or of God.[71] The hermetic vessel in which the opus was to take place was supposed to be perfectly round, in imitation of the shape of the cosmos. It is possible, of course, that what was involved was a real chemical procedure, which was supposed to be "activated by" or "infused with" a concomitant psychic act, a magical spell. The dual physical and psychical nature of the alchemical opus is perhaps reflected in the recommendation by the author of the *Liber Platonis quartorum* that the skull be used as the vessel of transmutation.[72]

If alchemy can be understood as a mystical doctrine, why then is it expressed in such unwieldy and often grotesque physicalistic language? Julius Evola, writing of alchemy as it existed in Christian times, states that alchemists went "into hiding": "And the Royal Art [i.e., the art of acquiring the wisdom of God] was presented as the alchemical art of transmuting base metals into gold and silver. By so doing it no longer fell under the suspicion of heresy, and even passed as one of the many forms of 'natural philosophy' that did not interfere with the faith; even among the ranks of Catholics we can discern the enigmatic figures of hermetic masters, from Raymond Lully and Albertus Magnus to Abbot Pernety."[73]

69. See Weeks, *Paracelsus*, 152–53.

70. Coudert, *Alchemy*, 96.

71. Gray, *Goethe the Alchemist*, 20–21.

72. This work was probably written in the tenth century. The text is Harranian, and exists in both Arabic and Latin versions. Jung notes that it is "of great importance for the history of alchemy" (Jung, *Psychology and Alchemy*, 267, 88).

73. Evola, *The Hermetic Tradition*, xviii. Recall also, from chapter 1, Luther's approving remarks on alchemy. The German alchemist Heinrich Khunrath (1560–1601), a Christian Kabbalist and friend of John Dee, held the transmutation to be a process occurring within the soul of the alchemist. In China, where alchemy also flourished, the art had already become exclusively mystical and contemplative by the thirteenth century. See Coudert, *Alchemy*, 83, 91.

In the *Opus Mago-Cabbalisticum* of Georg von Welling (a work of uncertain date known to have been read by Goethe[74]), it is said that "our intention is not directed towards teaching anyone how to make gold, but something much higher, namely how Nature may be seen and recognized as coming from God, and God in Nature."[75] Welling's alchemy was *theosophy*: his object was the knowledge of God, in Hegel's phrase, "as He is in His eternal essence before the creation of nature and a finite Spirit," and of God's expression in nature. The Paracelcist Oswald Croll writes:

> [The alchemists] leave themselves, and totally go out from themselves. . . . They hasten from the imperfect to that which is one and perfect, the knowledge and contemplation whereof . . . is a sacred, Heavenly and hid silence, the quiet or Rest of the sences and all things, . . . when at length . . . all minds . . . shall be altogether but one thing, in one MIND which is above every MIND. It is the intimate vision of God, which also hapneth by the Light of Grace to the separate Soul even in this world, if any man set himselfe about it now, and be subject to God. Thus many holy men by vertue of the Deifick Spirit have tasted the First fruits of the Resurrection in this life, and have had a foretaste of the Celestiall Country.[76]

The German alchemist Gerhard Dorn (known for having said "transform yourselves into living philosophical stones!"[77]) claimed that alchemists possessed the secret of freeing Spirit from Matter.[78] Jung writes that "For the alchemist, the one primarily in need of redemption is not man, but the deity who is lost and sleeping in matter."[79] Jung contrasts alchemy with traditional Christianity in that the latter holds that man is redeemed, whereas the former casts man as the *redeemer*: "man takes upon himself the duty of carrying out the redeeming *opus*, and attributes the state of suffering and consequent need of redemption to the *anima mundi* imprisoned in matter."[80] It is the task of the alchemist to help spirit to free itself from the bonds of the natural.

An eighteenth-century manuscript—*De summa et universalis medicinae sapientiae veterum philosophorum*—depicts a crucible in which Spirit, represented as a dove (a traditional Christian symbol) rises out of nature, represented by the four elements. Recall Hegel's "Böhme myth" of 1804–5 (chapter 4): "The consumed nature rises up in a newer, more ideal form, like a realm of shadows which has lost its first life, the appearance of its spirit after the death of its life. But this new form [Spirit] is the overcoming of the evil, the enduring of the glowing fire [*Glut*] of pain in the center point, where as purified it leaves all the flakes behind in the crucible

74. Gray, *Goethe the Alchemist*, 4.
75. Quoted in ibid., 19.
76. Oswald Croll, *Philosophy Reformed and Improved. . . . The Mysteries of Nature by . . . Osw. Crollius*, trans. H. Pinnell (London: Lodowick Lloyd, 1657), 214.
77. "Transmutemini in vivos lapides philosophicos!" (quoted in Jung, *Psychology and Alchemy*, 148).
78. Quoted in ibid., 269.
79. Ibid., 312.
80. Ibid., 306.

7. The dove of Spirit returning to God (the Father). Robert Fludd, *Utriusque Cosmi Maioris scilicet et Minoris Metaphysica, Physica Atque Techinica Historia*, vol. I (1619). Reprinted by permission of Phanes Press, Grand Rapids, Michigan.

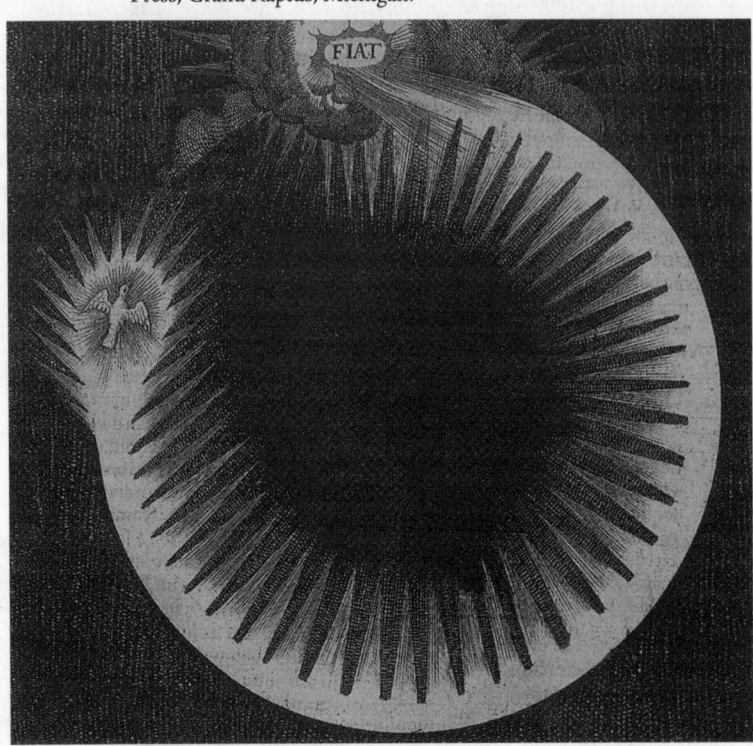

[*Tiegel*], a residuum, which is the pure nothing. It raises itself up as a freer spirit, which sees its radiance only in nature."[81]

A drawing accompanying a work by Robert Fludd (figure 7) depicts a jagged beam of energy projected from the Godhead, issuing in a dove and circling back again to God, representing the "completion" of God in Holy Spirit. The alchemical opus was often called *circulare* (circular), or represented as the *rota*, the wheel (see chapter 5 on Böhme's wheel). It was thought that the end of the opus returns to the beginning. As noted earlier, the Philosopher's Stone is simply a transformation of *prima materia*; the beginning is preserved in the end, but in a higher form; the Spirit hidden in *prima materia* is freed.[82] The stone was "alpha and omega," and the opus itself represented by the *ouroburos*, about which I have already had occasion to comment (see above and chapters 2 and 3). Given the obscurity of the texts in question, there is no way to decide if the alchemical opus is intended to be entirely figurative or symbolic, or if

81. Hoffmeister, *Dokumente*, 365.
82. See Jung, *Psychology and Alchemy*, 345. The Spirit in *prima materia* is explicitly identified by some alchemists with the Holy Spirit of the Christian Trinity.

there is both a literal, physical operation of some sort coupled with a mystical doctrine. Nevertheless, in some sense the alchemists believed that what they were doing involved the salvation of nature and/or the "completion" of God.

5. Hegel and Alchemy

I have already had occasion to mention alchemical ideas in Hegel a number of times. Hegel uses the alchemical phrase *caput mortuum* in the *Encyclopedia Logic* and the *Philosophy of Nature* (PN § 359; Petry 3:143). Elsewhere, Hegel employs the microcosm-macrocosm analogy, referring to the animal organism as the microcosm (*der Mikrokosmos*): "Within it, the whole of inorganic nature has recapitulated itself" (PN § 352, Z; Petry 3:108).

Statements in Hegel's *Philosophy of Nature* certainly indicate familiarity with Paracelsus's doctrines.[83] In fact, as H. S. Harris has shown, Hegel was quite attached to Paracelsianism. In Hegel's lectures of 1803 the division "metals-combustibles-neutrals-earths" is connected with Paracelsus's distinction "mercury-sulphur-salt."[84] In the Jena period, Hegel sometimes did not refer to Paracelsus by name, but instead employed the rubric "the elders" to refer to both Paracelsus and Böhme.[85] Most interesting of all, however, is the fact that even where Hegel is drawing from more recent sources he insists, as Harris puts it, "on finding an earlier pedigree . . . in Paracelsus and Böhme."[86]

In the mature *Philosophy of Nature*, just before beginning his discussion of the four elements, Hegel writes:

> It is a matter of history that Paracelsus said that all terrestrial bodies are composed of the four elements of mercury, sulphur, salt, and virgin earth [*jungfräulichen Erde*],[87] and that these correspond to the four cardinal virtues. Mercury is metalline, and as metal is abstract matter; it is self-identical in its fluid corporeality, and corresponds to light. Sulphur is rigidity, the possibility of combustion; fire is not alien to it, but constitutes its self-consuming actuality. Salt corresponds to water, which is the cometary principle, and its dissolution constitutes indifferent reality, or the subsidence of fire into independence. Finally, virgin earth is the simple innoxiousness of this movement, the subject which constitutes the extinction of these moments; this was the accepted expression for the abstract earthiness of pure silica.[88]

Against the charge that the theory is absurd because these components are obviously not to be found in all things, Hegel responds that "The essential point of such assertions [as Paracelsus's] is however that there

83. See in particular paragraphs 280 and 316; Petry 2:32; 117.
84. Harris, *Night Thoughts*, 274; 278–79; *Gesammelte werke*, vol. 6, 114, 4–17.
85. "Paracelsus and Böhme *together* are the 'elders'—i.e., the alchemists" (Harris, *Night Thoughts*, 274n).
86. Ibid., 278.
87. Recall Goethe's experiments with "virgin earth" (chapter 2).
88. Harris points out that Hegel is mistaken in attributing the "virgin earth" doctrine to Paracelsus. It actually originates with Böhme. See Harris, *Night Thoughts*, 274n.

are four moments to real corporeality, not that these materials are really present. Such theories should not be taken literally, for if they are, Jacob Böhme and others may well be thought of as nonsensical and lacking in experience" (PN § 280, Z; Petry 2:32). In short, Hegel is concerned—again—to defend Paracelsus and Böhme: if their work is not taken in a literal-minded way, it reveals important truths.

An even more interesting statement about Paracelsus and Böhme is to be found later in the text. Hegel writes that "According to an ancient and general opinion, each body consists of four elements. In more recent times, Paracelsus has regarded them as being composed of mercury or fluidity, sulphur or oil, and salt, which Jacob Böhme called the great triad." Again Hegel points out that such ideas are easy to refute if taken literally, but "It should not be overlooked . . . that in their essence they contain and express the determinations of the Concept" (PN § 316; Petry 2:117). This is a striking remark, for here Hegel is saying that if the alchemical language of Paracelsus, Böhme, and others is considered in a nonliteral way, its inner content is, in essence, identical to his system (i.e., to the "determinations of the Concept").

In an 1808 letter to Karl Ludwig von Knebel (a well-known Mason), Hegel employs fanciful alchemical imagery: "If this age is on the whole an age of iron, here it is still mixed with lead, nickel, and other base metals. Things are indeed always being reorganized to produce a nugget of gold as well. It is characteristic of gold, however, to grow all too slowly, and with all our sprinkling and greenhouse exertions no steady growth ensues."[89] It was believed by alchemists that metals contained a "seed of gold" that could be made to "sprout" by certain chemical procedures. The result would be that an inferior metal would "grow into" gold.[90] Hegel is drawing on that idea here, and using it as a figurative way of talking about his theory of the "cunning of reason" (List der Vernunft): bad times have a bright side, in that they are merely a vehicle, a "negative moment" through which something positive or better comes to be actualized. We are powerless, however, to force along a transformation in the fortunes of the world. Hegel's "cunning of reason" is his version of divine providence, over which mere mortals have no control. All "our sprinkling and greenhouse exertions" are in vain, for gold grows slowly. This example is sufficient to illustrate that Hegel was conversant with the basic ideas of alchemy, and that those ideas were a part of the "furniture" of his mind, which came to him quite naturally as a way of expressing his ideas, whether in a treatise such as the Logic (caput mortuum) or in a casual letter to a friend.[91]

In chapter 2, I discussed Goethe's interest in alchemy in order to argue that alchemy was still very much a part of the intellectual scene in Europe, but particularly in Germany. The articles on "alchemy" and

89. Butler, 147; Hoffmeister #131. Hegel is also, of course, playing on Hesiod's ages of Gold and Iron.
90. The metals in alchemy were ranked as follows, in order of increasing perfection: lead, tin, iron, copper, quicksilver, silver, and gold.
91. Hegel made Knebel's acquaintance in Jena. He was a member of Goethe's circle.

"alchemist" in Diderot's *Encyclopédie* (1746–59) were predominantly positive. In 1787, the Berlin Academy investigated the claims of a professor at Halle to have transmuted lead into gold.[92] Alchemy continued to be a part of life—although never quite a mundane part—in Germany until well into the nineteenth century. E. T. A. Hoffmann (1776–1822), in his short story "The Sandman" (*Der Sandmann*) (1816), has one character remark quite matter-of-factly to another, in an attempt to explain a strange occurrence that the latter had witnessed as a child, that it "was probably nothing other than secret alchemical experiments."[93] Charles Webster writes of Hegel's time that "There persisted a strong sense of the possibility that embedded in the accretions of alchemical literature lay important truths expressed in symbolic form."[94] Thus it is not surprising that alchemy would capture the imaginations of men like Oetinger, Goethe, Schelling, Steffens, Hegel, and others.

A systematic parallel can be drawn between each aspect of the opus and Hegel's philosophical project. As I have already noted, in alchemy each metal was said to contain a "seed of gold" that could be made to sprout and blossom. At the same time, the alchemist was expected to purify himself, or the process would not work. In this we can see an analogy to the "purification" function of the *Phenomenology* itself. In the phenomenological crucible, Spirit is separated from its impurities and, literally, perfected. As we have seen, the "seed" of Absolute Spirit is present in every flawed, imperfect form that Spirit takes. The work of this purification has happened, in part, through the historical process. But Hegel provides the final, secret ingredient necessary to synthesize Absolute Spirit. As I said in chapter 4, he has placed the historical forms of Spirit into his alembic and, through the fire of dialectic, has caused them to reorganize into a form that reveals the necessity within their apparent contingency. The *Phenomenology* is the *nigredo*, the stage in which the material (man) has its imperfections burned off. In Hegel the *albedo*, the pure white stone from which the Philosopher's Stone can be made, is Absolute Knowing, the pure aetherial consciousness from which the entire system develops.

As Ronald Gray writes of the alchemical process, "These very inferior metals . . . were to be transmuted in the alchemical work into a God-like form."[95] Hegel has utilized the dark will of Desire—and the blinkered perspectives of myriad forms of Desire sublimated as modes of consciousness—in order to produce not a "God-like form," but God Himself. Hegel's "magical power that converts [the negative] into being" is beyond the dreams of Agrippa, Paracelsus, or even Goethe's Faust. Hegel is the World-Historical Alchemist. His product is the Philosopher's Stone, the *lapis aethereus* or, as it was known to the Germans, *der Stein der Weisen*. The place of transformation is represented

92. Gray, *Goethe the Alchemist*, 3.
93. *Tales of E. T. A. Hoffmann*, ed. and trans. Leonard J. Kent and Elizabeth C. Knight (Chicago: University of Chicago Press, 1969), 101.
94. Webster, *From Paracelsus to Newton*, 10.
95. Gray, *Goethe the Alchemist*, 25.

in the *Phenomenology* as Golgotha, the Place of the Skull (*die Schädel-stätte*). As we have seen, the alchemical retort was sometimes a skull, and the *caput mortuum* was symbolized by a skull.

Hegel's "Philosopher's Stone" is a "transformation" of the *prima materia*, which is aether: a "solidification" of the eternal aether (Objective Spirit). Unlike the *prima materia* of traditional alchemy, though, it does not contain all things *in potentia*. Instead, all things are in actuality by being contained within it; it is "androgyne," a unity of opposites. Like the alchemists, Hegel's philosophical project is to free Spirit from nature. Just as alchemists believe that God is slumbering in matter and must be released by man, so Hegel holds that nature is "petrified intelligence" but that "God does not remain petrified and moribund however, the stones cry out and lift themselves up to spirit." Like Paracelsus, Hegel believes that nature has, in a sense, "excreted" man, that self-conscious man has arisen from nature and has developed his potentialities through history. His aim is the "redemption" of the nature from which he has arisen. Hegel believes that it is in philosophical thought that God and the world are "completed," exactly as "the elders" believed that man was the redeemer who must "save" nature and God.

Hegel's "stone," like Paracelsus's, is triadic. Hegel himself has claimed that the three materials of mercury, sulphur, and salt represent the three moments of the Concept. Just as each stage of the alchemical opus dies to the next, so each moment of the dialectic is negated and is superceded by another: each moment contains the "seed" of the Absolute, which blooms in the end. Just as Paracelsus holds that poison is a part of all things, so Hegel's account of the whole finds a place for and utilizes the negative. Hegel's dialectic is a "magical power that converts [the negative] into being." The dialectic is, of course, a circle. Idea issues in nature, which issues in Spirit, and Spirit returns to Idea in the form of Absolute Spirit or philosophical thought. The dove of Spirit emerges from a God-created nature, and circles back to God.

Hegel adopts the triadic preoccupation of Paracelsus and others, but his thought exhibits a tension between triads and tetrads. Recall Jung's comments on the tension in alchemy between three and four. Hegel identifies the mercury, sulphur, and salt of Paracelsus with the three moments of the Concept, but as we have also seen he conjoins Paracelsus's triad with the "virgin earth" and then states that the four represent the quadradicity of nature. Jung notes that sometimes three of the four elements are grouped together and the fourth separated off. This represents the tendency to regard three as the primary mystical number. In a similar fashion, Hegel argues in the *Philosophy of Subjective Spirit* that the five senses must be understood as three groups of senses, because the Concept has only three moments! (PS § 401, Z; Petry 2:167).

Alchemical texts seem to have both literal and symbolic levels. On the one hand, they describe actual laboratory work involving the physical manipulation and transformation of matter—although these processes also seem to involve psychic or magical operations as well. On the other hand, they seem to describe, in allegorical form, not the transformation of matter, but the transformation of the spirit of the alchemist himself, a process leading to psychic health and integration and even to mystical insight. There is a change in the alchemist's soul concomitant with a change in the retort. Hegel can be seen as separating the spiritual and the physical components of alchemy, discarding the physical as a mere *caput mortuum*. He has preserved the alchemists' aim of perfecting nature and completing God, but now the alchemical opus will take place entirely in the soul of man. God will achieve completion through man's speculative activity.

Although the ultimate consummation of reality takes place in Absolute Spirit, this level is preceded by Objective Spirit, which is the subject of chapter 7. We shall see there that alchemical imagery appears again, this time in the *Philosophy of Right*. In the following section, however, I shall discuss some aspects of Hegel's doctrine of Subjective Spirit.

6. Hegel on Mesmerism and ESP

The Philosophy of Subjective Spirit is divided into Anthropology, Phenomenology, and Psychology. Anthropology (like the other two) is itself divided into three subdivisions, which Hegel summarizes as follows:

Initially the Soul is—

a) In its immediate natural determinacy—the Natural Soul, which only *is*;

b) [Then] it is Feeling Soul, entering as an individual into relationship with its immediate being, with the determinatenesses of which it is abstractly for itself;

c) [Finally] it is Actual Soul, having this immediate being formed within it as its corporeality [*Leiblichkeit*]. (PS § 390; Petry 1:21)

If Hegel's account of nature seems calculated to disturb the "hard-headed" man of science, his *Philosophy of Spirit* seems positively "New Age." Hegel treats Natural Soul as the *anima mundi* (*Weltseele*; PS § 391; Petry 2:25): a universal soul of nature that is divided up into the individual souls of living beings. Hegel refers to the soul as "an immediate, unconscious totality" (PS § 440, Z; Petry 3:81) and as "the sleep of Spirit" (PS § 389; Petry 3:3). Kelly writes that "At its deepest, pre-individual level, the soul is identical with the living unity or immediate concrete universality of the cosmos. As such, it is the World Soul (*anima mundi*). . . . It is through the soul that each individual participates in the life of the cosmos."[96] Hegel's theory of Natural Soul is a direct consequence of his treatment of the Earth as a living organism.

The Natural Soul is, in effect, the Earth Soul, and all psychic activity ultimately has its origin in a kind of efflux of the Earth. Hegel writes that "The Soul is not only immaterial *for itself*, rather it is the universal immateriality of nature, its simple ideal life" (PS § 389; Petry 2:3). And: "The Soul is the all-pervasive [*Allesdurchbringende*], and is not simply that which exists in a particular individual" (PS § 406, Z; Petry 2:271).

96. Kelly, *Individuation and the Absolute*, 39.

As to the World-Soul's relationship to individual souls, Hegel states that "It is the substance, that is to say the absolute basis of all the particularizing and singularizing of Spirit, so that Spirit has within it all the material of its determination, and it remains the pervading identical ideality of this determination" (PS § 389; Petry 2:3).

We are, Hegel claims, "in ourselves a world of concrete content with an infinite periphery and have within us a multitude of numberless relations and connections, which even if it does not enter into our sensation and representation is always within us. . . . On account of its infinite wealth of content, the human soul may therefore be said to be the soul of a world, the individually determined World-Soul [Weltseele]" (PS § 402, Z; Petry 2:211). Hegel writes further that "Just as light disperses into an infinite multitude of stars, so the universal Soul of nature disperses into an infinite multitude of individual souls, the only difference being that whereas light appears to have a subsistence independent of the stars, it is only in individual souls that the universal Soul of nature attains actuality" (PS § 390, Z; Petry 2:23).

Recall that during his association with Schelling and Hölderlin in Tübingen, Hegel was attracted to the pantheistic-Spinozistic ideal of hen kai pan. His reflections on the World Soul seem to suggest that Hegel never entirely abandoned this ideal. In Anthropology, however, he explicitly rejects Pantheism while at the same time conceding, as one might expect, that it is not a bad place to begin:

> Organization and system remain entirely alien to pantheism. Where it appears in the form of presentation it is a tumultuous life, a bacchanalian intuition, for instead of allowing the single shapes of the universe to emerge in order, it is perpetually plunging them back into the universal, veering into the sublime and monstrous. Still this intuition is a natural point of departure for every healthy breast [Brust]. Especially in youth, through a life which ensouls us and all about us, we feel kinship and sympathy for the whole of nature, and we therefore have a sensation of the World-Soul, of the unity of spirit and nature, of the immateriality of nature. (PS § 389, Z; Petry 2:9)

Hegel believes that the Natural Soul bears within it certain influences from its native climate and geography.[97] Hegel writes that "In its substance, which is the Natural Soul, Spirit lives with the universal planetary life, difference of climates, the change of the seasons, the various times of day, etc. This natural life is only partly realized within it, as certain turbid feelings [trüben Stimmungen]" (PS § 392; Petry 2:26). As a result of this, there are different forms of Soul for different nations and peoples and races. Hegel attempts to characterize in general the Caucasian, Negroid and Mongoloid races, stating that "It is in the Caucasian race that Spirit first reaches absolute unity with itself,—It is here that it first enters into complete opposition to naturalness [i.e., rises above the mere natural],

---

97. This conception bears some similarity to Oetinger's views on the influence on the human soul of pre-human eras and forms of life. See Ernst Benz, The Theology of Electricity, 55.

apprehends itself in its absolute independence, disengages from the dispersive vacillation between one extreme and the other, achieves self-determination, self-development, and so brings forth world history" (PS § 393, Z; Petry 2:57). Hegel points out, however, that given that all men are implicitly rational they possess equal rights, no matter what level of advancement their race may find itself at (PS § 393, Z; Petry 3:45–47).

Hegel goes on to discuss national differences, and his remarks are interesting and perceptive, much like those of Kant in his *Anthropology from a Pragmatic Point of View* (1798). Hegel discusses in greatest detail the Italians, Spaniards, French, English, and Germans. As is typical with German authors, his harshest remarks are reserved for his fellow countrymen. Hegel, like Kant, accuses the Germans of an extreme formalism and of an absurd preoccupation with rank and title (PS § 394, Z; Petry 2:81–83). Hegel next has some interesting things to say about character, for instance, "A Person without character will either fail to assume determinateness or shift from one direction to the opposite" (PS § 395, Z; Petry 2:91). He holds that individual character is partly a product of the Natural Soul, and thus temperament may be affected by the climate or position on the earth into which one is born.

The section on Feeling Soul is notable chiefly for its treatment of extrasensory perception and animal magnetism, as well as madness. We know that Hegel lectured on animal magnetism as early as 1805 in Jena. Hegel mentions mesmerism as a cure for disease very briefly in the *Philosophy of Nature*. He states that "it is the finger-tips of the magnetizer [*des Magnetiseurs*] which fluidize the organism by conducting magnetism throughout the whole of it. Only sick persons can be magnetized, and put to sleep by this external means. Precisely considered, magnetism is the collection of the organism into its implicit entirety" (PN § 373; Petry 3:207). In other words, magnetism can help to "re-integrate" an organism in which one or more of the parts is working against the whole. As noted earlier, Hegel's treatment of animal magnetism in the *Philosophy of Spirit* falls under the "Feeling Soul" division of Anthropology. As Petry notes, "The treatment of animal magnetism is the most extensive and detailed exposition of any one topic in the *Philosophy of Subjective Spirit*, and one of the most extensive expositions of the whole *Encyclopedia*."[98] Thus it was obviously a topic of great importance for Hegel. Before dealing in detail with Hegel's discussion of animal magnetism—as well as other paranormal phenomena—I shall first briefly consider the background to Hegel's interest in magnetism: the history of the subject, possible influences on Hegel, when he first formulated his views, etc.

Franz Anton Mesmer (1733–1815), a Swabian physician, discovered that passing magnets or magnetized objects over the bodies of patients often seemed to have a curative effect.[99] Soon he found that he could achieve the same effect simply by passing his hands over his patients and

---

98. Petry, introduction to *Hegel's Philosophy of Spirit*, vol. 1, lviii.
99. Paracelsus was apparently the first to study the healing powers of magnets. Recently the idea has become fashionable again. See Benz, *Theology of Electricity*, 5.

lulling them into a trancelike state. This latter technique was also referred to as magnetism—though it was often called mesmerism, solarism, and tellurism—and is today almost universally referred to as hypnotism. Hegel refers to the relationship between the mesmerist and his subject as "magical" (ps § 406, Z; Petry 2:299). Mesmer made his techniques known in Paris in the 1770s. In 1784 a French royal commission led by none other than Benjamin Franklin investigated Mesmer's claims and declared them absolutely without foundation. This did not stop patients (particularly women) from flocking to Mesmer's salon. Celebrities like Mozart took an interest in Mesmer's work.[100] By this time, Mesmer had developed his own technology, chiefly represented by the *baquet*. According to Hegel, "This consists of a vessel, with iron rods which are touched by the persons to be magnetized, and constitutes the intermediary between them and the magnetizer" (ps § 406, Z; Petry, 2:297).

Scientific respectability, however, continued to elude Mesmer. In 1812 things began to change. The Prussian government took an interest in mesmerism and set up a commission to study it. The Germans proved more receptive than the French, and a number of sympathetic and open-minded studies began appearing, most of which Mesmer did not live to see.[101] Before long mesmerism became academically respectable. Therefore, Hegel was not risking censure by discussing it.

Schelling was the first among the German idealists to develop an enthusiasm for mesmerism. In a letter to Hegel dated January 11, 1807, Schelling discusses certain experiments concerning metal and water divining and pendulums. He recommends that Hegel perform these experiments himself, writing that "It is an actual magic incident to the human being, no animal is able to do it. Man actually breaks forth as a sun among other beings, all of which are his planets."[102] Schelling followed up with a letter dated March 22:

> As for the experiments about which I wrote you recently, things are nonetheless continuing to progress and prove indeed correct. [The Italian peasant dowser Francesco] Campetti's superior strength permits its employment in a manner excluding all illusion. Thin sheets of tin—as likewise broad and heavy plates of metal—revolve with the greatest regularity when placed on his index or middle finger. What is most profound in the matter is the undeniably nonmechanical, magical influence of the will, or of even the most fleeting thought, on these experiments. The pendulum—like the [divining] rod—behaves just like a muscle activated by free

100. Ibid., 21; Benz writes: "It is interesting to note that some Mozart compositions for glass harmonica were written for Mesmer, who had introduced Mozart to this instrument at his house."
101. See for example, C. A. F. Kluge, *Versuch einer Darstellung des animalischen Magnetismus* (Berlin: Salfeld, 1811; 2nd ed. 1816, 3rd ed. 1818); C. C. Wolfart, *Mesmerismus oder System der Wechselwirkungen* (Amsterdam: Bonset, 1966), and *Erläuterungen zum Mesmerismus* (Berlin: Nikolaischen, 1815).
102. Quoted in Petry, *Hegel's Philosophy of Spirit*, vol. 2, 517.

will, just as muscles on the other hand are veritable divining rods which oscillate now outward—extensors—and now inward—flexors.[103]

In the same letter, Schelling suggested to Hegel that he consult an article by his brother Karl on animal magnetism.[104] Karl Eberhard Schelling (1783–1854) was trained as a physician. In Jena in 1801–2 he attended some of Hegel's classes. In 1805 he settled in Stuttgart as a general practitioner, where he published a revised and expanded version of his thesis "Über das Leben und seine Erscheinung." In this work, Karl Schelling advanced a theory of life that involved a World Soul partitioning itself into individual souls. His treatment of the aether, sleep, disease, and death is also reminiscent of Hegel's.[105] In 1821, Hegel's sister Christianne came under the care of Schelling. She had been forced to quit her job as a governess in 1814 due to a nervous disorder. For a short time she had even committed herself to an asylum. On leaving it, she returned to Stuttgart. Hegel, of course, recommended that Christianne be treated by Schelling, who apparently did so without recompense. It is likely that the treatments included "magnetic" or mesmeric therapy.

Hegel shared the Schelling brothers' enthusiasm for animal magnetism and the paranormal. In an 1810 letter to van Ghert, Hegel writes:

I was very interested to hear that you are occupying yourself with animal magnetism. To me this dark region of the organic conditions seems to merit great attention because, among other reasons, ordinary physiological opinions here vanish. It is precisely the simplicity of animal magnetism which I hold to be most noteworthy. . . . Its operation seems to consist in the sympathy into which one animal individuality is capable of entering with a second, insofar as the sympathy of the first with itself, its fluidity in itself, is interrupted and hindered. That [sympathetic] union [of two organisms] leads life back again into its pervasive universal stream. The general idea I have of the matter is that the magnetic state belongs to the simple universal life, a life which thus behaves and generally manifests itself as a simple soul, as the scent of life in general undifferentiated into particular systems, organs, and their specialized activities.[106]

Hegel's letter is a response to van Ghert's letter, dated June 22, 1810, in which he described how he had been experimenting with animal magnetism on a relative for six months. Van Ghert asks Hegel to remind him about his (Hegel's) theory of animal magnetism, "which you provided us with in the Philosophy of Nature and which I have forgotten."[107] Van Ghert was Hegel's student at Jena in 1804–6. As we shall see, Hegel's views on animal magnetism summarized in the quote

103. Quoted in Butler, 78.

104. Karl Schelling, "Ideen und Erfahrungen über den tierschen Magnetismus," Jahrbücher für Medizin als Wissenschaft 2 (1807): 1–42; 158–90.

105. See Petry, Hegel's Philosophy of Spirit, vol. 2, 562.

106. Butler, 590; Hoffmeister #166. In the Philosophy of Spirit, Hegel mentions van Ghert's work on animal magnetism, along with that of the alchemist J. B. van Helmont (PS 406, Z; Petry 2:303–7).

107. Quoted in Petry, Hegel's Philosophy of Spirit, vol. 2, 560.

above are identical to the views later expressed in the mature *Philosophy of Subjective Spirit*, proving that Hegel's interest in the topic dates back at least to Jena and that his views on it remained fairly constant. Van Ghert published two works on animal magnetism—*Dagboek der magnetische Behandeling van Mejufvrouw B**** (1814), and *Mnemosyne, of aanteekeningen van merkwaardige verschijnsels van het animalisch magnetismus* (1815)—both of which Hegel read, admired, and mentioned in his lectures (e.g. PS § 406; Petry 2:303).

In an 1818 letter to Victor Cousin, written while Hegel was a professor in Heidelberg, Hegel states that "I have written a letter to Herr [Adam Karl] Eschenmayer on your behalf. A philosopher, he is above all a friend of animal magnetism."[108] (In the same letter, Hegel mentions that he will be moving to Berlin the following fall.) It is interesting to note that while in Heidelberg, Hegel sat in on mesmeric and spiritualist sittings (or "séances") with his friend Franz Josef Schelver.[109] While in Berlin, Hegel borrowed a book on the history of witchcraft and somnambulism from his teaching assistant Friedrich Wilhelm Carove.[110] During the same period, he also excerpted an essay by D. G. Kieser on "second sight."[111]

Hegel thinks that for magnetism to take place it is necessary that the will of the magnetizer be stronger than that of the patient. Hegel writes that "The main feature of this magical relationship is that a subject works upon an individual inferior to it in respect of freedom and independence of will. . . . It is for this reason that strong men are especially adept at magnetizing female persons" (PS § 406, Z; Petry 2:299–301). In explaining this phenomenon, Hegel introduces the concept of the *genius* (*Genius*): "By genius we are to understand the determining particularity of man, that which, in all situations and relationships, decides his action and his fate" (PS § 405; Petry 2:239). The genius is the "control" function of the individual.[112] In certain circumstances a man's genius can actually become *someone else*, as in mesmerism.

As I have already noted, Hegel regards the relationship between the mesmerist and subject as "magical." Hegel explains that this word is applied to "a relationship of inner to outer or to something else generally, which dispenses with mediation. A power is magical when its operation is not determined by the connectedness, the conditions and mediations of objective relationships" (PS § 405, Z; Petry 2:227). In chapter 3, I briefly mentioned K. J. H. Windischmann, a theologian who was engaged in the study of magic, and with whom Hegel corresponded. As

---

108. Butler, 633; Hoffmeister #344.
109. Helmut Schneider, "Dreiecks-Symbolik," 74.
110. Hoffmeister, vol. 2, 243.
111. Hegel, *Berliner Schriften*, ed. J. Hoffmeister (Hamburg: Felix Meiner, 1956), 691–92.
112. According to Petry, "In Hegel's day, 'Genie' was applied to Leonardo da Vinci, Michael Angelo, Mozart, etc., 'Genius' to the atmosphere of a locality, tutelary spirits, Descartes' demon, etc." See Petry, *Hegel's Philosophy of Spirit*, vol. 2, 496.

I discussed in chapter 3, Hegel was sympathetic to Windischmann's studies of magic. Further on in the *Philosophy of Spirit*, Hegel writes that "*Absolute magic* would be the magic of spirit as such. Spirit also subjects general objects to a magical infection, acts magically upon another spirit" (PS § 405, Z; Petry 2:229).[113] In private notes written in 1820–22, Hegel makes reference to the occultist Jean Baptiste van Helmont 1577–1644, father of the alchemist and Rosicrucian Francis Mercury van Helmont (see chapter 1), in connection with witchcraft and magic.

On the surface, it appears that all Hegel has in mind by "magic," and by the "magic" of magnetism, is simply psychological control. As we have seen, he speaks about magnetism being made possible by the strong-willed controlling the weak-willed. Hegel also speaks in the same context about various other kinds of "influence" that people can have on one another, none of which seems overtly "occult" or traditionally "magical." Hegel states that the most "unmediated" kind of magic that there is consists in the control that our mind has over our body. Again, it seems that there is nothing particularly "paranormal" here. Those who might be embarrassed by Hegel's interest in mesmerism will probably breathe a sigh of relief: At least he does not *really* believe in magic! They will be disappointed, however.

Hegel refers to the relationship of mother to child as a "magic tie" (PS § 405; Petry 2:223). In discussing the effects a mother can have on the unborn child, Hegel distinguishes between organic (*organische*) and psychic (*psychische*) causes. His use of "psychic" seems to be identical to our use of the term to refer to a supernatural influence of the mind, as the following lines bear out: "One hears, for example, of children coming into the world with an injured arm, either because the mother had actually broken hers or at least had knocked it so severely that she *feared* she had done so, or indeed on account of her having been frightened by the sight of someone else's broken arm" (PS § 405, Z; Petry 2:237). Hegel evinces no skepticism about such reports. He goes on to give examples of clairvoyance, dowsing, "remote viewing" (as it would be called today), and even of a man who could read with his stomach! (PS § 406, Z; Petry 2:267). Hegel allows that frauds do exist, but he seems to regard his anecdotes as well-authenticated. In one amusing example, Hegel tells how the arch-rationalist Friedrich Nicolai, looking down his street one day, had a vision in which he seemed to see not the actual houses that were there, but structures which had stood there at some earlier time. Hegel dryly notes that "The predominantly physical basis of the poetic illusion of this otherwise entirely prosaic individual became apparent through its being dispelled by the application of leeches to his rectum" (PS § 406; Petry 2:269).

Hegel thought that mesmerism (and, by implication, other sorts of "supernatural" phenomena) was now thoroughly understood, and that

---

113. In *Six Mystical Points* (Point 5, § 1), Böhme writes that "Magic is the mother of eternity, of the being of all beings; for it creates itself, and is understood in desire."

no new data were likely to arise (PS § 406; Petry 2:303). He believed that the Understanding (or "finite thought") is incapable of comprehending supernatural phenomena precisely because, as he put it in his letter to van Ghert, "ordinary physiological opinions here vanish." The Understanding insists on a mechanistic explanation and refuses to believe in the existence of any kind of unmediated causal relationship—and that, recall, is exactly what a "magical" relationship is for Hegel. In other words, the Understanding is faulty because, among other things, *it does not believe in magic.* Hegel writes that "In the experience of animal magnetism . . . it is within this very region of external appearances that the Understanding's connection between causes and effects, with its condition of spatial and temporal determinations, loses its validity, and in sensuous determinate being itself, together with its conditionality, that the higher nature of Spirit makes itself effective and becomes apparent" (PS § *Ein Fragment zur Philosophie des Geistes,* 1822–25; Petry 1:99). Hegel writes, further, that comprehension of magnetism and psychic phenomena is impossible, "in so far as one presupposes personalities independent of one another and of the content of an objective world, and assumes spatial and material juxtaposition to be generally absolute" (PS § 406; Petry 2:253).

In the introduction to the *Philosophy of Spirit,* Hegel writes that "In recent times, especially in the case of animal magnetism, the substantial unity of the soul and the power of its ideality have even become apparent as a matter of experience. This has discredited all the rigid distinctions drawn by the Understanding, and it has become immediately obvious that if contradictions are to be resolved, a speculative consideration is necessary" (PS § 379; Petry 1:15). Hegel's "speculative consideration" consists in maintaining that in psychic states Spirit sinks down into identity with the "feeling subjectivity" of the Soul. In other words, in psychic states such as precognition or telepathy a regression to a subrational, "natural" state is involved (this would be most evident in the case of a trance state).

By leaving behind intellect and individuality, we lose ourselves in a primordial oneness with all things and are thus capable of "tapping into" lines of connection of which we are not ordinarily, consciously aware.[114] Phenomena such as mind-reading or remote viewing become possible in such a state. Hegel is quick to point out, however, that psychic states are not a "higher" faculty or level of Spirit. In fact, they involve a descent into the lowest depths of Spirit. Hence Hegel's suggestion that psychic phenomena are much more prevalent in rural areas, under primitive conditions, such as in the Scottish Highlands (PS § 406, Z; Petry 2:287). Hegel also points out that, although psychic phenomena are remarkable, they are usually unreliable and useless. Dreams

114. Sean Kelly argues that here Hegel has come close yet again to Jung's "collective unconscious" and especially his theory of "synchronicity" (Kelly, *Individuation and the Absolute,* 50–52).

sometimes present portents, but also much else that is meaningless, and so they are not reliable guides to action. The ability to levitate a teacup using the power of mind alone is remarkable, but much more difficult than simply lifting the cup with one's hand.

Nevertheless, given the nature of dialectic, we might expect that in some way the highest level of Spirit will be a "return" to and sublation of this, the lowest. Philosophy will "circle back" to psychic phenomena. This is indeed the case. In the introduction to the *Philosophy of Spirit*, Hegel writes that, in magnetism, "spirit visibly liberates itself from the limits of time and space and from all finite connections, and the phenomena have, therefore, something of an affinity with philosophy" (PS § 379; Petry 1:23). Hegel writes later that space pertains to external nature not to the Soul, and that when external nature is apprehended by the Soul, "it ceases to be spatial, for it is no longer external either to itself or us once the ideality of the Soul has transformed it. Consequently, when free and understanding consciousness sinks into that form of the Soul which is mere feeling, the subject is no longer bound to space" (PS § 406, Z; Petry 2:277). Hegel goes on to speak similarly regarding time.

The implication here is that in order to understand psychic states we must not regard the Soul as spatially distinct from the world. Further, in psychic states Soul and world overlap. This happens when we sink into a certain primitive mode of being, *but it also happens when we achieve philosophical understanding*, when the world really does cease to be "external either to itself or us once the ideality of the Soul has transformed it." Psychic states are a fleeting, unreliable, fundamentally subconscious and subrational way in which the subject-object division is overcome and the world is made our own. In philosophy, we can achieve, consciously, a state in which we rise above space and time, and in which external relation or "otherness" is canceled. With philosophy, and in general with the human project of remaking the given, the world becomes no longer other but rather that which is understood and willed. Hegel writes that "It is true that the human Spirit is able to raise itself above knowledge concerned exclusively with the singularity of what is sensuously present, but it is only in the Conceptual cognition of the eternal that this elevation is absolute. . . . In the magnetic state, however, there can be no more than a conditioned rising above knowledge of what is immediately present" (PS § 406, Z; Petry 2:281–83). In short, philosophy is a higher type of magic. In Hegel's own words, philosophy is "absolute magic," "the magic of Spirit as such."

It is interesting to compare Hegel's understanding of magic with Böhme's. In *Six Mystical Points* (1620), Böhme writes that "Magic is the mother of eternity, of the being of all beings; for it creates itself, and is understood in desire. . . . It is in itself nothing but a will, and this will is the great mystery of all wonders and secrets, but brings itself by the imagination of the desireful hunger into being. . . . In Magic are all forms of the Being of all beings."[115] As we have seen, Hegel holds merely that magic is action of one thing on another that is unmediated (so, for example, the control of the mind over the body is "magical," because there is no third thing acting as intermediary). This is obviously a much thinner conception of magic than what Böhme has explained. Nevertheless, there is a parallelism between Böhme's magic and what I have called the "high magic" of the dialectic itself.

Note that Böhme says that magic "creates itself." As we have seen, the speculative philosopher does not create or invent the dialectic; instead it unfolds itself before him (and this is why there is no distinction between form and content). Further, Böhme claims that in this self-creating magic are "all forms of the Being of all beings," which should remind us of the *Logic*. Böhme also refers to the "first *Magia*" as "God in his triad."[116] This is a reference to the initial dialectic of sour-sweet-bitter, of God in Himself. Böhme is treating his own proto-dialectic of the "source-spirits" as a kind of high magic. Finally, and most striking of all, Böhme refers to magic as that "which makes within itself where there is nothing; which makes something out of nothing."[117] This comes close to Hegel's treatment of magic as an unmediated act, an act employing no medium or matter or "raw material." The dialectic of the *Logic* is precisely such a creation of something (*Etwas*) out of nothing (*Nichts*). On Böhme's terms, Voegelin's treatment of Hegel as a magician becomes quite plausible.

115. *Six Mystical Points*, Point 5, §§ 1–6.
116. Ibid.
117. *Mysterium Pansophicum*, "Der Erste Text," in Nicolescu, 211.

"The Rose in the Cross of the Present"
Hegel's Philosophy of Objective and Absolute Spirit

Between Eternal Birth, Restoration from the Fall and the discovery of the Philosopher's Stone there is no difference.
—Jakob Böhme, *De Signatura Rerum*

1. Introduction

According to Hegel, Objective and Absolute Spirit constitute a man-made world that stands in opposition to mere nature. In the *Lectures on the Philosophy of World History*, Hegel states, "After the creation of the natural universe, man appears on the scene as the antithesis of nature; he is the being who raises himself up into a second world" (Nisbet, 44; VIG, 50). Objective Spirit is the Absolute Idea as embodied in human history, culture, and social institutions. Absolute Spirit is the Absolute Idea expressed in art, religion, and philosophy. Absolute Spirit is the highest form in which the Idea realizes itself. In Objective Spirit, we seek to approach the Absolute through social institutions and practices, but these are not the proper medium for its embodiment. In art we strive to represent the Idea sensuously, and it attains greater "objective presence" than it does through social practices. In religion we strive to make ourselves at one with the Idea, which is again approached in representational or imagistic form. But these media are not adequate either. For Hegel it is not enough simply to change the world or to change our selves. We must interpret the world, and ourselves. And the proper medium for this interpretation is philosophy. The philosopher recognizes Idea in the world and "returns" it to the pure aether of thought, while all the time remaining a being in the world. Philosophy is the highest form of Absolute Spirit, for in it the self-thinking thought of Absolute Idea (or God) is finally realized in the world.

2. Hegel's Philosophy of Religion: The Influence of Mysticism

Karl Löwith writes that "For an understanding of Hegel's system, his philosophy of religion is even more important than his philosophy of the state. It is not just one component of the whole system, but its spiritual center of gravity."[1] Hegel's theology is essentially Böhmean in its

1. Karl Löwith, *From Hegel to Nietzsche: The Revolution in Nineteenth-Century Thought*, trans. David E. Green (New York: Columbia University Press, 1964), 47.

developmental conception of God. The *Logic* represents God "in Himself." God expresses Himself through the forms of nature, but only returns to Himself and achieves self-knowing through Spirit, through human knowing. The philosopher thus serves to "actualize" or "complete" God. Because God *qua* Absolute Idea (God in Himself) is conceived of as abstract and lacking realization in the world, it follows that God's progressive worldly incarnation involves a progressive increase in "concreteness" or "embodiment." In the *Lectures on the Philosophy of Religion*, Hegel states that "Spirit *is* in the most *concrete* sense. The absolute or highest being belongs to it" (LPR 1:142). This aspect of Hegel's thought is strikingly similar to Oetinger's theory of *Geistleiblichkeit*, discussed in chapter 2. In the *Lectures*, Hegel refers to God as "the absolute substance," but then goes on, just as in the *Phenomenology*, to identify substance with subject (LPR 1:370). What this means is simply that God *becomes* absolute substance as Spirit. Spirit is the "mystical body" of God on earth.[2]

In the *Philosophy of Right*, Hegel states that "The content of religion is absolute truth, and consequently the religious is the most sublime of all dispositions" (Knox, PR § 270; 165–66). Speculative philosophy, Hegel insists, is not hostile to religious belief: "nothing is further from its intention than to overthrow religion, i.e., to assert that the content of religion cannot *for itself* be the truth." In other words, religion on its own, without the "assistance" of philosophy *is* absolute truth. Hegel states that "religion is precisely the true content but in the form of representation, and philosophy is not the first to offer the substantive truth. Humanity has not had to await philosophy in order to receive for the first time the consciousness or cognition of truth" (LPR 1:251). Humanity, then, can receive the truth through religion alone, without the need for philosophy. "Religion is for everyone," Hegel claims, unlike philosophy which is for the few (LPR 1:180). Philosophy and religion have the same content. Hegel explicitly identifies the moments of the Idea—Being, Essence, Concept—with the Holy Trinity. The fact that religion expresses truth in the form of representation does not mean that Hegel denigrates or rejects it. Nevertheless, Hegel holds that in philosophy the truth is expressed in a more adequate form, the form of pure thought.

Hegel believed that the truth has always been an unconscious possession of mankind. It has expressed itself in different forms, at different times, and through different thinkers. The philosopher "recollects" this unconscious wisdom and expresses it in a fully adequate form. This interpretation is supported by Hegel's remarks in the *Lectures on the Philosophy of Religion*. Hegel refers to religions as "sprouting up fortuitously, like the flowers and creations of nature, as foreshadowings, images, representations, without [our] knowing where they come from or where they are going to" (LPR 1:196; VPR 1:106). Hegel states that "Religion is a begetting of the divine spirit, not an invention of human beings but an

2. See O'Regan, *The Heterodox Hegel*, 274–75.

effect of the divine at work, of the divine productive process within humanity" (LPR 1:130; VPR 1:46).

Hegel does not, however, regard all religions as equally adequate expressions of eternal truth. He claims that Christianity is the "Absolute Religion" (e.g., LPR 1:112; VPR 1:29). Hegel claims that "God has revealed Himself through the Christian religion; that is, he has granted mankind the possibility of recognizing his nature, so that he is no longer an impenetrable mystery" (Nisbet, 40; VIG, 45). Christianity has penetrated the mystery of God by revealing his nature as *triune*. Hegel takes issue with theologians and clergy who hold that mankind cannot know God, or who consider the attempt to know God as impious or hubristic. Hegel claims not only that such knowledge is possible, but that it is our highest *duty* to obtain it (Nisbet, 36; VIG, 40; also LPR 1:88). "God does not wish to have narrow-minded and empty-headed children," Hegel states (Nisbet 42; VIG, 47).

For Hegel, knowing God is our highest duty because God only fully exists in the community of worshippers. Hegel holds that "God's Spirit is essentially in his community; God *is* Spirit only insofar as God is in his *community*" (LPR 1:164; VPR 1:74). And: "The concept of God is God's idea, [namely,] to become and make Himself *objective* to himself. This is contained in God as Spirit: God *is* essentially in His community and has a community; He is objective to Himself, and is such truly only in self-consciousness [so that] God's very own highest determination is self-consciousness." Beforehand, God is "incomplete," Hegel says (LPR 1:186–87; VPR 1:96). He refers to the community of worshippers as the *cultus*. "In the *cultus*," Hegel writes, "the formal consciousness frees itself from the rest of its consciousness and becomes consciousness of its essence; the *cultus* consists in the consciousness that God knows Himself in the human being and the human being knows itself in God" (LPR 1:181; VPR 1:90). Hegel refers to the *cultus* as involving "the mystical attitude, the *unio mystica*" (LPR 1:180; VPR 1:89). He describes the *cultus* in his lecture manuscript as "the eternal relationship, the eternal process [of knowing] in which the subject posits itself as identical with its essence" (LPR 1:193; VPR 1:102).[3]

Hegel's claim that God is dependent on the *cultus*, and his view of the union of God and man in the *cultus*, are strikingly similar to Meister Eckhart's mysticism. In fact, the only place Hegel quotes Eckhart is in the *Lectures on the Philosophy of Religion*: "The eye with which God sees me is the eye with which I see Him; my eye and His eye are one and the same. In righteousness I am weighed in God and He in me. If God did not exist nor would I; if I did not exist nor would He. But there is no need to know this, for there are things that are easily misunderstood (and that can be grasped only in the concept)" (LPR 1:347–48; VPR 1:248). As noted before, this is actually a "quilt quotation" made up of lines from several of Eckhart's sermons (certainly the reference to "the concept" looks suspiciously like an Hegelian interpolation).[4] In sermon 12—

3. The words "of knowing" were inserted by Hegel in the margin.
4. See O'Regan, "Hegelian Philosophy of Religion and Eckhartian Mysticism."

which seems to be one of the texts Hegel was drawing from—Eckhart remarks that "When all creatures pronounce His name, God comes into being."

In the winter of 1823–24, Hegel was actively discussing Eckhart's ideas with Franz von Baader.[5] Baader himself has left us a record of what was perhaps the first of the occasions on which they met: "I was often with Hegel in Berlin. Once I read him a passage from Meister Eckhart, who was only a name to him. He was so excited by it that the next day he read me an entire lecture on Eckhart, and at the end said: 'There, indeed, we have what we want!'[Da haben wir es ja, was wir wollen]"[6] In 1823–24, Hegel was, of course, preparing his Lectures on the Philosophy of Religion, in which the Eckhart reference appears. As I have said, Hegel offers only one quote from Eckhart and discusses him very briefly, so the "entire lecture on Eckhart" mentioned by Baader probably refers to the entire Hegelian discussion of religion in which the Eckhart passage occurs, and which Baader apparently mistook (not surprisingly) for a lecture on Eckhartian mysticism.

As further evidence of the "Eckhartianism" of Hegel's philosophy of religion, consider the following quotations. In the Encyclopedia Hegel states that "God is God only insofar as he knows Himself: this self-knowledge is, further, a self-consciousness in man and man's knowledge of God, which becomes man's self-knowledge in God" (PS § 564; Wallace, 298). Elsewhere, Hegel remarks that "Insofar as the individual man is at the same time received into the unity of the divine essence, he is the object of the Christian religion, which is the most tremendous demand that may be made upon him" (PN § 247, Z; Petry 1:205–6). Finally, Rosenkranz quotes a fragment from Hegel's manuscripts (probably written not later than 1804) in which Hegel states that "the history of God is the history of the whole race."[7] Hegel's philosophy of religion is from the beginning indebted to Eckhart's mysticism.

Hegel does not consider his views to be so "mystical" or "speculative" as to be alien to the ordinary believer, however. In fact, he holds that his way of looking at God and religion are much closer to real religion than to what was called in his time "rational theology" (LPR 1:129; VPR 1:45). We have seen that Hegel does not believe religion to be dependent on philosophy, but he does claim the reverse, that philosophy depends on religion. He writes that "It is the distinctive task of philosophy to transmute the content that is in the representation of religion into the form of thought; the content [itself] cannot be distinguished" (LPR 1:333; VPR 1:235). The philosopher first encounters the content of absolute truth in religion. Indeed, Hegel holds that before Christianity arrived on the scene it would have been impossible for philosophy to present absolute truth in a fully adequate or complete form.

5. Ibid., 250.
6. See Nicolin, Hegel in Berichten seiner Zeitgenossen, 261. It is, of course, not true that Eckhart was "only a name" to Hegel in 1823–24. According to H. S. Harris, Hegel may have been familiar with Eckhart as early as 1795 (Toward the Sunlight, 230).
7. Rosenkranz, Hegels Leben, 138.

The philosopher depends, then, not only on the community but specifically on the religious community. Speculative philosophy cannot be done in a vacuum: it requires a certain social and historical context. All his life Hegel claimed to be a pious Lutheran. The temptation is to take this claim as disingenuous, as the heretical philosopher attempting to cover his tracks to avoid the fate of Fichte and many others. Once it is realized, however, that Hegel's philosophy of religion originates out of the Eckhartian, Böhmean, Oetingerite-influenced Lutheranism of Württemberg, his claim can be seen as sincere. Hegel's brand of Lutheranism would have been nothing unusual to his fellow Swabians.[8]

3. Hegel's Philosophy of History: The Influence of Isaac Luria and Jewish Eschatology

Hegel's philosophy of world history is shaped entirely by his commitment to Christianity. In the last chapter I described how Hegel believes that in studying nature we assume that our object must have an underlying rational structure. Hegel takes the same approach with history. He states that "world history is governed by an ultimate design, that is a rational process—whose rationality is not that of a particular subject, but a divine and absolute reason—this is a proposition whose truth we must assume; its proof lies in the study of world history itself, which is the image and enactment of reason. . . . World history is merely a manifestation of this one original reason; it is one of the particular forms in which reason reveals itself, a reflection of the archetype in a particular element, in the life of nations" (Nisbet, 28; VIG, 30). Hegel claims further that we are compelled to ask whether "beneath the superficial din and clamour of history, there is not perhaps a silent and mysterious inner process at work, whereby the energy of all phenomena is conserved" (Nisbet, 33; VIG, 36).

In the context of the philosophy of world history, Hegel uses the term *World Spirit* (*Weltgeist*). In the *Encyclopedia Logic* he describes the World Spirit along the lines of Plato's demiurge as a "master workman" constructing *itself* through history (EL § 13; Geraets, 31). He likens the World Spirit elsewhere to the "true Mercury [= Hermes]," who is "the leader of nations" (Nisbet, 31; VIG, 33). "The world Spirit," Hegel states, "is the spirit of the world as it reveals itself through the human consciousness; the relationship of men to it is that of single parts to the whole which is their substance. And this World Spirit corresponds to the Divine Spirit, which is the Absolute Spirit. Since God is omnipresent, He is present in everyone and appears in everyone's consciousness; and this is the World Spirit" (Nisbet, 52–53; VIG, 60).

Perhaps the most famous concept in Hegel's philosophy of world history is that of the "cunning of reason" (*List der Vernunft*). This is the "mechanism" whereby the World Spirit makes use of the shortsighted

8. To be sure, Hegel held some views that would be "heretical" even by the standards of Swabian speculative Pietism. For instance, he rejected belief in personal immortality and held instead that human beings only achieve a measure of immortality insofar as they achieve wisdom and see into the eternal (see LPR 3:304; VPR 3:227–28).

passions and aims of particular men to bring about its universal purposes (see Nisbet, 89; VIG, 105). The "cunning of reason" bears some similarity to Smith's "invisible hand," and of course, to the concept of divine providence. Hegel himself draws attention to the latter parallel. "Christians," he says, "are initiated into the mysteries of God, and this also supplies us with the key to world history. For we have here a definite knowledge of providence and its plan" (Nisbet, 41; VIG, 46). What can Hegel mean by this claim? How does Christianity supply a key to world history? The answer is surprising, and it involves yet another connection to a heterodox Christian thinker. I will deal with Hegel's debt to this thinker, Joachim de Fiore, in section 3. It is to Joachim that we must trace Hegel's notorious doctrine of the "end of history." There are other influences on Hegel's eschatology, however. In this section I will first look to the influence—direct and indirect—of mystical Judaism.

Oetinger remarks in one of his works that "God is in Himself without space, but in the revelation of his hiddenness, he is Himself the space of all things."[9] This idea, that somehow in God's "hiddenness" He is the space of all things, is derived from the Kabbalistic speculations of Isaac Luria.

The "new Kabbalah" of Luria, who lived from 1534 to 1572, quickly spread through Europe in the late sixteenth and early seventeenth centuries, mostly by word of mouth and through the works of followers (Luria himself wrote little). Scholem writes that "The influence of the Lurianic Kabbalah, which from about 1630 onwards became something like the true *theologia mystica* of Judaism, can hardly be exaggerated."[10] As we will see, there is a strong correspondence between the theosophy of Böhme and Lurianic Kabbalah. Scholem acknowledges this correspondence.[11] The writings of Luria's followers circulated in Europe widely between 1572 and 1650. It seems likely that Böhme either obtained some of these works, or was instructed directly by a Lurianic Kabbalist. Luria (sometimes spelled "Loria") was born in Jerusalem, but when still a boy his mother took him to live in Egypt after his father's death. In Safed, Luria studied with the famous Kabbalist Moses Cordovero. After Cordovero's death, Luria gathered a group of disciples around himself.

Then and now, many Jews have attacked Luria for his unorthodox views. The major reason for this seems to be his treatment of *Ein-Sof*, the "infinite," which many Kabbalists identify with God. For Luria, the crucial question is this: How can the world exist at all if we grant the existence of God as *Ein-Sof*? If God is truly infinite, no space is left over for creation. Thus, given that the world exists, it must have come about through God's *self-limitation* of His infinite nature. This self-limitation is called by Luria the *tsimtsum* (frequently transliterated by German-speaking scholars as *zimzum*), which means "concentration" or "contraction." Thus, for Luria, God, the infinite, allows the finite to come to be

9. "Gott ist in sich selbst ohne Raum, aber in der Offenbarung seiner Verborgenheit ist er selbst der Raum aller Dinge" (*Sämmtliche Schriften*, vol. 1, 29; see Robert Schneider, *Geistesahnen*, 100).
10. Scholem, *Major Trends*, 284.
11. Ibid., 237.

within himself. (This is, of course, in essence identical to Hegel's view of the infinite and finite: the true [*Wahrhafte*] infinite contains the finite within itself.) Luria's view is radical because it denies that the world comes to be through God's revelation or emanation. Instead, it is precisely through God's limitation and concealment (Oetinger's *Verborgenheit*) that a world comes into being.[12] Scholem describes the *tsimstum* as a "withdrawing into oneself."[13]

Recall from chapter 5 that the *Sephirah* of *Din* is equivalent to a "contracting" force in God. The Kabbalah identifies *Din* with "fire," "wrath," and "severity."[14] *Din* is the opposite of *Hesed*, "mercy" or the "expanding" power. *Din* and *Hesed* balance each other: severity of judgment is balanced by mercy; sharp distinction, cutting-off or closedness are balanced by unity, embrace, or openness. Böhme's word for *Din* is the "Sour"—it is an indrawing, a pulling away, a shutting off and negation of all else. It is significant that Böhme's account of the source-spirits *begins* with the Sour, with the contracting element. Some followers of Luria describe the *tsimtsum* in terms of *Din*. In Scholem's words, "When the primal intention to create came into being, *Ein-Sof* gathered together the roots of *Din*, which had been previously concealed within Him, to one place, from which the power of mercy had departed. In this way the power of *Din* became concentrated."

Scholem describes *tsimtsum*, in connection with *Din*, as "an act of judgment and self-limitation."[15] Given that *Din* is the origin of evil, God's contraction is the root of all evil.[16] Luria's follower Israel Sarug, who helped spread the master's ideas in the late sixteenth century, speaks of *Ein-Sof before* the *tsimtsum* in a way which is even more strikingly Böhmean. As Scholem puts it, Sarug held that "In the beginning, *Ein-Sof* took pleasure in its own autarkic self-sufficiency, and this 'pleasure' produced a kind of 'shaking' (*ni'anu'a*) which was the movement of *Ein-Sof* within itself."[17] Scholem notes that Sarug's influence was felt in Italy, Holland, Poland, and Germany.[18]

Luria holds that each new act of creation or manifestation in the world is the result of a simultaneous contraction and expansion.[19] This pair of forces generally goes under the names of *histalkut* ("regression," or contraction) and *hitpashtut* ("egression," or expansion).[20] This is, of

---

12. See Scholem, *Kabbalah*, 129; and *Major Trends*, 261. There are striking analogies between Luria's *tsimstum*, the "clearing" in which beings come to be, and Heidegger's notion of the *Lichtung*, the clearing in which Being itself comes to presence. See Martin Heidegger, "The End of Philosophy and the Task of Thinking," in *On Time and Being*, trans. Joan Stambaugh (New York: Harper and Row, 1972).
13. Scholem, *Major Trends*, 261.
14. Ibid., 237.
15. Scholem, *Kabbalah*, 130; see also *Major Trends*, 263.
16. See Scholem, *Major Trends*, 263.
17. Scholem, *Kabbalah*, 132.
18. Scholem, *Major Trends*, 257.
19. Ibid., 261.
20. Scholem, *Kabbalah*, 131.

course, very similar to Goethe's theory of expansion and contraction, discussed in chapter 2. In chapters 4 and 5, I also discussed these concepts in connection with Hegel's "Böhmean myth" of the fall of Lucifer. Scholem states that "This double-facedness in the process of emanation is typical of the dialectical tendency of Lurianic Kabbalah."[21]

God's contraction in the *tsimtsum* does not create the world by itself, however. Luria and his followers envision the *Ein-Sof* as an infinite sphere, in which a smaller sphere of empty space comes into being through the *tsimtsum*; this is the place of creation. Into this space God injects a ray of light (Luria seems to identify the divine substance with light). At this point the theory becomes rather murky, but it seems that the light differentiates itself into the classical ten *Sephiroth*. These are depicted as concentric circles of light, filling the space within God (see figure 8). The circle and the straight line (the line of light entering the spherical space) become key symbolic forms for Lurianic Kabbalah. The circle is a "natural form." The circular form characterizes all of creation (for instance, the orbits of the planets, the endless cycle of the seasons, the menstrual cycle, etc.). The line comes to represent humanity. It is a *willed* form that represents a divergence from the natural. As I have said, the light that comes from *Ein-Sof* first takes the form of a line, before it is "deformed" into spherical states. Thus, in identifying man with the line (a topic to which I shall return to shortly), Luria is linking humanity with the divine nature.

Indeed, the first definite form that appears in the sphere of creation is that of *Adam Kadmon*, primordial man. *Adam Kadmon* exists in a realm above the four worlds of classical Kabbalah: *Atsiluth, Beriah, Yezirah*, and *Asiah* (see Hegel's discussion of these worlds in chapter 5). *Adam Kadmon mediates* the light of *Ein-Sof* to the four worlds: "From his eyes, mouth, ears and nose, the lights of the *Sephiroth* burst forth."[22] Obviously, this account has to be taken in a non-temporal sense. *Adam Kadmon* is an Aristotelian *final cause*: he is logically prior to the rest of creation, and simultaneously the end toward which creation is moving (a point to which I shall return shortly). *Adam Ha-Rishon* is Adam of the Bible, who is the (imperfect) earthly embodiment of *Adam Kadmon*. An analogy can be drawn between this doctrine and Hegel's thought. Lurianic *Ein-Sof* and its *Sephirotic* structure corresponds to the Absolute Idea, which is abstract, withdrawn "into itself." *Adam Kadmon* is Spirit, which in its purest form (Absolute Spirit) participates in the divine nature. *Adam Ha-Rishon* is Spirit as developing in history: from the "fall of man" and the loss of the immediate relationship to God, to the recovery of that relationship in its true form, in thought. (Luria's account of the restoration from the Fall is somewhat different from Hegel's, as I shall explain shortly.)

The light of the *Sephiroth* streaming from *Adam Kadmon* was collected in separate "vessels," but the vessels containing the differentiated light

21. Ibid., 131.
22. Scholem, *Major Trends*, 265.

8. The Lurianic Sephiroth. From Brucker, *Historia Critica Philosophiae*, vol. 2, 1742. Reprinted by permission of the Robert W. Woodruff Library, Special Collections and Archives, Emory University, Atlanta, Georgia.

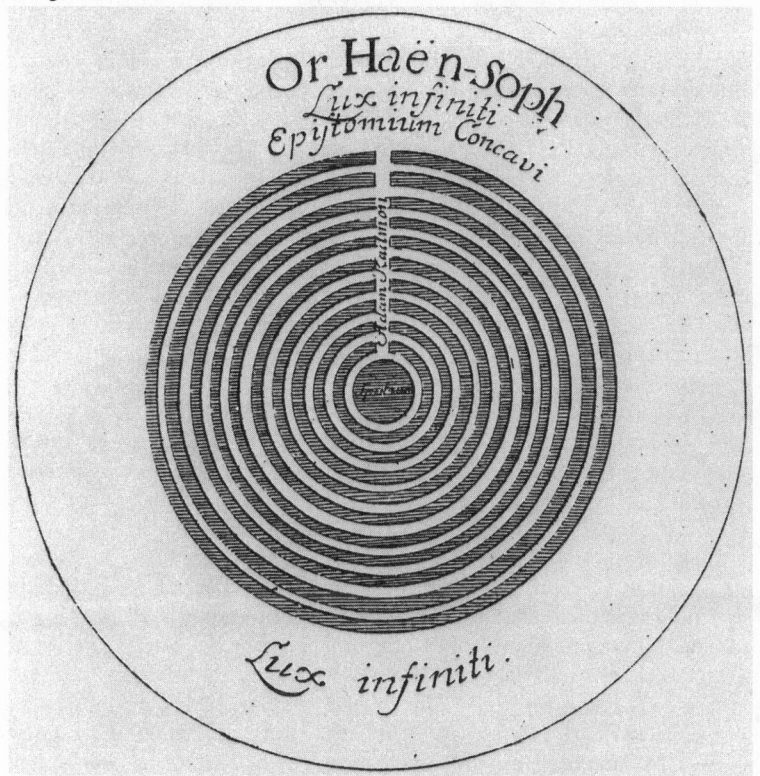

from the seven lower *Sephiroth* proved incapable of holding the light and shattered. The shards of these vessels are the source of matter. This cataclysm completely scrambled the divine cosmic structure, resulting in the emergence of an imperfect material order: nothing in nature is how it ought to be, all is imperfect. It is on this point—the account of the "breaking of the vessels"—that Luria's cosmology is particularly obscure. It all sounds like a cosmic accident, but according to Luria it was all predestined. If this is the case, then God's contraction and the subsequent creation of the imperfect universe are events that *had* to occur; in some way God needed them to happen. The picture again looks Böhmean. Indeed, Scholem remarks that "Luria is driven to something very much like a mythos of God giving birth to Himself; indeed, this seems to me to be the focal point of this whole involved and frequently rather obscure and inconsistent description."[23]

Before going on to the rest of Luria's doctrine, it would be helpful to

23. Ibid., 271.

consider what Hegel knew about Luria's Kabbalism as described thus far. In chapter 5, I briefly discussed Hegel's treatment of Kabbalism in his *Lectures on the History of Philosophy*. We cannot be sure that Hegel had any direct knowledge of Lurianic Kabbalah, but we know that he had at least three indirect sources. Both Böhme and Oetinger were deeply indebted to Lurianic Kabbalah (Böhme implicitly, Oetinger explicitly). But Hegel's principal source of information seems to have been Brucker's *Historia Critica Philosophiae*. Brucker's account of Kabbalah is almost entirely Lurianic in its orientation. As a consequence, the account Hegel gives of the Kabbalah in his *Lectures* is also decidedly Lurianic, even though Hegel never mentions Luria, as Brucker does. Instead, Hegel mentions one of Brucker's Lurianic sources, Abraham Cohen Irira (sometimes Herrera) and his work *Porta coelorum* (*The Gate of the Heavens*). Hegel cites this text directly, so it may possibly be that he actually read it in addition to reading about it in Brucker. Irira (d. Amsterdam 1635 or 1639) was a Spanish Jew whose two major works, the aforementioned *Gate of the Heavens*, and *Beth Elohim* (*The House of God*) were translated in the late seventeenth century from Spanish into Hebrew and exercised considerable influence. *Porta coelorum* was one of the texts published—in Latin translation—in Rosenroth's *Kabbala Denudata*, which was so well-known in Hegel's time that he very likely read it in preparing his remarks on the Kabbalah.

Hegel deals with the *Ein-Sof* and the origin of creation as follows: "The emanation connected [with *Ein-Sof*] is the effect of the first cause by the limitation of that first infinite whose boundary it is. In this one cause all is contained *eminenter*, not *formaliter* but *causaliter*" (LHP 2:396; *Werke* 19:427). This is obviously a description of Lurianic *tsimtsum*. Hegel goes on to say that "The second element of importance is the *Adam Kadmon*, the first man, *Keter*, the first that arose, the highest crown, the microcosm, the macrocosm, with which the world that emanated stands in connection as the efflux of light" (LHP 2:396; *Werke* 19:427). Again, this is Luria's Kabbalah: *Adam Kadmon* as the first and highest created being, as close to the divine nature, and as mediating the divine light to the rest of creation. *Adam Kadmon* was subsequently mentioned by Hegel several times in his *Lectures on the Philosophy of Religion* (see LPR 1:382 n. 41; 3:99, 288; VPR 1:278; 3:36, 213). Hegel goes on to mention the ten *Sephiroth* in general (not individually) and discusses the four lower worlds of *Atsiluth*, *Beriah*, *Yezirah*, and *Asiah* (for Hegel's treatment of these, see chapter 5).

Scholem notes that whereas Kabbalah before Luria had been concerned mainly with the beginning of time—with creation—Luria, to a great extent, shifted the focus of Kabbalists to the *end* of time.[24] This may seem surprising in light of Luria's highly original account of creation. Recall that Luria's doctrine of the "breaking of the vessels" involves a predestined "scrambling" of the cosmic order: the physical world that results is a flawed and imperfect expression of the divine

24. Ibid., 245.

order. The story cannot end there, of course. Luria insists that the world must be made whole, that the physical world must be completed or brought to perfection. This would "complete" the cosmic process begun in God's *tsimtsum* by making the finite within the infinite a faithful image of the infinite. This idea is called by Luria *Tikkun* (the term is, again, not original with Luria but his use of it is certainly original). *Tikkun* is the cosmic restoration at the end of time.

According to Scholem, Luria held that all things are interrelated. In other words, he held the idea of internal relations later made famous by Hegel.[25] The nature of the lowest regions of being is intimately linked to the highest, and just as the highest can affect the lowest (as in the tides, or the influence of the stars on the personality) so too the lowest can affect the highest.[26] Thus it is possible for created beings to benefit or to harm the cosmic order. Scholem writes that Luria believed that "The process in which God conceives, brings forth and develops Himself does not reach its final conclusion in God. Certain parts of the process of restitution are allotted to man."[27] The "cosmic assignment" of men on earth is to perfect themselves, to realize the nature of *Adam Kadmon* in *Adam Ha-Rishon* and thereby to "lift" the fallen, created world up to its pure, initial state of being in the light of God (this is not conceived of literally, of course, as a transformation of matter into light).

Man's task is to perfect himself and to build a social, cultural, and moral world in which material being is used for ends sanctioned by divine law. Scholem writes that "By fulfilling the commandments of the Torah, man restores his own spiritual structure; he carves it out of himself, as it were. And since every part corresponds to a commandment, the solution of the task demands the complete fulfillment of all the 613 commandments."[28] As a consequence, of this view, Scholem notes that Luria tended "to extreme conservatism" in his attitudes toward custom and law.[29] After all, these laws and customs had their origin in the covenant of the Jewish people with God. What can the real purpose of this covenant have been? Luria thinks that the Law is essentially an instruction manual for the restoration and completion of the divine order.[30] Thus if the *Tikkun* is to come to pass it is crucial that the Law must be strictly observed.

For Luria, the appearance of the Messiah is simply the achievement of *Tikkun*. Like the Pietist J. A. Bengel, whom I shall discuss in the next section, Luria even went so far as to give the specific year in which the *Tikkun* would be consummated: 1575. Summing up Luria's position, Scholem states that "it is man who adds the final touch to the divine countenance; it is he who completes the enthronement of God, the King

25. Ibid., 254.
26. Scholem discusses this idea in connection with Kabbalism as a whole (see ibid., 27, 223).
27. Ibid., 273.
28. Ibid., 279.
29. Scholem, *Kabbalah*, 426–27.
30. See Scholem, *Major Trends*, 268, 275–76.

and the mystical creator of all things, in His own Kingdom of Heaven; it is he who perfects the Maker of all things!"[31]

The similarity of these ideas to Hegel's is clear. Hegel holds that the true infinite (the Absolute Idea) "contains" the finite: nature is a "reflection" or "specification" of the Logos; it is an "other" to Idea yet at the same time is contained within its compass. Nevertheless, nature is an imperfect expression of Absolute Idea; it is the "fallenness" of Idea. In Spirit, a natural being, man, rises above nature and comes, through philosophy, to realize its true, eternal being as one with the Absolute Idea (*Adam Ha-Rishon*, or earthly man, realizing his identity with *Adam Kadmon*). Man is the being who "takes over" nature and transforms it according to the ideal, even bending his own passions and inclinations to conform to the "universal." We "return" to the pure light of Absolute Idea not only through philosophy—through the appropriation of the created world in thought—but through obedience to the edicts of the divine State, which is the guardian of the customs and laws of Ethical Life.

Hegel's doctrine of Objective Spirit is not only similar to Luria's Kabbalah but to Kabbalistic eschatology in general. Specifically, we must look at the Kabbalists' treatment of the tenth and final *Sephirah*, *Malkhut* or *Shekhinah*. *Malkhut* ("Kingdom," sometimes "Glory") is conceived of as feminine—in contrast to the "male" *Tiferet* and *Yesod* (the "organ" of *Tiferet*)—and is often referred to under the alternate name of *Shekhinah* or "Divine Presence." If one looks at a drawing of the Tree of Life, *Malkhut* seems almost like an extension of the Tree, a sort of appendage. This is not accidental, for *Malkhut* represents the divine presence in the world: with *Malkhut* the *Sephiroth* have reached down into the world of space and time. In chapter 5, I discussed how some Kabbalists take the *Ein-Sof* or Infinite to be identical to the *Ayin*, or Nothing. Scholem maintains that *Ayin* is a kind of primal unity that transcends the subject-object distinction.[32] Nevertheless, although *Ein-Sof/Ayin* is neither subject nor object, its telos is to develop into a true or absolute subject. According to the Kabbalists, "God willed to see God," to become fully manifest to Himself; to achieve perfect self-knowledge or self-relation.[33] The "I" of God is identified by many Kabbalists with *Malkhut* or "Kingdom."

Let us look more closely at what it means to identify *Malkhut*, God's "I," with *Shekhinah*. *Shekhinah* is the "Divine Presence." Scholem writes that *Shekhinah* is "the personification and hypostasis of God's 'indwelling' or 'presence' in the world. . . . In the literal sense, God's indwelling or *Shekhinah* means His visible or hidden presence in a given place, his immediacy."[34] Scholem speculates that *Shekhinah/Malkhut* is feminine because it was thought of as a "vessel" that receives all the other *Sephiroth*.[35] Thus, if

31. Ibid., 273–74.
32. Ibid., 221.
33. Halevi, *A Kabbalistic Universe*, 7.
34. Gershom Scholem, *On The Mystical Shape of the Godhead: Basic Concepts in the Kabbalah*, ed. Jonathan Chipman and trans. Joachim Neugroschel (New York: Schocken Books, 1991), 141–47.
35. Ibid., 160.

the *Sephiroth* are conceived as the aspects or moments of God's being, all the moments are contained within *Shekhinah*. Yet, the *Shekhinah* is conceived of as being in the world. Thus, the final and—perhaps it would not be misleading to say—highest moment of God's being is God's "indwelling" or "presence" in the world of space-time. Scholem writes that "The last *Sephirah* performs a different function from all the other *Sephiroth*: it is one with all the others and yet separate, because it performs a mission on their behalf to the world, like a princess coming from afar."[36] The parallel to Hegel is this: *Shekhinah* is like Objective Spirit; it is a "realization" of Absolute Idea in the world; it is "one" with Absolute Idea, yet the Idea, as formal and eternal, is also separate from it.[37]

"Objective Spirit" for Hegel, of course, refers to the realm of social institutions and practices. So far, however, *Shekhinah* simply sounds like the burning bush. Consider, however, the following lines from Joseph Gikatilla (thirteenth century):

[In the days of the Patriarchs] the *Shekhinah* was *in suspenso* [literally, "hanging in the air"], and found no resting place for its feet on earth, as in the beginning of Creation. But then came Moses, of blessed memory, and all of Israel together with him built the Tabernacle and the vessels, and repaired the broken channels, and put the ranks in order, and repaired the ponds, and drew live water into them from the House of Water Drawing, and then brought the *Shekhinah* back to its dwelling among the lower ones—into the Tent, but not upon the ground as in the beginning of Creation. And the hint of this is: "Let them make me a sanctuary, that I may dwell among them" [Exod. 25:8]. We find that the *Shekhinah* was like a guest, moving from place to place, and of this it is said "and I shall dwell among them" and not "I shall dwell below" but "among them"—i.e., like a lodger. Until David and Solomon came, and placed the *Shekhinah* on solid ground in the Temple of Jerusalem.[38]

The implication of this passage seems to be that *Shekhinah*—the living presence of God, containing all the attributes of God—came to be in the Temple of Jerusalem, the religious, cultural, and moral center of the people of Abraham.

Scholem quotes a popular Kabbalistic epigram: "Israel forms the limbs of the *Shekhinah*."[39] This appears to identify the nation of Israel (meaning the Jewish people, its culture and traditions) with God's presence in the world. In Jewish Gnostic circles in late antiquity the *Shekhinah* became hypostatized, that is, God's presence in the world came to denote a *specific* historical locus or conjunction of factors. From this arose the identification of *Shekhinah* with the *keneset Yisrael* ("the com-

36. Ibid., 168.
37. It is also interesting to note that Böhme, as discussed in chapter 1, viewed "God's Wisdom" as feminine, and saw the highest moment of God's Wisdom, Body (the seventh source-spirit) as a tangible presence. Scholem notes that Philo of Alexandria treated God's Wisdom as feminine in form (ibid., 142).
38. Quoted in ibid., 178.
39. Ibid., 175.

munity of Israel").[40] These Jewish Gnostics held to a doctrine of the "exile of the *Shekhinah*," according to which God's presence in the world is like the "divine spark" that exists in the terrestrial world and must be helped to ignite and fill the fallen world with divine presence. This is the mission of the *keneset Yisrael*. (Thus it appears that Luria's views about the role of man in redeeming the world were present in germinal form in earlier Kabbalah.) Unlike Christianity, Jewish Kabbalism sees redemption as occurring within time and within the world. As Scholem puts it, "Redemption is expressed as the end of the 'exile of the *Shekhinah*,' the restoration of the Divine unity throughout all areas of existence."[41] Thus, we find in the Kabbalah something very much like Hegel's concept of the "end of history": the "end" of the world and of man is realized in time and on earth through the "presence of God" coming to be in human institutions, in "Objective Spirit."

However, one might object that one crucial "Hegelian" element is missing from this Kabbalist account of "Objective Spirit": no indication has been given thus far that God *needs* to become present in the *keneset Yisrael*. In Hegel, however, Absolute Idea—God "in his eternal essence"—is abstract and formal, lacking full realization or actualization. Thus, God, to be God, must realize Himself in Spirit. Do the Kabbalists maintain something similar? Recall what was said earlier about God's achievement of "self-consciousness" or "ego" ("I") after emerging from the state of *Ein-Sof* = *Ayin*, the Being-Nothing beyond subject and object. This conception (held by some, but by no means all, Kabbalists) clearly implies that God develops and that the final stage of perfection involves self-reflection. As Scholem writes, "the *Zohar* identifies the highest development of God's personality with precisely that stage of His unfolding which is nearest to human experience, indeed which is immanent and mysteriously present in every one of us."[42] This is the evidence needed to make the Hegelian parallel stick: God, to be God, *does* require his hypostatization in the *keneset Yisrael*.

The influence of these Kabbalistic ideas on Hegel is almost entirely indirect, by way of Böhme and the Swabian Pietist movement. In the next section I will discuss the eschatology that Hegel inherited from his homeland, and its origins not only in Kabbalism but in the Christian mystical tradition.

4. Joachimite Mysticism and the End of History

In an article on the influence of Böhme on Hegel, David Walsh raises an interesting question: Why would Hegel believe that history has to have a structure (let alone an end) in the first place?[43] Walsh's answer is to point to the influence of Böhme, though I think he would agree with me in identifying the ultimate source as Joachim de Fiore (1135–1202).

40. Scholem, *Kabbalah*, 31.
41. Ibid., 335. It should be pointed out, as with everything in the Kabbalah, that this position was held by many but not all Kabbalists. There is seldom universal agreement about anything among Kabbalists.
42. Scholem, *Major Trends*, 216–17.
43. Walsh, "The Historical Dialectic of Spirit," 15.

Joachim was born in Calabria, the son of an official in the Sicilian court. As a young man he made a pilgrimage to the Holy Land, which led him to decide to devote his life to God. After a brief stint as a hermit on Mt. Etna, Joachim entered the Benedictine monastery of Corazzo, where he soon rose to the rank of abbot. In the 1180s, he fought to have the monastery incorporated into the Cistercian order. This brought Joachim into contact with Pope Lucius III, who suggested to Joachim that he commit his unusual views to writing. By the time the monastery was welcomed into the Cistercian order in 1188, Joachim and a group of followers had already broken off and founded their own house at San Giovanni de Fiore (sometimes written "Flora" or "Flore" or "Floris"). They were promptly repudiated by the Cistercians. By the time of his death, Joachim had become a celebrity, corresponding with and advising the great men of his age.

As Voegelin sees it, Joachim's great innovations were to conceive of history as having an *eidos*, a formal structure, and to "immanentize the eschaton," to hold that the end of time will take place in time.[44] Joachim held that history was not simply a series of contingent events. History consists of certain definite stages moving toward a final end. Joachim's immanentization of the eschaton is no more paradoxical than Hegel's end of history: time will continue, but there will be no new "ages," the story of man will come to an end, even though men will live on. Both Joachim and Hegel hold that at a certain point all the different forms of human life and society and culture will have revealed themselves, all meaningful struggles will be over. Anything that happens afterward is simply more of the same. Both Joachim and Hegel hold that the final phase of history involves the coming into being of certain "highest" or most perfect ways of life. It is unclear, however, whether they believe that these advances have to endure, or whether certain forms out of the past may reappear, temporarily, from time to time.

Joachim's *eidos* of history is the Christian Trinity. Ernst Benz writes that in Joachim, "Development and progress are not understood in human terms. . . . They are, rather, considered as steps in the progressive self-realization and self-revelation of the divine Trinity in the history of mankind."[45] Joachim speaks of the "Age of the Father," "Age of the Son," and "Age of the Holy Spirit" (the word he normally uses to refer to each is *status*, although he sometimes employs *tempus* and *aetas*; *regnum* or "Kingdom" was often employed by his followers). Each age is seen as representing an advance in spirituality and in freedom, and each is dominated by a different archetype: the layman, the priest, and the monk. The final stage of history, the final level of human spirituality, is literally an age of monks. One commentator writes that "For Joachim history was the story of the gradual triumph of spirit over flesh, of contemplation over literal-mindedness. This triumph was inseparable

44. Voegelin, *The New Science of Politics: An Introduction* (Chicago: University of Chicago Press, 1952), 119, 120.
45. Ernst Benz, *Evolution and Christian Hope*, trans. Heinz G. Frank (Garden City, N.Y.: Doubleday, 1966), 37.

from the history of monasticism." In the third age, organized religion simply ends—the church "withers away"—and is replaced by a highly individualistic form of worship.[46] The piety and contemplativeness of the individual are what is important, not the sacraments of the priesthood. Men will no longer be able to lead inauthentic lives and expect salvation: no longer will they be able to sin with abandon and receive absolution.

Joachim made frequent use of images to convey his ideas. Joachim saw the stages of the development of man's spirituality and redemption as unfolding like the growth of a tree, finally bearing fruit in the third age. Some of the other images he employed included circles, eagles, and a ten-stringed psaltery. He used interlocking circles to represent the three ages. Figure 9 shows the Tetragrammaton, the four-letter name of God, interpenetrating the circles of the three ages, perhaps indicating that the being of God or of God's presence is somehow bound up with the ages themselves. Joachim believed that the third age would begin in 1260. (Eschatologists cannot resist calculating the exact date of the end of time; we have already seen this with Luria, and we shall see it again with Bengel and Oetinger.)

Joachim's characterization of the third age as a time of pious, contemplative, monastic "inwardness," and his prediction that the organized Church would dissolve would seem to make him a "proto-Protestant." While Joachim himself was careful to avoid official censure, his followers were anything but cautious. For instance, Gerard of Borgo San Donnino, who published his major work, *Liber introductorious in Evangelium aeternum*, in 1249, declared that Joachim's prophecies were a new Gospel that nullified the authority of the church and Scripture. Another outgrowth of Joachimite prophecy were the notorious Flagellants, who believed that their self-torture was a necessary preliminary to the arrival of the Age of the Holy Spirit.

The origins of Joachim's thought are the topic of much speculation. Emma Jung, for example, sees an influence of Catharism and mystical Judaism: "Joachim's idea springs from a conception already extant in Judaism . . . of a kingdom to be established on earth by the Messiah at the end of time."[47] As to the matter of Joachim and Hegel, the similarity between the two was pointed out to Hegel himself in an 1810 letter from the occultist K. J. H. Windischmann.[48] Hegel himself never mentions Joachim. Nevertheless, in addition to Voegelin, such contemporary scholars as Clark Butler, Laurence Dickey, Antoine Faivre, Henri de

---

46. See Karl Löwith, *Meaning in History* (Chicago: University of Chicago Press, 1949), 151.

47. Emma Jung and von Franz, *Grail Legend*, 318.

48. Hoffmeister #155. The parallel has been developed by O'Regan (*The Heterodox Hegel*) and Clark Butler, "Hegelian Panentheism as Joachimite Christianity," in *New Perspectives on Hegel's Philosophy of Religion*, ed. David Kolb (Albany: State University of New York Press, 1992).

9. The Three Ages of Joachim de Fiore. From his *Book of Figures* (*Liber figurarum*, twelfth century). Reprinted by permission of the President and Fellows of Corpus Christi College, Oxford, MS 255A, fol 7 verso.

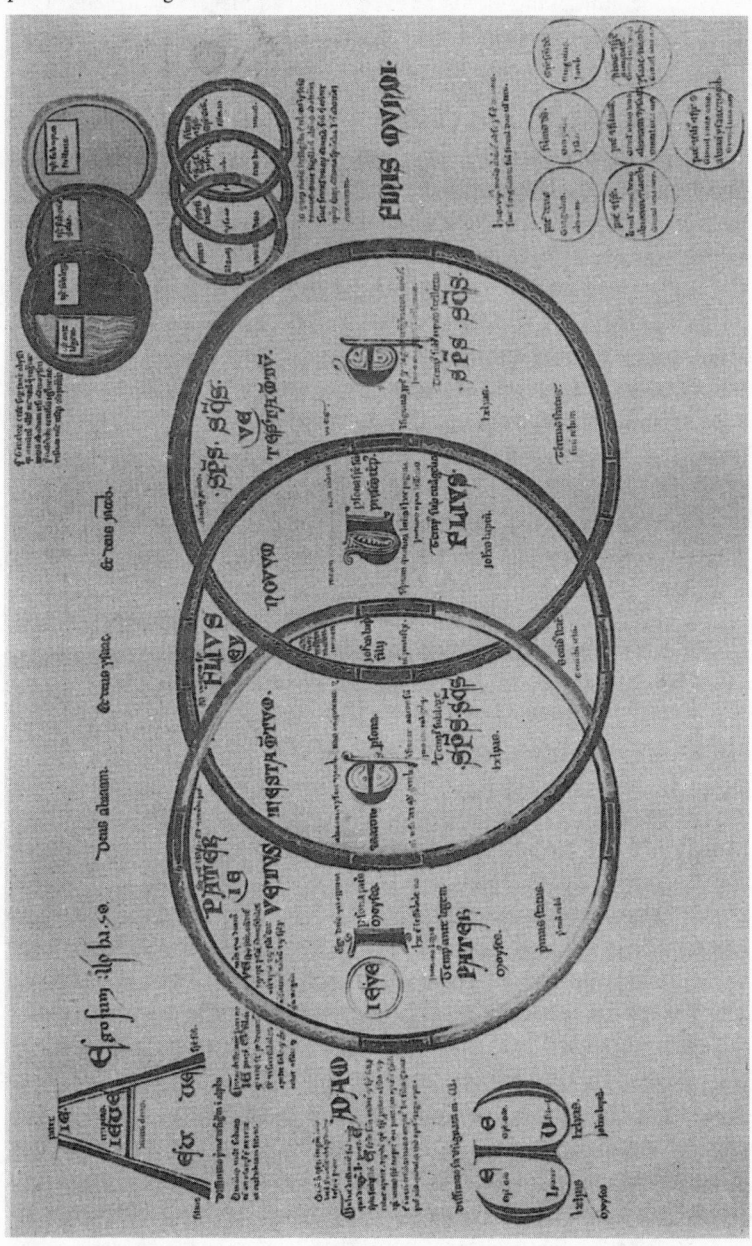

Lubac, Michael Murray, and Cyril O'Regan have argued for a Joachimite influence on Hegel.[49]

The Joachimite influence is most apparent in Hegel's treatment of the Trinity. In his *Lectures on the Philosophy of Religion*, Hegel deals in detail with the Trinity as constituting the "moments" of God (universality, diremption, and reconciliation).[50] In the 1831 version of the lectures, Hegel introduces a new twist: he begins calling Father, Son and Holy Spirit the "Kingdom [*Reich*] of the Father," "Kingdom of the Son," and "Kingdom of the Spirit." This use of "Kingdom" for the persons of the Trinity was employed widely by followers of Joachim. This alone, of course, does not necessarily prove a Joachimite influence. However, Hegel's treatment of the Trinity is, like Joachim's, temporal: he holds that the reconciliation of the diremption in God takes time; only at a certain point in human history is this accomplished. In the *Encyclopedia Logic* Hegel notes that "What underlies divine Providence at the level of thought will soon prove to be the Concept" (EL § 147, Z; Geraets, 222). Once it is realized that the Concept, as the crowning conception of the Logic, contains three moments which correspond to the Christian Trinity, the similarity to Joachim is striking: both Hegel and Joachim see the hand of God, Providence, playing out in history according to the pattern of the Trinity. Hegel does not repeat Joachim's treatment of the Age of the Father or of the Son, but there is a striking correspondence between Hegel's Kingdom of the Spirit and Joachim's.

There is a strong similarity between Joachim's conception of spirituality in the third age and the Pietist movement that arose in Germany centuries later. Both involve a rejection of the church as an intermediary between ordinary men and God and the claim that the lay community of worshippers can achieve salvation and knowledge of God unaided. Hegel explicitly identifies his Kingdom of the Spirit with the community of worshippers (LPR 3:371; VPR 3:287). He refers to the community as "existing Spirit" and refers to Spirit as "God existing as community" (LPR 3:331; VPR 3:254). Both men conceive the third stage as one of reconciliation, of higher spirituality or fully adequate knowledge, and of the actualization of human freedom. Further, as O'Regan notes, both Hegel and Joachim make the unusual move of locating the eschaton in time, Joachim believing that it is at hand, Hegel believing that it has already happened. Both Hegel and Joachim have Christ play a crucial role on the way to the achievement of the third age, Hegel insisting that the universality of human freedom (realized fully in the third age) was first revealed through Christianity.

Hegel's "Joachimite" treatment of the Trinity in the *Lectures* dovetails with his Böhmeanism. This is the case specifically with respect to the Kingdom of the Father. Not only is there a Trinity of Father-Son-Spirit,

49. See Butler, "Hegelian Panentheism"; Dickey, *Hegel*; Antoine Faivre, "Ancient and Medieval Sources of Modern Esoteric Movements," *Modern Esoteric Spirituality*; Henri de Lubac, *La Spiritualité de Joachim de Fiore* (Paris: Sycamore, 1979–81), vol. 2, 359–77; Michael Murray, *Modern Philosophy of History* (The Hague: Nijhoff, 1970), 89–113; O'Regan, *The Heterodox Hegel*.
50. See Peter C. Hodgson, introduction to *Hegel: Lectures on the Philosophy of Religion* (Berkeley: University of California Press, 1985), vol. 3, 50.

there is also a *secondary* Trinity immanent within the Father. Hegel identifies the Kingdom of the Father with the pure, *eidetic* realm of the *Logic*, thus the "Trinity of the Father" corresponds to the three divisions of the *Logic*.[51] In the 1831 *Lectures* Hegel speaks of the "Trinity of the father" (or, as O'Regan calls it, the "immanent Trinity") as involving, "the element of pure ideality and universality, in the silent abode of the thinking spirit." He goes on to say that in this abode, "God is immediately present to Himself through His differentiation, which, however, is not yet externalized at this stage. It is by virtue of this [inner] movement that God is spirit. Thus the doctrine of the Trinity pertains to this sphere, although it is preferentially termed the Kingdom of the Father" (LPR 3:362; VPR 3:281). Thus, in the "immanent Trinity" God is closed within Himself ("not yet externalized"). Hegel uses this language explicitly: in the 1824 lectures he states that "God is the true God, Spirit, because He is not merely Father, and hence closed up within Himself" (LPR 3:219; VPR 3:150). In the *Philosophy of Spirit* Hegel states that "God the Father is for Himself, shut up within Himself, abstract, and consequently not yet the God of Spirit and of truth" (PS § 384, Z; Petry 1:63). Hegel also refers to God in this sphere as "loving Himself" (LPR 1:124–25; 41). Thus, there is a clear parallel to Böhme's "immanent Trinity" of God "in Himself," the Sour, Sweet, and Bitter (see chapter 1).[52] In *Six Mystical Points*, Böhme refers to "God in his triad" as "the first *Magia*."[53]

The "immanent Trinity" is not an innovation of the *Lectures*; it is to be found in the Jena Triangle fragment in which the "triangle of triangles" represents the process of God's coming to consciousness of Himself. There are three triangles in all, with the triangle of triangles being the figure made up by the set of the three. The first triangle is described by Hegel as follows: "In this First, which is at the same time only One side of the absolutely unique Triangle, there is only the Godhead in reciprocal intuition and cognition with Himself." This is even more strikingly Böhmean than what Hegel says in the *Lectures*. David Walsh writes: "Hegel suggested, as Böhme also did, that the first Trinity of God in himself is not sufficient for the divine self-revelation."[54] Therefore a second triangle appears, "God the Son." Hegel writes: "In the Son, God is cognizant of Himself *as* God. He says to Himself: I am God. The within-itself ceases to be a negative."

The separated moment of that which stands opposed to the Godhead must be "transfigured" and brought into unity within God. Hegel writes that "the Son must go right through the Earth, must overcome Evil, and in that he steps over to one side as the victor, must awaken the other, the self-cognition of God, as a new cognition that is one with God, or as the Spirit of God: whereby the middle becomes a beautiful, free, divine

---

51. See O'Regan, *Heterodox Hegel*, 91, 108, 111. Hodgson speaks of it as a "pre-worldly Trinity," thus calling to mind the eternal character of the *Logic*. Hodgson, introduction to LPR 3:50.

52. O'Regan also recognizes the parallel to Böhme (*Heterodox Hegel*, 109, 130–31).

53. Nicolescu, *Science, Meaning and Evolution*, 229.

54. Walsh, *Boehme and Hegel*, 321.

middle, the Universe of God." This heralds the arrival of a new triangle, of the Holy Spirit. As we saw in chapter 3, this fragment is the "blueprint" for Hegel's system. The nature of his Logic is expressed here very clearly: the first "triad" of the system (in the later Logic, Being-Essence-Concept) is the "Idea of God." This Idea is expressed (made real) in the triads of the Son (Philosophy of Nature: Mechanics, Physics, Organics) and Spirit (Subjective, Objective, and Absolute Spirit). I noted in chapter 3 that this fragment seems to be influenced by Böhme, Baader, Oetinger, and Eckhart. I can now add Joachim to the list. In the *Lectures* Hegel speaks only of a Trinity immanent within the Father, but we know from the Philosophies of Nature and Spirit that the Son and Spirit must be triadically structured as well.

If we ask how Hegel could have encountered the ideas of the Calabrian monk, the answer is that, like so much else, those ideas were a part of the Württemberg cultural milieu to which he, Schelling, and other Swabian intellectuals were exposed. Joachim enjoyed a revival during the Reformation, when his ideas were used as a weapon against the papacy by the followers of Luther. As we have seen, Joachimism is remarkably "Protestant" in spirit. Ernest Renan marveled that the Reformation did not begin with Joachim in the thirteenth century.[55] Joachimite enthusiasm was very strong in the insular culture of Württemberg, where it became intertwined with indigenous mystical and Hermetic currents. Joachim's thought is not itself "Hermetic"—and it is even questionable whether it should be termed "mystical"—but it was co-opted by Hermeticists like Böhme, Andreae, Baader, and Oetinger.

As Laurence Dickey notes, Old Württemberg belonged to the tradition of what Gerhard Ladner has called "Christian reform." Dickey writes: "This tradition . . . took ethical and eschatological elements from widely divergent sources in the history of Christian thought and formed from them an anthropology of fallen and restored man that allowed for—indeed, demanded—man's participation in civil life as well as in his own salvation. The thrust of the tradition was to show that through ethical activism man could transform the world in accordance with God's wishes and, by doing so, make significant 'progress' not only toward transcending his own fallen nature, but toward establishing the Kingdom of God *on earth* as well."[56] Dickey argues that Joachimism was one of the influences on Württemberg "Christian reform."[57] He notes that the Württembergers viewed themselves as a "millennial people," chosen by God to realize the Kingdom of Heaven on earth.[58]

Dickey writes further that the sixteenth, seventeenth, and eighteenth centuries in Württemberg "constituted an age of apocalyptic expectation."[59] Nowhere was this more evident than among the Pietists. Ernst Benz writes of the atmosphere of Württemberg Pietism: "From all sides,

55. See Dickey, *Hegel*, 45.
56. Ibid., 12.
57. Ibid., 34.
58. Ibid., 36.
59. Ibid., 44.

one watches for the 'signs of the times,' one attempts to perceive in the great historical events the fulfillment of New Testament prophecies. . . . At the same time, the image of the 'Golden age,' the realization of the Kingdom of God, the Kingdom of a Thousand Years, the completion of the final phase of world history . . . appears more and more strongly in the spiritual considerations of the community."[60]

The Joachimism of the Pietists appears to have been influenced by the Rosicrucian movement. The influence of Joachim on the Rosicrucian manifestos has been discussed by a number of scholars, and J. V. Andreae himself actually mentions Joachim.[61] J. Montgomery has called Andreae "the single most important influence on the church history of the Württemberg territory for over two hundred years."[62] Phillip Jakob Spener (1635–1705), sometimes called the "father of German Pietism," explicitly acknowledged his intellectual debt to Andreae.[63] Spener divided the history of Christianity into three ages, corresponding to the Trinity, and claimed that the third age would involve the "Divine Light" penetrating and dispelling darkness.[64]

Perhaps the most striking example of Joachim's influence on Pietism, however, is that of J. A. Bengel (1687–1752). Robert Schneider has characterized Bengel as "the philosopher of history who anticipated the work of Schelling and Hegel."[65] Bengel's maternal great-grandfather was Matthias Hafenreffer (1561–1619), chancellor of the University of Tübingen and one of Andreae's teachers. Having lived through the wars of Louis XIV as a young boy, Bengel had seen much violence and grew up hoping for a time of perpetual peace. Unlike many such hopefuls, however, Bengel did not look for signs of progress. Instead he prophesied that corruption, violence, and blasphemy would only increase until the forces of the Antichrist burned themselves out. Bengel held that world history is an organic unity, in which revelation is playing itself out by degrees. As Ernst Benz puts it, for Bengel

> history is a series of alliances between God and the elect saved from the fall. This history of salvation is realized in a spiritual evolution through these alliances, until the final battle between the Kingdom of Light and the Kingdom of Darkness. In Bengel, these suggestions become even stronger as he also wishes to see a chronological conformity between the periods. His book *Weltalter*, a title that one finds again, significantly enough, in Schelling, represents an attempt

60. Benz, *Mystical Sources*, 34.
61. See J. V. Andreae, *Turris Babel sive Judiciorum de Fraternitate Rosaceae Crucis Chaos* (Argentorati: Sumptibus haeredum Lazari Zetzneri, 1619), 14–15. For scholars who have noted the Joachim-Rosicrucian connection see for example, Dickey, *Hegel*, 63–65; Roland Edighoffer, "Rosicrucianism from the Seventeenth to the Twentieth Centuries," *Modern Esoteric Spirituality*; J. Montgomery, *The Cross and the Crucible*, 57, 173, 198–99.
62. Dickey, *Hegel*, 61; J. Montgomery, *The Cross and the Crucible*, ix.
63. On the relationship of Andreae to Pietism, see Robert Schneider, *Geistesahnen*, 36–37.
64. Hanratty, "Hegel and the Gnostic Tradition: II," 319.
65. Robert Schneider, *Geistesahnen*, 38.

at a chronological fixation of the divine plan of redemptive history, with the aid of the varied numerical data from Old and New Testament prophetic books.[66]

Through a complex and eccentric interpretation of the Book of Revelation, Bengel determined that the Millennium would begin in the year 1836. 1809 would mark the return of Christ and the inception of the "Kingdom of a Thousand Years" (*Tausend-Jahre Reich*). Benz notes that Hegel's "cunning of reason" is clearly anticipated by Bengel in his account of how this Kingdom shall come into being:

> Viewed from outside, history is the place of the expansion of the private egotism of individuals and groups. Those with power act as they intend; each one wishes to attain his objective by his own action. But from the moment an act has taken place, the actor ceases to be the master of his actions. The act not only produces the repercussions its instigator desired, but also has boundless and unforseen consequences, leading to unimaginable and often completely unexpected primary and secondary results. . . . [In Bengel, this idea] is contained in a theological interpretation of history in its totality, which sees in every event, in the last analysis, an element of the divine plan of redemption.[67]

Bengel and his followers, who called themselves "The Free" (*Die Freien*), proclaimed the perennial ideal of the "invisible church," a conception which is similar to Joachim's informal "community of the faithful," which was supposed to characterize the third age.[68] As discussed earlier, the invisible church is a perennial theme of German mysticism, and also an important concept for both the Freemasons and the Rosicrucians (who also spoke of an "invisible college"). In a letter from Hegel to Schelling of January 1795, Hegel writes: "Reason and Freedom remain our watchword, and our rallying point the Invisible Church."[69] Robert Schneider holds that Hegel's use of the term *invisible church*, as well as the phrase "Kingdom of God" (see the following section) is evidence of the influence of Pietist theology.[70] As we have seen, Dickey argues that the "Protestant civil piety" of Old Württemberg involved, among other things, the goal of establishing the kingdom of God on earth through a transformation of ethics. Robert Schneider, in fact, refers to the "kingdom of God" (*Das Königreich Gottes*) as the "consummate idea" of Swabian Pietism.[71] In addition to Bengel, P. M. Hahn also preached a doctrine of the invisible church.

66. Benz, *Mystical Sources*, 35.

67. Ibid., 37.

68. See Hanratty, "Hegel and the Gnostic Tradition: II," 313.

69. Butler, 32; Hoffmeister #8. Harris writes: "It seems to me virtually certain that for Hegel, at any rate, the 'invisible Church' originally referred to the cosmopolitan ideal of Freemasonry as envisaged by Lessing in *Ernst und Falk*" (*Toward the Sunlight*, 105). Harris also seems to suggest that the "invisible church" should be understood as equivalent to Objective Spirit (*Night Thoughts*, 411).

70. Robert Schneider, *Geistesahnen*, 41.

71. Ibid., 146.

It is through Böhme and Oetinger that Joachimism and millenarianism in general are incorporated into the Hermetic tradition, and significantly, it is Böhme and Oetinger who are probably the chief sources of Hegel's Joachimism. F. Ernest Stoeffler makes reference to Oetinger's "rampant chiliasm," which "surpassed even that of Bengel."[72] While Bengel had put great stress on how we can know that the millennium is approaching (e.g., through his theories of biblical exegesis), Oetinger took Bengel's calculations for granted and focused instead on precisely what the end of time would bring. The picture that Oetinger paints of the "Golden Age" at the end of time is essentially indistinguishable from utopian socialism:

> In any kingdom, true happiness has three conditions [all of which will be satisfied in the millennium]: first, that despite all multiplicity, which is not against order, and despite all differences of rank, the subjects have equality among each other, as we have learned from the distribution of Israel where the equal share of land reminded everybody not to pride himself above others. Everybody is to find his happiness in the happiness of his neighbor, his joy in the joy of all the other people, and by that everybody is to be a free lord among others; secondly, that they have a community of goods and not take delight in goods because they are a property; thirdly, that they demand nothing from each other as an obligation. Because, if everything would be available in abundance, there would be no need of government, property, and of no liabilities forced and extorted by government.[73]

Of course, such a utopian conception is completely antithetical to the spirit of Hegel's *Philosophy of Right* (in the preface to which Hegel explicitly rejects utopianism).[74] Nevertheless, it must be remembered that in his youth, Hegel, like so many others of his generation, was infatuated with the utopian ideals of liberty, equality, and fraternity proclaimed by the French revolutionaries. As Hegel himself discusses, it is natural for young people to be idealistic and to dream of remaking the world. It is generally assumed that Hegel's youthful idealism was awakened by the revolution, but Ernst Benz suggests a different hypothesis: "German democratic ideas do not rest solely on the ideology of the French Revolution, but find roots in the Christian conscience of Swabian Pietism."[75] Benz is suggesting that the source of Hegel's idealism is the dream of the "Golden Age" of freedom and equality that he encountered in Bengelian, Oetingerite, Hahnian, and other Pietist "schools." It would have been hard to have avoided encountering these currents in late eighteenth-century Stuttgart. Hegel—and Schelling and Hölderlin—may have responded so quickly and enthusias-

---

72. Stoeffler, *German Pietism*, 117.
73. Quoted in Vondung, "Millenarianism, Hermeticism, and the Search for a Universal Science," 122.
74. It should be mentioned that Oetinger was in no way a revolutionary. He believed that his Golden Age would be brought about by God, not man. Until that time, he advocated obedience to authority and viewed existing social institutions positively. See Hayden-Roy, "A Foretaste of Heaven," 52–53.
75. Benz, *Mystical Sources*, 44.

tically to the French Revolution because they saw in it the imminent ful-fillment of ideals to which they were already committed, ideals transmit-ted to them by Swabian Pietism.[76]

Oetinger believed that at the end of time, not only would all men live in perfect harmony but science would be transformed. No longer would there be a multitude of disconnected sciences; a new "superscience" would arise that would unify all knowledge. Oetinger's New Science, as we might call it, is a version of *pansophia*. Benz describes Oetinger's sci-ence as it will exist in his utopia: "The coming together of these gifts of the spirit occurs in a central vision exalting the faith of the Kingdom's subjects to the level of knowledge, of an intellectual intuition. They will participate in a 'central knowledge.' The description of this knowledge of the future already constitutes a direct foreshadowing of the idealistic idea of knowledge such as we find in different forms in Schelling, Hegel, and Baader."[77] Oetinger describes his New Science in the following rap-turous language:

> It will be very easy to understand: God will present all things in an intuitive form; and we will see his reckonings in an architectural vision, in detail and in its totality, in the physical as in the moral; but above all we will have a very clear knowledge of the history of nations. What the Holy Revelation only outlined, will be recounted in all detail, drawn out of the abyss, set beside every kind of state or constitution and seen under the righteous enlighten-ment of the knowledge of God, of the soul, and of the human body. There will be no more than one basic wisdom. Jurisprudence and medicine will be inseparable from theology; history will be the public theatre of God's ways and of providence, of all the phrases of Solomon. . . . It will be the source of all knowledge. The law will come from theology, and medicine will be no more than an emblematic theology. We will see in souls and in bodies the imprint of the being from whom all things have come forth.[78]

Aside from the claim that this knowledge will be had in "intuitive form," this passage seems almost like a prophecy of Hegel's system. As we have noted, Hegel's philosophical project aims at a perfected form of life that will transform all aspects of man and his world: religious life, art, our understanding of history, of science, of government. Hegel's *Lec-tures on the Philosophy of History* can be seen as an attempt to make good on Oetinger's prediction that the New Science would include a theodicy, an attempt to show that "history [is] the public theatre of God's ways and of all providence." For Hegel as for Oetinger, science and philosophy become identical with theology. Hegel takes up "what the Holy Revela-

76. Hayden-Roy, in her study of the influence of Württemberg Pietism on Hölderlin, writes that "Chiliastic excitement was widespread among all ranks of the Württemberg Pietists at the time Hölderlin was studying at the *Stift*, and the French Revolution added to their conviction that they were drawing near to the fullness of time" ("A Foretaste of Heaven," 216).

77. Benz, *Mystical Sources*, 40.

78. Oetinger, *Sämtliche Schriften*, vol. 6, 47.

tion only outlined," the triune structure of the divine; he "recounts it in all detail" and "sets [it] beside every kind of state or constitution," in order that we may "see in souls and in bodies the imprint of the being from whom all things have come forth."

While the influence of Bengel and Oetinger on Hegel's thought is highly probable, in the case of Schelling it is certain. Schelling describes history as a "successively developing revelation of God."[79] In Die Weltalter Schelling states that "The peace of the Golden Age [das Goldne Zeitalter] will be made known first through the harmonious unification of all sciences."[80] In his System of Transcendental Idealism (1800), Schelling sets forth what he calls "the only true interpretation of history":

> History as a whole is a progressive, gradually self-disclosing revelation of the absolute. Hence one can never point out in history the particular places where the mark of providence, or God Himself, is as it were visible. For God never *exists*, if the existent *is* that which presents itself in the objective world; if He *existed* thus, then *we* should not; but He continually *reveals* Himself. Man, through history, provides a continuous demonstration of God's presence, a demonstration, however, which only the whole of history can render complete.[81]

In the same work, Schelling, like Joachim and his followers, divides history into three epochs, maintaining that in the third epoch God is finally "actualized."

5. Hegel and Prussian Rosicrucianism

The major difference between Hegel and the Swabian millennialists is that Hegel believes the end of time has already arrived. Indeed if it were not already finished we could not know it. To be sure, Hegel's theory of history is similar to Joachim's in being Trinitarian, but unlike Joachim, Hegel does not employ the Trinity as a device for making predictions about the future; he merely uses it to make sense of the past (Marx, not Hegel, is the true modern disciple of Joachim).

It was in Berlin that Hegel lectured on his philosophy of history, and in Berlin that he published his Philosophy of Right. Hegel came to Berlin in 1818, after having taught for just two years at Heidelberg. This was the crowning moment of his career, and he remained in Berlin until his death on November 14, 1831. The call to Berlin was a recognition of Hegel's importance as a thinker. In Berlin Hegel was a celebrity and enjoyed considerable influence. His lectures were attended by hundreds of people from all walks of life: "veterinary surgeons, insurance brokers, civil servants, operatic tenors and commercial clerks were rushing to his

79. Schelling, "Philosophie und Religion" (1804), Werke, vol. 4, 47.
80. Schelling, Die Weltalter (1813), Werke, vol. 4, 582. This and the preceding line from Schelling's "Philosophie und Religion" are quoted and discussed in Vondung, "Millenarianism, Hermeticism, and the Search for a Universal Science," 124.
81. Schelling, System of Transcendental Idealism, 211.

lectures."[82] If we look at Hegel's interests during the Berlin period it is clear that he viewed his new post as a pulpit from which to proclaim the nature of the legitimate state (the *Philosophy of Right*), the actualization of God in the world (the *Lectures on the Philosophy of Religion*), and the climax of the story of mankind (the *Lectures on the Philosophy of World History*). Hegel was no Oetinger: he was not the herald of a new age and of utopia; he was Minerva's wise old owl proclaiming that the Kingdom of God is already spread upon the earth, and men need only see it.[83]

In the preface to the *Philosophy of Right* Hegel attacks utopianism, at one point employing a now-famous metaphor: "To recognize reason as the rose in the cross of the present and thereby to enjoy the present, this is the rational insight which reconciles us to the actual . . ." (Knox, 12; PR, 27). In the *Lectures on the Philosophy of Religion* of 1824, Hegel employs the same metaphor, stating that "in order to pluck reason, the rose in the cross of the present, one must take up the cross itself" (LPR 2:248n45).

Such commentators as Knox, Löwith, Lasson, Hodgson, and Wood agree in attributing Hegel's metaphor to the Rosicrucians.[84] Oddly, however, none of them shows how this connection throws any light on Hegel's teaching. Löwith suggests that Hegel not only refers to the Rosicrucians but also to a device originated by Luther.[85] The problem with this suggestion is that Luther's device is a cross in a heart in a white rose, not a rose in a cross.[86] Furthermore, in a review essay published in 1829, Hegel himself identifies the reference as being to the Rosicrucians and suggests that only "ignorance" (*Unwissenheit*) could explain someone's failure to recognize the allusion.[87] He says nothing about Luther.

Earlier in the preface, Hegel draws an interesting contrast between people's attitude toward nature and their attitude toward the ethical world. "So far as nature is concerned people grant that it is nature *as it is* which philosophy has to bring within its ken, that *the philosopher's stone* [der Stein der Weisen] lies concealed somewhere within nature itself, that nature is inherently rational, and that what knowledge has to investigate and grasp in concepts is this actual reason present in it . . . in the sense of the law and essence immanent within it" (Knox, 4; PR, 16). The rose represents *reason*. Since Hegel uses the philosopher's stone to represent the reason inherent in nature and society, the philosopher's stone is

82. Rüdiger Safranski, *Schopenhauer and the Wild Years of Philosophy*, trans. Eswald Osers (Cambridge: Harvard University Press, 1991), 259.
83. My allusion is to the Gospel of Thomas, 114. See *The Other Bible*, ed. Willis Barnstone (San Francisco: Harper and Row, 1984), 307.
84. Knox, 303 n34; Löwith, *Hegel to Nietzsche*, 18; Hodgson, LPR 2:248 n45.; Allen Wood, editorial note in Hegel, *Elements of the Philosophy of Right*, ed. Allen W. Wood and trans. H. B. Nisbet (Cambridge, U.K.: Cambridge University Press, 1991), 391, n27.
85. Löwith, *Hegel to Nietzsche*, 18–19.
86. One is tempted to think that this implausible hypothesis has suggested itself to scholars simply because they are on more familiar territory dealing with Luther.
87. "Über die Hegelsche Lehre oder absolutes Wissen und moderner Pantheismus.—Über Philosophie überhaupt und Hegels *Enzyklopädie der philosophischen Wissenschaften* insbesondere," (1829), in *Werke* 11:466.

equivalent to the rose in the cross. Given the reputation of the Rosicrucians as alchemists, the equivalency of these two metaphors cannot have escaped Hegel.[88] Thus there is an alchemical-Rosicrucian metaphorical subtext to the preface. Hegel is again playing the role of "world-historical alchemist": having isolated the philosopher's stone (reason) in the realm of nature, he now turns to the ethical world and proposes to carry out a similar operation there, to find the philosopher's stone in what *is*.

Why does Hegel place a clear and publicly acknowledged reference to the Rosicrucians in the preface to the *Philosophy of Right*? Hegel seems an unlikely Rosicrucian. The Rosicrucian manifestos announced the aim of a "General Reformation of the Entire World." Hegel's aims, however, were not so grandiose, and by the time he arrived in Berlin his political philosophy had become distinctly conservative.

There is more to the Rosicrucian saga than has been discussed so far, however. Some time in the latter half of the eighteenth century the Rosicrucian movement was revived in Germany. There is disagreement about exactly when this took place—some say 1757, some 1777, others give a different date entirely. By the late eighteenth century, however, the Rosicrucians were anything but reformers. The new incarnation of the Rosicrucian brotherhood, christened the "Gold and Rosy-Cross" (*Gold-und Rosenkreuzer*) was a conservative organization, dedicated to combating the influence of the liberal Freemasons and Illuminati.[89] The Rosicrucian revival in the eighteenth century appears to have been sparked initially by Samuel Richter's *Die wahrhafte und volkommene Bereitung des philosophischen Steins der Brüderschaft aus dem Orden des Gülden und Rosen Kreutzes* (1710).[90] Richter (who wrote under the name Sincerus Renatus) was a Silesian Pietist pastor who preached Paracelcism and Böhmeanism from the pulpit. The order of the Gold and Rosy-Cross was probably founded by Hermann Fichtuld, who was in correspondence with Oetinger.[91]

The order was opposed to the rationalism and mechanistic materialism so much in vogue in the France and England of the Enlightenment. It was dedicated to combating rationalist attempts to "reform" religion, to "re-educate" the people, and to reshape or overthrow the state. The new Rosicrucians saw themselves as defenders of the faith and of public order, as the following quote from one of their number clearly indicates: "It is one of our foremost duties to serve the state into which we have been placed by Providence—to serve it with all our power and capacity. We must be obedient and loyal to the higher powers ordained by God,

88. Christopher MacIntosh argues that the members of the eighteenth-century Gold-und Rosenkreuzer were deeply involved in alchemy. Each of the order's lodges had its own alchemical laboratory, for the use of members. MacIntosh, *The Rose Cross*, 75; 84.

89. Epstein, *Genesis of German Conservatism*, 105; see also Heinrich Schneider, *The Quest for Mysteries*, 76–77. Epstein includes a long list of secondary sources for the Gold-und Rosenkreuzer (105).

90. MacIntosh, *The Rose Cross*, 30.

91. Ibid., 46–48.

and help to promote the public good even when it violates our private egotism."[92] The Gold and Rosy-Cross gained considerable influence throughout Germany, including Hegel's native Swabia. Its members included many prominent politicians, writers, and scientists, including the physiologist Samuel Thomas von Sömmering, whom Hegel cites in his *Philosophy of Nature* (*Werke* 9:451).

By far the most dramatic example of their influence was during the reign of Frederick William II of Prussia (1786–97). Frederick William was the nephew and successor of Frederick the Great. Whereas his uncle was an "enlightened" despot, interested in science, unmoved by superstition, and open to using the power of the state to effect limited reforms, Frederick William was a mystic and an opponent of Enlightenment. He was reputed to have visions, hear ghostly voices, and hold the occasional séance.[93] Frederick the Great had been a Mason, initiated into the order as a young man. During his reign the number of lodges in Berlin increased to thirteen. Frederick himself was Grand Master of a lodge called "At the Sign of the Three Globes."[94] Like his uncle, Frederick William had also been a Mason, but the order's emphasis on rationalism and its merely decorative mystification did not satisfy him.

During the War of Bavarian Succession in 1778–79, Frederick William encountered an officer in his uncle's army by the name of Johann Rudolf von Bischoffswerder (1741–1803). Bischoffswerder, a Saxon by birth, had also flirted with Masonry, but his burning desire was to be initiated into the secrets of alchemy, a desire the Masons could not satisfy. On Christmas Eve 1779 he was initiated into a Rosicrucian lodge, where he apparently found what he was looking for. Bischoffswerder is known to have been conversant with Kabbalistic and alchemical writings.[95] In 1780, learning of Bischoffswerder's friendship with the prince, Duke Friedrich August of Braunschweig-Öls, the chief of the Berlin Gold and Rosy-Cross, ordered him to entice Frederick William into joining their ranks. In the meantime, the prince had suffered an illness and Bischoffswerder had nursed him back to health, apparently using a mysterious elixir originating with the Rosicrucian brotherhood.[96] Grateful to Bischoffswerder and full of mystical enthusiasm, Frederick Wilhelm entered the Rosicrucian order on August 8, 1781, and was given the secret name Brother Ormesus Magnus.

Presiding at the prince's initiation ceremony was the lodge's founder, Johann Christoph Wöllner (1732–1800). Klaus Epstein has described Wöllner and Bischoffswerder, who were close allies, as "the first self-consciously Conservative politicians in German history, politicians in

92. Quoted in Epstein, *Genesis of German Conservatism*, 110.
93. See Henri Brunschwig, *Enlightenment and Romanticism in Eighteenth-Century Prussia*, trans. Frank Jellinek (Chicago: University of Chicago Press, 1974), 165; cf. Epstein, *Genesis of German Conservatism*, 353.
94. Brunschwig, *Enlightenment and Romanticism*, 185.
95. Epstein, *Genesis of German Conservatism*, 354.
96. Gilbert Stanhope, *A Mystic on the Prussian Throne* (London: Mills and Boon, 1912), 124.

the honorable sense of the term—men eager for power for the sake of implementing their principles."[97] That is to say, they were the first German politicians whose policies involved a conscious commitment to rolling back the forces of liberalism. Wöllner, the son of a Lutheran pastor, had married into the Prussian nobility over the objections of Frederick the Great, who refused to grant him a title. He became a Mason in 1765 and rose quickly in the ranks to become a Knight of the Strict Observance (a rank associated with the alleged link between the Masons and the Knights Templar) in 1776. Like Bischoffswerder, however, he became disillusioned with the Masons and joined the Rosicrucians in 1779, where he also attained a position of considerable authority, serving as *Oberhauptdirektor* over twenty-six *Zirkel*.[98] In the years leading up to Frederick William's coronation in 1786, Wöllner and Bischoffswerder worked hard to win the prince over to their mystical philosophy and conservative politics, which was not difficult.

Wöllner's ambition was to succeed the famous Karl Abraham Zedlitz, the Prussian minister of culture. He succeeded in this on July 3, 1788, when Frederick William, who had ascended the throne in the summer of 1786, appointed him *Staats- und Justiz-Minister* and *Chef des Geistlichen Departements* (minister of ecclesiastical affairs). While Wöllner's economic policy may have been progressive, he was a zealous defender of the traditional faith against rationalism. On July 9, 1788, just six days after acquiring his post, Wöllner persuaded the king to enact the "Edict Concerning Religion," which commanded orthodoxy of the clergy. The "Edict of Censorship" of December 19, 1788, suppressed writings considered to be atheistic or otherwise impious. In 1792, Wöllner's office published the *Landeskatechismus*, which defined the tenets of religious orthodoxy and proscribed all rationalist approaches to "reforming" religious practice or to "interpreting" scripture. Wöllner is famous for his censorship of Kant's *Religion Within the Bounds of Reason Alone* (1793). Despite this, Wöllner's "Edict Concerning Religion" granted the different religious sects of Prussia full freedom of worship, so long as they did not proselytize. Jews, for instance, enjoyed full religious toleration under the terms of the edict.

In 1797, the plans of Wöllner and Bischoffswerder were abruptly crushed by the death of the king and the ascension to the throne of his son, Frederick William III. The son had none of the father's mystical fervor or Rosicrucian connections. He was no rationalist either, but, by all accounts, merely a dullard without any convictions of his own. He reigned for forty-three years. The rationalists who had laid low during Frederick William II's reign saw their chance: they filled up the vacuum that was Frederick William III, persuaded him to purge the Rosicrucians from the cabinet and to cancel many of the measures enacted by Wöllner and company. Wöllner and Bischoffswerder retired into private life and died in obscurity.

97. Epstein, *Genesis of German Conservatism*, 354.
98. Ibid., 357.

This is the historical context required to understand what a reference to the "rose in the cross of the present" would have meant to readers—including censors—in 1821. Some Hegel scholars recognize this, but their treatment of the historical materials has, in some cases, been rather inadequate. For instance, Kenneth Westphal thinks that Hegel's reference to the "rose in the cross of the present" is a message to "the superstitious and reactionary king, Frederick William III." Westphal informs us that "The king belonged to the Rosicrucians, an anti-scientific cabalistic Christian sect devoted to the occult."[99] Thus, Hegel is denouncing the "other-worldliness" of the Rosicrucian king, telling him he must recognize the rose in the cross of the *present*.[100] The only problem with this, of course, is that Westphal has his Frederick Williams wrong: when Hegel published the *Philosophy of Right* in 1821, Frederick William II had been dead and the Rosicrucians out of power for twenty-four years! Westphal would make Hegel a liberal Don Quixote, dueling with nonexistent Rosicrucian villains, much like the American religious fundamentalists who see the Illuminati lurking under every bed. A further problem with Westphal's thesis is that with respect to their *political views*, the Rosicrucians were not "other-worldly": in fact, they espoused the very sort of anti-utopianism Hegel articulates in his preface.

The same blurring of historical fact occurs in a monograph on the preface by Adriaan Peperzak. Referring to the "rose in the cross of the present," Peperzak writes:

> In a veiled manner . . . Hegel could be understood here to be directing himself to the king and his reactionary advisers with the message that true philosophy . . . does precisely what they wish: it legitimizes the reconciliation and satisfaction with the existing political reality by showing that it is as beautiful as a rose—in spite of its painful aspects. The fact that Hegel is not on their side, however, but on the side of the modern, post-Napoleonic legal state . . . choosing in favor of enlightened ministers such as Herdenberg and Altenstein, is clear from the main text of the *Philosophy of Right*, but not from the *Preface*. This lack of clarity and *the appearance of agreement with the Rosicrucians among the politicians* are tricks employed in Hegel's rhetoric.[101]

But again, the Rosicrucians were simply not a political force in Prussia in 1821. Thus Hegel would have gained nothing by the "rhetorical trick" of "appearing to agree with the Rosicrucians"—far from it, in fact, since it was the reigning king who had long ago purged his government of Rosicrucian influence. Further, as I have shown, the Rosicrucians were not "paleo-conservatives," blindly reacting to all change and opposing all reform. Christopher MacIntosh writes that "Wöllner was in many ways

99. Westphal, "Context and Structure of Hegel's *Philosophy of Right*," 238.
100. Ibid., 239.
101. Adriaan Th. Peperzak, *Philosophy and Politics: A Commentary on the Preface to Hegel's Philosophy of Right* (Dordrecht: Martinus Nijhoff, 1987), 109; my italics.

a product of the Aufklärung."[102] He contributed articles to Friedrich Nicolai's *Allgemeine Deutsche Bibliothek*, the chief organ of the German Enlightenment, and wrote essays on agriculture and land reform. Moreover, many of the "reactionary" views of the Rosicrucians were shared by Hegel. For instance, Hegel opposed forces that would undermine traditional religion, particularly irreligious philosophies; he held that all citizens ought to be required to subscribe to a religion; he held that it is the "supreme duty" of citizens to belong to the state, etc. To be sure, Hegel *is* more liberal than Wöllner et al: he believes in greater freedom of religion and advocates greater freedom of expression than did the Rosicrucians, but his sentiments are decidedly paternalistic, pro-Christian, pro-tradition, and anti-individualistic. (The claim that conservatism means opposition to all reforms, including conservative ones, is simply a caricature and a canard.)

Peperzak claims that Hegel only "appears" to agree with the Rosicrucians in their opposition to utopianism and their advocacy of the conservative view that society as it is, warts and all, is at bottom "rational" and cannot and should not be otherwise. Given that Hegel had nothing to gain from merely appearing to agree with the Rosicrucians, we must consider the possibility that he *really does agree with them*. Thus, Hegel's metaphor of the "rose in the cross of the present" is hardly a bone thrown to the king's censors, but rather a *daring* move: an expression of sympathy with the discredited advisors of the previous monarch. My conclusion is that when, in 1821, Hegel set down his mature views on political philosophy, prefacing them with an attack on utopianism and political rationalism, he considered the place in which he was then working, Berlin, and found himself feeling some sympathy with the conservative Rosicrucians who had dominated the court of the previous king.

As we have seen, in Berlin Hegel allied himself with Franz von Baader, the reactionary occultist and opponent of Enlightenment. Baader was reputed to have been a member of the Gold and Rosy-Cross. This would certainly be a strange friendship for Hegel to publicly cultivate if he wanted to distance himself from the forces of "reaction" that were still alive in Prussia. Despite significant differences between Hegel's philosophy and Baader's, Hegel wrote to Baader in 1824, concerning the latter's *Fermenta Cognitionis*, "I think we are in agreement on the main issue. A few misgivings concerning a small number of points which you cite from my work probably would easily be removed." He closes by saying, "Please spare me an evening sometime soon. Let me know which evening this week you are free and could grant me the kindness of a visit. Most respectfully, Hegel."[103]

---

102. MacIntosh, *The Rose Cross*, 180.
103. Butler, 572–73; Hoffmeister #466a. In 1822, Baader and Baron Boris von Üxküll, a former Hegel student, set out for St. Petersburg to try and found an Academy for Religious Science. Baader invited Hegel along, but he declined (a good thing, since Baader and Üxküll were unceremoniously expelled from Russia; see Butler, 568–69).

As d'Hondt has discussed extensively, Hegel's early life was marked by numerous associations with Freemasonry. There is no evidence that Hegel ever actually became a Mason, but he was friends with many well-known Masons and, as we have seen in chapters 2 and 4, he employed some Masonic imagery in his writing. Hegel's correspondence with Schelling and Hölderlin contains Masonic allusions. Recall Hegel's January 1795 letter to Schelling: "May the Kingdom of God come, and our hands not be idle!" The last line before Hegel's signature reads, "Reason and Freedom remain our watchword, and our rallying point the Invisible Church."[104] In later years, however, Hegel realized that the Kingdom of God *had already come*. There was thus no need for busy hands, or for a rallying point. If we juxtapose these remarks from 1795 with Hegel's "rose in the cross of the present" of 1821, it is apparent that Hegel has, in effect, switched allegiances from the ideals of the radical, reforming Masons to those of the conservative Rosicrucians.[105]

The possibility that Hegel might actually have belonged to the Rosicrucians, or some other mystical sect, is tantalizing but, at present, devoid of proof. Nevertheless, in the sense in which Yates uses the term, Hegel is a Rosicrucian. Yates writes that "I should like to try to persuade sensible people and sensible historians to use the word 'Rosicrucian'. . . . The word could, I suggest, be used of a certain style of thinking which is historically recognizable without raising the question of whether a Rosicrucian style of thinker belonged to a secret society."[106]

In his *Enlightenment and Romanticism in Eighteenth-Century Prussia*, Henri Brunschwig discusses a certain character type prevalent in late eighteenth and early nineteenth century Germany: men who hunger after wisdom, particularly esoteric wisdom or forbidden ideas, and who are consequently attracted to "secret societies" like the Masons. They are disillusioned, inevitably, by the Masons, whose "mysteries" prove nonexistent. Brunschwig writes that such men

> believe that even if the lodges do not possess the secrets, that is no proof that the mystery does not exist. So they set to work in isolation. They read Jakob Böhme or Franz von Baader; they listen to Baron Eckhartshausen and Jung-Stilling in his old age, high priests who wrangle over each other's followers. They canvass such

104. Butler, 32; Hoffmeister #8.

105. In his *Lectures on the History of Philosophy* of 1805, Hegel bitterly dismisses Freemasonry: "Just as the Freemasons have symbols which are esteemed for their depth of wisdom—depth as a brook is deep when one cannot see the bottom—that which is hidden very easily seems to men deep, or as if the depth were concealed beneath. But when it is hidden, it may possibly prove to be the case that there is nothing behind. This is so in Freemasonry, in which everything is concealed to those outside and also to many people within, and where nothing remarkable is possessed in learning or in science, and least of all in philosophy" (LHP 1:89; *Werke* 18:110).

106. Frances A. Yates, "The Hermetic Tradition in Renaissance Science," in *Art, Science, and History in the Renaissance*, ed. Charles S. Singleton (Baltimore: Johns Hopkins Press, 1968), 263.

recent scientific discoveries as electricity, magnetism, and oxygen and combine experiments with them with the ideas of the ancient mystics in new systems based on a popularization of theosophy.[107] This is a description of the sort of men who identified themselves as "Rosicrucians," and—aside from the interest in Eckartshausen and Jung-Stilling—it is a very apt description of Hegel.

I have argued that Hegel is a Hermetic thinker. I have offered three kinds of evidence. First I have argued that Hegel displays the essential characteristic of Hermeticism: the doctrine that God alone is not complete, that He lacks self-knowledge, and that He therefore creates the world as the mirror in which He recognizes Himself, specifically through the speculative activity of the Hermetic adept, who by knowing God, allows God to know Himself. Hegel claims to be such an adept, having replaced the love of wisdom with the possession of wisdom, philosophy with theosophy. Second, I have argued that Hegel was interested in and influenced by strands of thought associated with most, if not all, Hermetic thinkers, such as alchemy, Kabbalism, mesmerism, extrasensory perception, spiritualism, dowsing, eschatology, *prisca theologia*, *philosophia perennis*, Lullism, Paracelcism, Joachimism, Rosicrucianism, Freemasonry, Eckhartean mysticism, and doctrines of occult "correspondences" and "cosmic sympathies." Third, by presenting ample evidence of Hegel's contacts with the Hermetic tradition throughout his intellectual career, I have shown that the parallels between Hegel and the Hermetic tradition are not accidental.

Have I proven my case? This question leads to another question: What are reasonable standards of evidence for asserting that a thinker belongs to or is influenced by an intellectual tradition? I ask the reader to evaluate the persuasiveness of my evidence by the standard used in a court case: proof beyond a "reasonable" doubt, as opposed to the unreasonable "paper" doubts philosophy professors are so facile in conjuring up. Imagine that Hermeticism is a crime and Hegel is on trial for it. This study could serve as a brief for the prosecution. Let the following serve as my final summation.

Hegel's writings contain numerous, and mostly approving references to Hermeticism: to leading Hermetic figures such as Eckhart, Paracelsus, Bruno, and Böhme, and to Hermetic movements or schools of thought such as alchemy, Kabbalism, Freemasonry, and Rosicrucianism. His library included Hermetic writings by Agrippa, Böhme, Bruno, and Paracelsus. He relied on histories of thought that discussed Hermes Trismegistus, Pico della Mirandola, Robert Fludd, Knorr von Rosenroth, and the Kabbalah alongside canonical figures like Plato and Descartes. He read widely on mesmerism, psychic phenomena, dowsing, precognition, and sorcery. He believed in an "Earth Spirit." He corresponded with colleagues about the nature of magic. He explicitly and

---

107. Brunschwig, *Enlightenment and Romanticism*, 187.

publicly aligned himself with the latter-day Rosicrucians and with the well-known occultist Franz von Baader.

Hegel was, furthermore, exposed to Hermetic ideas and influences throughout his career. Hegel was likely first exposed to Hermeticism during his boyhood in Stuttgart, from 1770–88. His homeland, the Grand Duchy of Württemberg, was a center of Hermetic activity and interest. In Württemberg, moreover, Hermeticism was not confined merely to secret societies. Such figures as Oetinger, Bengel, and Hahn injected the ideas of Joachim, Eckhart, Böhme, and Swedenborg, and of such traditions as Kabbalism, alchemy, and Rosicrucianism, into the Pietist movement, thereby influencing the society at large. The influence of Württemberg's speculative Pietism on Hegel's friends Schelling and Hölderlin is well-documented, and considering the parallels between some of Hegel's ideas and those of the speculative Pietists, it is reasonable to conclude that Hegel too felt their influence.

Rosenkranz calls the years 1793 to 1801, when Hegel worked as a private tutor in Berne and Frankfurt, the "theosophical phase" of his development. During this time, Hegel studied Böhme, Eckhart, and Tauler and associated with many known Freemasons. In Jena, from 1801–7, Hegel lectured at length, and approvingly, on Böhme and Bruno. He composed several works, preserved only in fragmentary form, employing Hermetic language and symbolism, including the "Böhme Myth," the Triangle fragment, and the triangle diagram, with its alchemical and astrological symbolism. His lectures on the Philosophy of Nature also display a knowledge of alchemy. It is also likely that Schelling introduced Hegel to his Jena associates, many of whom were heavily interested in Hermeticism.

During Hegel's years in Berlin, from 1818 until his death in 1831, his interest in Hermeticism became more intense and more explicit. It was during these years that Hegel developed his relationship with Baader. In the winter of 1823–24 Hegel studied Eckhart with Baader and subsequently produced a lecture on religion that Baader took to be a statement of Eckhartian mysticism. During these years, Hegel also began to acknowledge his Hermetic interests more explicitly in his writings. The image of the rose in the cross of the present in the preface to the 1821 *Philosophy of Right* publicly aligned him with the Rosicrucians, a fact that he made even more explicit in a review essay in 1829. The preface to the 1827 edition of the *Encyclopedia of the Philosophical Sciences in Outline* makes prominent mention of Böhme and Baader. The 1827 *Lectures on the Philosophy of Religion* introduce a doctrine of the "immanent Trinity" clearly inspired by Böhme's initial triad of "source-spirits." The 1831 *Lectures on the Philosophy of Religion* employ Joachimite terminology to speak of the Trinity. In the section on *Qualität* in the posthumous 1832 revised edition of the first part of the *Science of Logic*, Hegel makes an explicit reference to Böhme where the first edition has merely an allusion. In sum, all the evidence indicates that Hegel's Hermeticism was no mere folly of youth, abandoned with maturity. It was a lifelong interest, which grew deeper and richer with the passing years.

Finally, Hegel's system itself is Hermetic in both form and content. In addition to presenting the essential Hermetic doctrines concerning creation and man's role in it, Hegel also endorses the Hermetic ideas of the *prisca theologia* and the *philosophia perennis*. He structures his system using the Hermetic symbolic forms of the circle, triangle, and square. He also states more than once that the term *speculative* means the same thing as "mystical." I have shown that the *Phenomenology of Spirit* serves as a kind of initiation ritual, an initial stage of purification that raises the mind above the sensory and the mundane and prepares it for the reception of wisdom. It is a Hermetic ascent to the Absolute—which is set forth in Hegel's *Encyclopedia of the Philosophical Sciences*. I have also displayed a Böhmean subtext to the *Phenomenology*'s famous preface. The structure of Hegel's *Encyclopedia* describes the Hermetic circle of creation and also shows the influences of Lullism and pansophism. I have amply documented the explicitly ontotheological nature of Hegel's *Logic*, as well as its traces of Kabbalism, Böhmeanism, and Lullism. The *Logic* seeks to lay bare the mind of God before creation. As a Hermeticist, however, Hegel regards God before creation as incomplete. To complete himself, God must know himself, and the immediate self-cognition God possesses before creation is not self-knowledge. Self-knowledge requires mediated re-cognition. It requires that the self see itself reflected in another and recognize itself there. The *Philosophy of Nature* portrays the spatio-temporal world as a mirror of God. I have demonstrated its debts to alchemy, Paracelsus in particular. Hegel shows us how the world of Nature is shot through with intelligible anticipations of Spirit, how the very stones "cry out" for Spirit. The *Philosophy of Spirit* and related texts, *The Philosophy of Right*, *The Philosophy of World History*, and the lecture courses on the three moments of Absolute Spirit, art, religion, and philosophy, set forth the "return" of creation to the Divine by means of *man*, who brings about the actualization of God through progressively more adequate embodiments, first in the form of concrete institutions and practices, then in the realm of culture, particularly art and religion, and finally, and most adequately, in Hegel's system of speculative philosophy, which is the Word made flesh, the divine logos spiritually embodied in the pure aether of thought. With this, the Hermetic circle reaches closure. And here too the "prosecution" rests.

Bibliography

1. Works by Hegel

Hegel, Georg Wilhelm Friedrich. "Aphorisms from the Waste-Book." Translated by Susanne Klein, David L. Roochnik, and George Elliott Tucker. *Independent Journal of Philosophy* 3 (1979): 1–6.

——. *Berliner Schriften.* Edited by J. Hoffmeister. Hamburg: Felix Meiner, 1956.

——. *Berliner Schriften, 1818–1831.* Edited by Eva Moldenhauer and Karl Markus Michel. Frankfurt: Suhrkamp, 1986.

——. *Briefe von und an Hegel.* Edited by Johannes Hoffmeister and Rolf Flechsig. 4 vols. Hamburg: Meiner, 1952–61.

——. *The Difference Between Fichte's and Schelling's System of Philosophy.* Translated by H. S. Harris and Walter Cerf. Albany: State University of New York Press, 1977.

——. *Differenz des Fichteschen und Schellingschen Systems der Philosophie.* Vol. 1. *Jenaer Kritische Schriften.* Edited by Hans Brockhard and Hartmut Buchner. Hamburg: Meiner, 1979.

——. *Dissertatio Philosophica de Orbitis Planetarum. Philosophische Erörterung über die Planetenbahnen.* Translated by Wolfgang Neuser. Weinheim: Acta humaniora d. VHC, 1986.

——. *Early Theological Writings.* Translated by T. M. Knox. Chicago: University of Chicago Press, 1948.

——. *Elements of the Philosophy of Right.* Edited by Allen W. Wood. Translated by H. B. Nisbett. Cambridge, U.K.: Cambridge University Press, 1991.

——. *Encyclopedia Logic.* Translated by T. F. Geraets, W. A. Suchting, and H. S. Harris. Indianapolis: Hackett, 1991.

——. *Encyclopedia of the Philosophical Sciences.* Edited by Ernst Behler. Translated by A. V. Miller and Steven A. Taubeneck. New York: Continuum, 1990.

——. *Faith and Knowledge.* Translated by Walter Cerf and H. S. Harris. Albany: State University of New York Press, 1977.

——. "Fragment on the 'Life-Course' of God" (*Wastebook* excerpt 48). Translated by M. H. Hooheimer. *Clio* 11 (1982): 14–24.

——. *Gesammelte Werke.* Edited by Rheinisch-Westfaelischen Akademie der Wissenschaften. Hamburg: Meiner, 1968–.

——. *Glauben und Wissen, oder die Reflexionsphilosophie de Subjektivität, in der Vollständigkeit ihrer Formen, als Kantische, Jacobishe und Fichtesche Philosophie.* Vol. 3. *Jenaer Kritische Schriften.* Edited by Hans Brockhard and Hartmut Buchner. Hamburg: Meiner, 1986.

———. *Grundlinien der Philosophie des Rechts oder Naturrecht und Staatswissenschaft im Grundrisse.* Edited by Eduard Gans. Berlin: Akademie-Verlag, 1981.

———. *G. W. F. Hegel: Theologian of the Spirit.* Edited by Peter C. Hodgson. Minneapolis: Augsburg Fortress, 1997.

———. *Hegel: Three Essays (The Tübingen Essay, Berne Fragments, "Life of Jesus").* Edited and translated by Peter Fuss and John Dobbins. Notre Dame, Ind.: University of Notre Dame Press, 1984.

———. *Hegel: The Letters.* Translated by Clark Butler and Christianne Seiler. Bloomington: Indiana University Press, 1984.

———. *Hegel's Logic. (Encyclopedia Logic).* Translated by William Wallace. London: Oxford University Press, 1873.

———. *Hegel's Phenomenology of Spirit.* Translated by A. V. Miller. Oxford: Oxford University Press, 1977.

———. *Hegel's Philosophy of Mind.* Translated by A. V. Miller. London: Oxford University Press, 1971.

———. *Hegel's Philosophy of Nature.* Translated by A. V. Miller. Oxford: Clarendon, 1970.

———. *Hegel's Philosophy of Subjective Spirit.* 3 vols. Edited and translated by M. J. Petry. Dordrecht: Reidel, 1978.

———. *Hegels Theologische Jugendschriften.* Edited by H. Nohl. Tübingen: J. C. B. Mohr, 1907.

———. *The Jena System (1804–5): Logic and Metaphysics.* Translated by John W. Burbidge and George di Giovanni. Kingston and Montreal: McGill-Queens University Press, 1986.

———. *Jenenser Realphilosophie.* 2 vols. Edited by Johannes Hoffmeister. Leipzig: Meiner, 1931–1932.

———. *Lectures on Aesthetics.* 2 vols. Translated by T. M. Knox. Oxford: Oxford University Press, 1975.

———. *Lectures on the History of Philosophy.* 3 vols. Translated by E. S. Haldane and Francis H. Simson. Lincoln: University of Nebraska Press, 1995.

———. *Lectures on Natural Right and Political Science.* Translated by J. Michael Stewart and Peter C. Hodgson. Berkeley: University of California Press, 1995.

———. *Lectures on the Philosophy of Religion.* 3 vols. Edited by Peter C. Hodgson. Translated by R. F. Brown, P. C. Hodgson, and J. M. Stewart. Berkeley: University of California Press, 1984.

———. *Lectures on the Philosophy of World History.* Translated by H. B. Nisbet. Cambridge, U.K.: Cambridge University Press, 1975.

———. *Mythologie der Vernunft: Hegels "ältestes Systemprogram des deutschen Idealismus."* Edited by Christoph Jamme and Helmut Schneider. Frankfurt am Main: Suhrkamp, 1984.

———. *Phänomenologie des Geistes.* Edited by Hans-Friedrich Wessels and Heinrich Clairmont. Hamburg: Meiner, 1988.

———. *The Phenomenology of Mind.* Translated by J. B. Baillie. New York: Harper and Row, 1967.

———. *Philosophical Dissertation on the Orbits of the Planets (1801) Preceded by the 12 Theses Defended on August 27, 1801.* Translated by Pierre Adler. *Graduate Faculty Philosophy Journal* 11 (1987): 269–309.

———. *Philosophy of Nature.* 3 vols. Translated by M. J. Petry. London: Allen and Unwin, 1970.

———. *Philosophy of Right.* Translated by T. M. Knox. London: Oxford University Press, 1952.

——. Review of K. F. Göschel, *Aphorismen über Nichtwissen und absolutes Wissen in Verhältnisse zur christlichen Glaubenserkenntnis*. In *Berliner Schriften, 1818–1831*, edited by Eva Moldenhauer and Karl Markus Michel. Frankfurt am Main: Suhrkamp, 1986.

——. *Sämtliche Werke*. 20 vols. Edited by Hermann Glockner. Stuttgart: Fromann, 1936–57.

——. *Science of Logic*. Translated by A. V. Miller. Atlantic Highlands, N.J.: Humanities Press, 1969.

——. *System of Ethical Life and First Philosophy of Spirit*. Translated by H. S. Harris and T. M. Knox. Albany: State University of New York Press, 1979.

——. *System der Sittlichkeit*. 2nd ed. Edited by G. Lasson. Hamburg: Felix Meiner Verlag, 1923.

——. *Werke*. 20 vols. Edited by Eva Moldenhauer and Karl Markus Michel. Frankfurt am Main: Suhrkamp, 1971.

——. *Wissenschaft der Logik*. 3 vols. Edited by Leopold von Henning. Berlin: Duncker und Humblot, 1840–47.

——. *Wissenschaft der Logik*. 4 vols. Edited by Hans-Jürgen Gawoll. Hamburg: Meiner. *Das Sein* (1812), 1986; *Die Lehre vom Sein* (1832), 1990; *Die Lehre vom Wesen* (1813), 1992; *Die Lehre vom Begriff* (1816), 1994.

——. *Wissenschaftliche Behandlungsarten des Naturrechts*. In his *Gesammelte Werke*. Vol. 4. Edited by Harmut Buchner und Otto Pöggeler. Hamburg: Felix Meiner Verlag, 1968.

2. Works Treating Hegel

Adams, George Plimpton. "The Mystical Element in Hegel's Early Theological Writings." *University of California Publications in Philosophy* 2 (1910): 67–102.

Anonymous. *Berzeichniss der von dem Professor Herrn Dr. Hegel und dem Dr. Herrn Seebeck hinterlassen Bücher-Sammlungen*. Berlin, 1832.

Aulnis de Bourrouill, J.d'. "Het mystieke karakter van Hegel's logica." *Algemeine nederlands tijdschrift voor wijsbegeerte en psychologie* 10 (1916): 79–84.

Baur, Ferdinand Christian. *Die Christliche Gnosis*. Tübingen: Osiander, 1835.

Baur, Michael, and John Russon, eds. *Hegel and the Tradition: Essays in Honor of H. S. Harris*. Toronto: University of Toronto Press, 1997.

Bolland, Gerardus Johannes Petrus Josephus. *Schelling, Hegel, Fechner en de nieuwere theosophie: Eene geschiedkundige vooren in lichting*. Leiden: Adriani, 1910.

Bruaire, Claude. *Logique et religion chrétienne dans la philosophie de Hegel*. Paris: Éditions du Seuil, 1964.

Butler, Clark. "Hegelian Panentheism and Joachimite Christianity." In *New Perspectives on Hegel's Philosophy of Religion*, edited by David Kolb. Albany: State University of New York Press, 1992.

Cerf, Walter. "Speculative Philosophy and Intellectual Intuition: An Introduction to Hegel's *Essays*." In *Faith and Knowledge*, translated by Walter Cerf and H. S. Harris. Albany: State University of New York Press, 1977.

Chapelle, Albert. *Hegel et la religion*. 3 vols. Paris: Éditions Universitaires, 1964–71.

Clark, Malcolm. *Logic and System: A Study of the Transition from "Vorstellung" to Thought in the Philosophy of Hegel*. The Hague: Martinus Nijhoff, 1971.

Comoth, Katharina. "Hegels 'Logik' und die speculative Mystik." *Hegel-Studien* 19 (1984): 110–30.

Cottier, M.-M. *L'Atheisme Du Jeune Marx: Ses Origines Hegeliennes*. Paris: Vrin, 1969.

Darby, Tom. *The Feast: Meditations on Politics and Time*. Toronto: University of Toronto Press, 1982.

Desmond, William. *Desire, Dialectic and Otherness: An Essay on Origins*. New Haven, Conn.: Yale University Press, 1987.

de Vries, Willem A. *Hegel's Theory of Mental Activity*. Ithaca, N.Y.: Cornell University Press, 1988.

d'Hondt, Jacques. *Hegel in His Time*. Translated by John Burbidge. Lewiston, N.Y.: Broadview Press, 1988.

—— *Hegel Secret: Recherches sur les sources cachées de la pensée de Hegel*. Paris: Presses Universitaires de France, 1968.

—— *Verborgene Quellen des Hegelschen Denkens*. Translated by Joachim Wilke. 2nd ed. Berlin: Akademie Verlag, 1983.

Dickey, Lawrence. *Hegel: Religion, Economics and the Politics of Spirit 1770–1807*. Cambridge, U.K.: Cambridge University Press, 1987.

Düsing, Klaus. "Absolut Identität und Formen der Endlichkeit: Interpretationen zu Schellings und Hegels erster absoluter Metaphysik." *Schellings und Hegels erste absolute Metaphysik* (1801–1802). Edited by Klaus Düsing. Köln: Jürgen Dinter, 1988.

Fackenheim, Emil. *The Religious Dimension in Hegel's Thought*. Bloomington: Indiana University Press, 1967.

Figala, Karin. "Der alchemische Begriff der *Caput Mortuum* in der symbolischen Terminologie Hegels." In *Stuttgarter Hegel-Tage 1970*, edited by H. G. Gadamer. Bonn: Bouvier, 1974.

Findlay, J. N. *Hegel: A Re-Examination*. London: Allen and Unwin, 1958.

Gadamer, Hans-Georg. "Hegel's 'Inverted World.'" In his *Hegel's Dialectic: Five Hermeneutical Studies*, translated by P. Christopher Smith. New Haven, Conn.: Yale University Press, 1976.

Goedewaagen, T. "Hegel und der Patheismus." *Hegel-Studien* 6 (1971): 171–87.

Hanratty, Gerald. "Hegel and the Gnostic Tradition: I." *Philosophical Studies* (Ireland) 30 (1984): 23–48.

——. "Hegel and the Gnostic Tradition: II." *Philosophical Studies* (Ireland) 31 (1986–87): 301–25.

Harris, Errol. *Formal, Transcendental, and Dialectical Thinking: Logic and Reality*. Albany: State University of New York, Press, 1987.

——. *An Interpretation of the Logic of Hegel*. Lanham, Md.: University Press of America, 1983.

Harris, H. S. General Introduction. In *The Jena System (1804–5): Logic and Metaphysics*, translated by John W. Burbidge and George di Giovanni. Kingston and Montreal: McGill-Queens University Press, 1986.

——. *Hegel's Development: Toward The Sunlight (1770–1801)*. London: Oxford University Press, 1972.

——. *Hegel's Development: Night Thoughts (Jena 1801–1806)*. London: Oxford University Press, 1983.

——. "Hegel's *System of Ethical Life*: An Interpretation." In *System of Ethical Life and First Philosophy of Spirit*, translated by H. S. Harris and T. M. Knox. Albany: State University of New York Press, 1979.

——. Introduction to *Faith and Knowledge*. In *Faith and Knowledge*, translated by Walter Cerf and H. S. Harris. Albany: State University of New York Press, 1977.

———. Introduction to the *Difference* Essay. In *The Difference Between Fichte's and Schelling's System of Philosophy*, translated by H. S. Harris and Walter Cerf. Albany: State University of New York Press, 1977.

———. Introduction to the *First Philosophy of Spirit*. In *System of Ethical Life and First Philosophy of Spirit*, translated by H. S. Harris and T. M. Knox. Albany: State University of New York Press, 1979.

Hartmann, Klaus. "Hegel: A Non-Metaphysical View." In *Hegel: A Collection of Critical Essays*, Edited by Alasdair MacIntyre. Notre Dame University of Notre Dame Press, 1972.

Häussermann, Friedrich. "Das 'gottliche Dreieck' und seine Bedeutung für die Philosophie Hegels." *Zentrallblatt für Psychotherapie* 11 (1939): 359–79.

Haym, R. *Hegel und seine Zeit*. Leipzig: Heims, 1857.

Heidegger, Martin. "The Onto-Theo-Logical Constitution of Metaphysics." In *Identity and Difference*. Bilingual ed. Translated by Joan Stambaugh. New York: Harper and Row, 1969.

Hirsch, Emanuel. *Die idealistische Philosophie und das Christentum*. Gütersloh: Bertelsmann, 1926.

Hoffmeister, Johannes, ed. *Dokumente zu Hegels Entwicklung*. Stuttgart: Fromann, 1936.

Hyppolite, Jean. *The Genesis and Structure of Hegel's Phenomenology of Spirit*. Translated by Samuel Cherniak and John Heckman. Evanston: Northwestern University Press, 1974.

Iljin, Iwan. *Die Philosophie Hegels als kontemplative Gotteslehre*. Berne: Franke, 1946.

Jaeschke, Walter. *Reason in Religion: The Formation of Hegel's Philosophy of Religion*. Translated by J. Michael Stewart and Peter Hodgson. Berkeley: University of California, 1990.

———. *Die Religionsphilosophie Hegels*. Darmstadt: Wissenschaftliche Buchgesellschaft, 1983.

———. "Speculative and Anthropological Criticism of Religion: A Theological Orientation to Hegel and Feuerbach." *Journal of the American Academy of Religion* 48 (1980): 345–64.

Kelly, Sean. *Individuation and the Absolute: Hegel, Jung and the Path Toward Wholeness*. New York: Paulist Press, 1993.

Kimmerle, Heinz. "Dokumente zu Hegels Jenaer Dozententätigkeit (1801–1807)," *Hegel-Studien* 4 (1967): 21–100.

———. *Das Problem der Abgeschlossenheit des Denkens, Hegels 'System der Philosophie' in Jahren 1800–1804*. Bonn: Bouvier, 1970.

———. "Die von Rosenkranz uberlieferten Texte Hegels aus der Jenaer Zeit." *Hegel-Studien* 5 (1969): 83–94.

———. "Zur Chronologie von Hegels Jenaer Schriften." *Hegel-Studien* 4 (1967): 125–76.

Klaiber, Julius. *Hölderlin, Hegel und Schelling in ihren schwäbischen Jugendjahren*. Stuttgart: Cotta, 1877.

Kojève, Alexandre. *Introduction to the Reading of Hegel*. Edited by Allan Bloom. Translated by James H. Nichols Jr. Ithaca, N.Y.: Cornell University Press, 1969.

Kolb, David. *Critique of Pure Modernity: Hegel, Heidegger, and After*. Chicago: University of Chicago Press, 1986.

———, ed. *New Perspectives on Hegel's Philosophy of Religion*. Albany: State University of New York Press, 1992.

Lichtenstein, Ernst. "Von Meister Eckhart bis Hegel: Zur philosophischen Entwicklung des deutschen Bildungsbegriff." In *Kritik und Metaphysik*, edited by Friedrich Kaulbeck and Joachim Ritter. Berlin: De Gruyter, 1966.

Löwith, Karl. *From Hegel to Nietzsche: The Revolution in Nineteenth-Century Thought.* Translated by David E. Green. New York: Columbia University Press, 1964.

Mitscherling, Jeff. "The Identity of the Human and the Divine in the Logic of Speculative Philosophy." In *Hegel and the Tradition: Essays in Honor of H. S. Harris,* edited by Michael Baur and John Russon. Toronto: University of Toronto Press, 1997.

Mook, H.W. *Hegeliaansch-theosofische opstellen.* Amersfoort: Veen, 1913.

Müller, Gustav E. "The Hegel Legend of 'Thesis-Antithesis-Synthesis.'" In *The Hegel Myths and Legends,* edited by Jon Stewart. Evanston: Northwestern University Press, 1996.

Mure, G. R. G. *A Study of Hegel's Logic.* London: Oxford University Press, 1950.

Nicolin, Günther, ed. *Hegel in Berichten seiner Zeitgenossen.* Hamburg: Felix Meiner, 1970.

Noack, Ludwig. *Die Christliche Mystik nach ihrem geschichtlichen Entwicklungsgange im Mittelalter und in der neueren Zeit dargestellt.* 2 vols. Königsberg: Bornträger, 1853.

Olson, Alan M. *Hegel and the Spirit: Philosophy as Pneumatology.* Princeton, N.J.: Princeton University Press, 1992.

O'Regan, Cyril. "Hegelian Philosophy of Religion and Eckhartian Mysticism." In *New Perspectives on Hegel's Philosophy of Religion,* edited by David Kolb. Albany: State University of New York Press, 1992.

———. *The Heterodox Hegel.* Albany: State University of New York Press, 1994.

———. "Hegel and Anti-Judaism: Narrative and the Inner Circulation of the Kabbalah." *The Owl of Minerva* 28 (1997): 141–82.

Peperzak, Adriaan Th. *Philosophy and Politics: A Commentary on the Preface to Hegel's Philosophy of Right.* Dordrecht: Martinus Nijhoff, 1987.

Pöggeler, Otto. "Hegel der Verfasser des ältesten Systemprogramms des deutschen Idealismus." *Hegel-Studien,* Beiheft 4 (1969): 17–32.

Ralfs, G. "Lebensformen des Geistes Meister Eckhart und Hegel." *Kant Studien,* suppl. no. 86 (1966).

Redding, Paul. *Hegel's Hermeneutics.* Ithaca, N.Y.: Cornell University Press, 1996.

Rosenkranz, Karl. *G.W.F. Hegels Leben.* Berlin: Dunker und Humblot, 1944.

———. "Hegels ursprüngliches System, 1798–1806." *Literarhistorisches Taschenbuch* 2 (1844): 157–64.

Schneider, Helmut. "Anfänge der Systementwicklung Hegels in Jena." *Hegel-Studien* 10 (1975): 133–71.

———. "Zur Dreiecks-Symbolik bei Hegel." *Hegel Studien* 8 (1973): 55–77.

Schneider, Robert. *Schellings und Hegels schwabische Geistesahnen.* Würzburg: Tiltsch, 1938.

Schüler, Gisela. "Zur Chronologie von Hegels Jugendschriften." *Hegel-Studien* 2 (1963): 111–59.

Schultz, W. "Begegnugen Hegels mit der deutschen Mystik." In *Sammlung und Sendung vom Auftrag der Kirche in der Welt,* edited by Joachim Heubach and Heinrich-Hermann Ulrich. Berlin: Christlicher Zeitschriften Verlag, 1958.

———. "Der Einflüsse der deutschen Mystik auf Hegels Philosophie." In *Theologie und Wirklichkeit,* edited by Werner Schultz and Hans-Georg Pust. Kiel: Lutherische Verlagsgesellschaft, 1969.

Schussler, Ingrid. "Boehme and Hegel." *Jahrbuch der Schlesichen Friedrich Wilhelms Universitat* 10 (1965): 45–58.

Smith, John H. *The Spirit and Its Letter: Traces of Rhetoric in Hegel's Philosophy of Bildung*. Ithaca, N.Y.: Cornell University Press, 1988.

Stallmach, Josef. "Das Absolute und die Dialektik bei Cusanus im Vergleich zu Hegel." *Scholastik* 39 (1964): 495–509.

Verene, Donald Phillip. *Hegel's Recollection: A Study of Images in the Phenomenology of Spirit*. Albany: State University of New York Press, 1985.

——. "Two Sources of Philosophical Memory: Vico versus Hegel." In *Philosophical Imagination and Cultural Memory: Appropriating Historical Traditions*, edited by Patricia Cook. Durham, N.C.: Duke University Press, 1991.

Voegelin, Eric. *In Search of Order*. Vol. 5. *Order and History*. Baton Rouge: Louisiana State University Press, 1987.

——. "On Hegel: A Study in Sorcery." In *Published Essays 1966–1985*. Vol. 12. *The Collected Works of Eric Voegelin*, edited by Ellis Sandoz. Baton Rouge: Louisiana State University Press, 1990.

——. "Response to Professor Altizer's 'A New History and a New but Ancient God.'" In *Published Essays 1966–1985*. Vol. 12. *The Collected Works of Eric Voegelin*, edited by Ellis Sandoz. Baton Rouge: Louisiana State University Press, 1990.

——. *Science, Politics, and Gnosticism: Two Essays*. Translated by William J. Fitzpatrick. Washington, D.C.: Regnery, 1968.

Walsh, David. *The Esoteric Origins of Modern Ideological Thought: Hegel and Boehme*. Ph.D. dissertation, University of Virginia, 1978.

——. "The Historical Dialectic of Spirit: Jacob Boehme's Influence on Hegel." In *History and System: Hegel's Philosophy of History*, edited by Robert L. Perkins. Albany: State University of New York Press, 1984.

Westphal, Kenneth. "The Basic Context and Structure of Hegel's *Philosophy of Right*." In *The Cambridge Companion to Hegel*, edited by Frederick C. Beiser. Cambridge, U.K.: Cambridge University Press, 1993.

Wiedmann, Franz. *Hegel: An Illustrated Biography*. Translated by Joachim Neugroschel. New York: Pegasus, 1968.

White, Alan. *Absolute Knowledge: Hegel and the Problem of Metaphysics*. Athens, Ohio: Ohio University Press, 1983.

Winfield, Richard Dien. "On Individuality." In his *Freedom and Modernity*. Albany: State University of New York Press, 1991.

Yack, Bernard. *The Longing for Total Revolution: Philosophic Sources of Social Discontent from Rousseau to Marx and Nietzsche*. Berkeley: University of California Press, 1992.

3. Other Sources

Abrams, M. H. *Natural Supernaturalism: Tradition and Revolution in Romantic Literature*. New York: W. W. Norton, 1971.

Aesch, Alexander Gode-von. *Natural Science in German Romanticism*. New York: AMS Press, 1966.

Agrippa, Heinrich Cornelius (von Nettesheim). *Of the Vanitie and Uncertaintie of Artes and Sciences*. Edited by Catherine M. Dunn. Northridge, Calif.: California State Press, 1974.

——. *Three Books of Occult Philosophy*. Edited by Donald Tyson. Translated by James Freake. St. Paul, Minn.: Llewellyn Publications, 1995.

Andrae, John Valentin. *The Chemical Wedding of Christian Rosenkreutz.* Translated by Joscelyn Godwin. Introduction and commentary by Adam McLean. Magnum Opus Hermetic Sourceworks #18. Grand Rapids, Mich.: Phanes Press, 1991.

——. *Turris Babel sive Judiciorum de Fraternitate Rosaceae Crucis Chaos.* Argentorati: Sumptibus haeredum Lazari Zetzberi, 1619.

Anonymous. *The Theologia Germanica of Martin Luther.* Translated by Bengt Hoffman. New York: Paulist Press, 1980.

Aristotle. *De Anima.* Translated by Hippocrates G. Apostle. In *Aristotle: Selected Works,* edited by Hippocrates G. Apostle and Lloyd Gerson. Grinnell, Iowa: Peripatetic Press, 1982.

Augustine, Aurelius (Saint). *The City of God.* Translated by Marcus Dods. New York: Modern Library, 1950.

Baader, Franz von. *Fermenta Cognitionis.* 6 vols. (Berlin: G. Reimer, 1822–25).

Barnstone, Willis, ed. *The Other Bible.* San Francisco: Harper and Row, 1984.

Bartsch, Gerhard. "Zur Geschichte der Dialektik im alteren deutschen Pantheismus (vom Cusanus bis Böhme)." *Deutsche Zeitschrift für Philosophie* 16 (1968): 503–604.

Basnage, Jacques. *The History of the Jews from Jesus Christ to the Present Time: Containing their Antiquities, their Religion, their Rites, the Dispersion of the Ten Tribes in the East, and the Persecutions this Nation has suffered in the West. Being a Supplement and Continuation of the History of Josephus.* London: T. Bever and B. Lintot, 1708.

Baumgardt, David. *Franz von Baader und die philosophische Romantik.* Halle: Max Niemeyer, 1928.

Beach, Edward Allen. *The Potencies of Gods: Schelling's Philosophy of Mythology.* Albany: State University of New York Press, 1994.

Beck, Lewis White. *Early German Philosophy.* Cambridge, Mass.: Harvard University Press, 1969.

Beiser, Frederick C. *The Early Political Writings of the German Romantics.* Edited and translated by Frederick C. Beiser. Cambridge, U.K.: Cambridge University Press, 1996.

——. *Enlightenment, Revolution, and Romanticism: The Genesis of Modern German Political Thought, 1790–1800.* Cambridge, Mass.: Harvard University Press, 1992.

——. *The Fate of Reason: German Philosophy from Kant to Fichte.* Cambridge, Mass.: Harvard University Press, 1987.

Benz, Ernst. *Adam der Mythus vom Urmenschen.* Munich: Barth, 1955.

——. *Der Christliche Kabbala.* Zurich: Rhein Verlag, 1958.

——. *Evolution and Christian Hope: Man's Concept of the Future from the Early Fathers to Teilhard de Chardin.* Translated by Heinz G. Frank. Garden City, N.Y.: Doubleday, 1966.

——. *The Mystical Sources of German Romantic Philosophy.* Translated by Blair R. Reynolds and Eunice M. Paul. Allison Park, Pa.: Pickwick Publications, 1983.

——. "Die Mystik in der Philosophie des deutschen Idealismus." *Euphorion* 46 (1952): 280–300.

——. *The Theology of Electricity.* Translated by Wolfgang Taraba. Allison Park, Pa.: Pickwick Publications, 1989.

Berlin, Isaiah. *The Magus of the North: J. G. Hamann and the Origins of Modern Irrationalism.* Edited by Henry Hardy. London: John Murray, 1993.

Blau, Joseph Leon. *The Christian Interpretation of the Cabala in the Renaissance.* New York: Columbia University Press, 1944.

Böhme, Jakob. *Aurora, oder Morgenröte im Aufgang.* Edited by Gerhard Wehr. Frankfurt am Main: Insel, 1991.

———. *The Aurora.* Translated by John Sparrow. London, 1656. Edited by C. J. Barker and D. S. Hehner. London: John M. Watkins, 1914.

———. *Jakob Böhme: Essential Readings.* Edited by Robin Waterfield. Wellingborough, England: Crucible/Thorsens, 1989.

———. *Sämtliche Schriften.* 11 vols. Edited by Will-Erich Peuckert. Stuttgart: Frommann, 1955–61. Reprint of *Theosophia revelata. Das ist: Alle Göttliche Schriften des Gottseligen und Hocherleuchteten Deutschen Theosophi Jacob Böhmens.* 11 vols. Edited by Johann Georg Gichtel and Johann Wilhelm Ueberfeld. Amsterdam, 1730.

Bonardel, Francoise. "Alchemical Esotericism and the Hermeneutics of Culture." In *Modern Esoteric Spirituality,* edited by Antoine Faivre and Jacob Needleman. New York: Crossroad, 1995.

Bonner, Anthony. Editor's Introduction. In *Doctor Illuminatus: A Ramon Llull Reader,* edited by Anthony Bonner. Princeton, N.J.: Princeton University Press, 1985.

Bracken, Ernst von. *Meister Eckhart und Fichte.* Würzburg: Triltsch, 1943.

Brann, Henry Walter. "Spinoza and the Kabbalah." In *Speculum Spinozanum 1677–1977,* edited by Siegfried Hessing. London: Routledge and Kegan Paul, 1977.

Brinton, Howard Haines. *The Mystic Will, based on a study of the philosophy of Jacob Boehme.* New York: Macmillan, 1930.

Broek, Roelef van den. "Gnosticism and Hermetism: Two Roads to Salvation." In *Gnosis and Hermeticism From Antiquity to Modern Times,* edited by Roelef van den Broek and Wouter J. Hanegraff. Albany: State University of New Press, 1998.

———, and Wouter J. Hanegraff, eds. *Gnosis and Hermeticism From Antiquity to Modern Times.* Albany: State University of New Press, 1998.

Brown, Robert. *The Later Philosophy of Schelling: The Influence of Boehme on the Works of 1809–1815.* Lewisburg, Pa.: Bucknell University Press, 1972.

Brucker, Johann Jacob. *Historia Critica Philosophiae.* 5 vols. Leipzig: Breitkopf, 1742–44

Bruno, Giordano. *The Ash Wednesday Supper.* Translated by Stanley L. Jaki. The Hague: Mouton, 1975.

———. *The Expulsion of the Triumphant Beast.* Edited and translated by Arthur D. Imerti. New Brunswick, N.J.: Rutgers University Press, 1964.

———. *On the Composition of Images, Signs, and Ideas.* Edited by Dick Higgins. Translated by Charles Doria. New York: Willis, Locker, and Owens, 1991.

———. *Oratio valedictoria.* Wittenberg, 1588.

Brunschwig, Henri. *Enlightenment and Romanticism in Eighteenth-Century Prussia.* Translated by Frank Jellinek. Chicago: University of Chicago Press, 1974.

Burger, H. O. *Schwabentum in der Geistesgeschichte.* Stuttgart and Berlin: J. G. Cotta, 1933.

Campbell, Joseph. *The Hero with a Thousand Faces.* 2nd ed. Princeton, N.J.: Princeton University Press, 1968.

———. *The Masks of God: Primitive Mythology.* New York: Penguin Books, 1959.

——. *The Masks of God: Occidental Mythology*. New York: Penguin Books, 1964.

——. *Transformations of Myth Through Time*. New York: Harper and Row, 1990.

Capková, Dagmar. "Comenius and His Ideals: Escape from the Labyrinth." In *Samuel Hartlib and Universal Reformation*, edited by Mark Greengrass, Michael Leslie, and Timothy Raylor. Cambridge, U.K.: Cambridge University Press, 1994.

Cassirer, Ernst. *The Individual and the Cosmos in Renaissance Philosophy*. Translated by Mario Domandi. New York: Harper and Row, 1963.

Clucas, Stephen. "In Search of 'The True Logick': Methodological Eclecticism Among the Baconian Reformers." In *Samuel Hartlib and Universal Reformation*, edited by Mark Greengrass, Michael Leslie, and Timothy Raylor. Cambridge, U.K.: Cambridge University Press, 1994.

Comenius, John. *The Labyrinth of the World and the Paradise of the Heart*. Translated by Howard Louthan and Andrea Stark. New York: Paulist Press, 1998.

Copenhaver, Brian. *Hermetica: The Greek Corpus Hermeticum and the Latin Asclepius in a New English Translation with Notes and Introduction*. Cambridge, U.K.: Cambridge University Press, 1992.

Coudert, Alison. *Alchemy: The Philosopher's Stone*. London: Wildwood House, 1980.

——. *Leibniz and the Kabbalah*. Boston: Kluwer, 1995.

——. "Some Theories of a Natural Language from the Renaissance to the Seventeenth Century." *Studia Leibnitiana Sonderheft* (1978): 56–114.

Croll, Oswald. *Philosophy Reformed and Improved. . . . The Mysteries of Nature by . . . Osw. Crollius*. Translated by H. Pinnell. London: Lodowick Lloyd, 1657.

——. *Signatures of Internal Things*. In Croll, *Basilica Chymica*. Translated by John Hartman. London: John Stukey and Thomas Passenger: 1669–70.

D'Alembert, Jean Le Rond. *Preliminary Discourse to the Encyclopedia of Diderot* (1751). Translated by Richard N. Schwab. Chicago: University of Chicago Press, 1995.

Debus, Allen G. "Alchemy in the Age of Reason: The Chemical Philosophers in Early Eighteenth Century France." In *Hermeticism and the Renaissance: Intellectual History and the Occult in Early Modern Europe*, edited by Ingrid Merkel and Allen G. Debus. Washington, D.C.: Folger Books, 1988.

——. *The Chemical Philosophy: Paracelsian Science and Medicine in the Sixteenth and Seventeenth Centuries*. 2 vols. New York: Science History Publications, 1977.

——. *Man and Nature in the Renaissance*. Cambridge, U.K.: Cambridge University Press, 1978.

Deghaye, Pierre. "Jacob Boehme and His Followers." In *Modern Esoteric Spirituality*, edited by Antoine Faivre and Jacob Needleman. New York: Crossroad, 1995.

De Lubac, Henri. *La Spiritualité de Joachim de Fiore*. 2 vols. Paris: Sycamore, 1979–81.

Denslow, William R. *10,000 Famous Freemasons*. 4 vols. Trenton, Mo.: The Educational Bureau of the Royal Arch Mason Magazine, 1958.

Dickson, Donald R. *The Tessera of Antilia*. Leiden: Brill, 1998.

Dierauer, Walter. *Hölderlin und der spekulative Pietismus Württembergs: Gemeinsame Aunschauungshorizonte im Werk Oetingers und Hölderlins*. Zürich: Juris, 1986.

Dobbs, Betty Jo Teeter. *The Foundations of Newton's Alchemy or, the Hunting of the Greene Lyon*. Cambridge, U.K.: Cambridge University Press, 1975.

——. *The Janus Face of Genius: The Role of Alchemy in Newton's Thought*. Cambridge, U.K.: Cambridge University Press, 1991.

——. "Newton's Commentary on the *Emerald Tablet* of Hermes Trismegistus: Its Scientific and Theological Significance." In *Hermeticism and the Renaissance: Intellectual History and the Occult in Early Modern Europe*, edited by Ingrid Merkel and Allen G. Debus. Washington, D.C.: Folger Books, 1988.

——, and Margaret C. Jacob. *Newton and the Culture of Newtonianism*. Atlantic Highlands, N.J.: Humanities Press, 1995.

Dummett, Michael. *The Visconti-Sforza Tarot Cards*. New York: G. Braziller, 1986.

Eckermann, Johann Peter. *Conversations of Goethe*. Translated by John Oxenford. New York: Da Capo, 1998.

Eckhart, Meister Johannes. *Deutsche Predigten und Traktate*. Edited by Josef Quint. Munich: Carl Hanser, 1963.

——. *Meister Eckhart, An Introduction to the Study of His Works with an Anthology of His Sermons*. Edited by J. M. Clark. Edinburgh and London: Thomas Nelson and Sons, 1957.

——. *Meister Eckhart: A Modern Translation*. Translated by Raymond Bernard Blakney. New York: Harper, 1941.

——. *Meister Eckhart, die deutschen und lateinischen Werke*. Edited by Deutschen Forschungsgemeinschaft. Stuttgart: Kohlhammer, 1936–.

——. *Sermons and Treatises*. 3 vols. Translated by M. O'C. Walsh. Longmead, Shaftesbury, Dorset: Element Books, 1979.

Edighoffer, Roland. "Hermeticism in Early Rosicrucianism." In *Gnosis and Hermeticism From Antiquity to Modern Times*, edited by Roelef van den Broek and Wouter J. Hanegraff. Albany: State University of New Press, 1998.

——. "Rosicrucianism: From the Seventeenth to the Twentieth Century." In *Modern Esoteric Spirituality*, edited by Antoine Faivre and Jacob Needleman. New York: Crossroad, 1995.

Engelhardt, Dietrich von. "Natural Science in the Age of Romanticism." In *Modern Esoteric Spirituality*, edited by Antoine Faivre and Jacob Needleman. New York: Crossroad, 1995.

Epstein, Klaus. *The Genesis of German Conservatism*. Princeton, N.J.: Princeton University Press, 1966.

Erb, Peter C. Editor's introduction. In *Pietists: Selected Writings*. New York: Paulist Press, 1983.

——, ed. *Pietists: Selected Writings*. Translated by Peter C. Erb. New York: The Paulist Press, 1983.

Evola, Julius. *The Hermetic Tradition*. Translated by E. E. Rehmus. Rochester, Vt.: Inner Traditions, 1995.

——. *The Mystery of the Grail*. Translated by Guido Stucco. Rochester, Vt.: Inner Traditions, 1994.

Faivre, Antoine. *Access to Western Esotericism*. Albany: State University of New York Press, 1994.

——. "Ancient and Medieval Sources of Modern Esoteric Movements." In *Modern Esoteric Spirituality*, edited by Antoine Faivre and Jacob Needleman. New York: Crossroad, 1995.

——. *The Eternal Hermes: From Greek God to Alchemical Magus*. Grand Rapids, Mich.: Phanes Press, 1995.

——. *The Golden Fleece and Alchemy*. Albany: State University of New York Press, 1993.

——. *Mystiques, Théosophes et Illuminés au siècle des Lumières*. Hildesheim: Georg Olms, 1977.

——. *Physica Sacra: Etudes sur Franz von Baader et les Philosophes de la Nature*. Paris: Albin Michel, 1995.

——. "Renaissance Hermeticism and the Concept of Western Esotericism." In *Gnosis and Hermeticism From Antiquity to Modern Times*, edited by Roelef van den Broek and Wouter J. Hanegraff. Albany: State University of New Press, 1998.

——. *Theosophy, Imagination, Tradition: Studies in Western Esotericism*. Translated by Christine Rhone. Albany: State University of New York Press, 2000.

Faivre, Antoine, and Jacob Needleman, eds. *Modern Esoteric Spirituality*. New York: Crossroad, 1995.

Festugière, A. J. *Hermétisme et mystique païenne*. Paris: Aubier-Montaigne, 1967.

——. *La Révélation d'Hermès Trismégiste*. 4 vols. Paris: J. Gabalda, 1950–54.

Fichte, Johann Gottlieb. *Philosophy of Freemasonry: Letters to Constant*. Translated by Roscoe Pound. In his *Masonic Addresses and Writings of Roscoe Pound*. New York: Macoy Publishing and Masonic Supply Company, 1953.

Fideler, David. *Jesus Christ, Sun of God: Ancient Cosmology and Early Christian Symbolism*. Wheaton, Ill.: Quest, 1993.

Fine, Lawrence. *Essential Papers on Kabbalah*. New York: New York University Press, 1995.

Fowden, Garth. *The Egyptian Hermes: A Historical Approach to the Late Pagan Mind*. Princeton, N.J.: Princeton University Press, 1993.

Freher, Dionysus Andrew. *An Illustration of the Deep Principles of Jacob Behmen, the Teutonic Philosopher, in Thirteen Figures*. In *The Key of Jacob Boehme*, translated by William Law. Magnum Opus Hermetic Sourceworks #9. Grand Rapids, Mich.: Phanes Press, 1991.

Friedenthal, Richard. *Goethe: His Life and Times*. London: Weidenfeld, 1963.

Gadamer, Hans-Georg. *Truth and Method*. 2nd rev. ed. Translated by Joel Weinsheimer and Donald G. Marshall. New York: Crossroad, 1989.

Gaier, Ulrich. *Der gesetzliche Kalkül: Hölderlins Dichtungslehre*. Tübingen: Max Niemeyer, 1962.

Gettings, Fred. *Dictionary of Occult, Hermetic, and Alchemical Sigils*. London: Routledge and Kegan Paul, 1981.

Godwin, Joscelyn. *Robert Fludd: Hermetic Philosopher and Surveyor of Two Worlds*. Grand Rapids, Mich.: Phanes Press, 1991.

——. *The Theosophical Enlightenment*. Albany: State University of New York Press, 1994.

Goethe, Johann Wolfgang. *Goethe's Fairy Tale of the Green Snake and the Beautiful Lily*. Edited and translated by Adam McLean. Magnum Opus Hermetic Sourceworks #14. Grand Rapids, Mich.: Phanes Press, 1993.

——. *The Sorrows of the Young Werther*. Translated by Bayard Quincy Morgan. New York: Frederick Ungar Publishing, 1957.

——. *Wilhelm Meister's Apprenticeship*. Translated by Eric A. Blackall. Princeton, N.J.: Princeton University Press, 1989.

Goodrick-Clark, Clare. "The Rosicrucian Afterglow: The Life and Influence of Comenius." In *The Rosicrucian Enlightenment Revisited*, edited by Ralph White. Hudson, N.Y.: Lindisfarne Books, 1999.

Gray, Ronald D. *Goethe the Alchemist: A Study of Alchemical Symbolism in Goethe's Literary and Scientific Works.* Cambridge, U.K.: Cambridge University Press, 1952.

Gutekunst, Eberhard, and Eberhard Zwink, eds. *Zum Himmelreich gelehrt. Friedrich Christoph Oetinger: 1702–1782. Württembergischer Prälat, Theosoph und Naturforscher.* Stuttgart: Württembergische Landesbibliothek and Landeskirkliches Archiv, 1982.

Habermas, Jürgen. *Das Absolute und die Geschichte: Von der Zweispältigkeit in Schellings Denken.* Ph.D. dissertation, Rheinische Friedrich Wilhelms Universität, 1954.

Halevi, Z'ev ben Shimon. *A Kabbalistic Universe.* York Beach, Maine: Samuel Weiser, 1977.

———. *Kabbalah: Tradition of Hidden Knowledge.* London: Thames and Hudson, 1979.

Hall, Manly P. *An Encyclopedic Outline of Masonic, Hermetic, Quabbalistic and Rosicrucian Symbolical Philosophy, Being an Interpretation of the Secret Teachings concealed within the Rituals, Allegories and Mysteries of all Ages.* Los Angeles: The Philosophical Research Society, 1988.

Hanegraaff, Wouter J. "Romanticism and the Esoteric Connection." In *Gnosis and Hermeticism From Antiquity to Modern Times,* edited by Roelef van den Broek, and Wouter J. Hanegraaff. Albany: State University of New Press, 1998.

Hatab, Lawrence J. *Myth and Philosophy: A Contest of Truths.* Lasalle: Open Court, 1990.

Hayden-Roy, Priscilla A. *"A Foretaste of Heaven": Friedrich Hölderlin in the Context of Württemberg Pietism.* Amsterdam: Rodopi, 1994.

Heidegger, Martin. *Being and Time.* Translated by John Macquarrie and Edward Robinson. New York: Harper and Row, 1962.

Hertz, J. H. *The Pentateuch and Haftorahs.* London: Soncino Press, 1961.

Hoffmann, E. T. A. *Tales of E. T. A. Hoffmann.* Edited and translated by Leonard J. Kent and Elizabeth C. Knight. Chicago: University of Chicago Press, 1969.

Hölderlin, Friedrich. *Essays and Letter on Theory.* Translated and edited by Thomas Pfau. Albany: State University of New York Press, 1988.

———. *Hymns and Fragments.* Translated by Richard Sieburth. Princeton, N.J.: Princeton University Press, 1984.

———. *Hyperion and Selected Poems.* Edited by Eric L. Santer. New York: Continuum, 1994.

Horn, Friedemann. *Schelling and Swedenborg: Mysticism and German Idealism.* Translated by George F. Dole. West Chester, Pa.: Swedenborg Foundation, 1997.

Iamblichus. *On the Mysteries of the Egyptians, Chaldeans, and Assyrians.* Translated by Thomas Taylor. San Diego: Wizards Bookshelf, 1984.

Idel, Moshe. "Hermeticism and Judaism." In *Hermeticism and the Renaissance: Intellectual History and the Occult in Early Modern Europe,* edited by Ingrid Merkel and Allen G. Debus. Washington, D.C.: Folger Books, 1988.

———. Introduction to the Bison Books Edition of Johann Reuchlin, *De Arte Cabalistica/On the Art of the Kabbalah.* Bilingual ed. Translated by Martin Goodman and Sarah Goodman. Lincoln: University of Nebraska Press, 1993.

———. *Kabbalah: New Perspectives.* New Haven, Conn.: Yale University Press, 1978.

———. *The Mystical Experience in Abraham Abulafia.* Albany: State University of New York Press, 1988.

———. *Studies in Ecstatic Kabbalah*. Albany: State University of New York Press, 1988.

Jung, Carl Gustav. *Alchemical Studies*. Translated by R. F. C. Hull. Princeton, N.J.: Princeton University Press, 1967.

———. *Jung on Alchemy*. Edited by Nathan Schwartz-Salant. Princeton, N.J.: Princeton University Press, 1995.

———. *Mysterium Coniunctionis: An Inquiry into the Separation and Synthesis of Psychic Opposites in Alchemy*. 2nd ed. Translated by R. F. C. Hull. Princeton, N.J.: Princeton University Press, 1963.

———. *Psychology and Alchemy*. 2nd ed. Translated by R. F. C. Hull. Princeton, N.J.: Princeton University Press, 1968.

Jung, Emma, and Marie-Louise von Franz. *The Grail Legend*. Translated by Andrea Dykes. Boston: Sigo Press, 1986.

Jüngel, Eberhard. *The Doctrine of the Trinity: God's Being is in Becoming*. Translated by Horton Harris. Edinburgh: Scottish Academic Press, 1976.

Kaplan, Aryeh. *Sefer Yetzirah: The Book of Creation in Theory and Practice*. York Beach, Maine: 1990.

———, ed. *The Bahir*. York Beach, Maine: Samuel Weiser, 1979.

Kiesewetter, Carl. *Faust in der Geschichte und Tradition, mit besonderer Berücksichtigung des okkulten Phänomenalismus und des mittelalterlichen Zauberwesens*. 2 vols. Berlin: Herman Barsdorf, 1921.

Kluge, C. A. F. *Versuch einer Darstellung des animalischen Magnetismus*. 3rd ed. Berlin: Salfeld, 1888.

Kroll, Josef. *Die Lehren des Hermes Trismegistos*. Münster: Aschendorffsche Verlagsbuchhandlung, 1914.

Langen, August. *Der Wortschatz des Deutschen Pietismus*. Tübingen: Max Niemeyer, 1968.

Leeses, Kurt. "Von Jakob Böhme zu Schelling." Ph.D. dissertation, University of Erfurt, 1927.

Leibniz, G. W. F. "Introduction to a Secret Science." In *Philosophical Writings*, edited by G. H. R. Parkinson and translated by Mary Morris and G. H. R. Parkinson. London: Everyman, 1973.

———. *Theodicy*. Translated by E. M. Huggard. LaSalle, Ill.: Open Court, 1985.

Lessing, Gotthold Ephraim. *Ernst and Falk, Dialogues for Freemasons*. Translated by Chaninah Maschler. *Interpretation: A Journal of Political Philosophy* 14 (1986): 14–48.

———. *Nathan the Wise: A Dramatic Poem in Five Acts*. Translated by Bayard Quincy Morgan. New York: Ungar, 1955.

Llull, Ramon. *Doctor Illuminatus: A Ramon Llull Reader*. Edited by Anthony Bonner. Princeton, N.J.: Princeton University Press, 1985.

Löwith, Karl. *Meaning in History*. Chicago: University of Chicago Press, 1949.

Lütgert, Karl. *Die Religion des deutschen Idealismus und ihr Ende*. Gütersloh: Bertelsmann, 1923.

Luther, Martin. *Heidelberg Disputation*. In his *Early Theological Writings*, translated by James Atkinson. Philadelphia: Westminster Press, 1962.

McGinn, Bernard. Introduction. In *Apocalyptic Spirituality: Treatises and Letters of Lactantius, Adso of Montier-En-Der, Joachim of Fiore, the Franciscan Spirituals, Savonarola*. New York: Paulist Press, 1979.

———, ed. *Apocalyptic Spirituality: Treatises and Letters of Lactantius, Adso of Montier-En-Der, Joachim of Fiore, the Franciscan Spirituals, Savonarola*. New York: Paulist Press, 1979.

MacIntosh, Christopher. *The Rose Cross and the Age of Reason*. Leiden: E. J. Brill, 1992.

——. "The Rosicrucian Legacy." In *The Rosicrucian Enlightenment Revisited*, edited by Ralph White. Hudson, N.Y.: Lindisfarne Books, 1999.

McKnight, Stephen A. *The Modern Age and the Recovery of Ancient Wisdom: A Reconsideration of Historical Consciousness, 1450–1650*. Columbia: University of Missouri Press, 1991.

——. *Sacralizing the Secular: The Renaissance Origins of Modernity*. Baton Rouge: Louisiana State University Press, 1989.

——, ed. *Science, Pseudo-Science, and Utopianism in Early Modern Thought*. Columbia: University of Missouri Press, 1992.

Mahé, Jean-Pierre. *Hermès en haute-Egypte*. 2 vols. Québec: Presses de l'Université Laval, 1978–82.

Masters, G. Mallary. "Renaissance Kabbalah." In *Modern Esoteric Spirituality*, edited by Antoine Faivre and Jacob Needleman. New York: Crossroad, 1995.

Mayer, Paola. *Jena Romanticism and Its Appropriation of Jacob Böhme: Theosophy, Hagiography, Literature*. Montreal: McGill-Queen's University Press, 1999.

Mazet, Edmond. "Freemasonry and Esotericism." In *Modern Esoteric Spirituality*, edited by Antoine Faivre and Jacob Needleman. New York: Crossroad, 1995.

Mead, G. R. S. *Thrice Greatest Hermes: Studies in Hellenistic Theosophy and Gnosis*. 3 vols. York Beach, Maine: Samuel Weiser, 1992.

Merkel, Ingrid, and Allen G. Debus, eds. *Hermeticism and the Renaissance: Intellectual History and the Occult in Early Modern Europe*. Washington, D.C.: Folger Books, 1988.

Merkur, Dan. *Gnosis: An Esoteric Tradition of Mystical Visions and Unions*. Albany: State University of New York Press, 1993.

Montgomery, J. *The Cross and the Crucible*. 2 vols. The Hague: Nijoff, 1973.

Montgomery, J. W. "Cross, Constellation, and Crucible: Lutheran Astrology and Alchemy in the Age of Reformation." *Ambix* 11 (1963): 65–86.

Murray, Michael. *Modern Philosophy of History*. The Hague: Martinus Nijhoff, 1970.

Nehunia ben haKana. *The Bahir*. Translated by Aryeh Kaplan. York Beach, Maine: Samuel Weiser, 1979.

Neumann, Erich. *The Origins and History of Consciousness*. Translated by R. F. C. Hull. Princeton, N.J.: Princeton University Press, 1954.

Nicholas of Cusa. *Of Learned Ignorance*. Translated by Germain Heron. New Haven, Conn.: Yale University Press, 1954.

Nicolescu, Basarab. *Science, Meaning and Evolution: The Cosmology of Jacob Böhme*. Translated by Rob Baker. New York: Parabola Books, 1991.

Nilsson, Martin P. *Greek Folk Religion*. Philadelphia: University of Pennsylvania Press, 1978.

Novalis. *Hymns to the Night*. Bilingual ed. 3rd ed. Translated by Dick Higgins. Kingston, N.Y.: McPherson and Company, 1988.

——. *Philosophical Writings*. Translated and edited by Margaret Mahony Stoljar. Albany: State University of New York Press, 1997.

——. *Pollen and Fragments*. Translated by Arthur Versluis. Grand Rapids, Mich.: Phanes Press, 1989.

Oetinger, Friedrich Christoph. *Biblisches und Emblematisches Wörterbuch*. Reprint: Hildesheim: Georg Olms, 1969.

——. *Friedrich Christoph Oetingers Leben und Briefe, als urkundlicher Commentar zu dessen Schriften*. Edited by Karl Christian Eberhard Ehmann. Stuttgart: Steinkopf, 1859.

——. *Die Lehrtafel der Prinzessin Antonia.* Edited by Reinhard Breymayer and Friedrich Häusserman. Berlin, 1977.

——. *Die Philosophie der Alten, wiederkommend in der güldenen Zeit.* 2 vols. Frankfurt and Leipzig, 1762.

——. *Theologia ex idea vitae deducta.* Frankfurt and Leipzig: Aug. Lebr. Stettin, 1765.

——. *Die Wahrheit des sensus communis oder des allgemeinen Sinnes, in den nach dem Grundtext erklärten Sprüchen und Prediger Salomo oder das beste Haus- und Sittenbuch für Gelehrte und Ungelehrte.* Tübingen: Johann Nicolaus Stoll, 1753.

——. *Des Württembergischen Prälaten Friedrich Christoph Oetinger sämtliche Schriften.* Edited by Karl Christian Eberhard Ehmann. 11 vols. Stuttgart: Steinkopf, 1858–64.

Pagel, Walter. *Paracelsus: An Introduction to Philosophical Medicine in the Era of the Renaissance.* Basel: Karger, 1958.

Paracelsus [Philippus Theophrastus Bombastus von Hohenheim]. *Aurora of the Philosophers,* or *Monarchia.* In *The Hermetic and Alchemical Writings of Paracelsus the Great.* 2 vols. Translated by Arthur Edward Waite. Edmonds, Wash.: The Alchemical Press, 1992.

——. *Concerning the Nature of Things.* In *The Hermetic and Alchemical Writings of Paracelsus the Great.* Translated by Arthur Edward Waite. Edmonds, Wash.: The Alchemical Press, 1992.

——. *Sämtliche Werke, I Abteilung. Medizinische, naturwissenschaftliche und philosophische Schriften.* Edited by Karl Sudhoff. Vols 6–9, Munich: O. W. Barth, 1922–25; 1–4, 10–14, Munich, Berlin: R. Oldenbourg, 1928–33.

——. *Selected Writings.* Edited by Jolande Jacobi. Translated by Norbert Guterman. Princeton, N.J.: Bollingen, 1951.

——. *1. Abteilung. Die theologischen und religionsphilosophischen Schriften.* Edited by Karl Sudhoff and Wilhelm Matthiessen. Vol. 1. Munich: O.W. Barth, 1923.

——. *2. Abteilung. Theologische und religionsphilosophische Schriften.* Edited by Kurt Goldhammer. Wiesbaden and Stuttgart: Steiner, 1955ff.

Patai, Raphael. *The Jewish Alchemists: A History and Sourcebook.* Princeton, N.J.: Princeton University Press, 1994.

Paulin, Roger. *Ludwig Tieck: A Literary Biography.* Oxford: Clarendon Press, 1985.

Pennick, Nigel. *Magical Alphabets.* York Beach, Maine: Samuel Weiser, 1992.

Peuckert, Will-Erich. *Pansophie.* 3 vols. Berlin: Erich Schmidt. Vol. 1, *Pansophie: Ein Versuch zur Geschichte der weissen un schwartzen Magie,* 1973; Vol. 2, *Gabalia: Ein Versuch zur Geschichte der magia naturalis im 16. bis 18. Jahrhundert,* 1967; Vol. 3, *Das Rosenkreutz,* 1973.

——. *Die Rosenkreutzer: Zur Geschichte einer Reformation.* Jena: E. Diedericks, 1928.

Piatigorsky, Alexander. *Who's Afraid of Freemasons? The Phenomenon of Freemasonry.* London: Harvill Press, 1997.

Pico della Mirandola, Giovanni. *On The Dignity of Man, On Being and the One, Heptaplus.* Translated by Charles Glenn Wallis, Paul J. W. Miller, and Douglas Carmichael. New York: Macmillan, 1985.

——. Pico della Mirandola, Giovanni. *Oration on the Dignity of Man.* Translated by A. Robert Caponigri. Chicago: Regnery Gateway, 1956.

Popkin, Richard. "Newton's Biblical Theology and his Theological Physics." In *The Third Force in Seventeenth-century Thought.* Leiden: E. J. Brill, 1992.

———. "Philosophy and the History of Philosophy." In *The Third Force in Seventeenth-century Thought*. Leiden: E. J. Brill, 1992.

———. "The Religious Background of Seventeenth Century Philosophy." In *The Third Force in Seventeenth-century Thought*. Leiden: E. J. Brill, 1992.

———. "Roads that Led Beyond Judaism and Christianity." In *The Third Force in Seventeenth-century Thought*. Leiden: E. J. Brill, 1992.

———. "Spinoza, Neoplatonic Kabbalist?" In *Neoplatonism and Jewish Thought*, edited by Lenn E. Goodman. Albany: State University of New York Press, 1992.

———. "The Third Force in Seventeenth-Century Thought: Scepticism, Science and Millenarianism." In *The Third Force in Seventeenth-Century Thought*. Leiden: E. J. Brill, 1992.

———. *The Third Force in Seventeenth-Century Thought*. Leiden: E.J. Brill, 1992.

Pring-Mill, R. D. F. "The Trinitarian World Picture of Ramon Lull." *Romantisches Jahrbuch* 7 (1955–56): 229–56.

Proclus. *Elements of Theology*. Edited and translated by E. R. Dodds. 2nd ed. London: Oxford University Press, 1963.

Reuchlin, Johann. *De Arte Cabalistica/On the Art of the Kabbalah*. Bilingual ed. Translated by Martin Goodman and Sarah Goodman. New York: Abaris, 1983.

Ritschl, Albrecht. *Geschichte des Pietismus in der lutherische Kirche des 17. und 18. Jahrhunderts*. 3 vols. Bonn: Adolph Marcus, 1880–86.

Ross, George MacDonald. "Leibniz and Alchemy." *Studia Leibnitiana*, Sonderheft 7: 166–77.

———. "Leibniz and the Nuremberg Alchemical Society." *Studia Leibnitiana* 6 (1974): 22–48.

———. "Leibniz and Renaissance Neoplatonism." *Studia Leibnitiana*, Supplementa 23: 125–34.

———. "Rosicrucianism and the English Connection." *Studia Leibnitiana* 5 (1973): 239–45.

Rossi, Paolo. *Francis Bacon: From Magic to Science*. London: Routledge, 1968.

———. "The Legacy of Ramon Lull in Sixteenth-Century Thought." *Mediaeval and Renaissance Studies* 5 (1961): 181–213.

Safranski, Rüdiger. *Schopenhauer and the Wild Years of Philosophy*. Translated by Eswald Osers. Cambridge, Mass.: Harvard University Press, 1991.

Schelling, Friedrich Wilhelm Josef. *The Ages of the World*. Translated by Frederick de Wolfe Bolman Jr. New York: A.M.S. Press, 1967.

———. *Bruno, or On the Natural and Divine Principle of Things*. Translated by Michael G. Vater. Albany: State University of New York Press, 1984.

———. *Sämtliche Werke*. 14 vols. Edited by Karl Friedrich A. Schelling. Stuttgart/Augsburg: J. G. Cotta'scher Verlag, 1856–61.

———. *System of Transcendental Idealism*. Translated by Peter Heath. Charlottesville, VA: University Press of Virginia, 1980.

———. *Werke*. Edited by Manfred Schröter. 6 vols. and 6 supplementary vols. Munich: Beck, 1927–59.

Schelling, Karl Eberhard. "Ideen und Erfahrungen über den tierschen Magnetismus." *Jahrbücher für Medizin als Wissenschaft* 2 (1807): 1–42, 158–90.

Schiller, Friedrich. *Sämtliche Werke*. 4 vols. Edited by Gerhard Fricke, Herbert G. Göpfert, and Herbert Stubenrauch. 6th ed. Munich: Hanser, 1974–80.

Schipperges, Heinrich. "Paracelsus and His Followers." In *Modern Esoteric Spirituality*, edited by Antoine Faivre and Jacob Needleman. New York: Crossroad, 1995.

Schlegel, F. *Prosaische Jugendschriften*. 2 vols. Edited by J. Minor. Vienna: Konegen, 1906.

Schmitt, Charles B. "Perennial Philosophy: From Agostino Steuco to Leibniz." *Journal of the History of Ideas* 27 (1966): 505–32.

Schneider, Heinrich. *Quest for Mysteries: The Mystical Background for Literature in Eighteenth Century Germany*. Ithaca, N.Y.: Cornell University Press, 1947.

Scholem, Gershom G. *Kabbalah*. New York: New American Library, 1974.

———. *Major Trends in Jewish Mysticism*. New York: Schocken, 1946.

———. *On the Kabbalah and its Symbolism*. Translated by Ralph Manheim. New York: Schocken, 1965.

———. *On the Mystical Shape of the Godhead: Basic Concepts in the Kabbalah*. Edited by Jonathan Chapman and translated by Joachim Neugroschel. New York: Schocken, 1991.

———. *Origins of the Kabbalah*. Edited by R. J. Zwi Werblowsky. Translated by Allan Arkush. Princeton, N.J.: Princeton University Press, 1987.

Scott, Walter, ed. and tr. *Hermetica: The Ancient Greek and Latin Writings Which Contain Religious or Philosophic Teachings Ascribed to Hermes Trismegistus*. Boston: Shambhala, 1993.

Sladek, Mirko. *Fragmente der hermetischen Philosophie in der Naturphilosophie der Neuzeit*. Frankfurt am Main: Peter Lang, 1984.

Snow, Dale. *Schelling and the End of Idealism*. Albany: State University of New York Press, 1996.

Stanhope, Gilbert. *A Mystic on the Prussian Throne*. London: Mills and Boon, 1912.

Stoeffler, F. Ernest. *German Pietism During the Eighteenth Century*. Leiden: E. J. Brill, 1973.

Stoudt, John Joseph. *Sunrise to Eternity: A Study in Jacob Böhme's Life and Thought*. Philadelphia: University of Pennsylvania Press, 1957.

Thompson, C. J. S. *Alchemical Symbols and Secret Alphabets*. Edmonds, Wash.: The Alchemical Press, 1988.

———. *The Lure and Romance of Alchemy: A History of the Secret Link between Magic and Science*. New York: Bell, 1990.

Tilliette, Xavier. *Schelling im Spiegel seiner Zeitgenossen*. Turin: Bottega, d'Erasmo, 1974.

Tuveson, Ernest Lee. *The Avatars of Thrice Great Hermes: An Approach to Romanticism*. Lewisburg, Pa.: Bucknell University Press, 1982.

Versluis, Arthur. "Christian Theosophic Literature of the Seventeenth and Eighteenth Centuries." In *Gnosis and Hermeticism From Antiquity to Modern Times*, edited by Roelef van den Broek, and Wouter J. Hanegraff. Albany: State University of New Press, 1998.

———. *Theosophia: Hidden Dimensions of Christianity*. Hudson, N.Y.: Lindisfarne Press, 1994.

———. *Wisdom's Children: A Christian Esoteric Tradition*. Albany: State University of New York Press, 1999.

Vickers, Brian. "On the Function of Analogy in the Occult." In *Hermeticism and the Renaissance: Intellectual History and the Occult in Early Modern Europe*, edited by Ingrid Merkel and Allen G. Debus. Washington, D.C.: Folger Books, 1988.

Voegelin, Eric. *The New Science of Politics: An Introduction*. Chicago: University of Chicago Press, 1952.

Vondung, Klaus. "Millenarianism, Hermeticism, and the Search for a Universal Science." In *Science, Pseudo-Science, and Utopianism in Early Modern Thought,* edited by Stephen McKnight. Columbia: University of Missouri Press, 1992.

Waite, A. E. *The Brotherhood of the Rosy Cross: A History of the Rosicrucians.* New York: Barnes and Noble, 1993.

——. *The Holy Kabbalah.* New York: Citadel Press, 1992.

Walker, D. P. *Spiritual and Demonic Magic: From Ficino to Campanella.* London: The Warburg Institute, 1958.

Walsh, David. *The Mysticism of Innerworldly Fulfillment: A Study of Jacob Boehme.* Gainesville: University Presses of Florida, 1983.

——. "A Mythology of Reason: The Persistence of Pseudo-Science in the Modern World." In *Science, Pseudo-Science and Utopianism in Early Modern Thought,* edited by Stephen A. McKnight. Columbia: University of Missouri Press, 1992.

Webster, Charles. *From Paracelsus to Newton: Magic and the Making of Modern Science.* Cambridge, U.K.: Cambridge University Press, 1982.

Weeks, Andrew. *Boehme: An Intellectual Biography of the Seventeenth-Century Philosopher and Mystic.* Albany: State University of New York Press, 1991.

——. *German Mysticism from Hildegaard of Bingen to Ludwig Wittgenstein.* Albany: State University of New York Press, 1993.

——. *Paracelsus: Speculative Theory and the Crisis of the Early Reformation.* Albany: State University of New York Press, 1997.

——. *Valentin Weigel (1533–1588): German Religious Dissenter, Speculative Theorist, and Advocate of Tolerance.* Albany: State University of New York Press, 2000.

Westfall, Richard S. "Newton and the Hermetic Tradition." In *Science, Medicine and Society in the Renaissance,* edited by Allen G. Debus. New York: Science History Publications, 1972.

Wetzels, Walter. *Johann Wilhelm Ritter: Physik im Wirkungsfeld der deutschen Romantik.* Berlin: De Gruyter, 1973.

White, Ralph, ed. *The Rosicrucian Enlightenment Revisited.* Hudson, N.Y.: Lindisfarne Books, 1999.

Wilson, John A. "Egypt." In *The Intellectual Adventure of Ancient Man,* edited by Henri Frankfort et. al. Chicago: University of Chicago Press, 1977.

Wolfart, C. C. *Erlauterungen zum Mesmerismus.* Berlin: Nikolaischen, 1815.

Wolfson, Elliot R. *Through a Speculum that Shines: Vision and Imagination in Medieval Jewish Mysticism.* Princeton, N.J.: Princeton University Press, 1994.

Yates, Frances A. *The Art of Memory.* Chicago: University of Chicago Press, 1966.

——. "The Art of Ramon Lull: An Approach to it Through Lull's Theory of the Elements." *Journal of the Warburg and Courtauld Institutes* 17 (1964): 115–73.

——. *Giordano Bruno and the Hermetic Tradition.* Chicago: University of Chicago Press, 1964.

——. "The Hermetic Tradition in Renaissance Science." *Art, Science, and History in the Renaissance.* Edited by Charles Singleton. Baltimore: Johns Hopkins, 1968.

——. *Lull and Bruno.* London: Routledge, 1982.

——. *The Occult Philosophy in the Elizabethan Age.* London: Routledge, 1979.

——. *Renaissance and Reform: The Italian Contribution.* London: Routledge, 1983.

——. *The Rosicrucian Enlightenment.* London: Routledge, 1972.

——. *Theatre of the World.* Chicago: University of Chicago Press, 1969.

Zeydel, Edwin H. *Ludwig Tieck, the German Romanticist: A Critical Study.* Princeton, N.J.: Princeton University Press, 1935.

Zimmerman, Rolf Christian. *Das Weltbild des jungen Goethe: Studien zur hermetischen Tradition des deutschen 18. Jahrhunderts.* 2 vols. Munich: Fink, 1969, 1979.

Index

Abgrund (Abyss), 24, 38, 82, 163
Absolute Idea, 4, 16, 88, 95, 151, 155–156,
  160, 165, 177, 180, 189–190, 223,
  234–235
Absolute Knowing, 14, 96, 98, 120,
  127–128, 131, 137, 141, 145, 146, 211
Absolute Spirit, 13, 68, 95, 107, 117, 146,
  148, 164, 211, 213, 223
Abulafia, Abraham, 32, 179
Adam Ha-Rishon, 230, 233
Adam Kadmon, in Luria, 230–233
Adams, G. P., 6
aether: Aristotle on, 118; Böhme on,
  198n. 33; Hegel on, 95, 102, 117,
  196–200; in Kabbalah (ru'ah), 168,
  170; Plotinus on, 118; K. E. Schelling
  on, 217
Agrippa, Cornelius, 2, 30–33, 58, 70, 129,
  166, 182, 186, 211; Hegel owned works
  of, 32–33, 195
Albertus Magnus, 22–23, 206
alchemy, 1–2, 3, 22, 30, 32, 36, 46, 64, 70,
  80, 184, 191, 249–250; albedo, 146, 203,
  211; in China, 206n. 73; citrinatis, 203;
  description of doctrines of, 200–209;
  as influence on Goethe, 57–61, 207,
  210–211; as influence on Hegel, 3, 48,
  103, 119, 123, 132, 143–146, 191–196,
  209–213; nigredo, 145–146, 165, 203, 211;
  rubedo, 165, 203
Anaxagoras, 196
Andreae, Jakob, 52
Andreae, J. V., 52–53, 62, 70, 83, 183–184,
  242–243
animal magnetism. See Mesmer, F. A.
Antonia, Princess of Württemberg, 65
Apollonius of Tyana, 22
Aquinas, St. Thomas. See Thomas
  Aquinas, Saint
Arians, 16n. 39
Aristotle, 16, 17, 24, 30, 31, 66, 87, 92n.
  28, 93, 102, 118, 128, 137, 141, 150, 160,
  189–191, 194, 196–197, 200, 230

Arndt, Johann, 36
Arnold, Gottfried, 36, 47
Arnold of Villanova, 148
Asclepius, 22
Ashmole, Elias, 53
Augustine, Saint, 28

Baader, Franz von, 2, 47–48, 80n. 171,
  134, 176, 246, 254; and Böhme, 47; and
  Hegel, 4, 25, 48, 105, 110, 157–158, 226,
  242, 253
Bach, Joseph, 5
Bacon, Sir Francis, 7n. 12, 48, 53, 182,
  186
Bacon, Roger, 179
Bauer, F. C., 5
Beach, E. A., 83n. 188
Becco, Anne, 185
Beck, L. W., 28, 30, 35, 63
Beiser, Frederick, 77, 77n. 155
Bengel, J. A., 3, 64, 72, 72n. 121, 79–81,
  233, 238, 243–245, 247
Benz, Ernst, 5, 23, 24n. 9, 29, 37n. 56,
  79–80, 191, 216, 237, 242–243, 245
Berlin Academy, 211
Bischoffswerder, J. R. von, 250–251
Blake, William, 47
Blau, Joseph, 29
Böhme, Jakob, 2, 5, 13, 28, 36–50, 60n.
  54, 61, 70, 102–103, 105–107, 119–120,
  122–123, 134, 136, 138–145, 166,
  172–173, 186, 190, 206, 227–228, 231,
  235n. 37, 236, 240–242, 245, 249, 254;
  Alles and Nichts, 40, 162, 168;
  Begreiflichkeit, 42; "darkness and
  light," 40; developmental concept of
  God, 38–39; Etwas, 162, 222; "Flash"
  (Schrack), 41, 82, 170; followers of,
  46–47; historical significance of,
  37–38; influence on Hegel, 3–4, 7,
  48–50, 59n. 42, 100, 109–110,
  132–133, 138–145, 157–165, 167, 193,
  209–210, 223–224; influence on

Böhme, Jakob (continued)
  Newton, 191n. 11; influence on
  Oetinger, 64–68, 137; influence on
  Pietism, 63; influence on Schelling,
  79–83; and Jesus Christ, 45; life of,
  36–37, 46; Natursprache, 44; quale, 157;
  and Qualierung (Inqualierung),
  158–159, 163; Ungrund, 38, 40–43,
  137n. 47, 162–163, 168; Works, Aurora
  (Morgenrothe im Aufgang), 36, 39–40,
  42–45, 161; —, Clavis, 44, 161; —,
  Mysterium Magnum, 40–41, 48, 162,
  191n. 11; —, Six Mystical Points, 42,
  221, 241. See also evil; "source spirits"
Bolland, G. J. P. J., 5
Bolos of Mendes, 201
Bonner, Anthony, 178
Bourignon, Antoinette, 47
de Bourrouill, J., 5–6
Boyle, Robert, 70
Bracken, Ernst von, 74, 74n. 134
Bradley, F. H., 14
Braunschweig, Duke Ferdinand of, 57
Breckling, Friedrich, 47
Brinton, H. H., 37n. 55
Broad, C. D., 7n. 12
Brown, Robert, 83
Bruaire, Claude, 15
Brucker, J. J., 166, 176, 232
Bruno, Giordano, 2–3, 13, 26, 28–29,
  32–34, 46, 65, 77, 85n. 4, 103, 122, 129,
  135n. 40, 166, 182, 184; Hegel on, 33,
  49, 180; Schelling on, 83
Brunquell, Ludwig, 63
Brunschwig, Henri, 254
Burbidge, John, 74, 74n. 138, 130
Burger, H. O., 63n. 66
Burton, Robert, 182
Butler, Clark, 48, 75, 75n. 146, 85n. 3,
  238

Cambridge Platonists, 166, 191n. 11
Camillo, Giulio, 180–181
Campanella, Tommaso, 166, 183
Campbell, Joseph, 130
Campetti, Francesco, 216
Čapková, Dagmar, 183
caput mortuum, 112, 145, 203; Hegel on,
  102, 146, 164–165, 209, 210, 213
Carove, F. W., 218
Cassirer, Ernst, 26
Cerf, Walter, 92n. 25
Chapelle, Albert, 15
Charlier, John, 179
circularity, 2, 10, 14, 25, 100–102, 106n.
  73, 154–155, 161–162, 170, 179, 180–181,
  196, 208, 212, 230, 231; in Böhme, 43,
  170

Clark, Malcolm, 15
Clement of Alexandria, 28
Clement XII, Pope, 54
Cobenzl, Count Johann, 57
Coincidence of Opposites (Coincidentia
  Oppositorum), 24, 26–27, 127, 135, 137;
  in Schelling, 82
Colberg, E. D., 47
collective unconscious, 103
Comenius, J. A., 53, 182–183, 185
Concept (Begriff), 16n. 40, 49n. 114,
  136n. 42, 151, 156, 160–161, 165,
  190n. 8, 210, 212, 240; in Weigel, 36,
  42
concrete universal, 95
"contraction and expansion," 60, 60n. 54,
  66, 173, 229–230; in Hegel and
  Schelling, 82
Copenhaver, Brian, 22
Copleston, Frederick, 6
Cordovero, Moses, 168–169, 175, 228
Corpus Hermeticum, 1, 9, 11–12, 21–22, 24,
  46, 56, 69, 99n. 47, 129n. 9, 138
correspondences, 2, 46, 122, 188,
  193–195
Cotta, C. F., 57
Cottier, M.-M., 5n. 6
Coudert, Allison, 7, 184
Cousin, Victor, 218
Creuzer, G. F., influence on Hegel, 85n. 3
Croll, Oswald, 207
Cudworth, Ralph, 166
cultus, 225
"cunning of reason," 110, 142, 210,
  227–228

d'Alembert, Jean Le Rond, 182
Debus, Allan, 7, 191, 204
Deghaye, Pierre, 62
Democritus, 196
Descartes, Rene, 7n. 12, 53, 53n. 8, 65, 181,
  197, 218n. 112
Desire (Begierde); Böhme on, 45; Hegel
  on, 139–143, 173, 177, 211
de Wette, W. M. L., 157
d'Hondt, Jacques, 6, 57, 74n. 138, 75, 75n.
  144, 130, 254
dialectic, Hegel on, 89–90, 99, 120, 145,
  154–155, 161, 175, 211–212,
  221–222
Dickey, Laurence, 61–62, 70, 238, 242,
  244
Dickson, D. R., 53n. 12
Diderot, Denis, 166, 182, 211
Dierauer, Walter, 78
Dietrich of Freiburg, 23
Dilthey, Wilhelm, 4

Divine Triangle. *See* Hegel: Works: Triangle fragment
Divisch, Prokop, 68
Dobbs, Betty Jo Teeter, 7
Dorn, Gerhard, 207
Dove, K. R., 15
dowsing, 2, 16
Dummett, Michael, 7n. 12
Dupré, Louis, 15
Düsing, Klaus, 135n. 40
Dury, John, 182–183, 185

Earth Spirit, 201; Hegel on, 2, 201, 213–214
Eckermann, Peter, 78n. 160
Eckhart, Meister, 1–2, 22–26, 27, 32, 35, 38–39, 43, 63n. 70, 74, 82, 119, 122, 133, 136, 163, 205; as influence on Fichte, 74; as influence on Hegel, 3–4, 74, 106, 110, 116, 225–227, 242
Eckhartshausen, Baron Karl von, 254–255
Edighoffer, Roland, 52n. 3
Egidius of Viterbo, Cardinal, 31
Egyptian Mythology/Religion, 12, 33, 37, 94, 131
Eleusinian mysteries, 11, 75, 86n. 10, 123; Hegel on, 130–132, 139, 148
Eliade, Mircea, 201
Emerald Tablet of Hermes Trismegistus, the, 13, 22, 44, 58, 187, 201
Empedocles, 194
encyclopedism, 12, 177–186; and Hegel, 14, 185–186
"end of history," doctrine of, 236–247; in Hegel, 88, 119–120, 127, 236, 247; in Joachim de Fiore, 228; in the Kabbalah, 235–236. *See also* millenarianism
Enlightenment, the (*die Aufklärung*), 56–58, 182, 253; in Germany, 58, 63, 77
ennead, the, 100–101
Epstein, Klaus, 56n. 31, 249n. 89, 250–251
Erasmus, 181n. 94, 204
Eschenmayer, A. K., 218
esotericism, 1, 46
evil, 35, 173, 177; Hegel on, 108, 142–143, 241
Evola, Baron Julius, 40n. 74, 52, 101n. 57, 102n. 62, 148, 200–201, 203, 206

Fackenheim, Emil, 15
Faivre, Antoine, 7, 8n. 14, 22, 28, 45n. 97, 46, 52–53, 56n. 29, 83, 99, 166, 238
fall of man, Böhme on, 45, 73, 87, 176
Febvre, Lucien, 70

Fessler, J. K. C., 55
Fichte, J. G., 3, 71, 81, 117, 119, 134–135, 138, 227; "Letters to Constant," 55; as Mason, 55, 74
Fichtuld, Hermann, 249
Ficino, Marsillio, 28, 31–33, 196
Figala, Karin, 146, 164n. 29
Findlay, J. N., 6, 16, 49n. 115, 178n. 83
Fischer, Gottfried, 5
Flagellants, 238
Fludd, Robert, 2, 53, 70, 166, 182–183, 208
"folk religion," 72–73, 84
Force and its Utterance, 164
four elements, 101–102, 117, 122, 191–196, 202, 210
"four worlds," 174–175, 230, 232; Hegel on, 175
Fowden, Garth, 9–10, 129
Franck, Sebastian, 34–36, 54
Frankfort, H. A., 94, 97
Frankfort, Henri, 94, 97
Franklin, Benjamin, 216
Frauenmystik, 23
Frederick the Great, King of Prussia, 58, 250–251
Frederick-William II, King of Prussia, 250–252
Frederick-William III, King of Prussia, 251–252
freedom, Hegel on, 140
Freemasonry, 2–3, 35, 53–56, 113, 210, 244, 249, 250; and German Pietism, 64n. 73; and Hegel, 3, 73–74, 105, 130–131, 254, 254n. 105; and Hiram, legend of, 131; initiation into, 146; and Knights Templar, 54, 251; Scottish Rite, 54; Strict Observance, 54
French revolution, 75, 245–246
Fricker, J. L., 68, 70, 196n. 21
Friedenthal, Richard, 58
Friedrich August, Duke of Braunschweig-Öls, 250
Fries, J. F., 157

Gadamer, H.-G., 64n. 75
Gaier, Ulrich, 78, 78n. 165
Geistleiblichkeit (corporealization); in Böhme, 42–43, 162, 190; in Hegel, 68, 95, 122, 190, 213, 224; in Oetinger, 66, 68, 95, 122, 190, 224; in Schelling, 81; in Schwenkfeld, 66
gematria, 32
genius (*Genius*), 218
Geraets, T. F., 164
Gerard of Borgo San Donnino, 238
Gichtel, J. G., 47

Gikatilla, Joseph, 235
Gnosticism, 5, 10, 75, 165, 167n. 36, 175, 235–236
Godwin, Joscelyn, 182
Goethe, J. W. von, 57–61, 77, 79, 122, 207, 210n. 91, 211, 230; botanical theory, 60; color theory, 60; *Die Geheimnisse*, 61; and Hegel, 78n. 160, 83; as Mason, 55–56, 61; as member of Illuminati, 57; and Schelling, 83; *Sorrows of the Young Werther*, 59
Göschel, K. F., 71
Gogel, J. N., 75
Gospel of Thomas, 248n. 83
Gotha, Duke Ernst of, 57
Grail, Holy, 148–149
Gray, Ronald, 58, 61, 64n. 74, 203, 211
Groote, Gerald, 26
Grotius, Hugo, 74
Gruppe, O. H., 62

Habermas, Jürgen, 38n. 61
Hafenreffer, Matthias, 243
Hahn, J. M., 69, 80
Hahn, P. M., 62, 64, 68–70, 72n. 121, 78, 244–245; influence on Schelling, 80
HaKana, Rabbi N. ben, 166
Halevi, Z'ev ben Shimon, 168
Hamann, J. G., 28n. 28, 77; influence on Hegel, 77–78, 78n. 160
Hanratty, Gerald, 75
Hardenberg, Karl von, 57
Harris, H. S., 6, 12n. 30, 17, 48–49, 59n. 42, 71–73, 74–75, 75n. 144, 77, 82, 86n. 8, 87, 92n. 25, 100, 105–106, 107n. 76, 107n. 79, 110, 129, 132, 140n. 54, 142n. 60, 150n. 1, 155, 194–195, 196n. 20, 196n. 22, 197, 198n. 31, 198n. 34, 200, 209, 226n. 6
Hartlib, Samuel, 53, 182–183, 185
Hartmann, Klaus, 14–15
Haselmayer, Adam, 51
Hatab, L. J., 96–98
Häussermann, Friedrich, 111
Hayden-Roy, P. A., 78, 246n. 76
Haym, R., 107n. 76, 117n. 103
Hegel, Christianne, 217
Hegel, G. W. F.: on *aufheben*, 92n. 26; in Berlin, 3, 101n. 57, 150, 247–248, 253; in Berne, 3, 74, 84, 106, 116; conservatism of, 253; early, four-part system of, 117; as esoteric writer, 137; in Frankfurt, 3, 78, 105, 116; in Heidelberg, 150, 247; as Hermetic thinker, 1–4, 6, 10–14, 103–104; in Jena, 3, 25n. 13, 101, 132–134, 149, 151, 163, 209, 210n. 91, 215; lectures of, 247–248; Mythology of Reason,

84–123; "non-metaphysical reading" of, 14–17; in Nuremberg, 150; periods of Hermetic influence, 2–4; religious views of, 16, 16n. 38, 104, 227; Schelling, critique of, 135–138; in Stuttgart, 2; Swabianism of, 62, 70, 116 (*see also* Württemberg); "theosophical phase," 3, 105, 116; in Tübingen, 70; Works, "Böhme Myth" (of 1804–5), 143–144, 173, 207, 230; —, *Differenzschrift*, 79, 86n. 8, 90; —, "Dissertation," 101n. 57, 187, 195, 196n. 21; —, "Earliest System Program of German Idealism," 84–96, 104; —, "early theological writings," 71–72; —, "Eleusis," 75–76, 130, 198n. 35; —, *Encyclopedia Logic*, 85–86, 100–101, 106n. 73, 120, 135, 139, 147, 150–151, 159, 167n. 36, 168, 187, 189, 209, 240; —, *Encyclopedia of the Philosophical Sciences*, 4, 94, 150, 159, 185, 215, 226; —, *Faith and Knowledge*, 146; —, "First Philosophy of Spirit," 192–193, 199; —, *Lectures on the History of Philosophy*, 2, 21, 29, 30, 33, 41n. 78, 48–50, 85n. 3, 102, 107, 117, 132, 138, 143, 157, 159, 166, 246; —, *Lectures on the Philosophy of Religion*, 4, 48, 85n. 5, 86n. 10, 120–121n. 108, 132n. 21, 135, 136n. 42, 139, 152–153, 163, 223–227, 240–241, 248; —, *Lectures on the Philosophy of World History*, 92–93n. 28, 95, 113, 223, 248; —, *Logic*, 2, 14, 16, 81, 89, 95, 97n. 41, 101, 105, 109, 119, 128, 131, 150–186, 156, 187–188, 190, 198, 222, 224; —, purpose of, 150–152, 210; —, "On Mythology," 87; —, *Phenomenology of Spirit*, 1–2, 4, 14, 28, 34, 48, 59, 90n. 18, 92–93, 97n. 40, 98, 100, 105, 113, 122–123, 127–149, 160, 178, 180, 188, 190, 195, 199, 211–212, 224; as Grail quest, 149, 193; —, *Philosophy of Nature*, 2–4, 13, 30, 48, 59n. 42, 89, 95, 98n. 45, 100, 101n. 57, 105, 109n. 85, 128, 140, 142n. 60, 144, 151n. 3, 155, 158, 187–200, 209, 215, 250; —, *Philosophy of Right*, 2, 4, 155, 213, 224, 245, 247–249, 252; —, *Philosophy of Spirit*, 4, 24n. 11, 89n. 16, 95, 117n. 102, 128, 140, 142n. 59, 159, 174, 209–213, 189–190, 212–222, 241; —, *Realphilosophie*, 85–86, 192n. 13; —, *Science of Logic*, 4, 48, 85, 100, 103n. 64, 109, 150–165, 176–177; —, *System of Ethical Life*, 93n. 29; —, triangle diagram, 2, 105, 110–119, 132; —, Triangle fragment, 25n. 13, 104–110,

117, 132, 241; —, "Wastebook," 102, 106n. 72; See also aether; Concept; Desire; speculative philosophy
Heidegger, Martin, 15, 132, 150, 229n. 12
Heine, Heinrich, 78
Helmont, F. M. van, 58, 70, 166–167, 184–186, 201, 217n. 106, 219
Helmont, J. B. van, 184, 219
Hemsterhuis, Frans, 71
hen kai pan, 33, 77, 102, 135, 203, 206, 214
Herder, J. G., 69n. 102, 71, 77–78; Hermeticism of, 69, 69n. 103, 197; as member of Illuminati, 57; as Mason, 55
Hermes Trismegistus, 1–2, 22–23, 28, 35, 46, 53, 56, 69, 99, 166, 201
Hermetica. See Corpus Hermeticum
Hermeticism, 39, 98–99, 101n. 57, 102–103, 110, 116, 118–119, 123, 145, 192, 201; defined, 1, 8–14; and Enlightenment, 58
Hesiod, 210n. 89
Heydon, John, 53
Hildegard of Bingen, Saint, 23, 43, 63n. 70, 205
Hinrichs, H. F. W., 190
Hirsch, Immanuel, 5
Hobbes, Thomas, 49, 74
Hodgson, P. C., 241n. 51, 248
Hoffmann, E. T. A., 211
Hölderlin, Friedrich, 33, 35, 62, 69, 75, 77–78, 84, 135, 198n. 35, 214, 246n. 76, 254
Homer, 152
Humboldt, Alexander von, 48
Hume, David, 49, 74
Husserl, Edmund, 120
Hyppolite, Jean, 90

Ibn al-'Arabi, Muhyi al-Din, 177n. 79
Iljan, Iwan, 15
Illuminati, the, 56–57, 130, 249, 252
imagination, 46, 93, 176; Hegel on, 98–104, 122; and memory, 46
Indian mysticism, 85n. 3, 176–177n. 77
infinite, the, Hegel on, 147–148, 152, 229, 234
ingenium, 99
initiation, 10–11, 123, 129–130, 146, 154. See also Freemasonry: initiation into
internal relations, doctrine of: as Hermetic, 13, 14, 26, 205; in Luria, 233
"invisible church," 35, 55, 73, 244, 254. See also Objective Spirit

Irira, A. C., cited by Hegel, 232
Ishmael, Rabbi, 175

Jacobi, F. H., 49, 71, 77, 77n. 155, 89n. 15, 135n. 40
Jaeschke, Walter, 15, 105n. 67
Jager, J. W., 70
James, William, 7n. 12
Joachim de Fiore, 22, 63n. 70, 65, 228, 236–247; influence on Hegel, 238–242
Job, Book of, 72
John of Rupescissa, 196
Jung, C. G., 111n. 89, 200, 201n. 46, 203, 206n. 72, 212, 220n. 114
Jung, Emma, 148–149, 201, 238
Jung-Stilling, J. H., 254–255

Kabbala Denudata. See Rosenroth, Knorr von
Kabbalah, 1–2, 13, 28, 30–32, 37, 37n. 56, 41n. 79, 43n. 86, 77, 119–120, 122, 165–177, 181, 184, 186, 191, 228–236, 250; Christian, 13, 29, 31, 46, 62, 65, 166, 176–177, 179, 182, 185, 203, 206n. 73; "dialectic" in, 175; Ein-Sof, 168, 170, 176, 228, 229–230, 234, 236; Hegel on, 103, 166–167, 176–177; as influence on Goethe, 58, 61, 173; as influence on Oetinger, 65–66, 167, 173; Keneset Israel, 174, 235–236; Shekinah, 43n. 86, 174, 234–235 (see also Objective Spirit); Texts, Bahir, 166, 175; —, Ma'arekhet ha-Elohut, 169; —, Sefer Ha Zohar, 166, 167n40, 168, 174, 179, 236; —, Sefer Yezirah, 165–166, 167n40, 169–170; —, Tikkun, Luria on, 233. See also Adam Kadmon; "four worlds"; Sephiroth
Kant, Immanuel, 3, 7n. 12, 34, 48, 56, 67, 71, 74, 78, 81, 83, 100, 117, 119–120, 165, 215, 251; Hegel's critique of, 153–154
Kaplan, Aryeh, 170n. 57, 175
Karl-August, Duke of Weimar, 57
Karl Theodor, Elector of Bavaria, 57
Kelly, Sean, 117n. 102, 213, 220n. 114
Kepler, Johannes, 188
Khunrath, Heinrich, 146, 206n. 73
Kieser, D. G., 218
Kimmerle, Heinz, 101, 104
Kingdom of a Thousand Years (Tausend-Jahre Reich), 244
Kingdom of God, doctrine of, 54, 62, 73, 242, 243–244, 248, 254
Klettenberg, Susanna von, 58–59
Knebel, K. L. von, 210
Knigge, Freiherr Adolph von, 56

Knights Templar, 54, 251
Knox, T. M., 12n. 30, 248
Kober, Tobias, 37
Köstlin, N. F., 72n. 121, 80
Kojève, Alexandre, 120, 129, 141n. 57,
    155n. 6
Kolb, David, 14
Kristeller, P. O., 7, 191
Kuhlmann, Quirinius, 47

Lactantius, 28
Ladner, Gerald, 242
Langen, August, 145
Langer, E. Th., 58
Lanz, Jakob, 57
Lasson, Georg, 101n. 57, 248
Lavater, J. K., 7n. 12, 145n. 71
de Lavinheta, Bernard, 181
Law, William, 47
Lead, Jane, 46
Leeses, Kurt, 82n. 184
Leiblichkeit. See Geistleiblichkeit
Leibniz, G. W., 7n. 12, 27, 36, 65, 69, 74,
    167, 180, 184–186; as Rosicrucian, 53,
    184–185
de Leon, Moses, 166, 168
Leonardo da Vinci, 218n. 112
Lessing, G. E., 77, 130; Ernst and Falk, 55,
    73, 244n. 69; as Mason, 55; Nathan the
    Wise, 55, 73, 77n. 155, 127
Leutwein, Magister, 72
Locke, John, 49, 74
Logos, 16, 25, 107n. 79, 122, 151
Löwith, Karl, 223, 248
de Lubac, Henri, 238–239
Lucifer: Böhme on, 44, 108; Hegel on,
    143–144, 173, 230
Lull, Ramon, 1–2, 13, 22, 33, 122, 166,
    177–182, 201, 206; Hegel on, 179–180;
    names of God, 178; parallels to Hegel,
    178–181
Luria, Isaac, 38n. 62, 168, 170, 228–234;
    on Adam Kadmon, 230–233; and
    Hegel, 167, 229–230, 232, 234;
    influence on Böhme, 229–232;
    influence on Oetinger, 65, 232; Tikkun,
    233; tsimtsum, 228–230, 232–233. See
    also Kabbalah
Lütgert, Wilhelm, 5
Luther, Martin, 29–30, 34–35, 71, 78, 87,
    242, 248, 248n. 86

Machiavelli, Niccolò, 74
MacIntosh, Christopher, 55, 58, 249n.
    88, 252
macrocosm-microcosm doctrine, 32, 61,
    202; in Böhme, 45; in Hegel, 209; in
    Paracelsus, 205

magic, 2, 12, 31–33, 113–116, 191, 197, 200;
    in Böhme, 42, 162n. 27, 219n. 113,
    221–222; Hegel on, 93, 98, 110,
    122–123, 129, 212, 216, 218–222
Maier, Heinrich, 5
Maier, Michael, 53
Maker, William, 15
Martensen, Hans, 4
Marx, Karl, 247
Masonry. See Freemasonry
Mayer, Paola, 134
Mazet, Edmond, 54
McKnight, Stephen, 7, 191
Medici, Cosimo de, 28
memory: art of, 34, 46, 99, 103, 122,
    180–181, 184, 186. See also
    recollection
memory magic. See memory: art of
Merkur, Dan, 179n. 86, 181n. 95
Mesmer, F. A., 2, 16, 62, 68, 255; Hegel
    on, 215–218; Schelling on, 216–217
Messina Colloquium on Gnosticism,
    10n. 22
millenarianism, 183–184, 236–247; and
    Hermeticism, 245. See also "end of
    history," doctrine of
Minerva, 74, 74n. 139
Mitscherling, Jeff, 10n. 22
Mnemosyne, 85n. 4, 87, 90, 180
modernity, Hegel on, 97
Molay, Jacques de, 54
Montaigne, Michel de, 31
Montesquieu, Baron, 71, 74
Montgomery, J., 243
Mook, H. W., 6
More, Henry, 166, 191n. 11
Moses, 120
Mozart, W. A., 216, 218n. 112
Müller, Gustav, 100n. 55
Murray, Michael, 240
mysticism, 1, 10, 102, 129, 133, 135–138,
    157, 179, 223–227
myth, nature of, 94–98
mytho-poetic thought, 91–123

national differences, Hegel on, 215
natural science, Hegel's critique of, 97
Natural Soul, 213
Neoplatonism. See Plotinus
Neumann, Erich, 94, 102
Newton, Sir Isaac, 7n. 12, 188, 191n. 11,
    197
Nibelungenlied, 23
Nicholas of Cusa, 1, 26–28, 39, 82, 122,
    135–136, 181, 183, 205
Nicolai, Friedrich, 219, 253
Nicolescu, Basarab, 41–42
Nietzsche, Friedrich, 51

Nilsson, M. P., 131
Noack, Ludwig, 5
Novalis (Friedrich von Hardenberg), 47,
  78, 133–134; as Mason, 55

Oberberger, J. K., 64
Objective Spirit, 2, 68, 117, 164, 213, 223;
  and "invisible church," 244n. 69;
  parallels to Keneset Israel, 174, 236;
  parallels to Shekinah, 234–235
occultism, 1
Oetinger, F. C., 3, 13, 48, 60, 60n. 48,
  60n. 54, 62, 64–71, 72n. 121, 78n. 165,
  107n. 76, 120, 133, 138, 148, 156, 162,
  176, 186, 211, 227–228, 238, 245–247,
  248–249; balm leaf experiment,
  80–81; Bible translations quoted by
  Schelling, 81; chiliasm of, 245;
  conservatism of, 245n. 74; on fire and
  water, 192n. 13; followers of, 68–69; on
  Geist, 65–66; generative method, 67;
  and Hegel, 68, 95, 106, 109–110, 119,
  143, 162n. 21, 192n. 13, 196n. 20, 214n.
  97, 224, 242, 246–247; influence on
  Schelling, 69, 79–81, 79n. 169, 247; on
  Intensum, 65–66, 68, 122, 137; on
  nature and spirit, 189n. 6; theologia
  emblematica, 68, 122; "truth is a whole,"
  67–68, 137; Works, Aufmunternde
  Gründe . . . , 64; —, Biblisches und
  Emblematisches Wörterbuch, 66; —,
  Öffentliches Denckmal der Lehrtafel, 65;
  —, Reden nach dem Allgemeinen
  Wahrheitsgefühl. . . , 65; —, Swedenborgs
  und anderer irdische . . . , 65; —,
  Theologia ex idea vitae deducta, 79; —,
  Die Wahrheit des Sensus Communis, 67;
  Zentrallerkenntnis, 67. See also
  Geistleiblichkeit; Sensus communis
Olympiodorus, 201
ontotheology, 15–16, 150
O'Regan, Cyril, 6, 14–15, 50n. 118, 94n.
  32, 164, 167, 176n. 76, 238n. 48, 240,
  241n. 52
ouroburos, 102, 203, 208

pansophia, 2, 22, 52, 79n. 169, 177–186; in
  Oetinger, 246
pantheism (Pantheismusstreit), 8–9, 24,
  33, 39, 48, 59, 76–78, 119, 135–136,
  214
Paracelsus (Theophrastus Bombastus
  von Hohenheim), 2, 13, 30, 35–37, 48,
  53, 58, 65, 70, 105, 133, 138, 182–183,
  197, 201, 203–206, 211–212, 215n. 99,
  249; Hegel on, 49, 59n. 42, 100, 123,
  209–210; on sulphur-mercury-salt, 35,
  41, 132, 204, 212

Parzival. See Wolfram von Eschenbach
Patrizzi, Francesco, 183, 185
Paulus, H. E. B., 188
Peirce, C. S., 7n. 12
Peperzak, Adriaan, 252–253
perennial philosophy, 2, 53, 103; Hegel
  on, 84–90, 100, 122, 224
Petry, J. M., 192n. 12, 218
Philadelphian Society, 46
Philo of Alexandria, 235n. 37
philosopher's stone (Stein der Weisen),
  146, 148, 201–204, 206, 208, 211–212,
  248–249
philosophia perennis. See perennial
  philosophy
philosophy, 87; as magic, 221–222; and
  religion, 15n. 35, 120–121n. 108, 152,
  224, 226
phrenology, 145n. 71
Piaget, Jean, 138
Piatigorsky, Alexander, 131
Pico della Mirandola, 2, 11, 28, 31–33, 179,
  181
Pietism, 2–3, 5, 22, 47, 53n. 12, 58,
  62–63, 70–72, 71n. 114, 72, 78, 120, 137,
  145, 167n. 39, 227n. 8, 236, 240,
  242–244
Pimander, 28
Pinkard, Terry, 15
Plato, 2, 17, 28, 30, 71, 90n. 18, 196, 227;
  Platonic dialectic, 89
Plocquet, Gottfried, 69, 71
Plotinus, 8n. 13, 10, 21, 23, 172, 189, 204
Pöggler, Otto, 84
Poiret, Pierre, 47
Popkin, Richard, 7
Pordage, John, 46
Postel, Guillaume, 167n. 40
Pound, Roscoe, 55n. 23
Pre-Socratic philosophers, 199
prisca theologia, 31, 52, 54
Proclus, Hegel on, 21, 33, 49, 119, 122
psychic phenomena, 2; Hegel on,
  213–222
Pythagoras, 89

race, Hegel on, 214–215
Ramon of Sabunde, 179
recollection (Erinnerung), 86–87, 98–99,
  122, 180, 224
reflection, Hegel on, 120
Reformation, 29–30
Reinhold, K. L., 78; as Mason, 55
Renaissance, 8, 28–29, 34, 46, 181–182
Renan, Ernst, 242
Renatus, Sincerus. See Richter, Samuel
Reuchlin, Johannes, 29, 62, 65, 166, 176
Reuss, J. F., 72n. 121

Revealed Religion, 144–145
Ricci, Agostino, 31
Richter, Samuel, 249
Rieger, F. P. von, 80
Romanticism, 3, 88n. 14, 89,
    133–135
"Rose in the cross . . ." See
    Rosicrucianism: imagery of
Rosenkranz, Karl, 3, 12, 25n. 13, 48, 62,
    78, 93, 104–109, 116, 117n. 103, 122, 151,
    226
Rosenkreuz, Christian, 51–52, 86
Rosenroth, Knorr von, 2, 65, 167, 176,
    184, 232
Rosicrucianism, 2, 35–36, 51–53, 99,
    182–183, 244; Gold and Rosy-Cross,
    248–255; and Hegel, 248–249,
    252–253; imagery of, 52
Rösler, G. F., 68
Rossi, Paolo, 182
Rosslyn Chapel, 75n. 145
Rothe, Johann, 37
Rousseau, Jean-Jacques, 49

Saint-Martin, L. C. de, 47, 56
Salm, Hugo von, 54
Sartre, J.-P., 138
Sarug, Israel, 229
Schelling, F. W. J., 3–5, 7n. 12, 28, 35, 62,
    64, 70, 72, 73, 74n. 139, 77–84, 119,
    133–138, 192, 202, 211, 214, 242,
    243–244, 246, 254; on art, 91; and
    Böhme, 47, 133–134; Identity
    philosophy of, 79–83, 86n. 8, 90n. 18,
    137n. 47; influence on Hegel, 79–83; as
    Mason, 55; on medicine, 83, 205;
    philosophy of nature of, 81–83, 188,
    191, 195, 197; transcendental idealism
    of, 79, 82; Works, Bruno, 83, 131; —,
    Exposition of my System, 82; —,
    Freiheitschrift, 79; —, System of
    Transcendental Idealism, 88n. 14, 247;
    —, Die Weltalter, 61, 81, 243, 247
Schelling, Karoline, 83n. 191
Schelling, K. E., 192, 217
Schelver, F. J., 218
Schiller, J. C. F. von, 62, 71, 83; Die
    Freundschaft, 59, 146–149; as Mason,
    55
Schipperges, Heinrich, 205
Schlegel, A. W., 133
Schlegel, Friedrich, 77–78, 88n. 14,
    133–134
Schleiermacher, F. E. D., 78
Schneider, Heinrich, 47, 52, 54, 56,
    62–63, 64n. 73
Schneider, Helmut, 106n. 74, 110n. 88,
    111–113, 116, 117n. 101

Schneider, Robert, 5, 60–61, 63–64, 67,
    69n. 102, 70–71, 72–73, 79, 81, 107n.
    76, 143, 189n. 6, 196n. 21, 243–244
Scholem, Gershom, 38n. 62, 46, 79n.
    169, 165, 168–173, 175, 177, 228–229,
    231, 233, 235n. 37, 236
Schopenhauer, Arthur, 7n. 12
Schubart, C. F. D., 78
Schüler, Gisela, 84
Schwäbischen Magazin, 64
Schweighardt, Theophilus, 53
Schwenkfeld, Caspar, 66
Self-Consciousness, 141–142
Sense-Certainty, 141, 144
Sensus communis, 64n. 75, 67, 122; as
    influence on Hölderlin, 78
Sephiroth, 32, 41n. 79, 166, 169–174, 230,
    234; Binah, 172, 174; Da'at, 172, 174;
    Din (Gevurah), 67, 172–174, 177, 229;
    Hesed (Gedulah), 66, 172–174, 229;
    Hod, 172, 174; Hohkmah, 170–172, 174;
    in Luria, 230–232; Keter, 170–171, 174,
    232; Malkhut, 169, 174, 234–235; Nezah,
    172, 174; Tiferet, 172, 174; Yesod, 172,
    174
Shaftesbury, A. A. C., 74
Shakespeare, William, 182
Sinclair, Isaak von, 75, 75n. 145
skull: as image in Hegel (die
    Schädelstätte), 145–149, 212; as
    Masonic image, 146; as vessel of
    alchemical transmutation, 145–146,
    206, 212. See also caput mortuum
Smith, Adam, 228
Sömmering, S. T. von, 250
"source spirits" (Quellgeister), 42–43, 61,
    66, 74, 107, 136, 147, 160–161, 163, 169,
    172, 222, 229; Bitter, 40–42, 107–108,
    159; Body, 40, 42–43, 164, 235n. 37;
    Heat, 40–42, 159; Love, 40–42, 164;
    Sour, 40–42, 107–108, 144, 159;
    Sweet, 40–42, 107–108; Tone
    (Sound), 40, 42–43, 107n. 79,
    164
Sparrow, John, 37n. 54, 46
Späth, J. J., 167
speculative philosophy, 82, 86, 95–96,
    110, 120; and mysticism, 2, 86, 104, 138;
    and recollection, 88–90
Spener, P. J., 47, 53n. 12, 243
Sperber, Julius, 53
Spinoza, Baruch, 7n. 12, 33, 39, 74, 77,
    77n. 155, 81–82, 119, 136, 160, 163, 180,
    214
Spiritus, 196; in Böhme, 117n. 102; in
    Hegel, 111, 117–118, 194, 195
squareness, 2, 100–101, 117, 179, 181,
    192

Steffens, Heinrich, 195, 202, 211
Stephanos of Alexandria, 201
Stoeffler, F. E., 39, 47, 64, 245
Stoics, 196, 205
Storr, G. C., 72, 72n. 121
Stuhlfauth, G., 111
Swabia. See Württemberg
Swedenborg, Emanuel, 7n. 12, 58, 65, 83n. 191
symbolic forms, 98–104, 111, 122, 154
Synesius, 201

Tauler, Johannes, 3, 63n. 70, 106, 116
Tetragrammaton, 31, 238
Teutonic order, 35
Theologia Germanica, 35
theosophy, 1, 53, 137–138
Thomas Aquinas, Saint, 22–23
Thompson, C. J. S., 165
Tieck, Ludwig, 47, 133–134
triads, 2, 16, 27, 36, 39, 41, 49, 65–66, 86n. 10, 100–101, 106–107, 117–118, 122, 154–155, 157, 161, 172, 175, 178–179, 181, 192, 204, 208n. 82, 210, 212, 225, 237, 240–242, 247
Trismosin, Solomon, 203
Trithemius, John, 31n. 37
Tshugg, C. F. Steiger von, 74
Tuveson, E. L., 8–9

Understanding, 98, 118, 136n. 42, 188, 220
Üxküll, Baron Boris von, 253n. 103

Valentine, Basil, 58, 201n. 46
van den Broek, Roelof, 10n. 22
van Ghert, P. G., 132–133, 159, 217–218
Verene, D. P., 86n. 7, 87, 92, 99, 134n. 36, 148n. 77, 156n. 7, 180–181
Versluis, Arthur, 44, 154n4
"virgin earth," 59, 59n. 42, 132, 209, 212
Vischer, F. T., 4
Voegelin, Eric, 5n. 6, 6–7, 150, 187, 222, 237–238
Voltaire, 74

Vondung, Klaus, 12, 69n. 103, 79n. 169, 197, 247n. 80

Waite, A. E., 179n. 88
Walker, D. P., 7, 191
Walsh, David, 6–7, 8n. 13, 28n. 28, 37–39, 43n. 87, 44, 48, 48n. 112, 50, 59, 63, 74, 107–108, 133, 138, 144, 162, 192, 201–202, 204, 241
Walter, Balthasar, 37
Webster, Charles, 211
Weeks, Andrew, 31n. 36, 35, 37, 52, 205
Weigel, Valentin, 35–37
Weishaupt, Adam, 56–57
Welling, Georg von, 58, 207
Westphal, Kenneth, 252
Wiedmann, Franz, 70
Wierus, Johann, 33
Windischmann, K. J. H., 113–114, 123, 130, 218–219, 238
Winfield, R. D., 15, 141n. 56
witchcraft, 218–219
Wolff, Baron Christian von, 64–65, 166
Wolfram von Eschenbach, 148–149
Wöllner, J. C., 250–251
Wood, A. W., 248
World Soul (*Anima Mundi*), 32; Hegel on, 16, 213–214
World Spirit (*Weltgeist*), 227
Württemberg, culture of, 61–63, 70–71, 116, 227, 242–243, 245–246

Yates, Frances, 7, 28, 31, 34, 53, 85n. 4, 178–180, 182–184, 191, 254

Zedlitz, K. A., 251
Zimmerman, J. J., 63
Zimmerman, R. C., 60
Zinzendorf, Count Nikolaus von, 58
zodiac, signs of, 32
Zoroaster, 28
Zosimos of Panopolis, 201
Zuichemus, Viglius, 181n. 94
Zusätze, 7n. 11, 150